To: LISA ,

MW01285398

PRACTICES OF POWER

It's been a pleasure having Andrew in class this semester. You have a wonderful son. Hope to meet you one day.

Best Wishes,

Robert Errola Moses

04/14/2022

PRACTICES OF POWER

REVISITING THE PRINCIPALITIES AND POWERS IN THE PAULINE LETTERS

ROBERT EWUSIE MOSES

Fortress Press
Minneapolis

PRACTICES OF POWER

Revisiting the Principalities and Powers in the Pauline Letters

Copyright © 2014 Fortress Press. All rights reserved. Except for brief quotations in critical articles or reviews, no part of this book may be reproduced in any manner without prior written permission from the publisher. Visit http://www.augsburgfortress.org/copyrights/ or write to Permissions, Augsburg Fortress, Box 1209, Minneapolis, MN 55440.

An earlier version of the section "Church Discipline: Physical and Spiritual Exclusion (1 Cor. 5:1-13) in chapter 5 appeared in *NTS*; cf. "Physical and/or Spiritual Exclusion? Ecclesial Discipline in 1 Corinthians 5," *NTS* 59 (2013): 172-91.

Cover design: Alisha Lofgren

Library of Congress Cataloging-in-Publication Data is available

Print ISBN: 978-1-4514-7664-4

eBook ISBN: 978-1-4514-7993-5

The paper used in this publication meets the minimum requirements of American National Standard for Information Sciences — Permanence of Paper for Printed Library Materials, ANSI Z329.48-1984.

Manufactured in the U.S.A.

This book was produced using PressBooks.com, and PDF rendering was done by PrinceXML.

To:
William and Regina Moses
and
Sam and Janice Jackson

It takes a village to raise a child. — African Proverb

CONTENTS

Acknowledgments

This book is a revision of my dissertation at Duke University. I want to thank all the members of my dissertation committee: Richard B. Hays, Esther Acolatse, Douglas Campbell, Susan Eastman, and C. Kavin Rowe. Each member raised important questions during the defense, a number of which have been addressed in the course of revising the dissertation for publication. Richard Hays chaired this august committee. His interest in the project, encouragement, and insightful suggestions were invaluable in bringing this project to fruition. Douglas Campbell also deserves special mention. The numerous conversations we shared over lunches and tea—especially discussing his projects—helped me nuance and articulate lucidly my own positions.

I have also incurred many debts of gratitude from others along the way. I have been blessed over the years with many mentors and friends whose guidance and friendships have meant so much to me: Debra and Curtis Freeman, Ellen Davis, Randy Maddox, William C. Turner Jr., Willie Jennings, Sam Thompson, Ron Turner, Steve Bland Jr., (the late) Charles and Barbara Walker, Lewis Anthony, Bernard Richardson, Fay Acker, Joseph Hargett. Of course, in a short acknowledgments page like this, I have had to leave out the names of others whose friendships mean no less to me. To all my friends in Duke's Th.D. and Ph.D. programs, it is an honor to call you friends and conversation partners. To my wonderful colleagues in the Religion and Philosophy Department at High Point University, I am deeply grateful for your friendship and support. I would also like to express my gratitude to the editorial team at Fortress Press. The hard work and attention to details exhibited by this team are nothing short of remarkable.

My family has always been a constant source of support and delight; I am forever blessed to have them. Thanks are also due to my amazing wife, Erin, whose companionship makes every Herculean task joyous and feasible. May the good Lord continue to bless us with many more wonderful years together. This book is dedicated to my parents—biological and adoptive: William and Regina Moses and Sam and Janice Jackson. It is unfair that anyone should enjoy the warm embrace of two sets of wonderful parents. I am indeed blessed to have them in my life and I hope that this work is worthy of them. May they accept this gift as a tiny token of my enormous gratitude.

Abbreviations

11QT	The Temple Scroll
ABSA	The Annual of the British School at Athens
Abod. Zar.	Abodah Zarah
BT	The Bible Translator
b. Sabb.	Shabbat
BWANT	Beiträge zur Wissenschaft vom Alten und Neuen Testament
Disc (Epictetus)	The Discourses
EKKNT	Evangelisch-katholischer Kommentar zum Neuen Testament
EvQ	Evangelical Quarterly
FThSt	Freiburger Theologische Studien
HNT	Handbuch zum Neuen Testament
IRM	International Review of Mission
JSNTSup	Journal for the Study of the New Testament: Supplement Series
KD	Kerygma und Dogma
KEK	Kritisch-exegetischer Kommentar über das Neue Testament (Meyer-Kommentar)
L.A.E.	Life of Adam and Eve
LNTS	The Library of New Testament Studies
LUTH	The Luther Bible
Mek. Bahodesh	Mekilta Bahodesh
Mek. Yitro	Mekilta Yitro
MSJ	The Master's Seminary Journal
NETS	A New English Translation of the Septuagint
OG	Old Greek
SCJ	Studies in Christianity and Judaism
Sm. (Ignatius)	To the Smyrnaeans
NovTSup	Supplements to Novum Testamentum
TJ	Trinity Journal
Tr. (Ignatius)	To the Trallians
Tract. Ps. (Hilary of Poitiers)	Tractates on the Psalms
Yebam	Yebamot

PART I

Hermeneutical Issues

1

Introduction

Since World War I and II many scholars have argued for a recovery of the biblical concept classified under the rubric "principalities and powers."[1] The horrors of these wars and the catastrophic events in the years surrounding the wars forced the language of "principalities and powers" upon those who were attempting to find explanations for what many deemed to be beyond modern psychological analysis.[2] People saw destructive forces behind these horrific events.[3] Nonetheless, while scholars agree that the concept of the

---

1. Karl Barth's *Rechtfertigung und Recht* (1938) was one of the pioneering works in this area (ET *Church and State*, trans. Ronald Howe [London: Student Christian Movement, 1939]). As noted by Marva J. Dawn, Barth's work was preceded by the works of Johann Christoph Blumhardt and Christoph Friedrich Blumhardt; see Dawn, *Powers, Weakness, and the Tabernacling of God* (Grand Rapids: Eerdmans, 2001), 1–5. Blumhardt's biography is narrated by F. Zuendel, *The Awakenings: One Man's Battle with Darkness* (Farmington, PA: Plough Publishing House, 1999). See also W. A. Visser't Hooft, *The Kingship of Christ: An Interpretation of Recent European Theology* (New York: Harper and Brothers, 1948), 15–31.

2. Among the works that issued in this period, we mention the following: Hooft, *Kingship of Christ*; O. Cullman, *Christ and Time: The Primitive Christian Conception of Time and History* (Philadelphia: Westminster, 1950); J. S. Stewart, "On a Neglected Emphasis in New Testament Theology," *SJT* 4 (1951): 292–301; G. H. C. MacGregor, "Principalities and Powers: The Cosmic Background of Paul's Thought," *NTS* 1 (1954): 17–28; E. G. Rupp, *Principalities and Powers: Studies in the Christian Conflict in History* (London: Epworth, 1952); H. Berkhof, *Christ and the Powers* (Scottdale, PA: Herald, 1977 [orig. 1953]); G. B. Caird, *Principalities and Powers: A Study in Pauline Theology* (Eugene, OR: Wipf and Stock, 2003 [orig. 1956]); D. E. H. Whitley, *The Theology of Saint Paul* (Oxford: Blackwell, 1964) 18–80; A. N. Wilder, *Kerygma, Eschatology and Social Ethics* (Philadelphia: Fortress Press, 1966).

3. In his lecture, "The Church is Dead," delivered on August 29, 1932, Dietrich Bonhoeffer wrote: "How can one close one's eyes at the fact that the demons themselves have taken over the rule of the world, that it is the powers of darkness who have here made an awful conspiracy and could break out at any moment?—How could one think that these demons could be driven out, these powers annihilated with a bit of education in international understanding, with a bit of goodwill?" (*A Testament to Freedom: The Essential Writings of Dietrich Bonhoeffer*, rev. ed., ed. G. B. Kelly and F. B. Nelson [San Francisco: HarperSanFrancisco, 1995] 104).

powers is crucial for understanding the theology of the NT, there is little agreement on how to interpret the powers. How are we to interpret Paul's language of ἐξουσίαι ("authorities";[4] 1 Cor. 15:24; Col. 1:13, 16; 2:10, 15; cf. Eph. 1:21; 2:2; 3:10; 6:12), δυνάμεις ("powers"; Rom. 8:38; 1 Cor. 15:24; cf. Eph. 1:21), κυριότητες ("lordships"; Col 1:16; cf. Eph. 1:21), θρόνοι ("thrones"; Col. 1:16), ἄγγελοι ("angels"; Rom. 8:38; 1 Cor. 4:9; 6:3; 11:10; 13:1; 2 Cor. 11:14; 12:7; Gal. 1:8; 3:19; 4:14; Col. 2:18; 2 Thess. 1:7), δαιμόνια ("demons"; 1 Cor. 10:20-21), στοιχεῖα ("elements"; Gal. 4:3, 9; Col. 2:8, 20), ἀρχαί ("principalities"; Rom. 8:38; 1 Cor. 15:24; Col. 1:16, 18; 2:10, 15; cf. Eph. 1:21; 3:10; 6:12), ἄρχοντες ("rulers"; Rom. 13:3; 1 Cor. 2:6, 8; cf. Eph. 2:2), σατανᾶς ("Satan"; Rom. 16:20; 1 Cor. 5:5; 7:5; 2 Cor. 2:11; 11:14; 12:7; 1 Thess. 2:18; 2 Thess. 2:9), Βελιάρ ("Beliar"; 2 Cor. 6:15), ἁμαρτία ("sin"; Rom. 5–8 [e.g., 5:21, 6:6, 6:12, 7:11, 7:13, 8:2]), θάνατος ("death"; Rom 5–8 [e.g., 5:12, 5:14, 6:9, 8:2, 8:38]; 1 Cor. 15:26, 54-56), σάρξ ("flesh"; Rom 7:5, 18, 25; 8:4-9; 8:12-13; 13:14; Gal. 3:3; 5:13, 16, 17, 19; 6:8)? Can we relegate the NT conception of the powers to primitive myths (and what are the implications of such a move)? Is there a way to bridge the hermeneutical gap between the NT and early church's conception of the powers and modern critical approaches to Scripture?

These are very difficult questions. In order to be able to address these difficult questions and to chart a possible way forward, it is essential to look at a representative cross-section of approaches to the NT language of the powers throughout the last half-century. By critically engaging the various approaches, we can gain a sense of the strengths and pitfalls of each approach and what is at stake when we choose to embrace a particular approach. Such an analysis will in turn help us to articulate better our own view concerning the powers. Thus, we begin our study with a survey of four modern interpreters of the principalities and powers: Clinton Arnold, Rudolf Bultmann, Hendrik Berkhof, and Walter Wink. Each of these scholars represents for us a distinct model for understanding the powers. Arnold's approach to the powers attempts to recover the traditional premodern Christian belief in the existence of evil supernatural beings. This approach takes seriously the "real" existence of a spiritual realm of demons ruled by a figure named Satan. It is this first approach that Bultmann seeks to reinterpret. Bultmann argues that the biblical language of the powers belongs to a historical epoch where thought forms had not yet been shaped by scientific thinking. Thus, the only way to make the "mythical" mode of thinking relevant for the modern era is to "demythologize" it.

A third approach, exemplified in the work of Berkhof, argues that the NT writers themselves, Paul in particular, attempted to demythologize the

---

4. All translations in this work are our own, unless otherwise indicated.

prevailing view of the powers (that is, the view that the powers are personal spiritual beings). This third approach to the powers identifies the powers exclusively with structures of human existence. A fourth approach is proffered by Wink, who argues that the powers are the invisible interiority of inner and outer materiality. Wink argues that the physical and spiritual aspects of the powers are always simultaneously present. While these four approaches may not be exhaustive, other proposals on how to interpret the powers largely fit within one of these approaches, though with some variation and exegetical disagreements. We will note these throughout our study. In part 1 of this work, we present these models in detail and critically engage each model. We will offer some suggestions on how to best understand the principalities and powers in Paul.

The main contribution of this study is to offer "practice" as a category for understanding the powers in Paul. To a certain extent, this study hopes to move beyond modernity's unfortunate dichotomy between theory and practice, or understanding and application. The study approaches Paul's view of the powers through investigating the actual practices that Paul recommended to the early Christian congregations in his letters. We do not begin by asking what Paul or his contemporaries may have believed about the powers or a spirit world; rather, this study proceeds from the assumption that Paul's conception of the powers is unintelligible without a developed account of the practices he advocated for the early believers.

Thus, we offer a definition of what we have labeled as "practices of power" that will guide our investigation: *practices of power are either activities that guard believers from the dominion of the powers, or activities that expose believers and unbelievers to the dominion of the powers.* Paul advocated certain practices for believers that will shield them from the principalities and powers. There were also certain practices that, if adopted by believers, would make them vulnerable to the powers. We will draw on two contemporary accounts of practices—in the writings of Alasdair MacIntyre and Pierre Bourdieu—to contribute to a practical understanding of Paul's theology of the powers. In part 2 of this work, we will investigate the Pauline letters in canonical order (Romans, 1 and 2 Corinthians, Galatians, and Colossians) to identify these practices. In part 3 of this work we hope to bring a cross-cultural perspective to this study by considering how African traditional beliefs and practices shape the interpretation of the NT language of the powers in the African context.

Finally, we should mention upfront our decision to include Colossians and 2 Thessalonians in the Pauline evidence presented in this work. While we remain open to the possibility that these letters might be pseudonymous, the evidence for pseudonymity of these two letters remains, in our view, inconclusive.[5] Any treatment of Paul's conception of the powers that excludes these letters will be deficient. While we do not devote an entire chapter to 2 Thessalonians, we should note that the 2 Thess. 2:1-12 presents an apocalyptic worldview that is consistent with what we encounter in the undisputed letters of Paul. This letter presents a conflict that is cosmic in scope: Satan and his minion line up on the other side of the battlefront against God. The conflict involves a rebellion and the revelation (ἀποκάλυψις) of "the lawless one," who is destined for destruction (2 Thess. 2:3). The lawless one is an ambassador for Satan (2:9). Satan (σατανᾶς) uses all power (δύναμις), signs, false wonders (τέρασιν ψεύδους), and wicked deception (ἀπάτῃ ἀδικίας) on those who are perishing (τοῖς ἀπολλυμένοις), because they refused to love the truth (ἀλήθεια) (2 Thess. 2:9-10).

Satan's deceptive work will be noted throughout this study. For now, we observe that the apocalyptic concept presented in 2 Thessalonians 2 is analogous to Paul's arguments in 2 Corinthians 4 and 11.[6] In 2 Corinthians 4, Paul asserts that the gospel is veiled to those who are perishing (τοῖς ἀπολλυμένοις), because the "god of this age" has blinded the minds of unbelievers to the light (truth [ἀλήθεια; 2 Cor. 4:2]) of the gospel of glory (2 Cor 4:4). In 2 Corinthians 11, just as Satan (σατανᾶς) masquerades as an angel of light (2 Cor. 11:14), so also Satan's servants—the false apostles (ψευδαπόστολοι) and deceitful workers—are masquerading as apostles of Christ (2 Cor. 11:13). And just as the serpent deceived (ἐξαπατάω) Eve in the garden, so also these false apostles are leading believers astray (2 Cor. 11:3).

According to 2 Thessalonians, at the manifestation of his coming the Lord Jesus will destroy the lawless one with the breath of his mouth (2 Thess. 2:8). The ultimate destruction of the powers and the works of the powers is an apocalyptic theme that we encounter in Paul (1 Cor. 15:24-28; Rom. 16:20). In this regard, to exclude Colossians from a treatment of Paul's powers would lead to imprecise results, since Colossians introduces a significant discrepancy: Colossians does not envision the ultimate destruction of the powers; but rather, Colossians envisions the ultimate reconciliation of the powers to God through Christ (Col. 1:15-20). We give adequate attention to Colossians in this study;

---

5. For careful discussion on the authorship of Colossians, see J. M. G. Barclay, *Colossians and Philemon*, NTG (Sheffield: Sheffield Academic, 1997), 18–36. On the authorship of 2 Thessalonians, see A. Malherbe, *The Letters to the Thessalonians*, AB 32B (New York: Doubleday, 2000) 364–70.

6. An author who has noted the convergences between 2 Thessalonians 2 and 2 Corinthians 4 & 11 is Sigve K. Tonstad, "The Restrainer Removed: A Truly Alarming Thought (2 Thess 2:1-12)," *HBT* 29 (2007): 133–51, esp. 147–50.

suffice it to say for now that the concept of the ultimate reconciliation of the powers represents an important development and tension in the presentation of the powers in the Pauline corpus; and, as such, it cannot be ignored. The concept of reconciliation of the powers may suggest either that Colossians is pseudonymous or that the letter represents a significant shift in Paul's view concerning the powers. Both of these possibilities will be weighed in our detailed discussion of Colossians in chapter 7.

2

Four Models for Interpreting the Powers

In this chapter, we survey the works of four major twentieth-century interpreters of the principalities and powers: Clinton Arnold, Rudolph Bultmann, Hendrik Berkhof, and Walter Wink. Each of these scholars represents a distinctive approach to the powers, and all are influential voices in different circles. We do not claim that this survey represents a comprehensive typology of approaches to the powers. All the above scholars, for example, are European and American males. Thus, at the end of our study we will put them in conversation with non-European and non-American perspectives in our cross-cultural study. Readers are invited to expand the range of possibilities. In this chapter, nonetheless, we concentrate on these four scholars, because they represent an instructive spectrum of approaches to the powers, and they help us to raise important issues.

While Clinton Arnold's work is the most recent among the scholars surveyed, we have chosen to begin our discussion with him, because he represents an attempt to recover the "traditional" view of the powers that sees the powers as personal spiritual beings. Rudolf Bultmann's approach is a reaction against this traditional understanding of the powers. Thus, we will discuss Bultmann after Arnold. We then proceed to Berkhof and, finally, to Wink, whose approach is a reformulation of the position articulated by Berkhof. After engaging the works of these scholars, we will offer some overall assessments about a way forward for the study of the NT's principalities and powers.

CLINTON ARNOLD: PERSONAL SPIRITUAL BEINGS

"Belief in the real existence of [the] powers continued through the entire history of the church, including the Reformation,"[1] writes Clinton Arnold. If

Arnold is correct, then the position he defends may be labeled as the traditional understanding of the powers.[2] Arnold's work is a reaction against Western scholarship's tendency to demythologize the principalities and powers in the NT. Arnold's study pushes back against the approaches to the powers that do not take seriously the existence of a spiritual realm of demons ruled by a figure named Satan. He argues against the post–Enlightenment impulse to relegate the NT's portrayal of a struggle with evil spirits ("powers of darkness") to outmoded primitive myth, or that attempts to demythologize the powers. All such approaches to the powers are, for Arnold, characterized by one impulse: "A denial of the real existence of evil spirits."[3] Paul's conception of evil spiritual powers, in contrast, serves, for Arnold, as an important source for forming a Christian worldview in Western culture.

Arnold begins by conducting an archaeology of the worldview of the Greek, Roman, and Jewish populace, in order to situate Paul's belief within first-century Greco-Roman culture and Judaism. He contends that everyone in Paul's day agreed on one thing: "The supernatural realm exercises control over everyday life and eternal destiny."[4] Arnold cites evidence from papyrus texts, amulets, curse tablets (*defixiones*), and other sources to demonstrate how magic and divination, widespread practices in the Mediterranean world, were ways people manipulated good and evil spirits in order to assist or harm others. Such practices not only assumed the existence of a spiritual realm but also that these spirits were involved in the lives of humans and could be manipulated.[5]

Arnold argues that the Hellenistic age saw a rise in "personal religion," in which the gods were perceived as less remote and more personal, concerned with the affairs of people.[6] People sought relationships and union with the gods through ritual acts, such as Eleusis mystery rites and Cybele initiation rites; and the existence of dozens of gods and goddesses (Asclepius, Hekate, Dionysus, Isis, Mithras, and so on) was taken for granted, even by early Christians. The early Christians, however, attributed the activities of these gods and goddesses

---

1. C. E. Arnold, *Powers of Darkness: Principalities and Powers in Paul's Letters* (Downer's Grove, IL: InterVarsity, 1992) 169–70. See also Arnold, *Ephesians: Power and Magic. The Concept of Power in Ephesians in Light of Its Historical Setting*, SNTSMS 63 (Cambridge: Cambridge University Press, 1989); Arnold, *The Colossian Syncretism: The Interface between Christianity and Folk Belief at Colossae*, WUNT 77 (Tübingen: Mohr Siebeck, 1995). Our discussion in this section is mainly based on *Powers of Darkness*.

2. We remain a bit skeptical, however. Arnold's claim may be an oversimplification of history.

3. Arnold, *Powers of Darkness*, 172.

4. Ibid., 19.

5. Ibid., 27.

6. Ibid., 37.

to the influence of Satan (cf. Acts 14:8-20; 17:16-34; 19:23-41; 28:1-11). In addition, astrological belief and practice were widespread and varied in the Greco-Roman world: some believed that the heavenly bodies represented spirits or deities, while others believed that the heavenly bodies were actual spirits, deities, or supernatural powers. The Stoics believed that the movement of the heavenly bodies determined the fate of people on earth. Most people, however, believing the heavenly bodies to be gods or spirits, prayed to, invoked, or propitiated the planets and stars to alter their fate. Arnold argues that it was this concern about fate and the influence of the stars that Paul addressed in his letters when he spoke of the astral spirits as the *stoicheia* ("elementary spirits" [Gal. 4:3, 9; Col. 2:8, 20]). Paul spoke of God's election and predestination to combat this concern about fate.[7]

Having discussed what first-century pagans believed about evil spirits, Arnold turns his attention to first-century Judaism to shed light on what Paul believed about the powers of darkness. Arnold traces demonology in the Old Testament through the intertestamental period to rabbinic literature. He lists Old Testament references that link the worship of idols to demons (Deut. 32:16-17; Pss. 106:37-38; 96:5), a belief that Paul inherited (1 Cor. 10:19-21). He points to the OT references to the "Night Hag" (Isa. 34:14) and "goat spirits" (Isa. 13:21; Lev. 17:7; 2 Chron. 11:15) as references to evil spirits. He also points to the OT censuring of occult practices, divination, sorcery, magic and witchcraft (Deut. 18:10-12; Amos 5:26; Jer. 7:18; 44:17-19; Deut. 4:19; 1 Sam. 28:3-25; Lev. 19:26, 31), passages redolent of evil spirits (Judg. 9:23; 1 Sam. 16:14-23; 18:10-11; 19:9-10; 1 Kgs. 22:1-40), and the OT conception of angels of the nations (Deut. 32:8-9; Dan. 10:13-14, 20-21). He discusses Satan in the OT (Job 1–2; Zech. 3:1-2; 1 Chron. 21:1), arguing that Satan is portrayed in the OT as a supernatural enemy to both God and humanity. The intertestamental period reveals an increased preoccupation with the spirit realm, as demonstrated in Old Testament apocryphal writings, the Dead Sea Scrolls, pseudepigraphic testaments, and Jewish apocalyptic literature. These documents were interested in the origin of demons, attributing it to the fall of angels; they were also interested in the names and classes of these angelic beings (see, e.g., *Jub.* 5, 10; *1 En.* 6–36). These early Jewish writings portray the angelic beings as both influencing humans, leading them astray from God and society, and causing the propagation of pagan religions or war among the nations. Finally, Arnold takes a look at the ministry of Jesus, arguing that Jesus' confrontation with Satan,

---

7. Ibid., 53–54.

conflict with the powers of darkness, and teaching about evil powers greatly influenced the apostle Paul.[8]

An important observation from Arnold's study is the extraordinary amount of syncretism among all first-century religions and Judaism: each religion mixed together various elements of beliefs and practices from other religions. Greek, Egyptian, Persian, Phrygian, and Roman deities were all invoked in incantations, sometimes freely combined with names from the Bible. In the words of Arnold, "A very thin line separated Jewish and gentile religious belief in many quarters during the first century."[9] Paul's vocabulary for the principalities and powers drew on the vast reservoir of terms in first-century Jewish angelology and demonology.[10] But Paul's gentile audience would have clearly understood him, since different religions shared the same concepts and terminology.

Unlike the approaches to the powers that see Paul demythologizing the views of his contemporaries, Arnold agues that Paul was "a man of his times."[11] Like his Jewish and pagan contemporaries, Paul also assumed the existence of a realm filled with evil spirits hostile to humanity. For Paul, these personal demons were a given, not needing to be argued for. Paul never doubted the real existence of the principalities and powers. Arnold notes that belief in the real existence of the spirit realm spanned the history of Christianity until the church inherited a materialistic and rationalistic worldview from the Enlightenment. Paul saw the demonic forces as a well-organized world under the command of Satan, their head. In Paul's view, Satan and his powers worked to oppose at every point the purpose of God in Christ and in the life of believers. Satan and his demons were also manifest in non-Christian religions. The gods of the pagans were not lifeless images; rather, Satan used these lifeless images to hold humans in bondage. Paul, therefore, admonished the members of his congregation to "flee from idolatry" (1 Cor. 10:14), because involvement with pagan temples not only compromised their allegiance to the one true God but also exposed them to powerful demonic activity. Here Paul inherits from his Jewish tradition a link between idolatry and witchcraft (cf. *Jub.* 11:4-5; *T. Jud.* 23:1; *T. Naph.* 3:1).

---

8. Ibid., 75–86.

9. Ibid., 91.

10. Ἀρχαί ("principalities"), ἐξουσίαι ("authorities"), δυνάμεις ("powers"), κυριότητες ("lordships"), θρόνοι ("thrones"), ἄγγελοι ("angels"), κοσμοκράτορες ("world rulers"), δαιμόνια ("demons"), στοιχεῖα ("elements"), ἄρχοντες ("rulers").

11. Arnold, *Powers of Darkness*, 89.

Yet it is important to note, as Arnold argues, that Paul did not merely adopt the demonology and angelology of his Jewish and pagan world. For Arnold, Paul's views are firmly secured in the Old Testament and the life, death, and resurrection of Jesus. Thus, key differences emerge between Paul's approach to the powers and his Jewish and pagan contemporaries. For example, while Paul believed that the pagan gods were alive, he did not, like his pagan contemporaries, think the gods could help people in practical ways. Paul believed the pagan gods were inspired and perpetuated by Satan and his demons. Rather than being helpful resources for his gentile converts, Paul saw these evil spirits as a hindrance to the gospel he proclaimed. The only spirit that Paul favored was the Holy Spirit, whose indwelling and regular operation among believers meant ongoing spiritual progress for the body of Christ. In addition, while Jewish sources demonstrate a keen concern to elucidate the origins, names, and rank of the demonic forces, Paul shows no interest in these concerns. Furthermore, Paul was not concerned with the specific activities of specific demons or the territories ruled by evil angels. Paul, by contrast, often lumped all the demons together, pointing to Christ's lordship over all powers and Christ as the source to overcoming the evil powers.

The death and resurrection of Christ, Arnold avers, marks the pivotal point of defeat of the powers. In Christ's death, God disarmed the powers, making a public spectacle of them in the process. The believer's own defeat of the powers is, therefore, rooted in the death, resurrection, and exaltation of Christ. It is only in being "in Christ" that a person escapes the bondage of the hostile powers.[12] Believers, as a result of their union with Christ and bond with one another, have the strength to resist the powers of darkness. Although the powers may enjoy temporary victories in their ongoing campaign against the church, their ultimate doom is certain. Arnold, following Oscar Cullmann,[13] draws on a World War II analogy to shed light on the nature of the church's ongoing struggle with the powers: the church lives in the period between the D-Day invasion at Normandy and the VE-Day final victory a year later.[14]

Arnold argues further that Paul perceived a threefold nature of evil (Eph. 2:1-3): the world, the devil, and the flesh.[15] With regard to the world, Arnold notes that there is much in society that leads people away from God. In addition to the influence of the structures of society throughout a person's life, Paul

---

12. Ibid., 112–13.

13. O. Cullman, *Christ and Time: The Primitive Christian Conception of Time and History* (Philadelphia: Westminster, 1950) 84, 139–45.

14. Arnold, *Powers of Darkness*, 123.

15. Ibid., 125–26. Arnold assumes Pauline authorship of Ephesians.

perceived the influence of Satan and evil spirits over the lives of individuals. Finally, Paul also discerned an internal inclination toward evil in humans. Thus, the source of evil is internal to people as well as supernatural. In the end, however, for Arnold, the "demonic explanation for evil behavior needs to be seen as the thread that ties together all the evil influences." Arnold continues: "In practice Satan exploits the depraved tendencies of the flesh and exercises a measure of control over all levels of a social order."[16] Forces of darkness intensify the cravings of the flesh, exploit sinful activity in the life of believers as a means of control over a believer's life, inspire false teachings (and false teachers) among believers, hinder the mission of the church, and sometimes afflict believers with physical ailments. But, as Paul demonstrates in 2 Cor. 12:7 and 1 Cor. 5:1-13, God on occasion uses Satan and his forces in a positive way, either as a providential means to ensure the believer's continued dependence on God or as a tool for discipline.

Arnold devotes an entire chapter to the subject of "spiritual warfare."[17] The nature of spiritual warfare, according to Arnold, has to do primarily with Christian conduct and spreading the gospel, not exorcism or eliminating structural evil. He summarizes the essence of spiritual warfare as "resistance" and "proclamation."[18] In Ephesians 6, Paul lists the weapons of truth and righteousness, stressing the need for believers to cultivate moral integrity and holiness in their lives. A lack of these qualities impedes the Christian's ability to resist Satan's host. Paul lists weapons of salvation and the word of God to assure believers of their secure identity in Christ and to remind believers of the importance of the study and understanding of Scripture in engaging in spiritual warfare. These measures are all defensive forms of resistance. But spiritual warfare is also offensive: Christians must wield the "sword" of the Spirit. This is a call to primary aggression through proclamation and spread of the gospel. Finally, prayer is the primary way for gaining access to the power of God in order to wage successful spiritual warfare. This warfare is waged corporately, not individually.[19]

So what is the relationship between the powers, as Arnold interprets them, and structures? Arnold demonstrates a deep-seated aversion to equating the powers with the structures of existence. For Arnold, the two are ontologically distinct, one being personal and the other being nonpersonal. He, therefore,

---

16. Ibid., 126.

17. For a more detailed treatment of this subject, see Arnold, *3 Crucial Questions about Spiritual Warfare* (Grand Rapids: Baker Books, 1997).

18. Arnold, *Powers of Darkness*, 154.

19. Ibid., 159.

resists the impulse to use Paul's references to the "principalities and powers" as a tool for developing a theology of society. Paul is concerned about individuals' struggle with the powers of darkness. To the extent that Paul's theology can be applied to the structures, it has to do with the realization that it is *people* who control the structures and it is people whose ideas, affections, and activities represent the composite result of structures: "The lesson to be learned from Paul . . . is that Christians should place the primary focus of their energy on changing people. Society can change only to the extent that the hearts of the people are changed."[20] When the evil powers take control of key people they use these people to influence institutions. In sum, the powers influence people, who in turn influence society. Paul's theology, therefore, calls on no one to work toward reforming the social and political order.

Arnold's work stands in the tradition of studies of the powers that seek to move beyond the tendency in Western scholarship to avoid or trivialize the spirit realm.[21] His distance from the demythologizing tendencies of Western scholarship can be summed up under one statement: "The powers of darkness are real, we need to be conscious of their influence, and we need to respond to them appropriately."[22] His work makes a cogent case for the view that we cannot dismiss outright the existence of a spiritual realm inhabited by spiritual forces, at least if we are willing to take the biblical witness seriously. Arnold is also to be commended for situating Paul well within his Jewish milieu and establishing continuity between Paul and his Jewish contemporaries. We may also concur with Arnold that Paul gives Satan and the principalities and powers ontological reality, though, in our view, this does not tell the whole story. Thus, we note that in Arnold's study, the personal interpretation of the powers fails to give an adequate account of the complex view of the powers Paul presents in his letters.

The main deficiency of this approach is that it falls short of offering the church a comprehensive view of the nature and method of the powers, and arming the church with the adequate tools needed to combat the powers. In passing, one has to note that Arnold's target audience is the evangelical

---

20. Ibid., 217.

21. For other works that view the powers as personal spiritual beings, see J. R. W. Stott, *God's New Society: The Message of Ephesians* (Downer's Grove, IL: InterVarsity, 1979); P. O'Brien, "Principalities and the Relationship to Structures," *Evangelical Theological Review* 6 (1982): 50–61; R. E. Webber, *The Church in the World: Opposition, Tension, or Transformation* (Grand Rapids: Zondervan, 1986); G. Williams, *The Spirit World in the Letters of Paul the Apostle: A Critical Examination of the Role of Spiritual Beings in the Authentic Pauline Epistles*, FRLANT (Göttingen: Vandenhoeck & Ruprecht, 2009).

22. Arnold, *Powers of Darkness*, 182.

community.[23] And to this extent, his work comes across as a bit idiosyncratic. There are assumed positions in his work not argued for that will be readily accepted only among those who inhabit his symbolic world.[24] For example, Arnold writes that by an extension of Paul's thought, all non-Christian religions of today, including Judaism, are manifestations of the demonic powers.[25] It is questionable, however, whether Paul would have included Judaism under the demonic powers (as in pagan worship). On the one hand, Paul's critique of pagan idolatry is typically Jewish.[26] On the other hand, Paul does on occasion find a point of contact between certain Jewish practices *demanded of gentile converts* and the practices of their pagan past (cf. Gal. 4:1-11; Col. 2:8-23).[27] But this relationship is extremely complex and does not easily translate into Paul saying that Judaism is under the influence of demons. We will not take up here the complex topic of Paul's relationship to Judaism. We note only in passing that increasingly scholars have sensed a more nuanced and extremely complex relationship between Paul and Judaism. Krister Stendahl, for example, has argued that Paul never converted from Judaism,[28] and J. Louis Martyn has argued that in instances where Paul expresses negative views toward Judaism, his statements are neither directed at Jews nor the Jewish cult; rather, Paul was addressing the Jewish-Christians of his congregations.[29] Such findings should cause Arnold to argue for a more nuanced position.

More importantly, however, when it comes to dealing with the varied and complex nature of the work of the powers in the world as Paul sees it—from the bondage of creation to the disintegration of personal lives—Arnold's approach is deeply deficient. Take, for example, Arnold's call for the church to focus on individuals as a means to deal with the powers; he contends that the church's

23. The work contains numerous references to the "evangelical community," "evangelical works," "evangelical thinkers," "evangelical perspective," "evangelical ministers," and so on.

24. In addition to the ensuing discussion, we note Arnold's claim that Jesus' temptation scenes in the Gospels influenced Paul's words on spiritual warfare (Arnold, *Powers of Darkness*, 77); his inclusion of 1 & 2 Timothy and Titus as authentic letters of Paul for his study; and that Paul confirms John's account of Satan's role in Jesus' crucifixion (Arnold, *Powers of Darkness*, 101). These are all claims that require extended treatment.

25. See Arnold, *Powers of Darkness*, 97–98, 131. Arnold is not as cautious here as he is in his article, "Returning to the Domain of the Powers: *Stoicheia* as Evil Spirits in Galatians 4:3, 9," *NovT* 38 (1996): 55–76.

26. See our chapter on Galatians.

27. We discuss this in detail in our chapters on Galatians and Colossians.

28. See K. Stendahl, *Paul among Jews and Gentiles: And Other Essays* (Minneapolis: Fortress Press, 1976); Stendahl, *Final Account: Paul's Letter to the Romans* (Minneapolis: Fortress Press, 1995).

29. See J. L. Martyn, *Theological Issues in the Letters of Paul* (Nashville: Abingdon, 1997).

focus should be the individual, because the way to change society is to change one person at a time.[30] Contrary to Arnold's view, Paul has something to say about how structures of human existence can be co-opted by higher powers. And in our view, this helps to account for certain modern phenomena in a way that Arnold's approach does not. We will pick an example from American history to illustrate this point.

In his fine study of the American church's complicity, and inability to deal, with the institution of slavery, Clarence C. Goen points to the church's obsession with converting souls, rather than finding ways to confront the social system (and institutional bondage) of slavery.[31] The church condemned slaveholders as sinners, viewing the conversion of individuals as the surest route to change the social order. Speaking of antislavery evangelicals, Goen writes: "For the most part, they were content to emphasize individual conversion as the most direct way to reach their goal of Christianizing the social order."[32] As more individuals are changed for Christ, so the church thought, society would improve. Yet this approach rarely did much to shake the foundation of slavery.

Goen's study is very instructive for an approach to the powers that views them in purely personal spiritual terms. The only solution for a world wrenched by complex social demonic institutions, in this approach, is "spiritual warfare," and its accompanying attempts at trying to convert one person at a time. But how many people can the church exorcise or convert, and how long will this take? One can only weep for those who are suffering under oppressive structures, who have to wait for desirable structural changes through the conversion of individuals. The truth is that such changes may never come about. The church needs to come to terms with the complex and myriad schemes and methods of the powers. In the end, one wonders if the purely personal interpretation of the powers has not itself succumbed to the "powers" of modern individualism and Romanticism.

As we shall argue below, Paul's account of the powers presents us with comprehensive features of reality, and a purely personal interpretation of the powers is too simplistic to capture adequately Paul's complex presentation of the powers.[33] One, for example, struggles to find a place in this scheme for Paul's

---

30. See Arnold, *Powers of Darkness*, 217. Cf. O'Brien, "Principalities and the Relationship to Structures," 61: "The Biblical emphasis is that the powers of evil work in and through people, rather than impersonal structures. In speaking of the latter we are inclined to remove any responsibility for action from those who are responsible human agents."

31. C. C. Goen, *Broken Churches, Broken Nation: Denominational Schisms and the Coming of the American Civil War* (Macon, Ga.: Mercer University Press, 1985), 141–90.

32. Ibid., 155.

personification of abstract concepts as powers, such as Sin, Death, and the Flesh. We cannot do justice to Paul's presentation of the powers without accounting for personified nouns as powers in Paul.[34] We will take this up in detail in our chapter on Romans. Suffice it to say for now that when the full spectrum of Paul's presentation of the powers is taken into account, we cannot help but acknowledge the all-pervasiveness of the powers and the difficulty involved in categorizing them—a crucial point that the purely personal interpretation fails to bring out. And personification may be a way of acknowledging not only how pervasive and complex the powers are, but also a way to give language to that which defies language and categorization. Personification is very much a part of Paul's theology of the powers, and overlooking this runs the risk of distorting Paul's complex presentation of the powers.

Rudolf Bultmann: Demythologizing and Existentialist Interpretation

Rudolf Bultmann's approach to the powers is a reaction against the traditional understanding of the powers embodied in much of Christian history and in such approaches as Clinton Arnold's. Bultmann begins from the assumption that every author can only think and write through the thought forms of his or her time and culture.[35] Consequently, for the gospel to have any meaning in its Hellenistic world, the NT authors had to find terms and concepts with which to make their message intelligible to their world. This they found in Gnosticism, which provided the NT writers with a stock of terminologies and concepts with which to convey their message.[36] Thus, the biblical language of the powers,

---

33. So also J. M. G. Barclay, "Why the Roman Empire Was Insignificant to Paul," in *Pauline Churches and Diaspora Jews*, WUNT 275 (Tubingen: Mohr Siebeck, 2011), 363–87.

34. Occasional glimpses are found in Arnold's work on Ephesians (*Ephesians: Power and Magic*), but not a developed treatment. Arnold, for example, notes that the Ephesian "dimensional terms" may have parallels in the magical tradition (*Ephesians: Power and Magic*, 90–94): "The dimensional terms seem to appear as spiritual hypostases, but this is uncertain. It is difficult to determine in the magical papyri when an expression for power actually fades into a personalized power."

35. See R. Bultmann, "Is Exegesis without Presuppositions Possible?" in *New Testament and Mythology: And Other Basic Writings*, ed. and trans. Schubert M. Ogden (Philadelphia: Fortress Press, 1984), 145–53; also Bultmann, *Theology of the New Testament*, 2 vols (Waco, TX: Baylor University Press, 2007 [orig. 1951–55]), 1:164–65; 1:228–32; 1:257–58.

36. See Bultmann, *Theology of the New Testament*, 1:164–83. While Bultmann argues that Christianity and Gnosticism at times combined concepts, he also does note that some differences remained between the two. See *Theology of the New Testament*, 1:168–72.

for Bultmann, is best situated within ancient Jewish apocalypticism and Gnostic redemption myths.[37] Bultmann writes:

> It is Gnostic language when Satan is called "the god of this world" (αἰῶνος) (II Cor. 4:4), the "ruler of this world" (Jn. 12:31; 14:30; 16:11), "the prince of the power of the air" (Eph. 2:2), or "the ruler of this Aeon" (Ign. Eph. 19:1). Both in name and meaning "the rulers of this age" who brought "the Lord of glory" to the cross (I Cor. 2:6, 8) are figures of Gnostic mythology—viz. those demonic world-rulers who are also meant by the terms "angels," principalities," "authorities," "powers" (Rom. 8:38f.; I Cor. 15:24, 26; Col. 1:16; 2:10, 15; Eph. 1:21; 3:10; 6:12; I Pet. 3:22) and are at least included in the "many gods and many lords" of I Cor. 8:4. As in Gnosticism, they are conceived to be in essence star-spirits; as such they are called "elemental spirits of the universe" (Gal. 4:3, 9; cf. Col 2:8, 20) who govern the elapse and division of time (Gal. 4:10). Also Gnostic are the "world rulers of this present darkness" and the "spiritual hosts of wickedness in the heavenly places" (i.e. in the region of air, the lower sphere of the firmament, Eph. 6:12).[38]

According to Bultmann, it is gnostic belief that human life in this world is ruled by demonic powers and as such destined for destruction, and the NT authors appropriated this concept and its language. Yet these concepts and terminologies belong to a historical epoch where thought forms had not yet been formed by scientific thinking. The worldview of the biblical writers is best described as "mythical." Bultmann defines "myth" as "the report of an occurrence or an event in which supernatural, superhuman forces or persons are at work."[39] Mythical thinking is "the opposite of scientific thinking. It refers certain phenomena and events to supernatural, 'divine' powers, whether these are thought of dynamistically or animistically or are represented as personal spirits or gods."[40] For Bultmann, the advances of science and technology have rendered the biblical world picture obsolete, and no one in the modern era can take seriously the mythological biblical world picture.

---

37. Bultmann attributes to Jewish apocalypticism the concept of the imminent turn of the ages that puts an end to the old age and ushers in a new age. See Bultmann, "New Testament and Mythology," in *New Testament and Mythology*, 14–15.

38. Bultmann, *Theology of the New Testament*, 1:173.

39. Bultmann, "On the Problem of Demythologizing," in *New Testament and Mythology*, 95.

40. Ibid.

Bultmann contends that mythical thinking is opposite to scientific thinking, because mythical thinking proceeds from the assumption that the world is an "open" system, that is, occurrences in the world and personal life of humans can be influenced by the intervention of otherworldly powers. Scientific thinking, on the contrary, views the world and its occurrences as a "closed" continuum of cause and effects; the forces that govern natural processes are embedded within them, and this causal continuum of the world process cannot be disrupted by supernatural powers. Also, scientific thinking has taught us that everything that happens to humans can be attributed to ourselves, and that our existence is a unity not open to the intervention of transcendent powers.[41] All decisions and acts have their motive or cause and consequences, which the historical method seeks to uncover, thereby establishing the entire historical process as a closed unity.

Bultmann notes that myth can have an etiological function, for it may seek to explain extraordinary natural phenomena.[42] Myth also speaks about reality, though in an inadequate way; and it is an objectifying kind of thinking: "Myth objectifies the transcendent into the immanent, and thus also into the disposable."[43] Myth allows transcendent powers to fit within the human plane and endows these powers with the ability to break through the course of natural occurrences. But the real intention of myth is to give expression to an understanding of human existence. Myths do not aim at presenting an objective world picture; on the contrary, the point of myth is to relate an understanding of humans in existential terms:

> What is expressed in myth is the faith that the familiar and disposable world in which we live does not have its ground and aim in itself but that its ground and limit lie beyond all that is familiar and disposable and that this is all constantly threatened and controlled by uncanny powers that are its ground and limit. In unity with this myth also gives expression to the knowledge that we are not lords of ourselves, that we are not only dependent within the familiar world but that we are especially dependent on the powers that hold sway beyond all that is familiar, and that it is precisely in dependence on them that we can become free from the familiar powers.[44]

41. Ibid., 97.
42. Ibid.
43. Ibid., 99.
44. Bultmann, "New Testament and Mythology," 10.

This is the truth that the NT wishes to express using cosmological mythology; and this truth is not bound with, rather is independent of, the NT's mythical worldview. Therefore, in keeping with the real intention of myth, and in light of the fact that modern scientific thinking has "destroyed" the mythical world picture of the Bible, the only way the NT witness can retain its validity in the modern world is for us to "demythologize" it.[45]

Demythologizing not only criticizes the mythical world picture but it also seeks to reveal the real intention of the myth, which is to express a certain understanding of human existence. Thus, demythologizing is "existential interpretation." The NT proclamation that has been presented in mythical terms must be demythologized to disclose the truth of the kerygma that stands behind the myths: "The proclamation of the church refers me to scripture as the place where I will hear something decisive about my existence."[46] The demythologizing interpretation, which strips Scripture of its outmoded world picture, discloses the NT understanding of human existence relevant for our modern era. Thus, for example, when Paul speaks of creation's bondage to the powers in Rom. 8:20-39, Paul is using gnostic cosmological mythology to enable him to convey the truth that perishable creation becomes a "destructive power" whenever humans choose to base their lives on creation rather than God.[47] Paul's relating of the cosmic powers to creation is dependent upon what it means for human existence. The mythological presentation of the powers is not meant to speculate about cosmology. Rather, the mythological language of the powers seeks to articulate a certain understanding of existence:

> The spirit powers represent the reality into which man is placed as one full of conflicts and struggle, a reality which threatens and tempts. Thus, through these mythological conceptions the insight is indirectly expressed that man does not have his life in his hand as if he were his own Lord but that he is constantly confronted with the decision of choosing his lord. Beyond this, they also contain the conviction that natural man has always already decided against God, his true Lord, and has let the threatening and tempting world become lord over him.[48]

45. Ibid., 9; "On the Problem of Demythologizing," 99.
46. Bultmann, "On the Problem of Demythologizing," 106.
47. Bultmann, *Theology of the New Testament*, 1:230–31.
48. Ibid., 1:259.

According to Bultmann's demythologizing, the unmythological meanings of the powers are the dangers, tribulations, distresses, and temptations that ultimately threaten the Christian's existence.

Bultmann's work has greatly influenced subsequent scholarship on, and modern understanding of, the powers.[49] While many have sought to dispose of the NT passages dealing with the powers or the entire NT altogether, Bultmann is to be commended for taking the NT message seriously. Bultmann sought to translate the references to the powers and the message of the NT to his modern milieu. His genius lies in the clarity with which he sees the problem. We are all products of our time and culture, and new ways of thinking may require discarding old beliefs and modes of thought. An important implication of Bultmann's insight may be, for example, that our use of modern devices (such as cars, airplanes, microwaves, and so on) means that we all invest scientific materialism and predictability with a certain measure of authority. Thus, if one were suffering from meningitis, for example, one would have to go see a doctor and not first attempt an exorcism.[50]

But Bultmann's approach and solution raise a number of issues. We shall pass over quickly Bultmann's anachronistic appeal to Gnosticism as the appropriate matrix within which to situate the NT conception of the powers. This view hails from mid-twentieth-century German scholarship's fascination with Gnosticism's relation to the NT. The approach has since been largely discredited. There is no evidence of a gnostic Redeemer figure prior to or contemporary with the NT.[51] Thus, appeal to Gnosticism as background for the NT powers runs the risk of imposing thought forms from later centuries onto the NT's message. As we shall see throughout this study, Paul's presentation of the powers is very much at home in Jewish apocalyptic thought.

49. Other scholars who agree that the NT powers must be demythologized are E. Käsemann, "The Eschatological Royal Reign of God," in *Your Kingdom Come: Mission Perspectives. Report on the World Conference on Mission and Evanglism, Melbourne, Australia, 12–25 May, 1980* (Geneva: World Council of Churches, 1980), 65; G. H. C. MacGregor "Principalities and Powers: The Cosmic Background of Paul's Thought," *NTS* 1 (1954): 17–28; and A. Wilder *Kerygma, Eschatology and Social Ethics* (Philadelphia: Fortress Press, 1966). MacGregor and Wilder, while themselves exhibiting a demythologizing tendency, reject Bultmann's mode of demythologizing.

50. We will see how such insight becomes especially salient in our treatment of the powers in the African context in part 3 of this study.

51. See Carsten Colpe's paradigm shifting work, *Die religionsgeschichtliche Schule: Darstellung und Kritik ihres Bildes vom gnostichen Erlösermythus*, FRLANT 78 (Göttingen: Vandenhoeck & Ruprecht, 1961). Also, E. M. Yamauchi, *Pre-Christian Gnosticism: A Survey of the Proposed Evidences* (Grand Rapids: Eerdmans, 1973).

We should also raise an objection to Bultmann's dubious claim that scientific theories have rendered belief in supernatural forces and demons incredible for the modern person. One merely has to travel around the world to such continents as Africa, Asia, and Latin America, where indigenous religions and practices take for granted the existence and operation of supernatural forces.[52] And if by "modern man" Bultmann means the modern Westerner, even here his claim cannot be sustained. We only have to point to Hollywood's obsession and success with horror and fantasy films: as of 2012, the Harry Potter film series ranks number one on the highest-grossing film series of all time.[53] A 2008 extensive survey of the U.S. religious landscape by the Pew Forum on Religion and Public Life found that close to seven in ten Americans (68 percent) believe that angels and demons are active in the world and nearly eight in ten American adults (79 percent) agree that miracles still occur today as in ancient times.[54] It is fair to say that Bultmann's claim is palpably false, and the survey results may suggest to us that reliance on scientific theories does not necessarily rule out belief in the agency of invisible powers.

In addition to the above, we also have to observe the problematic nature—and inconsistence use—of Bultmann's definition of "myth."[55] To define myth as "the report of an occurrence or an event in which supernatural, superhuman forces or persons are at work"[56] is to imply that any talk of the supernatural—which would include symbolical or analogical talk of God—is mythical. To be sure, Bultmann sees God's action in the world as distinct from "wonders." This is because while myths represent divine action as "wonders" disrupting the closed continuum of occurrences in the natural world, God's action, according to Bultmann, takes place "between" occurrences in the world. God's action, therefore, does not disrupt the world's closed continuum since it takes place "in" them.[57] Is Bultmann trying to eat his cake and have it too? Bultmann cannot escape the charge that, by his own definition, any talk of God is mythical; and since Bultmann would not accept the latter claim, a serious tension runs through his work.

52. See our cross-cultural discussion in part 3.

53. See CNBC's "The Highest Grossing Movie Franchises of All Time." Online: http://www.cnbc.com/id/40259653/The_Highest_Grossing_Movie_Franchises_of_All_Time.

54. Pew Forum on Religion & Public Life, *U.S. Religious Landscape Survey* (2008). Online:http://religions.pewforum.org/pdf/report2religious-landscape-study-key-findings.pdf.

55. Cf. R. H. Ayers, "'Myth' in Theological Discourse: A Profusion of Confusion," *AThR* 48 (1966): 200–17, on 206.

56. Bultmann, "On the Problem of Demythologizing," 95.

57. See ibid., 110–12.

In his appropriation of Bultmann's program, Robin Attfield suggests that Bultmann's demythologizing is best applied when "myth involves *notions once symbolic but now obsolete.*"[58] To this end, Attfield notes that the concept of God cannot be subjected to demythologization, since "the concept of God . . . is neither obsolete nor reducible into notions of human powers or qualities."[59] It is not clear, however, what criteria should be used to determine which concepts were once symbolic but are now obsolete and which are reducible to human powers or qualities. As our detailed treatment of the powers in subsequent chapters will demonstrate, the language of the powers cannot be reduced to mere symbols for the NT authors. Moreover, some contemporary atheists have argued that science has (or at least should) make belief in God obsolete.[60] Herein lies the challenge of binding the NT message too closely to any worldview. Bultmann is correct in his astute recognition that every author can only think and write through the thought forms inherited from his or her time and culture. Our thoughts, language, and habits are socially constructed; we moderns have been formed by the language and habits of our times and place. Yet one wonders if demythologizing is not too closely bound to a modern scientific worldview and if this does not set up Bultmann's own demythologizing interpretation as a "myth"—albeit a twentieth-century myth, a perspective only possible within his twentieth-century matrix.[61]

The force of the NT proclamation lies in the claim that its message demands an epistemological transformation, and is, therefore, a scandal to all who have not experienced this epistemological transformation. Indeed, Paul's gospel is predicated on the fact that God's apocalyptic invasion of the world has ushered in a new epistemology that is in keeping with the turn of the ages. Paul writes, "From now on, we know no one according to the flesh [κατὰ σάρκα]" (2 Cor. 5:16). Thus, to call the powers "mythical" is to continue to see the world, in Paul's complex theology, κατὰ σάρκα. To attempt to demythologize the powers, then, may be an epistemological failure that fails to come to grips

58. R. Attfield, "On Translating Myth," *The International Journal for the Philosophy of Religion* 2 (1971): 228–45, at 239. Emphasis in the original.

59. Attfield, "On Translating Myth," 240–41.

60. See, for example, V. J. Stenger, *God: The Failed Hypothesis—How Science Shows That God Does Not Exist* (Amherst, NY: Prometheus Books, 2007); C. Hitchens, *God Is Not Great: How Religion Poisons Everything* (New York: Warner 12, 2007); S. Pinker, *The Language Instinct* (New York: W. Morrow and Co., 1994).

61. See Hans-Georg Gadamer, *Truth and Method*, 2nd rev. ed. (New York: Continuum, 2004 [orig. 1975]).

with the test the powers present to our modern (scientific, common sense) modes of perceiving the world, which could itself be immensely deceiving.[62]

Here Karl Barth's treatment of the powers may be helpful, for while Barth accepts the superiority of modern cosmology over ancient cosmology, Barth detects that the NT writers were less determined by their inherited cosmology than we are by our contemporary worldview.[63] Barth asseverates:

> In this matter [i.e. on the subject of the powers] we have one of the not infrequent cases in which it has to be said that not all people, but some to whom a so-called magical view of the world is now ascribed, have in fact, apart from occasional hocuspocus, seen more, seen more clearly, and come much closer to the reality in their thought and speech, than those of us who are happy possessors of a rational and scientific view of things, for whom the resultant clear (but perhaps not wholly clear) distinction between truth and illusion has become almost unconsciously the criterion of all that is possible and real.[64]

For Barth, even if we may label the world picture of the NT authors as "magical," this "magical" world picture did not prevent the NT authors from taking seriously the efficacy of the powers:

> It would be better for us if we were to learn again with the same fearlessness and freedom to see and to reckon with the fact that even today we still live in a world that has been basically dedemonized already in Jesus Christ, and will be so fully one day. But in the meantime it still needs a good deal of dedemonizing, because even up to our own time it is largely demon-possessed, possessed, that is, by the existence and lordship of similar or, at times, obviously the same lordless forces which the people of the New Testament knew and which have plainly not been broken or even affected, but in many ways intensified and strengthened, by the fact that our view of the world has since those days become a rational and scientific one.[65]

Thus, for Barth, if we are to undertake a demythologizing, it should not be a demythologizing of the concept of the principalities and powers in the NT, but

---

62. See Barclay, "Why the Roman Empire Was Insignificant to Paul," 384.

63. See K. Barth, *The Christian Life (Fragment): Church Dogmatics* 4.4, trans. G. W. Bromiley (Grand Rapids: Eerdmans, 1981) 213–33.

64. Ibid., 216.

65. Ibid., 218.

rather the myths of modern powers. What is needed, according to Barth, is for Scripture to demythologize our modern world picture, not the reverse.

Paul would certainly agree with the latter claim: rather than allowing our worldview to serve as a corrective to the NT, the NT proclamation presents a challenge to every worldview it encounters.[66] The modern scientific worldview has given us the tools to read Scripture critically—and for this we ought to be grateful. But does our critique of Scripture—using modern tools—not drown out Scripture's critique of us and our world picture? Do we not remain largely oblivious to Scripture's timeless message to us? In the words of Richard Hays, "We should indeed be suspicious when we read scripture—suspicious of ourselves, whose minds need to be transformed."[67] For Paul and the NT authors, the power of the Christian proclamation lies in its ability to challenge and provide a corrective to any and every worldview it encounters, including ours.

HENDRIK BERKHOF: STRUCTURAL INTERPRETATION OF THE POWERS

If Bultmann's approach seeks to demythologize the concept of principalities and powers in the NT for our day, there is another approach to the powers that posits that Paul himself attempted to demythologize the concept of the powers of his day. This approach to the principalities and powers identifies the principalities and powers exclusively with structures of human existence. As representative of this approach, we take a look at the work of Hendrik Berkhof.[68] Berkhof formulated his thesis during the period following the devastation of World War II and the nascent years of the Cold War that divided Germany into East and West. These two events profoundly influenced his work, as he and others found strong resonances of the NT's principalities and powers in the turmoil of those years. The thesis of Berkhof's work, simply put, is that "the powers *are* the structures."[69]

To defend his thesis, Berkhof first enumerates passages in the Pauline corpus dealing with the powers. For Berkhof, the various names of the powers suggest their variety of expressions, "the number and diversity of the powers."[70] Having noted that Paul's language of the powers must be situated within

---

66. See E. Acolatse, *Cosmology and Pastoral Diagnoses: A Psycho-Theological Anthropology for Pastoral Counseling in Ghana*, Ph.D. dissertation, Princeton Theological Seminary, 2002 (Ann Arbor, MI: University Microfilms, #3061046), 44–45.

67. R. B. Hays, "A Hermeneutic of Trust," in *The Conversion of the Imagination: Paul as Interpreter of Israel's Scripture* (Grand Rapids: Eerdmans, 2005), 190–201.

68. Hendrik Berkhof, *Christ and the Powers* (Scottdale, PA: Herald, 1977 [orig. 1953]).

69. Ibid., 21.

70. Ibid., 15.

Jewish apocalyptic writings as the clear background to Paul's doctrine on the powers, Berkhof discerns that Paul on occasion classifies the angelic names of the powers with other nouns that do not designate spiritual beings (Rom. 8:38-39).[71] On other occasions, Berkhof avers, in discussion of the powers, Paul drops out the angelic names, opting instead for the names of experienced realities. Citing 1 Cor. 3:22, he writes: "It is clear that these entities [world, life, death, present, future] are not at all thought of as persons, much less as angels."[72] Paul, according to Berkhof, also relates the powers to human history (1 Cor. 2:8); in and behind "the rulers of this age"—the visible, human authorities—Paul sees invisible powers at work. And, finally, in Colossians 2 and Gal. 4:1-11, Berkhof argues that Paul's mention of the *stoicheia* locates the manifestation of the powers within human traditions. All these prove, for Berkhof, that the powers are the structures of human existence that rule over human life: the state, politics, class, social struggle, national interest, public opinion, accepted morality, the ideas of decency, humanity, democracy.[73] By his cross, Christ has exposed and disarmed the quasi-divine authorities of the structures; and apart from Christ humans are at the mercy of these powers.[74]

Paul, then, adopted Jewish apocalyptic terminology for the powers, but gave this terminology a content different from what it normally meant in his context. Paul, in essence, unlike the apocalypticists who thought of the powers as angelic heavenly beings, demythologized the powers: "In comparison to the apocalypses a certain 'demythologising' has taken place in Paul's thought. In short, the apocalypses think primarily of the principalities and powers as heavenly angels; Paul sees them as structures of earthly existence."[75] Paul discovered various ways in which people are held in bondage. Paul appropriates familiar names for superterrestrial powers only to give expression to the myriad forms and weight of such bondage.

Citing Col. 1:15-17, Berkhof argues that the powers are not evil in themselves: "From their very creation, by their very nature, they were 'made to measure' to serve as instruments of [God's] love."[76] The powers, for Berkhof, were initially created to be the link between God's love and visible human experience; the structures were intended to give order to human life. Diverse human traditions (ethics, religious rules, the state) are not evil in themselves;

71. Ibid., 18–19.
72. Ibid., 19.
73. Ibid., 32.
74. Ibid., 21–22.
75. Ibid., 23.
76. Ibid., 28.

they protect human life and creation from chaos. But the powers have fallen; bound by sin, the powers now act in diametric opposition to God. While the powers fulfill half their divinely fixed function (that is, give order to human life and society), they also in the process prevent people from serving God. The task of the Christian is not to strive against the powers, but to work for their God-intended purpose to be realized. Christ has disarmed the powers in the cross, yet the battle with the powers continues; the church battles to make the powers instruments of God's purpose. "Christianizing" the powers would make the powers fulfill their God-intended functions: provide aid, give direction to human life as children of God and neighbor, spread resources to serve mankind, pass legislation that serves God's purpose, and so on.[77]

It was in the cross that Christ disarmed the powers; and whenever the cross is proclaimed the unmasking and disarming of the powers takes place. In the end, God's plan includes the redemption of the powers; God intends to reconcile the powers to himself under the lordship of Christ (Col. 1:19). Until that time when the powers are reconciled to God, the church is caught between the "already and not yet,"[78] that place where a limitation is placed on the powers. Whenever the church proclaims Christ she sets a limit on the work of the powers, a limitation that is a portent of their ultimate defeat.

Berkhof 's study and other structural interpretations of the powers are helpful for a church that needs to come to grips with the social and structural nature of sin and evil.[79] Locating the powers within the structures that determine human life cautions the church to evaluate how much its own way of life has been shaped by, and sometimes even constitutes a perpetuation of, oppressive structures. There are problems, however, with this approach. We may note the greatest flaw in this approach with a reverse formulation of Berkhof's thesis: the powers are *not* the structures for Paul. To equate the powers with structures of human existence is to fundamentally misread Paul. In a critique of the recent rise of scholarly interests in imperial readings of Paul, John Barclay correctly notes that, for Paul, the powers operate simultaneously

77. Ibid., 53–70.

78. Ibid., 43.

79. For other structural interpretations of the powers see E. G. Rupp, *Principalities and Powers: Studies in the Christian Conflict in History* (London: Epworth, 1952); G. B. Caird, *The Language and Imagery of the Bible* (Philadelphia: Westminster, 1980), 242; Caird, *Principalities and Powers: A Study in Pauline Theology* (Eugene, OR: Wipf and Stock, 2003 [orig. 1956]); M. Barth, *The Broken Wall: A Study of Ephesians* (Valley Forge: Judson, 1959); W. Stringfellow, *Free in Obedience* (New York: Seabury, 1964); R. J. Sider, "Christ and Power," *IRM* 69 (1980): 8–20; J. H. Yoder, *The Politics of Jesus*, 2nd ed. (Grand Rapids: Eerdmans, 1994), 134–62.

across all levels—individual, social, political, and cosmic.[80] Thus, the structures of human existence do not themselves constitute the powers, neither are they even one of the powers; but they may be co-opted by higher powers—divine or demonic. Take, for example, Paul's own treatment of the political structures in his letters—and here we cannot be deaf to the cacophony of research on the political dimensions of Paul's theology.[81] We do not think that Paul's theology is apolitical; on the contrary, Paul's theology has serious political implications. Nonetheless, we cannot include the political structures in our study of the principalities and powers, since Paul's complex theology on the powers denies the political authorities any significance in what Barclay has termed the cosmic drama of history.[82]

Barclay, in his critique of the "Paul and Empire" coalition, is correct to point out that Paul does not name any of the Roman emperors or governors in his letters;[83] nor does he make any special references to the imperial cult.[84] And while it was common knowledge that crucifixion was a Roman punishment, Paul does not attribute the crucifixion of Jesus to Rome; rather, he attributes it to "the rulers of this age" (1 Cor. 2:6-8). We should note that Barclay almost undermines his own position by interpreting "the rulers of this age" as nameless and generalized human authorities. Indeed, it seems to us almost impossible to posit that the Roman Empire "was insignificant to Paul" if Paul had attributed to human rulers the full weight of the title "the rulers of *this age*."

80. Barclay, "Why the Roman Empire Was Insignificant to Paul," 383–84. Barclay, however, does not deal fully with the concept of principalities and powers in Paul. His arguments are also mainly directed toward N. T. Wright.

81. The literature is immense. See, for example, R. A. Horsley, ed., *Paul and Empire: Religion and Power in Roman Imperial Society* (Harrisburg, PA: Trinity Press International, 1997); Horsley, ed., *Paul and Politics: Ekklesia, Israel, Imperium, Interpretatio: Essays in Honor of Krister Stendahl* (Harrisburg, PA: Trinity Press International, 2000); Horsley, ed., *Paul and the Roman Imperial Order* (Harrisburg, PA: Trinity Press International, 2004); N. Elliot, *Liberating Paul: The Justice of God and the Politics of the Apostle* (Maryknoll, NY: Orbis, 1994); Elliot, *The Arrogance of Nations: Reading Romans in the Shadow of Empire* (Minneapolis: Fortress Press, 2008); J. D. Crossan and J. L. Reed, *In Search of Paul: How Jesus' Apostle Opposed Rome's Empire with God's Kingdom* (San Francisco: HarperSanFrancisco, 2004); B. J. Walsh and S. C. Keesmaat, *Colossians Remixed: Subverting the Empire* (Downers Grove, IL: InterVarsity, 2004); N. T. Wright, "Paul and Caesar: A New Reading of Romans," in *A Royal Priesthood? The Use of the Bible Ethically and Politically*, ed. C. Bartholomew et al. (Grand Rapids: Zondervan, 2002), 173–93; Wright, *Paul: in Fresh Perspective* (Minneapolis: Fortress Press, 2005), 59–79.

82. Our analysis here is in large part in agreement with Barclay's argument against the Paul and Empire coalition ("Why the Roman Empire Was Insignificant to Paul," 363–87).

83. Paul makes reference to the "governor under King Aretas" of Damascus in 2 Cor. 11:32; but this mention is part of an autobiographical sketch.

84. Barclay, "Why the Roman Empire Was Insignificant to Paul," 374–75.

Nonetheless, Barclay's main contention is correct; and, in our view, nowhere is this more apparent than Paul's attribution of Christ's crucifixion to "the rulers of this age"—more pervasive, more powerful, spiritual forces operating on the cosmic scene.[85] The rulers of this age, Paul contends, crucified the Lord of glory (1 Cor. 2:8). This is a profound theological claim—one that perceives the religio-political context through an interpretive framework in which the political authorities are not the main actors in the cosmic drama of history. The political structures can be co-opted by higher powers—divine or demonic. Thus, to the extent that the work of the political authorities is discerned as aligning with God's purposes, then the political rulers can be identified as functioning as servants of God in those instances (Rom. 13:1-7). But when their work is discerned as lining up against God's will, then the political authorities must be unmasked as operating within the ranks of the powers of darkness. Paul's theology cautions us to desist from viewing the political structures as inherently evil, for they can at times serve as God's messengers. What is important to recognize is that Paul refuses to name the political structures among the classes of the principalities and powers, because their agency is subordinate and derived. As such, to equate the powers with the political structures would be to assign these human structures too much significance—far more than their due.

In addition, Berkhof's position, which requires Paul to demythologize the conception of the powers he had inherited from his Jewish tradition, raises the issue of continuity and discontinuity between Paul and early Judaism and early Christianity. Not many scholars, to my knowledge, would argue against the view that Jewish literature before Paul was characterized by a worldview that believed in an evil figure (Satan, Mastema, Belial, Beliar) and his demons in opposition to God's work and his angels.[86] Berkhof himself acknowledges this much: "[Paul's] terminology [of the powers] points us most clearly to . . . Jewish apocalyptic writings . . . Two things were always true of the Powers [found in the apocalyptic and rabbinic writings]: (1) they are personal, spiritual beings and (2) they influence events on earth, especially events within nature."[87] It is also the case that the NT authors—writing after Paul—often speak of the devil (or Satan), and evil spirits, with a will and intellect, actively opposing God's work and God's people.[88] In addition, later Christians (writing

85. See our chapter on 1 & 2 Corinthians for a detailed treatment of 1 Cor. 2:6-8.

86. For a study of Jewish literature in the period before and after Paul, see George W. E. Nickelsburg, *Jewish Literature between the Bible and the Mishnah: A Historical and Literary Introduction*, 2nd ed. (Minneapolis: Fortress Press, 2005).

87. Berkhof, *Christ and the Powers*, 17.

in the patristic period) were no different in viewing the devil and his minions as actively opposed to Christ's work.[89] Thus, the evidence unambiguously indicates that Paul inherited a tradition that viewed Satan and his evil cohorts as spiritual beings with will, intellect, and power to harm humans and oppose God's work. As a result, any view that makes Paul the only NT author to "demythologize" the powers, while it may highlight the distinctiveness of Paul, overstates the discontinuity between Paul and the Jewish tradition within which he stood and the Christian movement that came before and after him. Such deep discontinuity is unwarranted. At the root of this misconception is the anachronistic use of the term "demythologizing." This is a defective category that should not be applied to Paul. What Berkhof may be trying to characterize by his use of "demythologizing" may be the literary personifications in Paul's letters.[90] As we shall see later in this study, even in this move Paul is not unique but has Jewish predecessors.

WALTER WINK: INVISIBLE INTERIORITY OF MATERIAL AND OUTER MATERIALITY

Walter Wink, with his *Powers* trilogy, offers the most extensive investigation of the powers vocabulary and concept in the NT.[91] Wink sees his work as a "pilgrimage away" from the demythologizing perspectives on the powers that preceded his work. *Naming the Powers* develops the thesis that the powers consist of an outer manifestation and inner spirituality or interiority. Wink lays out some preliminary hypotheses about the powers:

1. The language of power pervades the whole New Testament.
2. The language of power in the New Testament is imprecise, liquid,

88. See, for example, the Gospel accounts of the temptation (Matt. 4:1-11 par.); also Matt. 12:26; 25:41; Mark 1:13; 3:26; 5:2; 7:25; Luke 8:12; John 13:2; James 4:7; 1 Pet. 5:8; 1 John 3:8; Rev. 12:9, etc. See J. B. Russell, *The Devil: Perceptions of Evil from Antiquity to Primitive Christianity* (Ithaca, NY: Cornell University Press, 1977); G. Twelftree, *Christ Triumphant: Exorcism Then and Now* (London: Hodder & Stoughton, 1985).

89. See J. B. Russell, *Satan: The Early Christian Tradition* (Ithaca, NY: Cornell University Press, 1981).

90. Cf. Berkhof, *Christ and the Powers*, 24: "One can even doubt whether Paul conceived of the powers as personal beings. In any case this aspect is so secondary that it makes little difference whether he did or not. He may be using personifications." Cf. 1 Cor. 5:5; 7:5; 2 Cor. 2:11; 11:14; 1 Thess. 2:18.

91. W. Wink, *Naming the Powers: The Language of the Powers in the New Testament* (Philadelphia: Fortress Press, 1984); Wink, *Unmasking the Powers: The Invisible Forces That Determine Human Existence* (Philadelphia: Fortress Press, 1986); Wink, *Engaging the Powers: Discernment and Resistance in a World of Domination* (Minneapolis: Fortress Press, 1992). See also Wink, *When the Powers Fall* (Minneapolis: Augsburg-Fortress Press, 1998); *The Powers That Be* (New York: Doubleday, 1999).

interchangeable, and unsystematic.

3. Despite all this imprecision and interchangeability, clear patterns of usage emerge.

4. Because these terms are to a degree interchangeable, one or a pair or a series can be made to represent them all.

5. These powers are both heavenly and earthly, divine and human, spiritual and political, invisible and structural.

6. These powers are also both good and evil.[92]

Wink, then, provides a very helpful analysis of the vocabulary of the powers in the NT: ἀρχή and ἄρχων; ἐξουσία; δύναμις; θρόνος; κυριότης; ὄνομα; angels; fallen angels, evil spirits, and demons; angels of the nations. This analysis arms Wink with the clues needed to add a further observation about the powers to the six preliminary hypotheses above:

7. Unless the context further specifies . . . we are to take the terms for power in their most comprehensive sense, understanding them to mean both heavenly and earthly, divine and human, good and evil powers.[93]

For Wink, the above observation serves as the key to unravel the puzzle of "disputed" NT passages on the powers (1 Cor. 2:6-8; Rom. 13:1-3; Rom. 8:38-39; 1 Cor. 15:24-27a; Col. 2:13-15; Eph. 1:20-23; Col. 1:16; Col. 2:9-10; Eph. 2:1-2; Eph. 6:12; Eph. 3:10). The powers, according to Wink, must be viewed as having a dual aspect: an outer, visible form *and* an inner, invisible spirit. Any other conclusion about the powers is inconsistent with their comprehensive portrayal in Scripture. Thus he rejects studies like that of Oscar Cullman's,[94] which views the powers as both earthly and heavenly, as too imprecise. For Wink, the powers cannot represent two distinct agents, human or institutional and divine or demonic: "*The Powers are simultaneously the outer and inner aspects of one and the same indivisible concretion of power.*"[95] The powers have no separate spiritual existence apart from reference to the material or earthly reality. The powers are like a mob spirit, which comes into being in the moment a crowd gathers and vanishes when the crowd disperses. Similarly, no spiritual reality exists at any moment in time without a material embodiment.

92. Wink, *Naming the Powers*, 7–12.

93. Ibid., 39.

94. See Cullman, *Christ and Time*.

95. Wink, *Naming the Powers*, 107; emphasis in the original.

The second book in the *Powers* trilogy, *Unmasking the Powers*, builds on the thesis argued in *Naming the Powers* through a detailed investigation of seven of the powers mentioned in the first volume:

> 1. Satan—the actual power that coagulates around injustice, idolatry, or inhumanity. This power increases or decreases depending on collective choices.[96]
> 2. Demons—the psychic or spiritual power emanated by subaspects of individuals or organizations. The energy of these powers seeks to subdue others.[97]
> 3. Angels of churches—the actual inner spirituality of a congregation as an entity, existing in, with, and under the material expressions of the church's life.[98]
> 4. Angels of nations—the actual invisible spirituality of a social entity or state that guides, sustains, and animates a nation.[99]
> 5. Gods—the very real archetype or ideological structures that govern or determine reality and the human brain.[100]
> 6. Elements of the universe—the invariances (or "laws") which, though many a time idolized by humans, preserve the self-consistency of each level of reality in its harmonious interrelationship with every other level and the Whole.[101]
> 7. Angels of nature—the patterning of physical things, the whole God-glorifying, visible universe.[102]

All these "powers" represent the invisible interiority of reality, and are forces that determine physical, psychic, and social existence.[103] In this respect, Wink proceeds with a functionalist approach. The functionalist approach identifies the "experiences" that the NT cosmology names. When these experiences named in the NT are recovered (the personal and social phenomena that transcend conscious grasp yet determine human existence), they give us the language to name our own experiences in our modern scientific milieu—experiences that materialism renders inexpressible.

---

96. Wink, *Unmasking the Powers*, 9–40.

97. Ibid., 41–68.

98. Ibid., 69–86.

99. Ibid., 87–107.

100. Ibid., 108–27.

101. Ibid., 128–52.

102. Ibid., 153–71.

103. The third book in the trilogy, *Engaging the Powers*, focuses on the more visible, institutionalized forms of the powers.

Wink's analysis of the "powers" terminology and passages in the NT is extremely valuable. Wink makes a convincing case that we cannot completely ignore or reject the spiritual dimension of existence. Of course, Wink's view, like Berkhof's interpretation of the powers, proceeds with the assumption that Paul took steps to "demythologize" the powers. Yet Wink brings a certain level of sophistication to an understanding of the powers as structures (or outer materialities) of human existence. He seeks to be both faithful to the ancient context of these texts and accessible and relevant to a modern context shaped by a worldview of scientific materialism. Wink is also to be commended for challenging our modern obsession with materiality. Henceforth, every work that addresses the biblical concept of the powers must grapple with Wink's provocative thesis.

Nonetheless, some of Wink's views are questionable. First, Wink does not give sufficient attention to or refutation of the view that the authors of the NT viewed the powers as spiritual forces with intellect and will, whose actions affect human life on earth.[104] To be sure, Wink sees himself as following the lead of Paul, who, for Wink, makes an important leap toward "depersonalizing"[105] the powers.[106] Yet is Wink's detection of Paul's attempt to "depersonalize" the powers not at the same time an implicit acknowledgement that Paul's contemporaries and predecessors viewed the powers as personal spiritual beings? If so, then how do Paul and the NT authors continue or discontinue this tradition? Wink's study has not armed us with the tools necessary to understand why and how the NT authors conceived of the powers differently from the commonly held belief of their contemporaries.

Second, in his treatment of the language of the powers, Wink's fourth hypothesis that the names of the powers are to a degree interchangeable,[107] so that one or a pair or a series can be made to represent them all, seems untenable. There are some differences between the NT's usage of terms such as ἐξουσίαι,

---

104. See, for example, John R. W. Stott, *God's New Society: The Message of Ephesians* (Downers Grove, IL: InterVarsity, 1979), 263–67.

105. Wink, *Naming the Powers*, 104.

106. This seems to us a confusion about personification. See our chapter on Romans for detailed discussion.

107. To my knowledge, this point was first made by H. Schlier. Cf. Schlier, *Principalities and Powers in the New Testament* (New York: Herder and Herder, 1961), 14–15: "Examination shows that the names given to the powers of evil are, to a large extent, interchangeable. Naturally, certain New Testament writers favour one name rather than another: we all know that the Synoptic Gospels usually speak of Satan, the devil, demons or spirits; St. Paul often uses the names principalities, powers, or virtues, while the Gospel of St. John prefers to speak of the prince of this world. But these names are not mutually exclusive; they are freely interchangeable."

θρόνοι, σατανᾶς, δαιμόνιον, and ἄγγελος.[108] Ἄγγελος, for example, receives an ambiguous treatment in the letters of Paul. On the one hand, Paul knows of good angels; he can, therefore, speak of an angel of light (2 Cor. 11:14), an angel of God (Gal. 4:14; cf. 3:19),[109] and mighty angels of heaven with Christ (2 Thess. 1:7; cf. Gal. 1:8).[110] But, on the other hand, Paul knows of an angel of Satan (ἄγγελος σατανᾶ; 2 Cor. 12:7)[111] and he includes angels in the list of "powers" attempting to separate believers from the love of God (Rom. 8:38). On other occasions, angels seem to be morally neutral in Paul; for example, in 1 Cor. 4:9, 6:3, 11:10 it is not clear whether the angels are good or evil. Paul's usage of terms like σατανᾶς and δαιμόνιον, however, contains no such ambiguity; Satan and demons are always evil entities in Paul—even if God can on occasion use them to serve his purposes (Rom. 16:20; 1 Cor. 5:5; 7:5; 10:20, 21; 2 Cor. 2:11; 11:14; 12:7; 1 Thess. 2:18; 2 Thess. 2:9). Thus, Wink's suggestion that all the terms for the powers can be used interchangeably cannot be correct.

Finally, can the view that the spiritual and physical aspects of the powers are always *simultaneously* present and indivisible survive scrutiny? Is Wink correct in his assertion that when ancient writers employed the language of the powers they always meant this indivisible unity between matter and spirit? Evidence from the early period seems to suggest otherwise. Early Jewish literature, for example, took for granted the existence of a spiritual realm that is independent of the natural. These writings perceived a natural order in the universe that demanded a certain pattern of life, one of the chief tenets of which was the preservation of the sexual boundaries between heavenly and earthly beings. An example of this view is found in a passage in the *Testament of the Twelve Patriarchs*:

> Sun, moon and stars do not alter their order; thus you should not alter the Law of God by the disorder of your actions. The gentiles, because they wandered astray and forsook the Lord, have changed the order, and have devoted themselves to stones and sticks, patterning themselves after wandering spirits. But you, my children, shall not be like that: in the firmament, in the earth, and in the sea, in all the products of his workmanship discern the Lord who made all

---

108. So also Marva J. Dawn, *Powers, Weakness, and the Tabernacling of God* (Grand Rapids: Eerdmans), 14.

109. We devote adequate attention to Gal. 3:19 in our chapter on Galatians.

110. Cf. 1 Cor. 13:1; 2 Thess. 1:7.

111. It is also possible that this verse should be rendered as "messenger of Satan."

things, so that you do not become like Sodom, which departed from the order of nature. Likewise the *Watchers departed from nature's order;* the Lord pronounced a curse on them at the Flood. On their account he ordered that the earth be without dweller or produce. (*T. Naph.* 3:2-5; emphasis mine)[112]

The sin of the Watchers was that they transgressed the natural boundaries between earth and heaven by having unnatural intercourse with women.[113] In traditions about this story, the result of this unnatural union was the release of a host of evil demons who plagued humanity (*Jub.* 7:20-28; 10:1-6; *1 En.* 6–15). That the origins of a devastated world should be attributed to a transgression of the boundaries between the heavenly and the earthly speaks to the fact that ancient writers held to a worldview that distinguished a spiritual, heavenly realm beyond the earthly realm. It also shows that they held this distinction to be sacred. We cannot exaggerate this distinction for the ancients; but we cannot obliterate the distinction either.

In the end, despite his constant castigation of the modern materialistic worldview, Wink's conflation of the spiritual with the material evinces an attempt to accommodate the ancient and biblical worldview to modern ideological assumptions. One wonders whether Wink has offered us exegesis of the biblical and ancient texts or a concession to the "powers" of modern materialism and psychology.

To summarize our discussion thus far, we have looked at four distinct approaches to the powers embodied in the works of Arnold, Bultmann, Berkhof, and Wink. The strength of Arnold's approach is that it takes seriously the existence of the reality of spiritual entities for Paul and early Jewish and Christian writers. But this purely personal interpretation of the powers cannot account for the complex presentation of the powers in Paul; and it offers very few resources for dealing with the structural nature of evil. Bultmann also accepts the fact that the early Christian writers believed in the existence of spiritual entities; but he dismisses this belief as "mythical." Bultmann is wrong exegetically to posit a gnostic background for the NT language of the powers; and his own demythologizing interpretation is too closely bound to his own worldview, thereby making him oblivious to the challenge the powers pose to our modern myths. Berkhof's structural interpretation of the powers may help us to wrestle with the nature of structural evil, but whereas Bultmann clearly recognizes the difference between Paul's worldview and his own, Berkhof

---

112. Translation by H. C. Kee in *OTP* 1:812.

113. Cf. *T. Reu.* 5:6; 2 Pet. 2:4; Jude 6.

anachronistically projects his own worldview back onto Paul. Thus, Berkhof introduces a confusion between exegesis and hermeneutics.[114] Finally, Wink's approach is a more nuanced formulation of the structural interpretation of the powers, attributing to the structures an inner spirituality. But Wink's position is fundamentally damaged by his misguided assumption that ancient writers could not conceive of a spiritual realm that is independent of the physical realm.

In the next chapter we propose "practice" as an important category with which to understand Paul's principalities and powers. It is our contention that Paul's conception of the principalities and powers is unintelligible without a developed account of the practices of the Pauline congregations. Thus, in part 2 of this work we will give a detailed study of the practices Paul recommends for engaging the principalities and powers in the early believing communities.

---

114. I am grateful to Richard Hays for this formulation.

3

A Proposed Way Forward: Practices

The contribution this study hopes to make is to approach Paul's theology of the principalities and powers by attending to practices of the early believers. It is our contention that the category of "practice" provides important clues for thinking about Paul's theology of the powers. Whatever we may consider to be Paul's theology of the powers, his understanding is embodied and social, disclosed by practices he performed or advocated for the early believers. Language of the powers can, therefore, not be isolated from early Christian practices. As a result, while this study hopes to make a contribution to a vital aspect of Pauline theology largely ignored in Western scholarship, it also hopes to expand the conversation on how theological conviction is embedded in Christian practices, illuminating this from the standpoint of the powers. Because Paul's view of the powers was intimately connected with his vision for reordering the life of the body of Christ, the powers cannot be given adequate treatment without an account of practices within the early church. Thus, a simple (though not necessarily simplistic) definition of what we are calling "practices of power" will guide our study of the principalities and powers in the Pauline letters: *practices of power are either activities that guard believers from the dominion of the powers, or activities that expose believers and unbelievers to the dominion of the powers.*

According to Paul, there are certain practices that shield believers from the domain of the principalities and powers. Conversely, other practices, if adopted by believers, would make them vulnerable to the powers. Practice becomes the means by which Paul and the early believers orient themselves to Christ in hopes of overcoming the powers of evil.

To contribute to a practical understanding of Paul's theology of the powers, we will sketch two contemporary accounts of practices—in the works of Alasdair MacIntyre and Pierre Bourdieu—and draw out their implications for Paul's theology of the powers.

Alasdair MacIntyre: Narratives and Practices

Alasdair MacIntyre diagnoses the modern liberal condition as one characterized by rival arguments that are conceptually incommensurable, because we have inherited fragments of formerly robust and coherent moral traditions.[1] According to MacIntyre, modern societies have lost any sense of a shared common good; modern liberal societies have lost the Aristotelian tradition of teleology and the notion of virtue based on this tradition. The heart of Aristotelian theory is that humans, by nature, move toward a certain *telos*.[2] The virtues are the dispositions possessed by a person that help a person move toward the *telos*. These virtues have to be cultivated within a *polis*, a community whose central bond is a shared vision of the good. MacIntyre appeals for a retrieval of this pre-Enlightenment tradition of the virtues. For virtues to be applied, they require the acceptance of some prior account of social and moral life by which to define or account for the virtues. Thus, if a core concept of a virtue is to be understood it requires a practice, a narrative of a single human life, and a moral tradition.[3] Human practice is the sphere in which the virtues are displayed. Practice serves for MacIntyre as the context for establishing the common background for differing accounts of the virtues. MacIntyre defines practice as

> any coherent and complex form of socially established cooperative human activity through which goods internal to that form of activity are realized in the course of trying to achieve those standards of excellence which are appropriate to, and partially definitive of, that form of activity, with the result that human powers to achieve excellence, and human conceptions of the ends and goods involved, are systematically extended.[4]

The goods are internal to a practice because they can be obtained and experienced only by engaging in a particular practice. This must be distinguished from external goods—goods not necessarily dependent on performing the practice well. To attain the goods internal to a practice requires

---

1. Alasdair MacIntyre, *After Virtue: A Study in Moral Theory*, 3d ed. (Notre Dame, IN: Notre Dame University Press, 2007), 1–5. See also MacIntyre, *Three Rival Versions of Moral Enquiry: Encyclopaedia, Genealogy, and Tradition* (Notre Dame, IN: University of Notre Dame Press, 1988); MacIntyre, *Whose Justice, Which Rationality?* (Notre Dame, IN: University of Notre Dame Press, 1988).

2. See Aristotle, *Nichomachean Ethics*, 1; 2.4–6; 3.6; 4; 5; 6.4–13.

3. MacIntyre, *After Virtue*, 186–87.

4. Ibid., 187.

the cultivation of the virtues: the virtues are those acquired human qualities the possession of which enable a person to achieve the goods internal to a practice and the lack of which prevent a person from achieving the goods.[5] And since the application of virtues requires the acceptance of some prior account of social and moral life, practices have a history and standards of excellence that have to be obeyed in order to achieve the goods internal to the practices. Practices are, consequently, also inherently communal, for it is in community that humans learn and narrate the history of the practice and the virtues required to attain the goods internal to the practice. In short, narratives and practices are essential for embodying, interpreting, and sustaining the virtues appropriate to a moral tradition.

In an extension of MacIntyre's account of narratives and practices as essential for the cultivation of virtues, Stanley Hauerwas argues that the virtues needed to sustain the Christian community can only be demonstrated by drawing on the community's account of the good, which takes the form of narrative.[6] The narrative of this community and the practice of their virtues are intertwined: "The nature of Christian ethics is determined by the fact that Christian convictions take the form of a story, or perhaps better, a set of stories that constitutes a tradition, which in turn creates and forms community."[7] Christian ethical practices do not begin with a set of rules or principles, but they first point to a narrative of God's work in creation.

Important for our purpose in MacIntyre's rehabilitation of narratives and practices as the framework for cultivating the virtues is that practices are narrative dependent; practices involve a story. Such a conception of practice is helpful for understanding an early Christian practice such as baptism as a practice of power. Since practices are essential for shaping communal identity, a particular narrative was required in the early church for the interpretation and maintaining of baptism as a practice of power—one that rescues believers from the realm of darkness and transfers them to the realm of light.[8] It is our contention that underlying the practice of baptism is a story of Christ's encounter with the principalities and powers at the cross. According to Colossians, on the cross Christ divested himself of the powers and unmasked the powers as enemies of God and humanity (Col. 2:15). It is this story that underlies the Christian practice of baptism, in which believers are said to divest

5. Ibid., 191.

6. Stanley Hauerwas, *The Peaceable Kingdom: A Primer in Christian Ethics* (Notre Dame, IN: University of Notre Dame Press, 1983), 1–22.

7. Ibid., 24.

8. See our chapters on Romans and Colossians.

themselves of the old human by being buried with Christ in baptism (Col. 2:11-12). In baptism Christians reenact the story of Christ's death by being stripped naked—a signification of the stripping of the old self who has been crucified with Christ (Rom. 6:6). Believers are "buried" under the water of baptism and "raised" with Christ (Rom. 6:1-7; Col. 2:11-12). Believers are mapped onto Christ's own trajectory and transferred into a new sphere, where the principalities and powers no longer hold sway but Christ reigns supreme (Rom. 6:7; Col. 2:13-14). This view of baptism as a practice of power is possible because of a narrative that recognized larger forces at work in Christ's death and burial: the rulers of this age crucified the Lord of glory, Paul claims (1 Cor. 2:6-8), and Colossians recounts that at his crucifixion Christ nailed the cheirographon with its legal demands against believers to the cross and divested himself of the principalities and powers (Col. 2:14-15). These are all part of the same story that underwrites baptism as a practice of power in which believers are delivered from the domain of the powers by reenacting Christ's story. As we shall see in our treatment of 1 Corinthians 1–2, to proclaim this story of Christ's encounter with the powers at the cross is to be swept into a battlefront inaugurated by the death of Christ (cf. 1 Cor. 1–2; 1 Thess. 1:5-10; 2:18-19).

PIERRE BOURDIEU: STRUCTURES AND *HABITUS*

French sociologist Pierre Bourdieu develops an account of practice that is helpful for dealing with the range of human social practices. Bourdieu develops his account from his ethnographic research on traditional Algerian communities and his study of contemporary French society. Bourdieu's main targets are structuralism—for its objectivism—and subjectivism, with its isolated Sartrean subject. For Bourdieu, when social scientists adopt the "objective" and external posture, their study of social life is, perforce, distorted. Social scientists and anthropologists in their preoccupation with interpreting practices are prone to construct patterns of regularity and excavate the underlying logic to account for the patterns; they, in turn, impose these constructs on the subjects of their study, because they are outsiders to the social realities of their subjects.[9] "It is significant," Bourdieu writes, "that 'culture' is sometimes described as a *map*; it is the analogy which occurs to an outsider who has to find his way around in a foreign landscape and who compensates for his lack of practical mastery, the prerogative of the native, by the use of a model of all possible routes."[10] For

---

9. P. Bourdieu, *Outline of a Theory of Practice*, trans. Richard Nice (Cambridge: Cambridge University Press, 1977 [orig. 1972]), 1–71.

10. Ibid., 2. Emphasis in the original.

this reason, the anthropologist needs to break with the presuppositions inherent in the position of an outside observer so as not to introduce into the object principles and an objective system of rules of his or her own creation. According to Bourdieu, social agents do not act according to rules or governing principles, nor do they have any need for such rules. This is because social agents know the practices of their culture better than the logical scheme developed by the researcher to account for their social practices. For Bourdieu,

> If practices had as their principle the generative principle which has to be constructed in order to account for them, that is, a set of independent and coherent axioms, then the practices produced according to perfectly conscious generative rules would be stripped of everything that defines them distinctively as practices, that is, the uncertainty and "fuzziness" resulting from the fact that they have as their principle not a set of conscious, constant rules, but practical schemes, opaque to their possessors, varying according to the logic of the situation, the almost invariable viewpoint which it imposes.[11]

The logic that actually generates practices is hidden from researchers and not apparent to social agents. This generative logic Bourdieu terms *habitus*. *Habitus* refers to "systems of durable, transposable dispositions, structured structures predisposed to function as structuring structures, that is, as principles which generate and organize practices and representations that can be objectively adapted to their outcomes without presupposing a conscious aiming at ends or an express mastery of the operations necessary in order to attain them."[12] The *habitus* helps us to understand the dialectic between structures and practices; and per this account, individuals adopt practical strategies and prior cultural and structural products of a society. Bourdieu contends that social agents internalize the perceptual structures of their social location and embody these structures in the way they act. The important points are that structures determine human actions and that the internalization and performance of these embodied social structures are unconscious: "Each agent, wittingly or unwittingly, willy nilly, is a producer and reproducer of objective meaning. Because his actions and works are the product of a *modus operandi* of which he is not the producer and has no conscious mastery, they contain an 'objective intention,' as the Scholastics put it, which always outruns his conscious intentions."[13] Social agents perform the

---

11. P. Bourdieu, *The Logic of Practice*, trans. Richard Nice (Stanford: Stanford University Press, 1990 [orig. 1980]), 12.
12. Ibid., 53.

practices imposed upon them by their social structures by means of the *habitus*. In short, social practices are governed by social realities—hidden from social agents—that are internalized and experienced as natural by social agents and orient their actions.

In their rehabilitation of Bourdieu's concept of the *habitus*, Greg Noble and Megan Watkins take issue with Bourdieu's emphasis on the unconscious embodiment of the social structures.[14] This emphasis on the unconscious nature of embodiment, Noble and Watkins insist, introduces a form of mechanistic determinism into Boudieu's application of the *habitus* and eliminates any account of the acquisition of the *habitus*. This makes the reproduction of the *habitus* a passive process, a mere mimesis that takes place "below the level of consciousness."[15] Using sporting performance as a template, Noble and Watkins argue that the *habitus* is not opposed to consciousness; rather, *habitus* must be developed over time through conscious learning:

> Habitus cannot develop except via habituation. Performativity is based on iteration. . . . Habituation, moreover, allows us to account for how conscious behavior can become unconscious. There is no doubt that much of what we do remains unconscious, yet throughout the training process we have the capacity to reflect upon our practical sense. Competence is achieved, however, when we return much of the bodily process to the realm of the unconscious.[16]

> The relationship between the conscious and the unconscious must be conceived as a dialectic of bringing behavior to consciousness ("remembering") and then habituating the behavior ("forgetting").[17]

This concept of *habitus* as habituated disposition provides a helpful resource for exploring Paul's attempt to nurture dispositions in believers that internalize the Christian message and that orient their actions in light of the knowledge of the all-pervasiveness of the powers. The former pagans had their own *habitus*. This involved, among other things, participation in meals offered to idols (1 Corinthians 8, 10). Such dispositions meant the gentiles were predisposed to

13. Bourdieu, *Outline of a Theory of Practice*, 79.

14. G. Noble and M. Watkins, "So, How did Bourdieu Learn to Play Tennis? Habitus, Consciousness and Habituation," *Cultural Studies* 17 (2003): 520–38.

15. Bourdieu, *Logic of Practice*, 73.

16. Noble and Watkins, "Habitus, Consciousness and Habituation," 535.

17. Ibid.

engage in certain practices of power—activities that will expose them to the powers of darkness. According to Paul, to participate in meals offered to idols is to leave oneself vulnerable to the demons behind the idols (1 Cor. 10:20-21). As such, Paul wanted to cultivate a new *habitus* in believers, one that would be reinforced through regular practice. The new social location of believers in Christ meant the need for the cultivation of new dispositions that would govern their social practices. He reminds them that their regular sharing in the Lord's Supper is a sharing in Christ's body; and this practice makes it impossible for them to also participate in the table of idols. While there may exist many lords and many gods outside the church, believers are now located in a realm ruled by one God and one Lord. As such, they cannot engage in practices that make room for other lords and other gods (1 Cor. 10:21-22).

The cultivation of a *habitus* as a means to engage the powers is also seen in 1 Thessalonians, where the proclamation of the Christian message is interwoven with discipleship and nurturing. The message proclaimed in power breaks the yoke of the unbelievers who were held in bondage by the power of idolatry (1 Thess. 1:5-10; cf. Gal. 1:4; 4:8-10). Yet these new converts have to be constantly nurtured, lest they fall prey to the "Tempter" (1 Thess. 3:1-5), who seeks to lead them astray. Nurturing of new converts includes guarding them against unsound teaching. Thus, 2 Thessalonians seeks to combat misinterpretations and false teachings concerning the Parousia. In the Thessalonian correspondence, nurturing of new converts is a crucial practice in producing believers who can overcome the temptations and deceptive schemes of the powers (cf. 1 Thess. 3:1-5; 2 Thess. 2:9-10; 1 Cor. 7:5).

The creation of a Christian *habitus* also involves the ability to discern the all-pervasive work of the powers in unanticipated places. Satan seeks to take more than his due with the church. That is why the way the church conducts herself in matters of church discipline can be Satan's point of entry into the church (1 Cor. 5:1-5; 2 Cor. 2:11). The powers can also penetrate the church through Christian apostles (2 Cor. 11:1-15). Believers, therefore, have to be vigilant in order to be able to detect and unmask the insidious works of the powers (cf. 2 Thess. 2:1-12).

But all this is possible only through the cultivation of a Christian *habitus*. And the fact that Paul kept writing letters to these congregations meant that the Christian *habitus* had to be developed over time through teaching and learning. In the next four chapters we devote adequate attention to practices of power in the Pauline letters. The goal of this study is not to treat every single passage in the Pauline corpus where the principalities and powers are invoked. Rather, we treat in detail only some representative passages where practices of power are present. It is our hope that by paying attention to these practices we can help shed light on an important aspect of Paul's theology.

PART II

Practices for Engaging the Powers in the Pauline Communities

4

Baptism as Deliverance from the Powers: Romans

Paul presents in Romans the most sophisticated account of the powers of any of his letters. We will discover later on in our study that Paul makes similar arguments in his other letters, even if his arguments in the other letters appear in polemical contexts and do not represent the kind of sober reflection we encounter in Romans.[1] Romans is, thus, a good place to begin. As in his other letters, readers are ushered in Romans into a drama in which God, by means of his invasion of the world in Christ, rescues humans from anti-God powers that hold them in thrall.[2] But in Romans the focus is rarely on figures such as Satan, demons, and the rulers of this age; rather, the powers mostly consist of figures that are *not* otherworldly, but more pervasive: Sin and Death. This observation should in no way downplay the presence of supernatural forces in Romans; we do encounter them in 8:38-39 and 16:20. However, the main players are Sin and Death. These actors, together with their supernatural counterparts, are evidence of how pervasive the powers are. The powers operate across all facets of human existence and the cosmos. The battlefield in Romans is much broader but also much closer to home. Thus, God's rectifying act must encompass all the spheres into which the powers have penetrated.[3]

---

1. This is especially the case with the Letter to the Galatians.

2. This theme is mostly concentrated in Romans 5–8, which is our focus in this chapter. To defend her argument that the cosmology Paul presents in Romans is a universe inhabited by anti-God powers that have taken creation captive, Beverly Gaventa points to the language of conflict that pervades the letter, most of which is located in chapters 5–8. See Gaventa, "Neither Height Nor Depth: Discerning the Cosmology of Romans," *SJT* 64 (2011): 265–78, esp. 269–75.

3. It is difficult to come to grips with Paul's theology of the powers and still maintain an anthropocentric notion of "salvation," one reserved only for individuals who profess faith in Christ. As we shall see, in Romans salvation is cosmic in scope, reaching beyond humanity to include a groaning

Attempting to pin down the source of Paul's terminologies may well require some supernatural ability. Yet if we pay close attention, we may hear echoes in Romans of terminologies and concepts in the Jewish Scriptures in which Paul was deeply immersed. In this chapter, we will focus on Romans 5–8.[4] We hope to set Paul's presentation of the powers alongside the author of Ps. 18:8-14 OG (Ps. 19:7-13 MT). The terminological and conceptual convergences make it probable that Paul was either giving an extensive reflection on this psalm in Romans 5–8 or responding to other interpretations of this psalm. While we remain cautious about positing direct dependence, we contend that it is likely that Paul was in dialogue with the Jewish tradition behind Psalm 18 OG, one that expressed delight in the Law of God and yet puzzled at human transgression. It is our hope that a careful treatment of the psalmist's presentation of some of the same concepts and vocabulary encountered in Romans will help to sharpen Paul's own message. Thus, in the following sections, we begin with a treatment of the message of Psalm 18 OG, and then proceed to a discussion of Paul's own presentation in Romans 5–8 of the themes present in Psalm 18.

PSALM 18:8-14 OG: THE LAW OF THE LORD AND TREE OF KNOWLEDGE

We begin our treatment of Psalm 18 with an extensive quotation of the pericope germane to our treatment of Romans 5–8: vv. 8–14. We have underlined key terms that feature prominently in Romans 5–8. Other conceptual overlaps will be noted in due cause.

ὁ νόμος τοῦ κυρίου ἄμωμος ἐπιστρέφων ψυχάς
ἡ μαρτυρία κυρίου πιστή σοφίζουσα νήπια
τά δικαιώματα κυρίου εὐθεῖα εὐφραίνοντα καρδίαν

---

creation subjected to bondage. Cf. J. Moo, "Romans 8.19-22 and Isaiah's Cosmic Covenant," *NTS* 54 (2008): 74–89.

4. As a number of scholars have observed, Romans 5–8 is a carefully crafted unit, framed by 5:1-11 and 8:14-39. Nils Dahl noted the connection between Rom. 5:1-11 and ch. 8; see Dahl, *Studies in Paul: Theology of the Early Christian Mission* (Minneapolis: Augsburg, 1977), 88–90 ("Appendix I: A Synopsis of Rom 5:1-11 and 8:1-39"); Dahl, "Two Notes on Romans 5," *ST* (1951): 37–48. See also N. T. Wright, "The Letter to the Romans: Introduction, Commentary, and Reflections," in *The New Interpreter's Bible*, vol. 10 (Nashville: Abingdon, 2002), 508–14. Cf. Robin Scroggs, "Paul as Rhetorician: Two Homilies in Romans 1–11," in *Jews, Greeks and Christians: Religious Cultures in Late Antiquity: Essays in Honor of William David Davies*, ed. Robert Hammerton-Kelly and Robin Scroggs, SJLA 21 (Leiden: Brill 1976), 71–98; Leander E. Keck, "What Makes Romans Tick?" in *Pauline Theology*, volume 3: *Romans*, ed. David M. Hay and E. Elizabeth Johnson (Minneapolis: Fortress Press, 1995), 3–29.

ἡ ἐντολὴ κυρίου τηλαυγής φωτίζουσα ὀφθαλμούς
ὁ φόβος κυρίου ἀγνός διαμένων εἰς αἰῶνα αἰῶνος
τὰ κρίματα κυρίου ἀληθινά δεδικαιωμένα ἐπὶ τὸ αὐτό
ἐπιθυμητὰ ὑπέρ χρυσίον καὶ λίθον τίμιον πολὺν
καὶ γλυκύτερα ὑπὲρ μέλι καὶ κηρίον
καὶ γὰρ ὁ δοῦλός σου φυλάσσει αὐτά
ἐν τῷ φυλάσσειν αὐτὰ ἀνταπόδοσις πολλή
παραπτώματα τίς συνήσει
ἐκ τῶν κρυφίων μου καθάρισόν με
καὶ ἀπὸ ἀλλοτρίων (MT זדים) φεῖσαι τοῦ δούλου σου
ἐὰν μή μου κατακυριεύσωσιν τότε ἄμωμος ἔσομαι
καὶ καθαρισθήσομαι ἀπὸ ἁμαρτίας μεγάλης.

D. J. A. Clines has argued forcefully that Psalm 19 (18 OG) is a poetic reflection on Genesis 1–3.[5] The first part of the psalm (vv. 1–7) is a poetic meditation on the wonder of creation, reminiscent of the creation narrative of Genesis 1. The second part of the Psalm (vv. 8–15) reflects on the depiction of the tree of knowledge in Genesis 2–3.[6] According to Clines, the psalmist shows how the Law of the Lord supplies the benefits that the tree of knowledge failed to provide for Adam and Eve in the Garden of Eden. Though the tree of knowledge looked good for food (Gen. 3:6), it failed to refresh the souls of those who ate of its fruit. For the psalmist, however, the Law of the Lord refreshes the souls (ἐπιστρέφων ψυχάς) of those who keep it. While the tree of knowledge may have been desirable to make one wise (Gen. 3:6), it is the witness of the Lord that makes the simple (or children) wise (σοφίζουσα νήπια).[7] Adam and Eve's eyes were opened after they ate the fruit from the tree of knowledge (Gen. 3:7); but, according to the psalmist, the true enlightening of the eyes (φωτίζουσα ὀφθαλμούς) comes from the commandment of the Lord. Finally, Clines notes that while the eating of the tree of knowledge denied Adam and Eve access to the tree of life that they might "live forever" (Gen. 3:22), the fear of

5. D. J. A. Clines, "The Tree of Knowledge and the Law of Yahweh (Psalm XIX)," *VT* 24 (1974), 8–14. Clines is commenting on the Hebrew text. In the ensuing discussion, we present Clines' argument using the Greek text, since this facilitates our comparison with Romans 5–8. We will show below that the psalm echoes Genesis 4 also.

6. A number of commentators have also noted the Gen 2–3 background to this psalm; see, e.g., J. Goldingay, *Psalms 1–41*, vol. 1 (Grand Rapids: Baker, 2006), 293–94; Samuel Terrien, *The Psalms: Strophic Structure and Theological Commentary* (Grand Rapids: Eerdmans, 2003), 214–16; cf. M. S. Smith, "The Levitical Compilation of the Psalter," *ZAW* 103 (1991): 258–63.

7. Clines argues that "rejoicing the heart" alludes to the tradition that views the tree of knowledge as a vine, whose wine gladdens the heart; Clines, "Tree of Knowledge," 9–10.

the Lord endures forever (διαμένων εἰς αἰῶνα αἰῶνος). With these claims, the psalmist elevates the Torah to a position far superior to the tree of knowledge.

In addition to Clines's findings, we note also that the personal prayer at the end of the psalm may echo the story of Cain and Abel in Genesis 4.[8] Having extolled God's majestic creation (vv. 1-7) and the beauty and necessity of the Law for life (vv. 8-12), the psalmist petitions God for strength to live a life that is pleasing to God (vv. 13-15). When the psalmist in prayer turns to God for help, he evinces puzzlement at the surprising outcome of human actions: παραπτώματα τίς συνήσει ("Who will understand transgressions"?). He acknowledges something sinister on the scene seeking to "rule" him (κατακυριεύω; MT מֹשֵׁל), the result of which would be to cause him to commit great sin (ἁμαρτίας μεγάλης).[9] In the Hebrew, the verb מֹשֵׁל establishes a link between Psalm 19 MT and Genesis 4. In Gen. 4:7, sin is portrayed as a crouching animal waiting to pounce on its prey. Sin desires to have Cain, and God admonishes Cain to "rule over" (תִּמְשָׁל) sin. As the story unfolds, however, it becomes clear that Cain has not ruled over sin; the reverse is true: Cain is ruled by sin, causing him to commit murder (Gen. 4:8).

Similarly, in Psalm 19 MT, the psalmist prays for God to preserve him from that which seeks to rule him: the זֵדִים. When God has preserved him from the זֵדִים, the psalmist will be clean from the Great Transgression. We agree with Mitchell Dahood that "the Great Transgression" (19:14 ;פֶּשַׁע רָב MT) is idolatry, because it is a fitting parallel to the Great Sin (חֲטָאָה גְדֹלָה) of Exod. 32:30-31.[10] Against, Dahood, however, we contend that if the Great Transgression is idolatry, then the זֵדִים that seek to rule over the psalmist are not "idols," but rather the "demons"[11] behind the idols who were perceived to be the cause of idolatry.[12]

It seems to us highly plausible that the OG translator of the psalm understood the Great Sin to be idolatry for a number of reasons. First, the

8. Cf. C. A. and E. G. Briggs, *A Critical and Exegetical Commentary on the Book of Psalms*, vol. 1 (New York: Charles Schribner's Sons, 1914), 170: "[It is] probable that the author had in mind the story of Cain."

9. We take ἐάν the subjunctive as a future more probable conditional (third class conditional), implying a great degree of probability: "If they [ἀλλοτρίων] do not rule over me, then I will be blameless and be cleansed from the Great Sin." On "the Great Sin" and ἀλλότριος see our discussion below.

10. M. Dahood, *Psalms I: 1–50*, AB (Garden City, NY: Doubleday, 1966), 125. It is also possible that with the echoes of Gen 4 the Great Transgression is murder, though murder is nowhere characterized in the OT as "the Great Sin/Transgression."

11. So also S. Mowinckel, *The Psalms in Israel's Worship*, 2 vols. (Oxford: Oxford University Press, 1962), 2:114.

12. See Deut. 32:17; Ps. 106:37-38; *1 En.* 19:1; 99:7; *Jub.* 22:17; 1 Cor 10:20.

Greek counterparts of the MT contain the same vocabulary in Exod. 32:30 and Ps. 18:14: ἁμαρτίαν μεγάλην (Exod. 32:30); ἁμαρτίας μεγάλης (Ps. 18:14). Second, Ps. 18:14 is the only place in the OG Psalm where זדים is translated with ἀλλότριοι. The translator's preferred word for זדים is ὑπερήφανοι (cf. Ps. 119:21 [118:21 OG]; 119:51 [118:51 OG]; 119:69 [118:69 OG]; 119:78 [118:78 OG]; 119:85 [118:85 OG]; 119:122 [118:122 OG]); the only exception is 85:14 (86:14 MT), where παράνομοι is used. Third, the word ἀλλότριος is often coupled with θεός in the LXX and OG to refer to the "alien/strange god(s)" of idolatry (e.g., Deut. 31:16, 18; 32:12, 16; Josh. 24:14, 23; Judg. 10:16; 1 Sam. 7:3; 1 Kgs. 9:9; 2 Chron. 34:25; Ps. 43:21; 80:10; Jer. 1:16; 11:10; 13:10; 16:11; 19:4; 22:9; 25:6; Dan. 11:39). Crucially, the word stands alone as shorthand for "alien god" in Isa. 43:12. Thus, the word, as used in its context in Psalm 18 OG—especially its connection with the Great Sin—should be understood as "alien powers." These observations are crucial, since Paul is dependent on the Greek translation; and Paul also held the view that demonic powers stood behind idolatry (1 Cor. 10:19-21).

In sum, there is acknowledgement in both Psalm 19 (18 OG) and Genesis 4 of powerful forces in the face of which humans seem powerless. The psalmist terms these forces זדים, which the OG renders as ἀλλότριοι ("alien powers"). Alternatively, the author of Genesis personifies "Sin" as the powerful force.

PAUL'S VERSION OF THEMES PRESENT IN PSALM 18 OG

It is always difficult to posit direct dependence, even if it is tempting in this case: not only does vocabulary from the rather brief pericope (Ps. 18:8-14 OG) echo resoundingly in Paul's diction in Romans 5–8,[13] but there are also many conceptual overlaps that make the convergences seem more than sheer coincidence. In addition, Paul explicitly quotes Ps. 18:5 (OG) in Rom. 10:18; this shows conclusively that Paul was well aware of this psalm and had it mind while writing this letter.[14] Thus, it is possible that with such verbal and thematic convergences from such a short pericope, Paul was giving an extensive reflection (or sermon) on the message of this psalm in Romans 5–8, or that Paul was responding to other interpretations or evangelistic uses of the psalm,

13. Cf., e.g., νόμος (Ps.18:8 OG; Rom. 5:13; 5:20; 6:14; 6:19; 7:7; 7:8; 7:12; 7:14); δικαίωμα (Ps. 18:9 OG; Rom. 5:16; 5:18 [cf. 5:1; 5:9; 5:17; 5:19; 5:21; 6:14-23]); ἐντολή (Ps. 18:9 OG; Rom. 7:8-12); κρίμα (Ps. 18:10 OG; Rom. 5:16; 5:18); δικαιόω (Ps. 18:10 OG; Rom. 5:1; 5:9); ἐπιθυμία (Ps. 18:11 OG adj.; Rom. 6:12; 7:5; 7:7-10); δοῦλός (Ps. 18:12, 14 OG; Rom. 6:15-23; 7:25); παράπτωμα (Ps. 18:13 OG; Rom. 5:14-18; 5:20); κυριεύω (Ps. 18:14 OG; Rom. 6:14; 7:1); ἁμαρτία (Ps. 18:14 OG; Rom. 5:18; 5:12; 5:13; 5:16; 5:19; 5:20; 5:21; 6:1-23; 7:1-25).

14. I am grateful to Richard Hays for this thought and reference.

interpretations which drew on this psalm to show the unique benefits of the Torah.[15]

In our treatment, however, we take a more cautious approach, only contending that Paul was in conversation with the tradition behind Psalm 18 OG. In what follows we point out the parallels between Paul and the psalmist in order to bring out Paul's message more forcefully. Paul does present some of the very themes of Psalm 18 OG in Romans 5–8; but, using Christ as the hermeneutical key to interpret the same concepts and vocabulary, he presents these concepts in a peculiar way.

THE TREE OF KNOWLEDGE UNLEASHES DEATH

As noted above, in Ps. 18:8-14 OG the psalmist attempts to show how the Torah provides a corrective alternative to the tree of knowledge. Paul, in Romans 5–6, wrestles with the legacy of the tree of knowledge. It is worth drawing the reader's attention to the psalmist's claim in Ps. 18:10 OG that τά κρίματα κυρίου ἀληθινά δεδικαιωμένα ἐπὶ τὸ αὐτό ("the judgments of the Lord are true; they are justified altogether"), for it is our contention that the underlying purpose of Romans 5–6 is to establish beyond all reasonable doubt that God's word is true and that God is "proved righteous" (δικαιόω) in his dealing with the world.[16]

Paul begins his treatment of the Genesis account with Christ (Rom. 5:1-11) and works backward. As Karl Barth recognized, Paul saw Adam in the light of Christ and sin in the light of grace.[17] The legacy of Adam's sin can only be comprehended if one recognizes how God has set things right in Christ Jesus.

15. May we infer the latter from Rom. 2:17-21 ("Now if you call yourself a Jew and rely on the Law and boast of your relationship to God and know his will and approve of what is best, having been instructed in the Law, if you are persuaded that you are a guide to the blind, a light to those who are in darkness, a corrector of the foolish, a teacher of children, having the embodiment of knowledge and truth in the Law, you then who teach others, why are you not teaching yourself?")? According to Paul, the Teacher of the Law saw himself as a guide to the blind, a light to those in darkness, and a teacher of children. These characterizations echo the psalmist's claim that the Law makes children (νήπιος) wise and enlightens the eyes. In addition, the Law as the embodiment of truth also recalls the psalmist's view that the precepts of the Lord are "true" (ἀληθινός). This psalm may have been a key text for Paul's rival missionaries, and Paul may have been responding to these missionaries. (I owe this possibility to a personal conversation with Douglas Campbell on the echoes of Psalm 18 [OG] in Romans 5–8.) It is also possible that Rom. 2:17-21 only reflects conventional notions about the role of the Law.

16. Cf. Rom. 3:4. As we shall see, the death that Adam brought to himself and to humanity was a sign of God's judgment on sin.

17. See, for example, Karl Barth, *The Doctrine of God: Church Dogmatics*, 2.2, trans. G. W. Bromiley et al. (Edinburgh: T & T Clark, 1957), 92: "The reality and revelation of this movement is Jesus Christ Himself.... It is only by grace that the lack of grace can be recognized as such." So also E. P. Sanders in

The death of Christ was God's rectifying act for a creation held in bondage through the legacy of Adam's transgression. Christ's death is God's initiative to set right a creation that has been groaning (8:22). The death of Jesus has resulted in believers' reconciliation with God. In Paul's words, if while enemies believers were reconciled to God through Christ's death, then believers can be assured that they will be saved in Christ's resurrection (lit. "his life"; 5:10).

Paul's reflection on the tree of knowledge deals with the unleashing of Sin and Death into the cosmos because of transgression of the divine commandment.[18] Sin entered into the world through one man and Death entered as a result of Sin.[19] Death then spread to all people because all sinned (5:12). Paul sees Adam's eating of the fruit of the tree of knowledge as the cause of death within the human race. While Paul derives this claim from a reading of Genesis, the Genesis story itself is, nonetheless, riddled with ambiguity. On the one hand, it seems as though eating of the tree of knowledge of good and evil is the cause of the eventual death of Adam and Eve. This seems to be implied in God's warning to Adam: "And the Lord God commanded Adam, saying, 'You shall eat of every tree for food that is in the garden, but of the tree for knowing good and evil, you shall not eat of it. Now, on the day that you eat of it, you shall surely die" (Gen. 2:16-17 LXX). This verse seems to support Paul's view that it was Adam's transgression that ushered in death, which might in turn imply that Adam and Eve would have enjoyed immortality had they not transgressed God's commandment. On the other hand, this picture is far from certain, since a few verses later the narrative implies that immortality was not part of the original plan; humans could achieve immortality only if they ate of the tree of life:

> The Lord God said, "Behold, Adam has become like one of us, having knowledge of good and evil, and now perhaps he might stretch forth his hand and take of the tree of life and eat, and he will live forever." So the Lord God sent him forth from the garden of delight to till the earth from which he was taken. And he drove Adam out and made him dwell opposite the garden of delight. And he stationed the cherubim and the flaming sword that turns to guard the way to the tree of life. (Gen. 3:22-24 LXX)

his claim that Paul's thinking moved from solution to plight (*Paul and Palestinian Judaism* [Minneapolis: Fortress Press, 1977], 442–47).

18. We capitalize both Sin and Death to show that Paul personifies these concepts as powers that have taken residence in the cosmos.

19. Cf. 1 Cor. 15:21-22, 45-49.

This verse suggests that the original human state did not include immortality.

What is important is the recognition that Paul constructs his views from Gen. 2:16-17, not Gen. 3:22-24. And in this, Paul is not alone, as other Jewish traditions also put the blame for sin and death in the human race on Adam (*4 Ezra* 3:7, 21-22; 4:30-32; 7:118-19; *2 Bar.* 17:2-3; 23:4; 48:42-43; 54:15-19; *Bib. Ant.* 13:8) or at Eve's feet (*Apoc. Mos.* 14:2; *L.A.E.* 49:2; Sir. 25:24; *2 En.* 30:16-17; cf. 1 Tim. 2:14).[20] Wisd. of Sol. 2:23-24 puts the blame on the devil (who Jewish and Christian tradition eventually equated with the serpent).[21]

By making use of the Genesis account in Romans 5–6 Paul presents another facet of an important theme that runs through Romans: *the gospel is the fulfillment of God's word*. If in Romans 1–4 the gospel is the fulfillment of God's word to Abraham, and if in Romans 9–11 the gospel is the fulfillment of God's word to Israel, in Romans 5–6 the gospel is the fulfillment of God's word to Adam. Paul appropriates the Genesis account in a way that honors God's words to Adam: "Now, on the day that you transgress the divine commandment, you shall surely die" (cf. Gen. 2:17). According to Paul, by means of Adam and subsequent human transgression, death spread to all humans, ruling even in the absence of the Law in the period between Adam and Moses (Rom. 5:12-14, 17). The penalty spelled out for Adam's transgression of the divine commandment was death (Gen. 2:16-17); and since Adam did transgress the divine commandment, God's word could not return void. The only way death was able to enter the world was through Adam's transgression; and the only way death was able to spread to all people was because all people sinned (Rom.

---

20. See A. J. M. Wedderburn, "The Theological Structure of Romans v. 12," *NTS* 19 (1972–73): 332–54; R. Scroggs, *The Last Adam* (Oxford: Blackwell, 1966): 17–20, 33–36.

21. Cf. Rev. 12:9; 20:2; *L.A.E.* 12:1; 2 En. 31:3, 6.

3:23; 5:12).[22] With this important qualification, Paul connects Adam's sin and all subsequent human sinning; all humans deserve their fate of death.

For Paul, then, the presence of death is indication of the presence of sin, for sin rules in death (5:21). Thus, we can know that sin was in the world even before the Law was given to Moses, because death "ruled" from the time of Adam to the time of Moses over all people, even over those who did not commit the same kind of sin Adam committed (5:14). Paul quotes a maxim, "But sin is not reckoned when there is no law" (5:13),[23] and proceeds to argue that despite this known maxim the late arrival of the Law did not mean that sin was not being reckoned, since death reigned from the time of Adam to the time of Moses. The widespread presence of death is the visible indicator of the universal presence and dominion of sin.

Important for us is the recognition that all of this speaks to the fact that God's word has not fallen. According to God's word, transgressing the divine commandment will result in death: "Let God be true and every man a liar" (Rom. 3:4). Thus, *any discussion on the plan of escape from sin must in some way include death, for all have sinned* (Rom. 3:23; cf. Rom. 6:23). Death, then, becomes not only the just penalty for sin but also the only means of release from sin's power.[24] When the theme that God's word is true has been established, then God's act of rectification in Christ Jesus can only be seen as a divine act of mercy. The death that has come upon humanity since Adam is deserved; God's act in Christ, however, is undeserved and exceedingly gracious. It is *God's initiative* from start to finish to rescue the world from the power of Sin, which had taken its (rightful) due with the world. That is why Paul can say that "where sin multiplied, grace abounded even more" (5:20).

---

22. There has been much debate on how to translate the phrase ἐφ᾽ ᾧ in 5:12. For a good summary of the various positions, see S. L. Johnson Jr. "Romans 5:12—An Exercise in Exegesis and Theology," in *New Dimensions in New Testament Study*, ed. R. N. Longenecker and M. C. Tenney (Grand Rapids: Zondervan, 1974), 303–13; J. A. Fitzmyer, *Romans*, AB 33 (New York: Doubleday), 413–16. We understand ἐφ᾽ ᾧ to be a contract form of the classical ἐπὶ τούτῳ ὅτι; the case of the relative pronoun is attracted to that of the unstated antecedent. With the dative case, the preposition ἐπὶ can express the cause of an action or result (that is, the grounds upon which an action or result is based) (cf. 2 Cor. 5:4). See Daniel B. Wallace, *Greek Grammar beyond the Basics: An Exegetical Syntax of the New Testament* (Grand Rapids: Zondervan, 1996), 376. Cf. B. Byrne, "'The Type of the One to Come' (Rom 5:14): Fate and Responsibility in Romans 5:12-21," *ABR* 36 (1988): 19–30; S. E. Porter, "The Pauline Concept of Original Sin, in Light of Rabbinic Background," *TynBul* 41, no. 1 (1990): 3–30. On the question of the anacoluthon in 5:12, see J. T. Kirby, "The Syntax of Romans 5.12: A Rhetorical Approach," *NTS* 33 (1987): 283–86. Kirby, however, ignores completely the critical fourth element in the sentence, v 12d.

23. Cf. G. Friedrich, "*Hamartia . . . ouk ellogeitai*—Rom. 5,13," *TLZ* 77 (1952): 523–28.

24. Cf. 2 Cor. 5:14–15.

Even so, Paul's account of God's act of rectification in Christ still holds God's word to be true, for it is in Christ's obedient *death*, bearing the sins of humanity, that God rectifies a fallen cosmos. Thus, in the death and resurrection of Jesus Christ, God's act of rectification also reveals the steadfastness of God's word. In short, by reading the Genesis narrative through God's rectifying act in the death and resurrection of Jesus, Paul is able to affirm both the truth of God's word and the graciousness of God's ways.

It is in his death that Christ destroys the power of Sin. According to Paul, God made him who knew no sin a sin offering for the world (Rom. 8:3; 2 Cor. 5:21); Christ died bearing the sins of others (Rom. 5:6, 8; 8:32; 2 Cor. 5:14-15; Gal. 2:20). Christ is the one who has died and has been acquitted from Sin (6:7). Because Christ died he is no longer under the power of Sin (6:10); and because Christ was raised from the dead, he is no longer subject to Death (6:9). In light of the arguments above, the latter statements are just two expressions of the same concept: to say that Christ no longer dies is to say that Christ is no longer under the realm of Sin (6:9). Paul's argument moves from Christ to believers and the world. Christ is the prototype of the person who is not ruled by Death. Since Christ is not ruled by Death, he is not under the sway or realm of Sin, for Sin reigns in death. Consequently, for believers to no longer be under the power of Sin, believers must be mapped onto Christ's trajectory; they must participate in Christ's "career":[25] believers must also die—"for the one who dies is acquitted from sin" (6:7)—and be raised from death. While this hope remains eschatological, believers can still live in this reality by participating in Christ.

In the course of his argument, it becomes clear that Paul has discovered an alliance between sin and the Law.[26] According to Paul, the Law "sneaked in" (παρεισέρχομαι) to multiply sin (5:20); but where sin increased, grace abounded even more (5:20). This leads to the natural question of whether believers should bring out the abounding grace of God by contributing to sin's proliferation; should believers continue to sin, in order that God's grace may continue to abound (6:1)?[27] Paul's response is not only an emphatic "God forbid" (μὴ γένοιτο) but also a lucid argument that this is *impossible*. The death of Christ has opened up a new reality for those for whom Christ died. By dying with Christ, believers have also died to sin; and, consequently, it is impossible for believers to live in sin any longer (6:2).[28]

---

25. B. Byrne, *Romans*, Sacra Pagina 6 (Collegeville: Liturgical Press, 1996), 190.

26. A fuller development of this point comes in Romans 7. See our discussion below.

27. This question is similar to the conundrum raised in 3:5 by the recognition that human unrighteousness brings out the righteousness of God.

To recap our argument thus far, Paul's position hinges on the fact that death is the means of release from sin's power and realm. He arrives at this through God's word to Adam in Gen. 2:16-17 viewed through the death and resurrection of Christ. The very presence of death in the world is indication of sin's reign. Thus, to die is to be released from sin's power and realm. Christ is the cosmic template for deliverance from the powers of Sin and Death. Christ has been raised from the dead and he no longer dies; Death no longer rules over him (6:9). This implies that Christ has been released from Sin's power and realm. That is why Paul can say that Christ's death was a once-for-all death to Sin (6:10). It follows, then, that if believers are also to be released from the power of Sin, believers must somehow die. This is possible if believers recognize that they participate in Christ's career. When believers participate in Christ's career, they are released from Sin's realm and can, therefore, no longer continue to live in sin. A similar argument is presented in chapter 8, where Paul states, "Those whom he [God] foreknew he appointed beforehand to be conformed together to the image of his Son, so that he [Christ] might be the firstborn among many brothers" (8:29). Christ has set the paradigm of release from the powers of Sin and Death, and God the Father had purposed, through his Spirit, to map humanity onto this Christological template.

BAPTISM AS DELIVERANCE FROM THE POWERS

The question remains as to how believers are able to participate in Christ's career. According to Paul, believers do so by being mapped onto Christ's trajectory in *baptism*; baptism is the means through which believers participate in Christ's career (6:3-4). Baptism is the practice of power by means of which believers escape the tyranny of Sin. Paul argues that to be baptized "into" (εἰς)[29]

28. The logic of Paul's argument forces one to distinguish between occasional acts of transgression in the lives of believers and willful persistence in sin. Paul is not a fool on matters of Christian perfection. The believers' objective location is deliverance from the power and realm of sin. The present subjective location, however, includes occasional lapses into sin. See D. Campbell, *The End of Religion* (forthcoming): "Despite what we 'see' and 'experience subjectively' the underlying realities in play in the cosmos are different, and are illuminated supremely by the Christ event. Christ gives a true, 'objective' account of matters, and not our own subjective location. . . . We need a different account of the apparent ambiguities of our present location" (77). This point becomes clearer in Paul's discussion of sin as a slave master in 6:13. See our discussion below.

29. The preposition εἰς must carry a spatial sense here. Cf. Gal. 3:27; 1 Cor. 12:13; J. W. Roberts, "The Preposition *Eis* after the Verbs *Pisteuo* and *Baptizo*," *ResQ* 5 (1961): 157–59. Here one must distinguish between "baptism into Christ" and "baptism into the name of" Christ. The latter is not Paul's point here. With E. Käsemann, *Commentary on Romans*, trans. Geoffrey W. Bromiley (Grand Rapids: Eerdmans, 1980), 165.

Christ Jesus is to be baptized into his death (6:3). God's rectifying act in Christ Jesus is made concrete in the life of those who undergo baptism. With a series of *syn*-prefixed verbs, Paul shows that it is in baptism that believers are mapped onto Christ's trajectory of death, burial, and resurrection: "Do you not know that as many as were baptized into Christ Jesus were baptized into his death? Therefore, we were buried with him through baptism in death, in order that just as Christ was raised from the dead through the glory of the father, we also might walk in newness of life" (6:4).[30]

Believers are not to undergo the same historical, physical death on the cross that Jesus underwent; rather, believers are united with Christ in the "likeness" (ὁμοίωμα) of his death (6:5), and this means they will also be united with Christ in the likeness of his resurrection (6:5). The crucifixion that believers are subject to is a crucifying of the "old self" (6:6; lit. the "old man"[31]). Nonetheless, the constant use of the aorist tense is perhaps significant: "we were buried [συνετάφημεν] with him" (6:4); "our old self was crucified [συνεσταυρώθη] with him" (6:6); "we died [ἀπεθάνομεν] with Christ" (6:8). It may suggest that the notion that believers were placed on the cross with Christ and laid in Christ's tomb with him cannot be easily dismissed (cf. 2 Cor. 5:14). According to this view, the death and resurrection of the believer is the death of Christ at Golgotha and his resurrection on Easter morning.[32] George R. Beasley-Murray writes, "'We were buried with him' indicates that the action of baptism

30. There have been attempts to locate the background of Paul's baptismal language within Hellenistic mystery religions, where the initiate shares in the death of the cult hero or heroine through ceremonial washings or sacred meals. In these mystery religions, such practices procure protection from powerful forces for the initiate and also hold out to the initiate a blissful life after death. Cf., e.g., Apuleius, *Metamorphoses* 11. Since Paul's thought differs from these mystery religion ideas, it may be unwise to posit dependence. On this subject, see A. Schweitzer, *The Mysticism of Paul the Apostle*, trans. William Montgomery (New York: Macmillan, 1956 [orig. 1931]), 18–24, 134–35, 138–40; G. Wagner, *Pauline Baptism and the Pagan Mysteries: The Problem of the Pauline Doctrine of Baptism in Romans VI.1–11, in the Light of its Religio-historical "Parallels"* (Edinburgh: Oliver & Boyd, 1967); U. Schnelle, *Gerechtigkeit und Christusgegenwart* (Göttingen: Vadenhoeck & Ruprecht, 1983), 74–89; 208–225; R. C. Tannehill, *Dying and Rising with Christ* (Berlin: Töpelmann, 1967), 7–43; A. J. M. Wedderburn, *Baptism and Resurrection: Studies in Pauline Theology against Its Graeco-Roman Background*, WUNT (Tubingen: Mohr, 1987), 90–163, 296–359; Wedderburn, "The Soteriology of the Mysteries and Pauline Baptismal Theology," *NovT* 29 (1987): 53–72; J. D. G. Dunn, *Romans 1–8*, WBC 38A (Nashville: Thomas Nelson, 1988), 308–11.

31. Ὁ παλαιὸς ἄνθρωπος. In the Genesis account, Adam is often referred to simply as ὁ ἄνθρωπος. See Byrne, *Romans*, 191; J. Ziesler, *Romans Paul's Letter to the Romans*, TPINTC (Philadelphia: Trinity, 1989), 159.

32. See, e.g., G. Bornkamm, "Taufe und neues Leben bei Paulus (Röm 6)," in *Das Ende des Gesetzes: Paulusstudien. Gesammelte Afusätze 1*, 2d ed., BEvT 16 (Munich: C. Kaiser, 1958), 34–50. A concise

primarily means, not that the baptistery becomes our grave, but that we are laid in the grave of Christ. To be buried along with Christ in a Jerusalem grave *c.* A.D. 30 means unequivocally that the death we died is the death *He* died on Golgotha."[33] In this reading, ὁμοίωμα in 6:5 is translated as "form":[34] "If we have become united with him in the form of his death, we will surely also be united with him in [the form of] his resurrection." The strongest evidence in favor of this interpretation is the second half of the verse; the resurrection that believers will experience will not be unlike that of Christ. But perhaps this view and the view that what believers undergo is in the "likeness" of Christ's death and resurrection are not mutually exclusive;[35] for even though Paul employs the future tense to speak of the resurrection of believers (6:4, 8), we cannot deny the present aspect of the new life made possible for believers upon their death in baptism and their reception of the Holy Spirit.[36] This is the decisive theme of chapter 8. The future "living" with Christ has already penetrated the present existence of the baptized believer. The believer can be assured of this because she or he has already received the Holy Spirit as the "first fruits" (ἀπαρχή) of the eschatological harvest (Rom. 8:23; cf. 2 Cor. 1:21-22). Thus, believers now share in the "likeness" of Christ's resurrection by partaking in the resurrection life in which the powerful hold of Sin has been definitively terminated: the future reality has already begun to unfold.[37] But this present partaking of the "likeness" of Christ's resurrection is done with the assurance that believers will partake of the "form" of Christ's resurrection in the future.

The former existence was lived in the old self, which was under the power and realm of Sin, and this is part of the old eon that is being nullified in Christ. That is why Paul can refer to the old self as "the body of sin" (τὸ σῶμα τῆς ἁμαρτίας)[38] that is being nullified (καταργέω) (6:6). To the extent that the old

---

summary of the debates can be found in S. Sabou, "A Note on Romans 6:5: The Representation (ὁμοίωμα) of his Death," *TynBul* 55, no. 2 (2004): 220–29.

33. G. R. Beasley-Murray, *Baptism in the New Testament* (Grand Rapids: Eerdmans, 1962), 133. Emphasis in the original.

34. Cf. LXX Deut. 4:12.

35. Cf. Rom. 5:14 and 8:3; in both verses the translation ὁμοίωμα as "likeness" seems more apt.

36. In Col. 2:2, the same point about baptism is made but the resurrection with Christ is not a future event; here the resurrection with Christ has already taken place. Cf. C. E. B. Cranfield, "Romans 6:1-14 Revisited," *ExpTim* 106 (1994): 40–43; E. Schweizer, "Dying and Rising with Christ," *NTS* 14 (1967–68): 1–14.

37. Cf. Wedderburn, *Baptism and Resurrection*, 46: "Christians participate proleptically in their Lord's resurrection only in the form of their new obedience, while, conversely, their service for him proclaims that the power of the resurrection has already grasped them and transported them to the new life and the new age."

self exists within the realm of Sin, Sin is the slave master of the old self. Thus, when the old self is crucified (that is, subjected to the likeness of Christ's death), believers are freed from Sin's dominion.

We are back to the theme we began with, that because God's word has not fallen, death is the means by which one may be freed from sin; death has now become the means of access to life. Christ's death, then, achieves deliverance from slavery for believers (much more so than forgiveness[39]).

Paul's dramatic portrayal of baptism depicts the practice as an immersion under water;[40] believers are plunged under the baptismal water and reenact the death and burial of Christ. When the baptismal candidate is raised from the water she or he shares in the resurrection of Jesus Christ.[41] As John Ziesler puts it, "The picture is that of going down into the water in baptism and of being covered by it, thus representing and conveying death and burial."[42] The image of συνετάφημεν οὖν αὐτῷ διὰ τοῦ βαπτίσματος εἰς τὸν θάνατον ("we were, therefore, buried with him through baptism into death") is suggestive of immersion; for in this image burial precedes death. It seems to be the reverse of the Christ experience: Christ died, was buried, and was raised.[43] Believers, however, experienced death when they were buried with Christ (6:4). Paul in 6:4 allows the practice to dictate his analogy. Two verses later in 6:6, nonetheless, we learn that believers have also undergone crucifixion: believers have been crucified with Christ and have crucified the old self in the process. When the old self is crucified and is buried in the baptismal water, it is left behind with the Old Age ruled by Sin; a new person is raised from the water, who dwells in the New Age in Christ.

We cannot emphasize enough the importance of baptism for Paul's argument. Paul's entire argument depends on believers' actual participation in Christ's trajectory in baptism. Or to put it more bluntly, Paul's argument demands that something concrete happen to the believer in baptism. Against

---

38. The σῶμα τῆς ἁμαρτίας is in essence the body that is under the dominion of Sin.

39. Cf. B. Gaventa, "The Cosmic Power of Sin in Paul's Letter to the Romans: Toward a Widescreen Edition," *Interpretation* 58 (2004): 229–40, on 235: "God's power revealed in the gospel . . . is far greater than God's mere ability to forgive the sins of those who assent to a set of propositions about Jesus Christ. It is God's own power to redeem all of creation (see [Rom.] 8:19-23) from the grasp of powers arrayed against God."

40. Contra Käsemann, *Romans*, 164.

41. Cf. C. H. Dodd, *The Epistle of Paul to the Romans*, MNTC (New York: Harper, 1932), 87: "Immersion is a sort of burial . . . emergence a sort of resurrection."

42. Ziesler, *Romans*, 157.

43. The entire presentation of Rom. 6:3-4 follows this movement of the primitive Christian kerygma (1 Cor 15:3-4): "Were baptized into his *death* . . . were *buried* with him . . . was *raised*."

those who seek to downplay the importance of the baptismal event for Paul's argument,[44] we contend that without a concrete reality flowing out from the baptismal event, Paul's whole argument collapses and believers remain under the power of Sin.[45] In other words, to the extent that the concrete (spiritual) reality in (physical) baptism is weakened, the argument for release from the powers of Sin and Death also loses its force.[46] While Paul postpones a discussion of the Holy Spirit until chapter 8, it is the Holy Spirit who especially effects this identification of believers and Christ in baptism. According to Paul, having died with Christ in baptism, believers will also live with him in his resurrection (6:8-11). Yet in chapter 8, God's resurrecting act in believers is mediated by the Holy Spirit: "And if the Spirit of the one who raised Jesus from the dead dwells in you, the one who raised Christ from the dead will also make alive your mortal bodies through the one who dwells in you, the Holy Spirit" (8:11). Paul's argument demands that baptism cannot be viewed as some arbitrary ritual; the event is fraught with significance and power. In the end, the baptismal font becomes the believer's grave: to accept to undergo baptism, or to subject another to baptism, is to accept, or subject another, to a death sentence.

LIFE AFTER BAPTISM

In 6:12-23 Paul's concern is similar to that expressed in 6:1. As discussed above, in 6:1-11, Paul's argument is that it is impossible for believers to continue to live in sin, since believers have died to sin. This is the objective location of believers achieved in Christ. But the subjective location of believers includes occasional lapses into sin. This point Paul addresses in 6:12-23 using the metaphor of Sin

---

44. See, e.g., Dunn, *Romans 1–8*, 311–12; 327–29. A concise summary of the history of interpretation of baptism in Rom. 6:1-14 is presented in H. Boers, "The Structure and Meaning of Romans 6:1-14," *CBQ* 63 (2001): 664–82; see esp. 664–71.

45. It is because of this that caution must be exercised when the view that believers' death took place at Golgotha in Christ's death is maintained. As noted by H. Halter, this position runs the risk of reducing baptism to a mere act of acknowledgment of what happened in the past for believers; H. Halter, *Taufe und Ethos: paulinische Kriterien für das Proprium christlicher Moral*, FThSt 106 (Freiburg im Breisgau: Herder, 1977), 43–46. So also Käsemann, *Romans*, 165.

46. Another way to look at this issue is to pay particular attention to the implications of illicit "unions" for believers, according to Paul. In 1 Cor. 6:13-19 believers' participation in Christ forbids them from uniting with prostitutes. This illicit union destroys their union with Christ. So also in 1 Cor. 10:14-21 partaking in idol sacrificial feasts poses a threat to believers' participation in Christ, since behind these feasts stand demons, who in Paul's theology represent "other gods and other lords" (1 Cor. 8:5). Our point is that if Paul does not think something concrete happens in baptism to effect an actual union with Christ, then he has no basis to be concerned about other "unions" posing a threat to believers' union with Christ.

as slave master. It is important to be clear that the argument in 6:12-23 applies only to those who have already "died" to Sin, that is, those who have crucified the old self. Nonetheless, as Paul's argument suggests, having died to Sin (in Christ), having been rescued from the dominion of Sin, believers can still yield themselves to Sin; they can place their "mortal bodies" (6:12) or "members" (6:13) at Sin's disposal.[47] If believers choose to present their members to Sin, Sin will readily employ their members as "weapons" of unrighteousness (6:13). Since it involves obedience to Sin (6:16), submitting one's members to Sin naturally means becoming a slave to Sin. This is what these believing gentiles used to be until they were freed from Sin and enslaved to righteousness.[48] Sin is presented in this section as crouching at the door of believers; its desire is for believers (cf. Gen 4:7).[49] Believers must battle Sin, presenting their members as "weapons of righteousness to God" (ὅπλα δικαιοσύνης τῷ θεῷ), or risk being ruled (again) by Sin.

The logic of Paul's argument suggests that the fading of the old age with the arrival of Christ demands the nullification of Sin's sphere of influence, which is variously characterized: "the old human" (6:6); "the body of sin" (6:6); "the flesh" (7:5; 7:18); "the body of death" (7:24). As long as these are alive, a person has not yet escaped the sphere of Sin's rule. The upshot of this argument is that all who are not united with Christ are under the realm and power of Sin;[50] and

47. This is implicit acknowledgement on Paul's part that believers may on occasion commit acts of transgression, though, as mentioned earlier, believers are still differentiated from those who are living under the power of Sin. Here Paul's choice of "members" is perhaps significant: believers must present their "selves" to God and not present their "members" to Sin (6:13). Since believers have crucified the old self with Christ, it is impossible for believers to present their "selves" to Sin; they can only present their "members" to Sin (see Wright, "Letter to the Romans," 542). In this, Paul admits that believers can commit sinful acts. In the end, however, we should not allow our cautions about perfectionism to blunt the force of Paul's argument: believers now belong to a new reality where the dominion of Sin has been broken.

48. Paul uses a curious expression here: the believers were obedient from the heart to the *typos* of teaching to which they were handed over (6:17). R. A. J. Gagnon argues that this verse should be understood as the "imprint stamped by teaching, to which (imprint) you were handed over" ("Heart of Wax and a Teaching that Stamps: [Rom. 6:17b] Once More," *JBL* 112 [1993] 667–87: on 687). Cf. J. Moffat, "The Interpretation of Romans 6:17-18," *JBL* 48 (1929): 233–38.

49. Cf. L. J. Waters' perceptive observation: "Victory over sin . . . is not easily or quickly realized. That is because sin still tries to assert authority in the believer's life, and believers often submit to sin's illegitimate authority. It is a lifelong process to experience the reality of 'death to sin.' As Paul argued later, believers must 'by the Spirit [be] putting to death the deeds of the body' (8:13)" ("Paradoxes in the Pauline Epistles," *BSac* 167 [2010]: 423–41, on 440). See also D. T. Ejenobo, " 'Union with Christ': A Critique of Romans 6:1-11," *AJT* 22 (2008): 309–323.

50. Paul has already asserted this point in Rom. 1–3, especially 3:9b-18.

it is only by dying and being raised with Christ in baptism that believers escape Sin's dominion. Yet even believers, having escaped the power of Sin, can yield themselves to Sin to be "ruled" again by Sin (6:14).[51]

The argument here is similar to what we encounter in 1 Corinthians 5. In our treatment of this passage, we will show that for Paul everyone outside the body of Christ is under the influence of the god of this age—Satan. Nonetheless, by persisting in sin, believers may give Satan entry into the body of Christ to work his schemes within the body. Paul's thought, then, concerning the powers shows a striking degree of consistency—whether he is speaking of concrete supernatural powers or personifying abstract nouns as powers. Believers are protected from the powers by being united with the body of Christ. But this protection is not absolute until Christ has destroyed all the powers at the end (1 Cor. 15:24-26). Until then, it is possible for believers to leave themselves exposed to the powers.

PAUL ON THE LAW: SIN'S USE OF THE LAW

To return to links to Psalm 19 (18 OG), so far we have noted that both the psalmist and Paul reflect on the tree of knowledge. For the psalmist the Law is the vital corrective to the failed promises of the tree of knowledge. Paul sees the eating of the tree of knowledge as the catalyst for the entrance of Sin and Death into the cosmos. But, for Paul, Christ, *not the Law*, is the proper response to the legacy of the tree of knowledge. And this is because Paul has detected a surprising alliance between the Law and the powers of Sin and Death. This point has had to wait until chapter 7 to receive full treatment; but all along Paul has been dropping hints of this discovery. For example, in 5:20, the reader is surprised to hear that the Law "sneaked in" to increase transgression. So also in 6:14, the reason why believers cannot present their members to Sin as weapons of unrighteousness is because "Sin no longer rules" believers (6:14). Paul presses beyond this point, however, to make a statement that will stump not only the author of Psalm 19 but his Jewish contemporaries as well: "Sin no longer rules you, for you are not under Law, but under grace"! To be under Law is tantamount to being under the realm of Sin! The Law's cooperation with Sin has also been indirectly hinted at in 5:12-14, where we learned that the transgression of the divine commandment by Adam unleashed a legacy that

---

51. Cf. Wright, "Letter to Romans," 541: "[Paul] is speaking of a different level of reality. If someone challenged him and said that sin and death were just as powerful to them as they had been before their coming to faith, he would reply that they had not yet considered the seriousness of their baptism; just as if someone claimed that, now they had been baptized, evil had no attraction whatever for them, he would no doubt reply that they had not yet considered the seriousness of sin."

the Law has been powerless to reverse: the powerful hold of Sin and Death. In the face of these powers, the Law is impotent. Thus, on one side, the powers of Sin and Death have formed an alliance with the Law by co-opting the Law; the Law is an unwilling participant on this side of the equation. On the other side, Christ has unleashed the power of grace by means of his sacrificial death for the sins of the world. Because Christ is no longer under the power of Sin, Christ is the prototype of the believer's escape from the powerful hold of Sin and Death, not the Law. Only those who have died with Christ are no longer subject to the power of Sin.

It is in Romans 7, however, that Paul develops in detail what he has only been hinting at up to this point—that the Law is secretly aiding the powers of Sin and Death. Romans 7 begins with an example Paul draws from the legal system to flesh out further the alliance between the Law and Sin. According to Paul's example, a woman is released from the law binding her to her husband when her husband dies (7:1-3). After her husband's death, she is free to unite with another man. From this example, Paul infers that believers have died to the Law through the body of Christ and are free to become united with the one who has been raised from the dead (7:4).[52] Paul can make this point only because he perceives the Law secretly, and unknowingly, forming an alliance with Sin. That is why in the very next verse after saying that believers have died to the Law through the body of Christ, Paul can turn to the subject of Sin: "For when we were in the flesh, *the passions of Sin, aroused by the Law*, were at work in our members to bear fruits unto death" (7:5; emphasis added). Because the Law has formed a secret partnership with Sin, by dying to Sin (through baptism), believers have also died to the Law (7:4). Paul does not have to repeat the argument in chapters 5 and 6 about believers' death to Sin.

---

52. As noted in most commentaries, Paul's analogy breaks down. In the legal example, it is the death of the husband that frees the woman to unite with another. In Paul's inference, however, it is the death of believers in Christ that frees believers to unite with Christ. Paul's analogy should not be pressed rigorously. The point he wants to make is that "death" brings freedom from the law. In the words of J. A. Little, "Paul is trying in this analogy to express the reality of a unique event in the world, an event which makes it possible for a man to die and yet live. There are no parallels for this experience. Nor are there any parallels in law for the process by which this new event makes it possible for a man to die into a new freedom before the Law. There are, however, parallels for how one man's death can free another person from a specific part of the law, and there are also parallels for how one person's death can free another person to a new way of life. In using the analogy of marriage, Paul has chosen an illustration which combines both of those parallels. In that sense, this analogy is quite good" (Little, "Paul's Use of Analogy: A Structural Analysis of Romans 7:1-6," *CBQ* 46 [1984]: 82–90, on 87). But cf. P. Spitaler, who sees perfect symmetry in Paul's analogy ("Analogical Reasoning in Romans 7:2-4: A Woman and the Believers in Rome," *JBL* 125 [2006]: 715–47).

In chapter 7, however, he seeks the attentive listener to make the appropriate hermeneutical transfer that death to Sin is also death to the Law, for the Law and Sin have formed an alliance. The example from legal experience, then, helps to demonstrate how the death of a person can totally alter the moral and legal situation of another. Christ's death has altered the moral and legal situation of those for whom he died. Believers are released from the Law into a new life lived under the power of the Holy Spirit (7:6).

A fairly strong consensus that seems to have emerged on Romans 7 is that Paul's ἐγώ is not necessarily autobiographical, yielding insight into Paul's personal life before or after his conversion. Paul's ἐγώ is a rhetorical device serving as representative for all humanity under the cloud of Adam. This should not necessarily exclude Paul himself.[53] Indeed, if Paul is giving a retrospective account of life outside of Christ,[54] then for him to be excluded from the pattern would mean that his own assessment of the human situation is deeply inaccurate, for in Paul we would have at least one person who does not fit his pattern.[55] Thus, it seems to me almost impossible to dismiss entirely all autobiographical references in Paul's use of ἐγώ.[56] Neither can Romans 7 be viewed as an account of the Christian life;[57] such a reading destroys completely

---

53. W. G. Kümmel provided the classic case against an autobiographical reading of Rom 7; Kümmel, *Römer 7 und die Bekehrung des Paulus* (Leipzig: J. C. Hinrichs'sche Buchhandlung, 1929). Kümmel, however, swung the pendulum too far in the opposite direction by making the "I" entirely fictive (*uneigentlich*) and denying any autobiographical elements. Against Kümmel, see G. Theissen, *Psychological Aspects of Pauline Theology* (Minneapolis: Fortress Press, 1987 [orig. 1983]), 179–265.

54. As many commentators now assume; see, for example, E. P. Sanders, *Paul and Palestinian Judaism*, 443; Ziesler, *Romans*, 183; S. Lyonnet, "L'histoire du salut selon le chapitre VII de l'épître aux Romains," *Bib* 43 (1962): 117–51; U. Wilckens, *Der Brief an die Römer*, vol. 2 (Neukirchen-Vluyn: Neukirchener Verlag, 1980), 86.

55. Phil 3:6 should not rule Paul out of the pattern he establishes in Romans 7 if Romans 7 reflects a Christian outlook. Phil. 3:6 must be read as an account of how things appeared to Paul before his encounter with Christ. Before his encounter with Christ all the credentials he lists (Phil. 3:4-6), when viewed from another standpoint, were "gains." After his own encounter with Christ all the "gains," when viewed from a Christian standpoint, he reckoned as "loss" (Phil. 3:7).

56. Also Paul's use of the first person plural (ἦμεν, 7:5; ἐροῦμεν, 7:7) seems to include himself in some way in the pattern he has established.

57. The view that Paul is describing the Christian life in Romans 7 is maintained by L. A. Jervis, "'The Commandment which Is for Life' (Romans 7.10): Sin's Use of the Obedience of Faith," *JSNT* 27, no. 2 (2004): 193–216; D. B. Garlington, "Romans 7:14-25 and the Creation Theology of Paul," *TJ* 11 (1990): 197–235; Dunn, *Romans 1–8*, 374–412; C. K. Barrett, *The Epistle to the Romans*, HNTC (New York: Harper & Row, 1957), 151–53; C. E. B. Cranfield, *The Epistle to the Romans*, vol. 1, ICC (Edinburgh: T & T Clark, 1975), 340–47; S. D. Toussaint, "The Contrast between the Spiritual Conflict in Romans 7 and Galatians 5," *Bibliotheca Sacra* 123 (1966): 310–14.

the antithesis Paul presents to Romans 7 in Romans 8 and stands in sharp tension with Romans 6, where Sin is no longer slave master to believers.[58] During the former life of the gentiles, they were slaves of Sin (6:17, 20); but Sin no longer rules the believer (6:14; cf. 8:15). This description dovetails well with the ἐγώ of Romans 7, who is described as sold under slavery to Sin (7:14). In addition, for the believer, the body of death from which the ἐγώ cries to be rescued in Rom. 7:24 has already been crucified with Christ (6:6; 8:10). In Romans 7 it is clear that one of Sin's bases of operations is the "flesh" (7:14; 7:25); indeed, nothing good dwells in the flesh of the ἐγώ (7:18), and the Law is made ineffective through the flesh (8:3). Yet in chapter 8, believers are those who no longer walk in the flesh, but rather walk in the Spirit (8:4, 8, 9, 12-13). Romans 7, then, cannot be an account of the Christian life[59]; rather, Romans 7 is a retrospective account of all of humanity outside Christ (under the cloud of Adam), whose existence, for Paul, is inescapably subject to the destructive power of Sin.[60]

According to the author of Psalm 18 OG, the Law creates a desire for itself, a desire that transcends all desires (18:11 OG). Desire for the Law is contrasted with Eve's desire for the tree of knowledge; it is a desire stronger than the yearning for gold, precious stone, and honey, since the Law is of utmost delight. Such a strong desire for the Law makes one essentially a "slave" to the Law (18:12 OG). Paul would agree with the psalmist that the Law engenders a desire not only for itself but also a desire for what is good (Rom. 7:12-13, 19). But for Paul, the Law, working in conjunction with Sin, also creates desire for that which is not to be desired (7:7-8).[61] It is only now becoming clear why Paul thinks that the Law multiplied sin (5:20). It begins

---

58. For a survey of the debates, see Ziesler, *Romans*, 191–95.

59. Cf. Hae-Kyung Chang, "The Christian Life in a Dialectical Tension? Romans 7:7-25 Reconsidered," *NovT* 49 (2007): 257–80.

60. Robert Jewett's proposal that Paul in Romans 7 is describing the dilemma of his former career as a zealot after discovering the destructive error of his pursuits is too limiting an account of Paul's ἐγώ. See Jewett, "The Basic Human Dilemma: Weakness or Zealous Violence? Romans 7:7-25 and Romans 10:1-18," *Ex Auditu* 13 (1997): 96–109; Jewett, *Romans: A Commentary*, Hermeneia (Minneapolis: Fortress Press, 2007), 443–49. So also are all accounts that limit Paul's "I" to Israel under Torah. If Romans 7 concerns only Israel, then Paul's solution to the dilemma of Romans 7 presented in Romans 8 must also be limited to Jews, a point which proponents of this view will not concede. In other words, if the plight expressed in Romans 7 only pertains to Israel under Torah, then it is difficult to see how the solution proclaimed in Romans 8 is of significance to all humanity. It seems to us that by alluding to *both* Adam (a figure of universal significance [Rom. 5:12-21]) and Israel in Romans 7 (by quoting the Tenth Commandment [see our discussion below]) Paul has covered all of humanity—both Jews and gentiles.

61. One again hears echoes of Eve's desiring of the fruit to make her wise (Gen. 3:6). Paul has already hinted at this allusion by associating the Law with "fruit for death" (καρποφορῆσαι τῷ θανάτῳ; 7:5). Noted in A. Busch, "The Figure of Eve in Romans 7:5-25," *BibInt* 12 (2004): 1–36, on 13.

with the Law's commandments, which awaken Sin (7:7-8): "I would not have known sin except through the Law; for I would not have known desire if the Law did not say, 'You shall not desire'" (οὐκ ἐπιθυμήσεις).[62] Once Sin has been awakened, it turns the Law into one of its lethal bases of operations to wage war against humans. Sin seizes the opportunity afforded it by the Law to produce all kinds of desire (7:8).[63] But Paul is adamant to stress that—despite their alliance—the Law should in no way be equated with Sin: the Law is not Sin (7:7). Nonetheless, these entities work together, because Sin is able to co-opt the Law into producing death. The Genesis account still looms in the background of Paul's discussion. Before the coming of the commandment to abstain from the tree of knowledge Adam and Eve were alive (7:9); but upon arrival of the commandment Sin sprang to life (7:9), seized the opportunity afforded by the commandment to deceive Adam and Eve, and effected death

---

62. This is a direct quotation of the Tenth Commandment (Exod. 20:17; Deut. 5:21). Both the Tenth Commandment and the prohibition of the tree of knowledge concern desire for that which is forbidden. By quoting the Tenth Commandment here, Paul is able to connect the giving of the Law to Israel at Sinai and the giving of the commandment to Adam in Genesis 2—a move that is already anticipated in Rom. 5:12-21. (See our discussion of Rom. 5:12-21 above). There are certain Jewish traditions that either connect the Adam narrative with the giving of the Law at Sinai or the commands not to eat and not to covet; cf. Philo, QG 1:477–48; Opif. 157–60; Alleg. Interp. 2:72, 74; Sirach 17; Apoc. Mos. 19:3; Tg. Neofiti on Gen. 2:15 and Gen 3:24; b. Sabb. 145b–146a; Yebam. 103b; Abod. Zar. 22b. See Lyonnet, "'Tu ne convoiteras pas,'" Neotestamentica et Patristica. Eine Freundesgabe Herrn Prof. Dr. Oscar Cullmann zu seinem 60. Geburtstag überreicht (Leiden: Brill, 1962), 157–65; Ziesler, "The Role of the Tenth Commandment in Romans 7," JSNT 33 (1988): 47. D. G. Moo can, therefore, not be correct to deny the allusion to Adam in Rom. 7:7-12 on the basis of Paul's quotation of the Tenth Commandment; see Moo, "Israel and Paul in Romans 7:7-12," NTS 32 (1986): 122–35. One only has to note traditions in which the entire Law or the Ten Commandments are summed up with "do not covet," or a great number of evils traced back to covetousness as their root cause. See, e.g., 4 Macc. 2:6; Apoc. Ab. 24:9–10; Apoc. Mos. 19:3; Philo, Spec. 4.84–94; Decal. 142, 150, 173. Cf. Theissen, Psychological Aspects, 205.

63. R.H. Gundry's attempt to limit ἐπιθυμία to sexual desire suffers a major setback in the face of this verse (Gundry, "The Moral Frustration of Paul before his Conversion," in Pauline Studies: Essays Presented to F.F. Bruce, ed. D. A. Hagner and M. J. Harris [Exeter: Paternoster, 1980], 228–245). See Ziesler, "Tenth Commandment," 45–46.

(7:11).[64] What this episode demonstrates is that Sin is able to use that which is intended for life to generate the exact opposite: death (7:10).

Paul's positive characterization of the Law is strikingly reminiscent of Psalm 18 OG: "The Law is holy and the commandment is holy and righteous" (7:12). Yet Paul, like the psalmist, expresses puzzlement at human deeds. Despite all the wonderful benefits the Law provides, the psalmist acknowledges that there is still an element of surprise in human action: παραπτώματα τίς συνήσει (Ps. 18:13 OG; cf. Rom. 7:15). The psalmist displays puzzlement with respect to certain transgressions, in spite of utmost delight for the Law. The surprising result of human action leads both Paul and the psalmist to deduce that there is something more sinister on the scene that produces sinful human behavior. As noted in our discussion of Psalm 19 MT (18 OG), the psalmist acknowledges that higher forces (זדים) can overpower even those who are under the Law and cause them to commit great sin. We observed that the זדים are best interpreted as "demons" that cause people to commit idolatry—the Great Transgression.

Paul's understanding is close to that of the psalmist but also distinct.[65] For Paul, the goodness of the Law is irrelevant in the face of the powerful force of Sin. The problem is this higher power that overrides humanity's desire for the Law and all that is good. Thus, like the psalmist, Paul also expresses puzzlement at the transgressive outcome of human action caused by a sinister force on the scene. As Paul Meyer has argued, the dilemma expressed in Rom 7 does not concern a person's inability[66] to fulfill the demands of the Law or a simple frustration of good intent.[67] Rather, it is the discernment that a sinister power

---

64. Paul is using *Law* and *commandment* synonymously in this pericope. We have already noted above that Paul's quotation of the Tenth Commandment in 7:7 allows him to connect the Adam event with the giving of the Law at Sinai. The interchange between *Law* and *commandment* also harkens back to Paul's contention that sin was being reckoned between the time of Adam and Moses, since death reigned in this period (5:13-14). Paul seems to think that the Law was in effect in the form of God's commandments before the time of Moses; cf. LXX Gen. 2:16: καὶ ἐνετείλατο κύριος ὁ θεὸς τῷ Αδαμ; *4 Ezra* 3:7. Cf. also Byrne, *Romans*, 181: "Under law, human sinning comes to resemble the sin of Adam, who deliberately disobeyed an explicit commandment of God."

65. If Paul is reading the psalm, then Paul correctly understands the psalmist to be acknowledging the existence of higher powers that can enslave a person, despite one's enslavement to the Law. He would then view ἀλλοτρίων as parallel to ἁμαρτίας in 18:14 (OG) or view 18:14b as restating the point of 18:14a and understand the higher power to be "Sin."

66. Contra, e.g., M. A. Seifrid, "The Subject of Rom 7:14-25," *NovT* 34 (1992): 313–33, on 328: "An initial confession of inability is supported by a narrative and a subsequent analysis aimed at convincing the reader of the validity of that confession."

67. See P. W. Meyer, "The Worm at the Core of the Apple," in *The Word in This World: Essays in New Testament Exegesis and Theology* (Louisville: Westminster John Knox, 2004), 57–77.

on the scene is capable of deceiving one and making the best devotion to God produce exactly what it was intended to eradicate. The outcome of one's religious devotion turns out to be the opposite of what one had hoped for. A higher power is at work that overpowers humans and uses the self as the agent of its own desires (7:15-17, 20).[68] In other words, Sin now does to the religious self—whether the "inmost self" (7:22) or the "members" (7:23)—exactly what it does to the Law of God. As Meyer puts it, the symptom of being "sold under sin" (7:14) is "good intention carried out and then surprised and dumbfounded by the evil it has produced, not despair but the same disillusionment so clearly described in v.10. What should have effected life has produced death."[69] The ability to effect death even in the best and most pious of human endeavors shows the exceedingly demonic character of Sin (ἵνα γένηται καθ' ὑπερβολὴν ἁμαρτωλὸς ἡ ἁμαρτία; 7:13).

Meyer rightly notes that Rom. 7:13-25 culminates in a cleavage, but the cleavage is not in the self but in the Law. Rom. 7:21-23 presents two diametrically opposed Laws: "the Law of God" (7:22, 25), which is also "the Law of the mind" (7:23); and a "different Law," which is also "the Law of Sin" (7:23, 25). The Mosaic Law of God has been co-opted by Sin to produce death, resulting in the "Law of sin and death" (8:2).[70]

LIFE IN THE SPIRIT

Romans 8 is the direct antithesis of the pattern Paul has established in Romans 7. This was already signaled in Rom. 7:6, where believers, having been released from the Law, are said to be enslaved in the newness of the Spirit. In the face of such a sinister actor as Sin, something more powerful (than the Law) must invade the human scene.[71] Thus, God sends his own Son; and it is through him that the Law of the Spirit sets believers free from the Law of Sin and Death.[72] If the Law has been impotent in the face of Sin, God has rectified this situation by

68. R. Bultmann, *Theology of the New Testament*, 2 vols (Waco, TX: Baylor University Press, 2007 [orig. 1951–55]), 1:248, correctly recognized that Greek and Latin parallels have very little in common with the purpose of Paul's vocabulary in this pericope (cf. R. V. Huggins, "Alleged Classical Parallels to Paul's 'What I Want to Do I do Not Do, but What I Hate, That I Do' (Rom 7:15)," *WTJ* 54 [1992]: 153–61); see, e.g., Ovid, *Metam.* 7:18–21; Euripides, *Med.* 1076–80; Euripides, *Hipp.* 375–85; Epictetus, *Disc.* 2:26.1–2, 4–5. The Greek and Latin parallels express either a perception of the good and yet an incapacity to perform it or a misperception of what the good is. For Paul, an alien force is at work.

69. Meyer, "Worm," 74.

70. Meyer, "Worm," 75–76. Cf. K. Snodgrass, "Spheres of Influence: A Possible Solution to the Problem of Paul and the Law," *JSNT* 32 (1988): 93–113.

71. See J. L. Martyn, *Galatians: A New Translation with Introduction and Commentary*, AB (New Haven: Yale University Press, 1997).

sending his own Son in order to deal with the power of Sin in a manner that the Law could not (8:3-4). In Romans 8 the Spirit creates freedom from bondage to Sin and a new ethical possibility. The Holy Spirit has replaced the Law as the ethical guide for believers. The Holy Spirit creates the conditions that make fulfillment of the righteousness leading to life possible.

SIN AS PERSONIFIED POWER

Sin in Romans 5–8 represents both human deeds of transgression[73] and a power under which humans can be enslaved.[74] It begins with Sin "entering" the world through Adam's transgression (5:12) and taking up residence in the cosmos; but everyone has also committed sin (5:12). Paul is able to move freely between both conceptions of sin. Rom. 5:20-21 is a good example of this. Here the Law is said to have "sneaked in" to increase "transgressions"; but where "sin" increased, grace abounded even more. The structure of 5:20 suggests that "sin" is being used as a synonym for "transgression":

ἵνα πλεονάσῃ τὸ παράπτωμα
οὗ δὲ ἐπλεόνασεν ἡ ἁμαρτία.

In 5:20, "sin" and "transgression" are parallel concepts. But in the very next verse, sin is said to have "ruled" in death (5:21). Sin is personified as a power whose dominion is experienced within a certain sphere of existence. Thus, in Romans 6, Paul can personify Sin as a slave master having authority over all within its household (6:15-16) and who recompenses humanity's services with death (6:23). And in Romans 7, Sin is a power that co-opts the Law and the religious self: Sin uses the Law to achieve the very things the Law is supposed to counter (7:7-11), and Sin uses the self to "work" (κατεργάζομαι; 7:17, 20) and "do" (ποιέω; 7:20-21) what is contrary to the self's wishes. Paul's presentation of Sin brings with it the complex tension between human agency and powerful forces seeking to usurp the will into performing actions whose outcome is contrary to the self's wishes.[75] That the tension is not entirely eliminated is undeniable, and this applies not only to Paul but also to Jewish theology and

---

72. The Law of the Spirit of life (8:2) is the rhetorical counterpart to the Law of Sin and Death, which in turn is a summation of Rom. 7:7-25: Sin has taken possession of the Law to produce Death. The Law of the Spirit of life, then, is the Law in the possession of the Spirit of Christ; the result is life. Cf. Gal. 6:2.

73. Cf. Rom. 2:12; 3:23.

74. Cf. Rom. 3:9.

75. From our analysis above, drawing from Meyer, the problem in Romans 7 is not so much the self's inability to do the good, but rather action whose result is the opposite of what is desired.

Christian theology more generally. Be that as it may, it seems fair to say that, for Paul, humans are not completely free agents who are able simply to choose what is right or what is wrong. Humans always operate within the realm of some power, divine or demonic.[76] On the one hand, outside of Christ, all are under the dominion of Sin. On the other hand, in Christ, it is the divine powers of grace (5:17, 21; 6:14) and the Holy Spirit (8:1-11) that create the conditions within which righteous living is possible.[77]

The two forms of sin—as transgression and as demonic power—are, nonetheless, intimately connected, for the rule of Sin is manifested in the performance of actions contrary to God's purposes. Rom. 6:14-16 provides a good example of this. Having stated that Sin no longer "rules" believers, Paul asks, "Are we to sin, since we are no longer under Law but under grace"? He then goes on to suggest that by submitting to Sin, believers, who have already died to Sin, would be in essence selling themselves into slavery under Sin. Those who are under the realm of Sin are held in bondage to Sin; and the result is that they bear fruit to all kinds of sinful behavior whose end result is death. This is the exact point Paul makes about the ubiquity of sin in Romans 1–3 and the sinful past of the Gentile believers he is addressing (6:17-21). Yet even here, human agency is not totally obliterated, for, as Paul puts it, the gentiles "presented" their members as slaves to uncleanness and lawlessness (6:19); the gentiles responsibly made their own decision to voluntarily embrace ἀκαθαρσία and ἀνομία. For Paul, it is only when a person dies with Christ that the will is liberated (through the power of grace) to perform deeds of righteousness, even if choosing to be (re)enslaved to Sin still remains a possibility (6:15-23). The arrival of the power of grace on the scene creates the conditions in which the "fruit leading to holiness" (6:22) is possible.[78]

It seems fair to infer from Romans 5–8 that Paul's personifying of Sin may at times serve as a literary device for speaking about concrete realities in the universe.[79] This is especially evident in Rom. 7:11, where Sin is said to have "deceived" (ἐξαπατάω) the self. The verse is a direct echo of Eve's

---

76. Even in Romans 1, humans sin because God has handed them over to corruptible passions and debased minds (1:24-28). I owe this insight to Susan Eastman's SBL presentation on sin and evil. Eastman, "'The Evil I Do Not Want Is What I Do': Sin and Evil in Romans," paper presented to the Society of Biblical Literature, Atlanta, 2010. See also Käsemann, *Perspectives on Paul*, trans. Margaret Kohl (Mifflintown, PA: Sigler Press, 1971 [orig. 1969]), 20–28; Käsemann, *Romans*, 176.

77. Cf. Byrne, "Living out the Righteousness of God: The Contribution of Rom 6:1—8:13 to an Understanding of Paul's Ethical Presuppositions," *CBQ* 83 (1981): 557–81.

78. We note that grace plays the same role in Romans 5–6 as the Holy Spirit plays in Romans 8 (cf. 6:12-14; 8:3, 10-11). Cf. also Gal. 2:20.

79. A full account of personification as a literary device is presented in our summary in chapter 8.

lament in Gen. 3:13: ὁ ὄφις ἠπάτησέν με ("the serpent deceived me"). Sin in Rom. 7:11 is playing for Paul—for whom Adam and Eve were historical figures— the role of the serpent in Gen. 3.[80] Sin—the serpent—exploited the arrival of the commandment as an opportunity (ἀφορμή) to turn the life-giving commandment of the Creator into a death-dealing encounter. That Paul has the Genesis narrative in mind is made all the more secure when we recognize that Paul makes a similar point in 2 Cor. 11:3: ὁ ὄφις ἐξηπάτησεν Εὕαν ("the serpent deceived Eve").[81] Second Corinthians 11:1-15 is quite telling for understanding Paul's personification of Sin. In this passage, Paul laments that just as Eve was deceived by the serpent (11:3), so also the false apostles who have infiltrated the Corinthian congregation are leading many astray. These false apostles—"deceitful workers" (11:13)—are also, according to Paul, messengers of Satan (11:14-15). In both Romans 7 and 2 Corinthians 11 the theme of "deception" is key.[82] Eve is deceived in both texts—by Sin in Romans 7 and by the serpent in 2 Corinthians 11. In 2 Corinthians 11 we discover that Satan's deception is possible because he is able to transform himself into an angel of light. A similar idea is presented in 2 Thess. 2:1-13, where the coming of the lawless one—who will parade himself as a god to be worshiped (2 Thess. 2:4)—is in accordance with Satan's deceitful schemes (2 Thess. 2:9-10).

Echoing Gen. 3:13, Sin as personified demonic power in Romans 7, then, fits with early Jewish/Christian tradition that identified the serpent with Satan.[83] N. T. Wright is, therefore, on target when he writes: "When we stand back and look at the two kingdoms, they are those of sin on the one hand and grace on the other; and if 'grace' is a periphrastic (or indirect) personification for 'God,'[84] we may suppose that 'sin' is an indirect way of saying 'Satan.'"[85] In our

---

80. Wright's detection of an underlying new exodus motif in Romans 5–8 allows him to posit that Sin and Death are also playing the role of Pharaoh (Wright, "Letter to the Romans," 525). If Wright is correct, this will also confirm our argument that personification is a way of representing concrete realities, though we ourselves find the new exodus motif a bit overworked in Wright's commentary.

81. Cf. 1 Tim. 2:14.

82. This crucial theme of deception in Romans 7 (and also present in 2 Corinthians 11 and 2 Thessalonians 2) poses a problem for those who want to read the "I" in Rom. 7:7-12 as solely a reference to Israel. See, e.g., D. Moo, "Israel and Paul in Romans 7.7-12," 122–35; D. Napier, "Paul's Analysis of Sin and Torah in Romans 7:7-25," ResQ 44, no. 1 (2002): 15–32. There is no mention in the Torah of Israel being deceived into breaking God's commandments.

83. Cf. Rev. 12:9; 20:2, where Satan is referred to as the "ancient serpent." In addition, Paul may have the serpent of Gen. 3:15 in the background in Rom. 16:20, where Satan will soon be crushed under the believer's feet. Also, Wis. of Sol. 2:23-24 echoes the Genesis 3 narrative but lays blame for death in the human race on the devil. Closer to our reading of Paul is the author of the *Apocalypse of Abraham*, who also interprets personified "Sin" in Gen. 4:7 as the "adversary" (*Apoc. Ab.* 24:5).

summary chapter at the end of part 2 (chapter 8), we will demonstrate in detail that personification is a way of speaking about the nature of the world.[86]

Suffice it to say for now that for Paul, Adam's transgression released a host of powers into the cosmos, including Sin and Death. Paul, unlike his Jewish contemporaries, is not interested in stories about fallen angels. Yet when Paul speaks of the bondage and groaning of creation in chapter 8 (cf. 8:20-23) it becomes apparent that Adam's transgression was of cosmic significance. There are hosts of principalities and powers (8:38-39) that hold creation in bondage and seek to sever humans from God. What is not clear is whether Paul thinks these powers were already in the world prior to Adam's transgression and whether they were even the catalyst behind Adam's transgression. For example, when Paul speaks of Sin deceiving Adam (7:11) it may suggest that Adam was not acting within a "neutral" situation;[87] there seems to be a force behind Adam's transgression, loitering and seeking the opportunity to make an insidious entrance—even if Adam's transgression gave this force free reign. Paul is not very lucid on this point; he does not seem to be interested in such speculation. Nonetheless, it is clear that after Adam's transgression, and in a manner unlike before, Sin—together with Death—and a host of forces took residence in the cosmos. That is why at the end of chapter 8 Paul can include "Death" (and by extension "Sin," since Death acts jointly with Sin) in a list of "powers" seeking to wrest humanity from God (8:38-39): "Death . . . life . . . angels . . . rulers . . . the present . . . the future . . . powers . . . heights . . . depths . . . any other creature." The list itself is intriguing because of the pattern Paul sets up:

θάνατος (A); ζωὴ (B)
ἄγγελοι (A); ἀρχαὶ (B)
ἐνεστῶτα (A); μέλλοντα (B)
δυνάμεις (C).

---

84. Here we would include "or the Holy Spirit." Cf. Rom. 8:1-11; see our discussion above.

85. Wright, "Letter to the Romans," 530.

86. It is possible that Paul's personification of "Sin" as a higher power stems from his reading of Gen. 4:7. We have already noted that the author of the *Apocalypse of Abraham* attributes the cause of Cain's breaking of the Law to the "adversary" (*Apoc. Ab.* 24:5). The author of the *Apoc. Ab.*, then, understood the personification of "Sin" in Gen 4:7 as an oblique reference to Satan. Wright has even gone so far as to posit that, while Rom. 7:7-12 is a reference to Adam, Rom. 7:13-20 is an allusive reference to Cain. See Wright, *The Climax of the Covenant: Christ and the Law in Pauline Theology* (Minneapolis: Fortress Press, 1991), 226–30.

87. Thus, those who posit Adam sinning on "neutral terrain" may need to nuance their views a bit; see, e.g., Byrne, "Living out the Righteousness of God," 561–62.

ὕψωμα (A); βάθος (B)
τις κτίσις ἑτέρα (C).

The list establishes the pattern:

AB AB AB C AB C.

And the AB pattern permits us to posit a list composed of opposite pairs.[88]

Of immense significance is the fact that δυνάμεις ("powers") is not paired with anything; it stands by itself. It is important to note that the words "principalities," "powers," "authorities" almost always occur in a cluster of "powers" terms (e.g., 1 Cor. 15:24-26; Col. 1:16; Col. 2:8-10; cf. Eph. 1:21; 6:12).[89] These terms are comprehensive in nature. Thus, the central location of δυνάμεις ("powers") in Paul's list suggests that the term must be understood as a comprehensive summary of everything that stands before and after it.[90] Death, life, angels, rulers, present, future, height, depth, any other creature must all be summed up as δυνάμεις ("powers").

The AB C pattern is repeated in the second half of the list, where τις κτίσις ἑτέρα ("any other creature") sums up what stands in front of it—ὕψωμα οὔτε βάθος. Ὕψωμα and βάθος are astronomical terms, and Paul may be using these astronomical terms to refer to celestial beings.[91] According to Georg Bertram, the term ὕψωμα denotes a sphere where "astrally conceived powers . . . hold sway."[92] Acts of John 23 lists ὕψωμα among the evil powers. If Paul has these celestial beings in mind, then τις κτίσις ἑτέρα is also a comprehensive summation of beings within creation: no being in creation (among those

88. Thus, the NIV committee may be justified in their decision to translate ἀρχαί as "demons," since it is paired with "angels." This interpretation corroborates our own reading of the "rulers of this age" in 1 Cor. 2:6-8 as hostile powers. See our chapter on Corinthians. Cf. 1 Cor. 15:24; Col. 1:16; 2:15; Eph. 1:21; 6:12.

89. See our summary chapter at the end of part 2 (ch. 8) for a more detailed discussion.

90. Walter Wink provides a structure of Paul's list similar to ours, but he goes on to assert that "the fact that *dynameis* and 'any other creature' violate the series of pairs may mean that Paul is not all that conscious of the poetic structure" (Walter Wink, *Naming the Powers: The Language of the Powers in the New Testament* [Philadelphia: Fortress Press, 1984], 49). Our own analysis suggests that such a view is misguided. Other commentators who do not present a structure equivalent to ours often make the claim that in Rom. 8:31-39 Paul speaks of "powers" seeking to separate believers from God's love (see, e.g. Byrne, *Romans*, 275–79; Gaventa, "Neither Height Nor Depth," 274–75; Gaventa, "Cosmic Power of Sin," 237). It is not clear in these discussions how we can encapsulate Paul's list in this term. Nonetheless, our structure does demonstrate that this assumption is correct.

91. See Dunn, *Romans 1–8*, 508. For a discussion of these celestial powers, see A. Toepel, "Planetary Demons in Early Jewish Literature," *JSP* 14 (2005): 231–238.

92. G. Bertram, "ὕψωμα" in *TDNT*: 8:613–14.

dwelling from the highest to the lowest sphere) can separate believers from the love of God.

The positioning of "powers" and "any other creature" in the structure we have presented raises the possibility that the powers are God's creatures who have fallen out of fellowship with their Creator.[93] This is certainly the view of the Colossian hymn (Col. 1:15-20). Thus, Wink, for example, writes, "The 'et cetera' Paul adds at the end ('nor any other creature') shows how much in agreement with Col. 1:16 he really is: all these Powers—human, structural, or divine—are 'creatures' of the good God. 'Any other creature' indicates that creaturehood is the generic category from which the whole preceding series is derived. Every power is a 'creature.'"[94] This view, however, cannot be maintained in light of the preceding discussions, which argued that Paul presents Sin and Death as personified powers. For Paul, Sin is not God's creation. Rather, Sin was unleashed into the cosmos as a result of Adam's transgression, and the entrance of Sin made way for Death. Thus, the view that Paul presents all the powers as God's creatures does not find support in Romans or anywhere else in Paul's writings.[95]

At the end of part 2 of this study, we will see that Paul's "powers" consist of both personifications of abstract nouns (for example, Sin and Death) and spiritual entities with will and intellect (for example, Satan, demons, rulers, angels).[96] When Paul sums up his list in Rom. 8:38-39 as "powers," he leaves readers with a catalogue of comprehensive features of reality that span the whole gamut of existence. Drawing on Colin Gunton's work on the use of metaphor in theological language,[97] we will show that Paul's personification of abstract nouns must be viewed as a way of expressing truth about the mysterious nature of our world. To represent the powers with personified concepts such as Sin and Death shows how pervasive the powers are; the work of the powers seem closer, since sin and death are normal everyday experiences. Nonetheless, personification, in our view, also helps to give language to realities that defy language, to give speech to realities whose identification defy our normal human classifications and categories. While we have attempted so far to give some hermeneutical shape to Paul's powers, we also have to stress the extreme difficulty in categorizing the powers. The powers are supernatural, but their

93. We discuss this issue in detail in our chapter on Colossians.

94. Wink, *Naming the Powers*, 50.

95. See our chapter on Colossians for further discussion.

96. We will encounter these spiritual entities with will and intellect in subsequent chapters.

97. See C. Gunton, *The Actuality of Atonement: A Study of Metaphor, Rationality and the Christian Tradition* (Grand Rapids: Eerdmans, 1989).

actions do affect the natural course of events on earth and in human lives. The powers are entities with will and intellect, but they are also capable of co-opting structures, institutions, and traditions of human existence (such as the Law). The powers cannot be spotted with our common sense and empirical outlook on the world (the powers are evidence of how humans may be "ever seeing but never perceiving" [Isa. 6:9]), but the Christian message demands a new epistemology so that believers no longer see κατὰ σάρκα (2 Cor. 5:16). The powers may hold humans in thrall, causing self-destructive behavior in the process, but their work extends to bondage of the entire created order. Thus, we contend, when Paul presents *both* spiritual entities with will and intellect *and* personifications of abstract nouns as "powers," this allows Paul to cover all the levels and dimensions of existence into which the powers penetrate; it allows Paul to give language to the mysterious nature of our world.

CONCLUSION

We have discovered in this chapter that for Paul, Adam's transgression unleashed the powers of Sin and Death and a host of other hostile powers into the cosmos. The powers pervade all aspects of the cosmos and human existence. Christ's death and resurrection is God's way of rectifying a cosmos held in bondage to the powers, and believers are set free from the dominion of the powers by participating in Christ's death and resurrection. Participation in Christ's death and resurrection takes place through the practice of baptism. In baptism believers are mapped onto Christ's career by dying, being buried, and being raised with Christ (Rom. 6:1-7). When believers are stripped naked before the baptismal water, they signify that they have crucified the old person belonging to the old age from which Christ has rescued believers. When believers are immersed ("buried") into the baptismal water, they signify their own death to the power of Sin; and they are raised from the water of baptism into a new life and into a new sphere where the powers of darkness no longer hold sway.

As we observed in part 1, practices involve narratives. It is our contention that the narrative that underwrites baptism as a practice of power—one that rescues believers from the domain of the powers of darkness—is the story of Christ's encounter with the powers on cross (so also Col. 2:11-15). Christ's crucifixion was a battle stage between forces of good and evil; it was the site where the powers committed their most heinous crime, and it was also, paradoxically, the site of their own undoing. As we shall see in the next chapter, the story of Christ's encounter with powers on the cross was well established in Christian tradition, and the Gospel writers narrate the same story in different ways. More importantly, in the next chapter we will see that Paul presents his own version of the story when he claims that "the rulers of this age" crucified the Lord of glory (1 Cor. 2:6-8). We shall see in the next chapter that such a story—in addition to the practice of baptism—also informs Paul's understanding of the practice of Christian preaching. To this we now turn.

5

Cross-Centered Preaching and Church Discipline as Confrontation with the Powers: 1 & 2 Corinthians

When one reads the Corinthian correspondence, one gets the sense that Paul sees behind many of the activities of everyday life a spiritual significance and reality: behind everyday activities of planting and watering stand the invisible work of God that ensures growth (3:7); the sexually deviant believer who has not repented of his ways is destroying the body of Christ (5:1-13); Christians cannot go before worldly judges to settle disputes because believers will judge the angels (6:3); because the Holy Spirit dwells in the believer, the believer cannot engage in sexual immorality (6:19); even sex in marriage, when not rightly ordered, could become a base of operations for Satan to attack the Christian couple (7:5); mere food might be harmful for believers who do not realize that demons may stand behind certain foods (8:1-13; 10). The list goes on and on. The point is clear: normal everyday activities have a spiritual significance and reality. Thus, in the Corinthian correspondence Paul calls the congregation to an epistemological transformation that will help them see the spiritual reality behind everyday activities, and as a result cause them to take everyday experiences seriously in that way. Some have argued that there is no direct connection between Paul's ethical instructions and his theological framework.[1] This view has been challenged, however.[2] Nonetheless, those who

1. See, for example, M. Dibelius, *A Fresh Approach to the New Testament and Early Christian Literature* (London: Ivor Nicholson and Watson, 1936), 143–44, 217–20; H. D. Betz, *Galatians*, Hermeneia (Philadelphia: Fortress Press, 1979), 292.

2. See, e.g., V. P. Furnish, *Theology and Ethics in Paul* (Nashville: Abingdon, 1968); R. B. Hays, "Christology and Ethics in Galatians: The Law of Christ," *CBQ* 49 (1987): 268–90; Hays, *The Moral Vision of the New Testament: Community, Cross, New Creation: A Contemporary Introduction to New*

have attempted to ground Paul's ethic in his gospel proclamation have often failed to integrate his ethic with his teaching on the powers. In this chapter we hope to show that Paul's ethic cannot be separated from the reality of cosmic powers. When this crucial point is missed, we run the risk of distorting Paul's message to the church at Corinth. In our treatment of Paul's letters to the Corinthians, we will focus on two practices of power in these terms: cross-centered preaching and church discipline.[3]

Preaching the Cross as Manifestation of Divine Power (1 Cor. 1:18—2:16)

Paul begins 1 Corinthians by calling the congregation's attention to divisions within the Corinthian body, as reported to Paul by Chloe (1:11). These divisions presumably have to do with factions siding with authoritative figures (1:12-14). To address these schisms Paul invokes two of his own missionary activities among the Corinthians: baptism (1:13-17) and preaching (1:17–2:16). Paul's reference to his own baptismal ministry at Corinth is curt; his point is that since his baptismal ministry was very limited at Corinth, none of these factions can claim allegiance to him on the basis of baptism. His appeal to his preaching ministry, however, is extensive; it sets the stage for a lengthy discourse concerning the nature of true "wisdom." The discourse on wisdom drawn from Paul's preaching practice is necessary because some at Corinth are boasting of their wisdom (3:18-21; cf. 8:1), a wisdom that, for Paul, empties the cross of its power. This "wisdom of the world" (1:20) stands in sharp antithesis to the preaching of a crucified Messiah (1:21-24). To those who possess this worldly wisdom, who together with their wisdom are being destroyed by God (1:19), the word of the cross is foolishness (1:18). But to the called, Christ crucified is the power and wisdom of God (1:24).

This transvaluation of wisdom is possible only for believers, because believers have experienced an epistemological transformation (cf. 2 Cor. 5:17).[4]

Testament Ethics (San Francisco: HarperSanFrancisco, 1996), 16–59; J. Barclay, *Obeying the Truth: A Study of Paul's Ethics in Galatians* (Edinburgh: T & T Clark, 1988).

3. We need to state upfront our decision to defer treatment of the issue of food offered to idols (1 Corinthians 8–10) until our discussion of the *stoicheia* in Galatians. There are two underlying reasons for this decision: first, as we shall argue in our chapter on Galatians, the *stoicheia* also concerns idolatry. Second, our forthcoming work is an extensive study on the subject of idolatry that also includes a detailed treatment of 1 Corinthians 8–10. Thus, in this work, we only offer a brief treatment of these passages in combination with our discussion of the *stoicheia* in Galatians.

4. Cf. J. L. Martyn, "Epistemology at the Turn of the Ages," in *Theological Issues in the Letters of Paul* (Nashville: Abingdon, 1997), 89–110.

According to the world's mode of perceiving (κατὰ σάρκα), the proclamation of a crucified Messiah is folly. But what the world perceives as foolishness and weakness is wisdom and power before God. Conversely, what the world perceives as wise and strong is foolishness and weakness before God.

The wisdom of the world is characterized by a form of sophisticated rhetoric. It is likely that other missionaries at Corinth employed such rhetoric and that the Corinthians accused Paul of being too insipid in his preaching.[5] Paul, therefore, reminds the Corinthians that while his own preaching was not conveyed in sophisticated rhetoric, the potency of the kerygma lay in the "proof of the Spirit and power" (2:4), a power that transforms the character and conditions of those whom the word encounters. For Paul, then, a power and spirit (or better, a "powerful spirit") accompany preaching (cf. 1 Cor. 12:10).[6] In other words, the preaching of the kerygma, for Paul, is a *Spirit*-ual practice. To load this message with sophisticated rhetoric is to void the proclamation of its power.

Paul's preaching at Corinth was not encumbered with the kind of sophisticated rhetoric characteristic of the wisdom of the world (2:1). Paul's own style of preaching was characterized by weakness (ἀσθένεια), fear (φόβος), and trembling (τρόμος) (2:3). The content of Paul's preaching was a simple message: "Jesus Christ and Jesus Christ crucified" (2:2). It is this same message that Paul describes in 1:18 as "the word of the cross."[7] In his death Christ exhibited strength in weakness. Paul's own style among the Corinthians, then, captured the essence of the content of his message: a God who reigned from a tree. This is not the *modus operandi* of credentialed orators, for their message is characterized by captivating eloquence and shrewd parlance (2:4). This could not be Paul's method, however; for to proceed like the professional orators would shift the focus of Paul's message away from God's power to human rhetorical dexterity (2:5). As simple and unimpressive as this message may seem, it is, nonetheless, accompanied by a divine power that is able to break the shackles and reverse the condition of those who believe this message, a fact that the Corinthians themselves have witnessed (6:11; cf. 1 Thess. 1:9).

---

5. See 2 Corinthians 10–11; 12:11-21.

6. This insight is crucial for a correct interpretation of 2 Corinthians. In 2 Corinthians, Paul's anxiety over the preachers at Corinth stems from his belief that their preaching is introducing another spirit—distinct from the Holy Spirit—into the Corinthian body (cf. 2 Cor. 11:4). See our discussion below.

7. Thus, a good paraphrase of 1:18 would be: "Jesus Christ crucified" is foolishness to those who are becoming undone; but to us who are being saved, "Jesus Christ crucified" is the power of God.

Furthermore, this simple message of the cross is also a mystery (2:1); it is wisdom accessible only to the mature (2:6).[8] This sort of wisdom is not accessible even to "the rulers of this age" (οἱ ἄρχοντες τοῦ αἰῶνος τούτου) who crucified the Lord of glory. The identity of these "rulers" has been the subject of much debate. In what follows, we devote adequate attention to the identity of the rulers of this age, since, as we shall see below, the identity of these rulers is crucial for a correct understanding of Paul's theology of preaching. Interpreters tend to view the rulers of this age as either human or spiritual, or both human and spiritual. In the ensuing discussion, we will critically engage each of these positions in increasing order of plausibility.

"THE RULERS OF THIS AGE" AS HUMAN AUTHORITIES

Gene Miller and Wesley Carr have offered the most detailed and developed arguments for the view that the rulers of this age are earthly powers.[9] Both Miller and Carr set up their arguments in opposition to the view that the rulers of this age are spiritual powers. Miller rejects, correctly, the notion that the rulers are some kind of gnostic demigods who diffuse wisdom.[10] Citing those who propose that 1 Cor. 2:6-8 teaches that the spiritual rulers were ignorant of the identity of Jesus, Miller argues that the Gospels depict demonic powers or spirits as discerning the identity of Jesus as "the Holy One of God" and "the Son of God."[11] A similar position had been argued prior to Miller by Julius Schniewind,[12] who argued that while Paul may have believed that the devil stood behind Jesus' opponents, the view that the rulers of this age are spiritual powers cannot be maintained because it would put Paul in tension with the Synoptic Gospels, which portray demonic spirits as recognizing the identity of Jesus.[13]

---

8. Paul's characterization of his message as "wisdom" in 2:6 is already anticipated by his identification of the crucified Christ with the "wisdom of God" for believers (1:24; 1:30).

9. See G. Miller, "ΑΡΧΟΝΤΩΝ ΤΟΥ ΑΙΩΝΟΣ ΤΟΥΤΟΥ — A New Look at 1 Corinthians 2:6-8," *JBL* 91 (1972): 522-28; W. Carr, "The Rulers of This Age — 1 Cor. ii:6-8," *NTS* 23 (1976): 20-35; Carr, *Angels and Principalities: The Background Meaning and Development of the Pauline Phrase Hai Archai kai hai Exousiai*, SNTSMS 42 (Cambridge: Cambridge University Press, 1981), 118-20. Among modern commentators who prefer this position, see Fee, *The First Epistle to the Corinthians*, NICNT (Grand Rapids: Eerdmans, 1987), 104; R. B. Hays, *First Corinthians*, Interpretation (Louisville: Knox, 1997), 43-44.

10. Miller, "ΑΡΧΟΝΤΩΝ ΤΟΥ ΑΙΩΝΟΣ ΤΟΥΤΟΥ," 523.

11. See Matt. 8:29; Mark 1:24; 1:34; 3:11; Luke 4:34; 4:41; Miller, "ΑΡΧΟΝΤΩΝ ΤΟΥ ΑΙΩΝΟΣ ΤΟΥΤΟΥ," 524.

12. J. Schniewind, *Nachgelassene Reden und Aufsätze* (Berlin: A. Töpelmann, 1952), 104-9. Cf. Carr, "Rulers of this Age," 27n4.

The latter argument is important not only for its flawed logic but also because it may provide for us an important window into the history of interpretation of the identity of the rulers of this age. Our earliest interpretations of 1 Cor. 2:6-8 understood the rulers to be spiritual powers.[14] Later centuries, however, saw a reversal, with many patristic exegetes opting for the earthly rulers interpretation.[15] It is probable, as Martin Werner has argued,[16] that this reversal was due to the perceived tension between these verses and the Gospels.[17] Patristic exegetes harmonized their reading of Paul with their reading of the Gospels.

Against Miller and Schniewind, however, the argument concerning the (perceived) tension between Paul and the Gospels on this subject is flawed for two reasons. First, Paul's opinions on a number of subjects (such as the Law and gentile inclusion) were by no means consensus positions in the early church;[18] Paul's theology was often controversial.[19] Thus, as a contentious figure, that Paul would disagree on an issue with the Gospels (or early church) is by no means remarkable. Second, interpreting the rulers as human authorities does not eradicate all tensions with the Gospels, for the Gospels *do* present some human rulers as discerning the identity of Jesus (Matt. 8:5-13; Luke 7:1-10; Mark 15:39

13. Miller does not cite Schniewind, however.

14. This is the view of Ignatius, *Eph.* 18–19 (cf. *Tr.* 5:2; *Sm.* 6:1); Marcion (Tertullian, *Marc.* 5.6), and the *Martyrdom and Ascension of Isaiah* 11:22–33. Cf. Justin, *Dial.* 36. But, as we hope to show below, evidence for our earliest interpretation may come from the NT itself—from the authors of Mark and Ephesians. Other patristic exegetes who hold this position include Cyril of Alexandria, *Commentary on 1 Corinthians*, in *Sancti patris nostri Cyrilli Archiepiscopi Alexandrini in D. Joannis Evangelium: accedunt fragmenta varia necnon tractatus ad Tiberium diaconum duo*, vol. 3:249–318, ed. Philip Edward Pusey (Brussels: Culture et Civilisation, 1965), 256–57; Ambrosiaster, *Commentary on Paul's Epistles*, CSEL 81:24; Origen, *Comm. Matt.* 13:8.

15. See, e.g., Tertullian, *Marc.* 5:6; Pelagius, *Commentary on the First Epistle to the Corinthians* 2 (PL 30:722D–723A); Chrysostom, *Homilies on the Epistles of Paul to the Corinthians* 7.5 (NPNF1 12:35–36); Theodoret, *Commentary on the First Epistle to the Corinthians* 176 (PG 82:242); Oecumenius, *Pauline Commentary from the Greek Church* (NTA 15:432).

16. M. Werner, *The Formation of Christian Dogma* (New York: Harper and Brothers, 1957), 97.

17. See, e.g., Tertullian, *Marc.* 5:6; 4:42; Cyprian, *Quod idola dii non sint*, 14; Lactantius, *Inst.* 4:16. Noted in Werner, *Formation of Christian Dogma*, 97.

18. This was F. C. Baur's thesis; see, *Paul, the Apostle of Jesus Christ, His Life and Works, His Epistles and Teachings: A Contribution to a Critical History of Primitive Christianity*, 2 vols., ed. E. Zeller, rev. A. Menzies (London: Williams and Norgate, 1873–75 [repr. 2003; Peabody, Mass.: Hendrickson]). See also E. Käsemann, *New Testament Questions of Today* (Philadelphia: Fortress Press, 1969 [1957]); Käsemann, *Perspectives on Paul* (Mifflintown, PA: Sigler, 1996 [1971]); G. Lüdemann, *Opposition to Paul in Jewish Christianity* (Minneapolis: Fortress Press, 1989); Martyn, *Theological Issues*.

19. See, e.g., Gal. 2; 2 Cor. 11:24-25; Phil. 3:2-6; cf. Acts 21:17-36.

par.).[20] Thus, we are trapped in the very pit that this interpretation seeks to escape. In the end, as we shall soon demonstrate, Paul may not be in conflict with the Gospel writers on this particular issue after all.

More important is the recognition that the ignorance about which Paul speaks does not concern the "identity" of Jesus. As the context of the passage suggests, the ignorance concerns the cross as the locus for the manifestation of God's power.[21] The rulers of this age could not see God's power in the event of utter degradation and weakness. Consequently, the rulers could not discern that the cross would be the site of their own undoing. If they had known this, they would not have crucified "the Lord of glory."[22] In contrast to the perceived tension between Paul and the Gospels on this subject, when these rulers are viewed as demonic forces, then Paul's theology of the cross actually dovetails well with Mark's presentation of the crucifixion of Jesus. Mark presents Jesus' death scene as the culmination of the battle between Jesus and demonic forces, which began immediately after Jesus' baptism (Mark 1:9-13; cf. Matt. 4:1-11; Luke 4:1-13), and extended throughout his ministry.[23] It will

20. We may even include the sages from the East in Matthew's birth narrative (Matt. 2:1-12), since it is commonplace to find the sages, scribes, and philosophers of this age (1 Cor. 1:20) included among the "earthly" rulers of this age (see, e.g., Miller, "ΑΡΧΟΝΤΩΝ ΤΟΥ ΑΙΩΝΟΣ ΤΟΥΤΟΥ," 527; Carr, "Rulers of this Age," 25; Schniewind, *Nachgelassene Reden*, 104–9; Fee, *The First Epistle to the Corinthians*, 104). But to those who see a connection between 1:20 and the "rulers of this age," the question remains as to what the philosophers and sages of this age have to do with the crucifixion of Jesus (2:8).

21. This should rule out the interpretation of *Mart. Ascen. Isa.* 10:1–31; 11:19–33. According to this legend, Christ disguised himself when he entered the world; thus, the spiritual and earthly rulers failed to recognize him. See also *Acts Thom.* 143; *Ep. Apost.* 13–14; *2 Apoc. Jas.* 56–58; *Gos. Phil.* 55:14–16; *Tri. Trac.* 64:28–66.5; *Paraph. Shem* 34:16–36:24; *Melch.* 6:10–22; *Great Pow.* 40:24–41.32. This legend has been influential for gnostic interpretations of this pericope; see, for example, R. Bultmann, *Theology of the New Testament*, 2 vols (Waco, TX: Baylor University Press, 2007 [orig. 1951–55]), 1:175; U. Wilckens, *Weisheit und Torheit. Eine exegetisch-religionsgeschichtliche Untersuchung zu 1 Kor. 1 und 2* (Tübingen: Mohr, 1959) 206; C. K. Barrett, *The First Epistle to the Corinthians*, HNTC (New York: Harper & Row, 1968), 71–72. The reluctance to embrace the interpretation of the rulers as spiritual powers has at times, therefore, stemmed from the misguided assumption that one needs this gnostic myth for the interpretation of the rulers as spiritual powers (see, e.g., Carr, "Rulers of this Age," 23–24; 28–29). This assumption must be rejected.

22. For this expression in apocalyptic literature, see *1 En.* 22:14; 25:3–7; 27:3–5; 36:4; 40:3; 63:2; 83:8. Cf. A. C. Thiselton, *First Epistle to the Corinthians*, NIGTC (Grand Rapids: Eerdmans, 2000), 246–48.

23. See James Robinson, *The Problem of History in Mark and Other Marcan Studies* (Philadelphia: Fortress Press, 1982 [1957]), 91–4; Susan R. Garrett, *The Temptations of Jesus in Mark's Gospel* (Grand Rapids: Eerdmans, 1998). Robinson and Garrett argue convincingly that human opposition to Jesus in Mark's Gospel is an extension of demonic opposition. See also J. Marcus's demonic interpretation of the sudden shift in the crowd's stance toward Jesus and cosmic darkness at the death scene in *Mark 8–16*, AB

not be an exaggeration to include the other Gospels as well, since both Luke and John identify Satan as the one who influences Judas to betray Jesus, thereby setting in motion Jesus' passion and crucifixion (Luke 22:3-6; John 13:21-30).

In addition to the above arguments, the view that the rulers are human authorities must also wrestle with the question of the identity of these human authorities. Paul never explicitly identifies the Roman government as the executioners of Jesus anywhere in his letters. When he speaks explicitly of the Roman authorities, they appear as servants of God (Rom. 13:1-7) who are denied any significant role in the drama of history, because their agency is subordinate and derived.[24] And while those who argue that the rulers of this age are human authorities often identify these rulers as the Jewish leaders (or at least include the Jewish leaders), the surrounding context of our passage presents problems for this identification. Miller, for example, notes: "[Paul] considered the Jewish leaders to be primarily responsible for the crucifixion."[25] But the argumentative context of 1 Corinthians 1–2 in general and 1 Cor. 2:6 in particular suggests that Paul's description and critique of the wisdom of

27A (New Haven: Yale University Press, 2009), 1036–37; 1061–64. It may well be that Mark is an interpreter of Paul (see Marcus, "Mark — Interpreter of Paul," *NTS* 46 [2000]: 473–87; cf. C. Black, "Christ Crucified in Paul and in Mark: Reflections on an Intracanonical Conversation," in *Theology and Ethics in Paul and His Interpreters: Essays in Honor of Victor Paul Furnish*, ed. Eugene H. Lovering and Jerry L. Sumney [Nashville: Abingdon, 1996], 184–206). If so, then our reading is corroborated by one of the earliest interpretations of Paul's theology. As we hope to show, the author of Ephesians is another early interpreter of Paul who gives support to our reading. In favor of the rulers as earthly powers, A. Robertson and A. Plummer have suggested that Acts 3:17 may be the earliest commentary on 1 Cor. 2:6-8; Robertson and Plummer, *First Epistle to the Corinthians*, 2d ed., ICC (Edinburgh: T & T Clark, 1958 [1911]), 37. But see Phillip Vielhauer, who has shown that Luke on occasion misunderstands Paul; P. Vielhauer, "On the 'Paulinism' of Acts," in *Studies in Luke-Acts*, ed. Leander E. Keck and J. Louis Martyn (Philadelphia: Fortress Press, 1980 [1963]), 33–50. For other possible contacts between 1 Cor. 2:6-16 and the Gospels, see Richard B. Gaffin, Jr., "Some Epistemological Reflections on 1 Cor 2:6-16," *WTJ* 57 (1995): 103–24. Gaffin makes the interesting observation that 1 Cor. 2:6-16 may be a commentary on Matt. 11:25-27 // Luke 10:21-22.

24. We have already argued this in part 1 of our study. See also J. M. G. Barclay, "Why the Roman Empire Was Insignificant to Paul," in *Pauline Churches and Diaspora Jews*, WUNT 275 (Tubingen: Mohr Siebeck, 2011), 363–87.

25. Miller, "ΑΡΧΟΝΤΩΝ ΤΟΥ ΑΙΩΝΟΣ ΤΟΥΤΟΥ," 525; cf. 528. Miller goes on to note that in Rom. 10:1-4 the Jews stand condemned because they sought to establish their own righteousness. 1 Cor. 2:6-8 presents a similar argument to Romans 10, except that "righteousness" is replaced by "wisdom" (527). This argument is unwarranted. Miller ultimately adopts A. T. Robertson's and A. Plummer's position that "the archontes are the men who actually took part in the crucifixion of the lord of glory and they primarily include the rulers of the Jews" (ibid.). Cf. Robertson and Plummer, *First Epistle to the Corinthians*, 36–37.

this age and its *modus operandi* evoke a backdrop of Greco-Roman rhetorical tradition, with its unrivaled rhetorical heritage and high regard for virtuoso public orators.[26] When Paul makes mention of the Jews in the context of his argument, he contrasts them with Greeks in a statement that almost undercuts the identification of the wisdom of the rulers of this age (2:6) as earthly Jewish leaders: "Jews ask for signs and Greeks seek wisdom" (1:22). The wisdom Paul denounces is the quest of Greeks.[27] Consequently, the preaching of a crucified Messiah, while "scandalous" to Jews, is to the gentiles "folly" (1:23). It is hard to see Paul making this distinction if the *wisdom* of the rulers of this age is of Jewish origin.[28]

The above criticism applies to another argument proffered in favor of the view that the rulers are human authorities: that the primitive Christian kerygma in Acts 13:27-29 affirms the view that human rulers (ἄρχοντες) crucified Jesus.[29]

26. For detailed treatments of the Greco-Roman rhetorical and sophistic traditions, see S. M. Pogoloff, *Logos and Sophia: The Rhetorical Situation of 1 Corinthians*, SBLDS 134 (Atlanta: Scholars Press, 1992); D. Liftin, *St. Paul's Theology of Proclamation: 1 Corinthians 1–4 and Greco-Roman Rhetoric*, SNTSMS 79 (Cambridge: Cambridge University Press, 1994); M. A. Bullmore, *St. Paul's Theology of Rhetorical Style: An Examination of 1 Corinthians 2:1-5 in the Light of First Century Greco-Roman Rhetorical Culture* (San Francisco: International Scholars Publication, 1995); B. W. Winter, *Philo and Paul among the Sophists*, SNTSMS 96 (Cambridge: Cambridge University Press, 1997). Alternatively, there have been attempts to situate the rhetorical practice at Corinth within Jewish wisdom traditions. For these attempts, see R. A. Horsley, "Wisdom of Word and Words of Wisdom," *CBQ* 39 (1977): 224–39; J. A. Davis, *Wisdom and Spirit: An Investigation of 1 Cor. 1:18—3:20 against the Background of Jewish Sapiential Traditions in the Greco-Roman Period* (Lanham, MD: University Press of America, 1984). But see Gordon Fee's perceptive critique of these attempts; Fee, *The First Epistle to the Corinthians*, 13–15, 64–5. The alternative view that attempts to explain 1 Corinthians against the background of Gnosticism has been largely discredited. For this view see W. Schmithals, *Gnosticism in Corinth: An Investigation of the Letters to the Corinthians* (Nashville: Abingdon, 1971); U. Wilckens, *Weisheit und Torheit*; R. Bultmann, *Exegetische Probleme des zweiten Korintherbriefs* (Upsala: Wretmans, 1947). For refutations of this view, see R. McL. Wilson, "How Gnostic Were the Corinthians?" *NTS* 19 (1972): 65–74; J. Kovacs, "The Archons, the Spirit, and the Death of Christ: Do We Really Need the Hypothesis of Gnostic Opponents to Explain 1 Cor. 2:2-16?" in *Apocalyptic and the New Testament: Essays in Honor of J. Louis Martyn*, eds. Joel Marcus and Marion L. Soards, JSNTSup 24 (Sheffield: JSOT Press, 1989), 217–36.

27. Cf. R. F. Collins, *First Corinthians*, Sacra Pagina 7 (Collegeville: Liturgical Press, 1999), 106: "Paul's choice of 'Hellenes' rather than 'Gentiles' to describe non-Jews may be due to his diatribal invective against dependence on Hellenistic wisdom."

28. Cf. Earle McMillan, "An Aspect of Recent Wisdom Studies in the New Testament," *ResQ* 10 (1967), 209: "There is no hint that would justify the conclusion that [Paul] felt himself to be expounding the true meaning of Jewish Wisdom speculation."

29. See Carr, "Rulers of this Age," 25–27; also Fee, *The First Epistle to the Corinthians*, 103. On the other hand, see G. Williams' observation that Christ's defeat of the spiritual powers may have been part of the early Christian message (G. Williams, *The Spirit World in the Letters of Paul the Apostle: A Critical*

A close reading of Acts 13 reveals that the passage relates the account of *Jewish rulers* (ἄρχοντες), who, having failed to discern the *identity* of Jesus, ask Pilate to execute Jesus.[30] But the two crucial tenets that form the backbone of this Lucan account—Jewish rulers and ignorance concerning Jesus' identity—have already been discredited as Pauline teaching on the rulers of this age.

"THE RULERS OF THIS AGE" AS BOTH HUMAN AND SPIRITUAL POWERS

When the notion that Paul has human rulers in view is set aside, this, by implication, also renders precarious the position that *both* human rulers and their demonic/angelic counterparts are in view, at least for 1 Cor. 2:6-8.[31] This view may be implied, since Paul is fully aware of the human agency in Jesus' death, and ancient Jews often connected political and spiritual powers.[32] But this point is not explicitly argued by Paul in 1 Cor. 2:6-8. When Paul wants to make this point explicit, he can do so (e.g., 2 Cor. 11:1-15). Thus, not only is this position exegetically unsupportable in 1 Cor 2:6-8, but it also has not wrestled adequately with the identity of the human rulers, often assuming the Jewish rulers of Acts, a view which we have refuted in light of the context of 1 Corinthians 2.

"THE RULERS OF THIS AGE" AS SPIRITUAL POWERS

We turn now to the most plausible interpretation: that the rulers of this age in 1 Cor. 2:6-8 are spiritual powers.[33] Our argument that Paul sees the preaching of the kerygma as a spiritual practice accompanied by power and the Holy Spirit,

Examination of the Role of Spiritual Beings in the Authentic Pauline Epistles [Göttingen: Vandenhoeck & Ruprecht, 2009], 133–34; cf. 1 Cor. 15:24; Eph. 1:20–21; 1 Pet. 3:22).

30. Cf. Ambrosiaster, *Commentary on Paul's Epistles*: "The Jewish rulers cannot be called rulers of this age, because they were subject to the Romans." Translation in *1–2 Corinthians*, ACCS 7, ed. Gerald Bray (Chicago: Fitzroy Dearborn Publishers, 1999), 22.

31. This position is argued by O. Cullmann, *Christ and Time: The Primitive Christian Conception of Time and History* (Philadelphia: Westminster, 1950), 191–201; G. B. Caird, *Principalities and Powers: A Study in Pauline Theology* (Eugene, OR: Wipf and Stock, 2003 [orig. 1956]), 82–101. A more nuanced presentation of this interpretation is given by W. Wink, *Naming the Powers: The Language of the Powers in the New Testament* (Philadelphia: Fortress Press, 1984) 13–15, 40–45; Thiselton, *First Epistle to the Corinthians*, 238–39.

32. See, e.g., 1QM.

33. The scholarly literature for this position is immense. See, for example, O. Everling, *Die paulinische Angelologie und Dämonologie: Ein biblisch-theologischer Versuch* (Göttingen: Vandenhoeck & Ruprecht, 1888), 11–25; M. Dibelius, *Die Geisterwelt im Glauben des Paulus* (Göttingen: Vandenhoeck & Ruprecht, 1909), 88–99; Wilckens, *Weisheit und Torheit*, 52–96; Barrett, *First Epistle to the Corinthians*, 70–72; H. Conzelmann, *1 Corinthians: A Commentary on the First Epistle to the Corinthians*, trans. James W. Leitch,

and the overall context of 1 Cor. 1:18–2:16, favors the view that the "rulers of this age" are spiritual powers. First, the introduction of the "rulers of this age" in 2:6 seems arbitrary and redundant if they are human. Paul's claim that the wisdom he proclaims is not of this age is enough to signal to the reader the fact that this wisdom is not accessible to the sages, scribes, and philosophers of this age (1:20). Yet Paul presses beyond these. Paul's claim is not only that this wisdom is inaccessible to these human characters, but also that not even the rulers of this age ("who are being rendered inoperative") are privy to this knowledge. This characterization of the "rulers" denies them certain important attributes assumed to be inherent to these "rulers": superior knowledge, superior power, and immortality. These properties were distinguishing marks of the gods in Greco-Roman religions,[34] all of which Paul regarded as demons (1 Cor. 10:19-21).

The argument prior to 2:6 concerns a reversal, in which God has "chosen" the foolish, weak, and ignoble things of this world, and the effect of God's election is that no "flesh" (σάρξ) might boast before God (1:29). The argument up to this point concerns a human realm in which God elects what appears to be foolish, weak, and ignoble before human eyes. That Paul is dealing with the human realm prior to 2:6 is obvious by the qualifiers he employs in 1:26—2:5, such as κατὰ σάρκα ("according to the flesh"; 1:26), τοῦ κόσμου ("this world"; 1:27-28), πᾶσα σὰρξ ("all flesh"; 1:29), σοφίᾳ ἀνθρώπων ("human wisdom"; 2:5). The theme of God's reversal within the human realm is well established prior to 2:6.

Paul's argument, however, takes a dramatic turn at 2:6, when Paul speaks of a wisdom hidden in mystery, which also existed before this age came into being.[35] The argument seems to move to a supraterrestrial realm whose

Hermeneia (Philadelphia: Fortress Press, 1975), 61; Kovacs, "The Archons, the Spirit, and the Death of Christ"; R. F. Collins, *First Corinthians*, 129; Williams, *Spirit World*, 133–34; 136–37; 232–40.

34. This is certainly Homer's portrayal of the gods in his *Iliad* and *Odyssey*. See Hans-Josef Klauck, *The Religious Context of Early Christianity: A Guide to Graeco-Roman Religions* (Edinburgh: T & T Clark, 2000).

35. This dramatic shift has led to some speculation that 1 Cor. 2:6-16 may be a non-Pauline fragment. This view was proposed by M. Windmann, "1 Kor 2:6-16: Ein Einspruch gegen Paulus," *ZNW* 70 (1979): 44–53. See J. Murphy-O'Connor's refutation of Windmann's arguments, "Interpolations in 1 Corinthians," *CBQ* 48 (1986): 81–94. Windmann's position has been revived by W. Walker, Jr., "1 Corinthians 2.6-16: A Non-Pauline Interpolation?" *JSNT* 47 (1992): 75–94. It is perhaps significant that Walker makes no mention of Kovacs's fine 1989 essay arguing for the unity of this pericope and its consistency with Paul's own theology and the entire context of 1 Corinthians (Kovacs, "The Archons, the Spirit, and the Death of Christ"). Our own argument is consonant with the consensus position that this pericope is a continuation of the previous argumentation, with its antithesis between the wisdom of

inhabitants existed before this age of humans (2:8).[36] These inhabitants seem to have superior knowledge, so that information kept from them must be shrouded in mystery (2:7). If Paul's reference is to humans, this information is unnecessary in light of his argument about the epistemological transformation available only to believers (1:26-31). Paul's argument, then, assumes entities thought to have superior knowledge and an otherworldly lifespan.[37]

Second, Paul employs concepts and terminologies encountered in apocalyptic literature to make his argument: the wisdom about which Paul speaks is hidden "in mystery" (θεοῦ σοφίαν ἐν μυστηρίῳ τήν ἀποκεκρυμμένην) and foreordained by God before "this age" (ἣν προώρισεν ὁ θεὸς πρὸ τῶν αἰώνων) for "the glory" of believers (εἰς δόξαν ἡμῶν).[38] The theme of the glory of the elect can be found in apocalyptic texts such as Dan. 12:3 and *1 En.* 50:1, 51:1–5; and the expression "the Lord of glory" (2:8) is also common in apocalyptic literature (see, e.g., *1 En.* 22.14; 25.3–7; 27.3–5; 36.4; 40.3; 63.2; 83.8).[39] In *1 En.* 16:3 angelic powers offer their own mysteries in opposition to God's mysteries.[40] Finally, the view that God's mysterious plan (which includes judgment on evil forces and salvation for the elect) is hidden yet revealed to the elect is also routinely encountered in Jewish apocalyptic texts (e.g., *1 En.* 1; 16:3; 83–90; 91; 93; Dan. 7–12; *4 Ezra; 2 Bar.*).[41]

Paul brings the latter point home in 1 Cor. 2:9 by quoting "Scripture." Paul's point is that the wisdom believers possess is God's mysterious wisdom, long hidden, and this wisdom is inaccessible even to spiritual entities that are thought to possess superior knowledge. At the center of this wisdom is the cross as the site of manifestation of God's power. That God would make his hidden wisdom available to believers is, by definition, unprecedented. It is unheard of that humans would be the bearers of a wisdom that has been long hidden, about which even spiritual powers are ignorant. But this knowledge, which "no

the cosmos and the wisdom of God. On the unity of 1 Corinthians, see J. C. Hurd Jr., *The Origin of I Corinthians* (London: SPCK, 1965), 43–47; Barrett, *The First Epistle to the Corinthians*, 11–17; Conzelmann, *1 Corinthians*, 4.

36. Cf. Conzelmann, *1 Corinthians*, 62: "This verse gives an impression of indefiniteness."

37. Or a lifespan not characteristic of humans.

38. As Clifton Black has observed, Paul's presentation of the death of Christ with apocalyptic terminologies and concepts portrays Christ's death as an apocalyptic event, the turning point of the ages (Black, "Christ Crucified in Paul and in Mark," 184–206, esp. 201). For Paul, then, the advent of Christ is the decisive moment in history that ushers in a new age and, in turn, sets in motion the gradual fading out of the old cosmos (1 Cor. 7:33).

39. Cf. Thiselton, *First Epistle to the Corinthians*, 246–48.

40. Noted in Williams, *Spirit World*, 235.

41. See Kovacs, "The Archons, the Spirit, and the Death of Christ," 219.

eye has seen, nor ear heard, nor entered the human heart," is "what God has prepared for those who love him" (2:9).[42]

Important for our purpose is the fact that an argument analogous to that of Paul is expressed by the author of Ephesians, one of our earliest interpreters of Paul:

> In order that now, through the church, the manifold wisdom of God might be made known to the rulers and authorities *in the heavenly realms*, according to his eternal purpose which he accomplished in Christ Jesus our Lord. (Eph. 3:10–11, emphasis added)

The author of Ephesians aptly captures the main contention of 1 Cor. 2:6–10. The wisdom of God is hidden from the rulers and authorities in the heavenly realm; yet this wisdom has been made available to those who are in the body of Christ (cf. Col. 1:26).[43] For Paul, God has chosen the weakness of the cross

---

42. As commentators have long noted, the source of this quotation is unknown. Origen attributes this quotation to the *Apocalypse of Elijah* (Origen on Matt. 27:9, *Comm. Matt.* 5:29), though Jerome disputes this claim (Jerome, *Comm. Isa.* bk. 17 chap. 14 [Isaiah 64:4–5] [PL 24:622]). The form in which Paul quotes the verse, however, occurs in none of our extant sources. But cf. Isa. 64:3 (OG); 65:16; Ps. 31:20; *Mart. Ascen. Isa.* 11:34; *b. Sanh.* 99a; *Gos. Thom.* 17. The irony should not be lost on the reader or listener; for if God's act to make believers the bearers of a wisdom long hidden is unprecedented, then Paul's logic suggests quoting a passage the source of which no eye has ever seen nor ear ever heard.

43. The same concept is expressed in *1 En.* 16:3: "And so to the Watchers on whose behalf you have been sent to intercede—who were formerly in heaven—(say to them), 'You were (once) in heaven, but not all the mysteries (of heaven) are open to you, and you (only) know the rejected mysteries'" (translation by E. Isaac, *OTP* 1:22). Also in 1 Pet. 1:12: "It was revealed to them that they were serving not themselves but you, in these things which have now been recounted to you by those who preached the good news to you through the Holy Spirit sent from heaven, things into which angels long to look." Cf. *2 En.* 24:3; *Zost.* 128:7–18. We may also note the theme of angelic jealousy of humans present in Jewish and Christian mystical texts. In these texts, angels are jealous of humans who ascend high into heavenly places to receive deep mysteries and, therefore, attempt to oppose the ascent of the mystic. In *Ascension of Isaiah* 9:1–5, when Isaiah reaches the seventh heaven, the angel in charge of the praise of the sixth heaven is heard saying, "How far is he who dwells among aliens to go up?" (*Mart. Ascen. Isa.* 9:1, translation by M. A. Knibb, *OTP* 2:169). Isaiah trembles, but Jesus intervenes and grants him permission to ascend higher. The same theme is encountered in rabbinic Hekhalot literature. In Hekhalot Zutarti and Merkavah Rabbah, the ministering angels are said to have attempted to prevent R. Aqiva from reaching the throne in the seventh palace and also attempted to kill him. But God rebukes the angels and tells them that R. Aqiva is worthy to gaze at his glory. The story is retold in *b. Hag.* 15b. See P. Schäfer, *Synopse zur Hekhalot-Literatur* (Tübingen: Mohr Siebeck, 1981), § 346 (Hekhalot Zutarti), § 673 (Merkavah Rabbah); Schäfer, *The Origins of Jewish Mysticism* (Tübingen: Mohr Siebeck, 2009). Implied in this motif of angelic jealousy of humans is the notion that humans can receive certain mysteries that some angels are not privy to.

(1:24; 2:2), the folly and unimpressive rhetoric of proclamation (1:21; 2:1, 3–5; 2 Cor. 1:10), and the lowly status of the church (1:26) as the locus of manifestation of God's wisdom and power. All this is possible through the revelatory work of the Holy Spirit. What Paul denies the rulers of this age he attributes to the Holy Spirit: the Spirit is omniscient, for the Spirit is the able investigator of all things, including the very depths of God (2:10). This is God's own Spirit who knows God and the things of God and is the channel for communicating this knowledge of God. More importantly, it is this same Spirit that believers have received from God (2:12); the Holy Spirit indwells believers. The message of God that believers proclaim, then, is a *spirit*-ual message discerned only by those who have the Spirit of God (2:13). To the carnal person this word is foolishness (2:14; cf. 1:18); to the person who does not have the Spirit of God, this message is unintelligible. But on account of the gift of the Spirit believers are the recipients of a wisdom that is otherwise inaccessible.

Third, Paul employs the same verb used to describe the rulers of this age, καταργέω (2:6), in 15:24 to characterize the ultimate destiny of Christ's enemies at the Parousia: "Then comes the end, when he hands over the kingdom to God the Father after rendering inoperative (καταργήσῃ) every rule and authority and power." At his coming, Christ will reign over all powers. Christ's dominion encompasses not only earthly kingdoms but also heavenly kingdoms. It is these heavenly powers who were responsible for Christ's crucifixion. Paul's use of the present passive participle, καταργουμένων, suggests an event currently in process. Indeed, what would be the point of Paul stressing that Caiaphas, Herod, and Pilate are presently being destroyed? This is the crucial insight that led Martin Dibelius to interpret the rulers as spiritual powers. As Dibelius notes, the high priest, Herod, and Pilate cannot bear the weight of the title "rulers of this age," for at the time of Paul's writing the earthly rulers who were involved in Jesus' death would have already passed away.[44] Paul's point is forceful when the verb καταργέω is applied to entities that were thought to be immortal. The irony of the crucifixion is that it is the cross itself that spelled doom for the powers who crucified Jesus.

The confession that the powers who engineered Christ's death also met their defeat in the cross is a recurrent theme in early Christian thought and liturgy.[45] In 1 Cor. 15:24, however, the destruction of the powers is an eschatological event;[46] and this is already anticipated in 2:6 by the use of the

---

44. Dibelius, *Die Geisterwelt*, 89–90; also Everling, *Angelologie und Dämonologie*, 12.

45. See, e.g., Col. 2:13-15; Phil. 2:5-11; cf. Eph. 1:20-22.

46. See Neil Elliott, *Liberating Paul: The Justice of God and the Politics of the Apostle* (Maryknoll, NY: Orbis Books, 1994), 114–24.

present passive participle, καταργουμένων. Believers are already the bearers of a revelation that the cross was the site of the powers' demise; but the powers are still at work in the world, though believers know that their days are numbered, for they are being rendered inoperative.

Fourth, interpreting Paul with Paul, the expression τῶν ἀρχόντων τοῦ αἰῶνος τούτου ("the rulers of this age") closely parallels the phrase ὁ θεὸς τοῦ αἰῶνος τούτου ("the god of this age") in 2 Cor. 4:4. According to Paul, the god of this age has blinded the minds of unbelievers to the light of the gospel of the glory of Christ.[47] The context of the passage suggests that "the god of this age" is Satan. The argument that ἄρχοντες cannot be spiritual powers in Paul because only the singular form of the noun, ἄρχων, is used for demonic powers in Paul's time[48] tells us more about Western individualism than Pauline theology.[49] It would be an egregious error to think that Paul would conceive of Satan (or some singular "ruler") as working against God's purposes individually. The god of this age does not operate alone; he works with his minions. For Paul, the powers span the whole gamut of existence, so much so that none of the powers can be judged in isolation from the others.

Finally, in 1 Cor. 4:9 Paul will describe his apostolic sufferings as being put on display to *the cosmos, angels, and men.* It is our contention that this is *the same tripartite division at work in 1 Cor. 1:18—2:16.* As we hope to have shown, Paul's argument moves through "the cosmos" (ὁ κόσμος; 1:27-28) and "human wisdom" (σοφία ἀνθρώπων; 2:5) to angelic powers (οἱ ἄρχοντες τοῦ αἰῶνος τούτου ["the rulers of this age"]; 2:6-8).

---

47. Cf. Eph. 2:1-2.

48. See, e.g., Carr, "Rulers of this Age," 23–24; Fee, *The First Epistle to the Corinthians*, 104.

49. Paul uses the plural, ἄρχοντες, in Rom. 13:3 in a context where earthly rulers are in view. But, as shown above, the argumentative context of 1 Corinthians 1–2 rules out this interpretation for 1 Cor. 2:6-8. In the end, one cannot stake one's argument on Romans 13, for this same passage also poses a problem for the earthly rulers interpretation, since it seems contradictory to what Paul says about the rulers in 1 Cor. 2:6-8: the rulers in Romans 13 are God's servants, but the rulers in 1 Cor. 2:6-8 are being destroyed. But cf. Dan. 10:13 (LXX), where the plural, ἀρχόντων, is used for the angels. In the LXX, ἄρχων translates the Hebrew שׂר ("prince"). In the Qumran documents, שׂר at times refers to the "Prince of Lights" (also known as "Angel of Truth" [1QS 3:24–25]), who is opposed to Belial or the "Angel of Darkness" (CD 5.18; 1QS 3:20; 1QSb 4:24–25; 1QM 13:10, 13:14; 4Q266f3ii.11; 4Q267f2.1; 6Q15f3.1). The word שׂר is also used for Belial, the "Prince of the Kingdom of wickedness" or the "Prince of Malevolence" (1QM 17.5; 4Q225f2ii.13–14). In addition, Matt. 15:41 speaks of "the Devil and his angels." Cf. also Matt. 9:34; 12:24; Mark 3:22; Luke 11:15; John 12:31; 14:30; 16:11; Eph. 2:2.

PREACHING AS SPIRIT-UAL PRACTICE

If the rulers of this age are spiritual powers, then Paul's theology of Christian proclamation becomes strikingly coherent. Preaching for Paul is a spiritual practice that involves the work of the Holy Spirit and other spirits.[50] Paul makes this point explicit in 2 Cor. 11:4, where he laments the Corinthians' tolerance of false teaching; for the preaching of false apostles at Corinth, according to Paul, is introducing a spirit different from the Holy Spirit into the community. To preach the message of the cross, then, is to be swept into a spiritual practice and spiritual battle not only because it involves the work of the Holy Spirit but also because the crucifixion was a spiritual confrontation between Christ and supernatural rulers.

In part 1 of our study we observed that Christian practices point to a story about God's work in the world. And as we showed in our chapter on Romans, the story of Christ's confrontation with the powers on the cross undergirds the practice of baptism as a practice of power. In 1 Corinthians 1–2, we contend, Paul has applied the same story of Christ's encounter with the powers on the cross to Christian proclamation. To preach the one crucified by the rulers of this age is to be swept into this cosmic battle. Such preaching can only be undertaken ἐν πνεύματος καί δυνάμεως ("in the Spirit and power"; 2:4). Preaching is a mediation of the Spirit's revelatory and empowering activity. It can only be undertaken in the Spirit because preaching conveys the mysteries of God's wisdom, known only to the one who searches the depths of God—the Holy Spirit. It can only be undertaken in power because the proclamation of one who was crucified by spiritual powers draws one into a cosmic battle that requires an empowering presence.[51] Herein lies the reason why the kerygma cannot be conveyed with sophisticated rhetoric: the preaching of the one crucified by the (supernatural) powers of this age is a spiritual practice that can *only* be endeavored ἐν δυνάμει θεοῦ ("in the power of God," 2:5; cf. 1 Thess. 1:5; 2:13).[52]

---

50. Paul finds an ally on this view in the author of 1 John, who admonishes the community to "test the spirits" (1 John 4:1) to determine which teaching is actually from God.

51. This point may help shed light on why believers are barred from entering pagan cultic settings in general (there are harmful demons in these places), but are allowed in these same settings for missionary preaching: since preaching is done in power and the Spirit, believers are covered. Cf. Acts 19:13-16, where the sons of Sceva attempt a powerful invocation without adequate preparation and spiritual protection and are "overpowered" by the demoniac.

52. The Spirit becomes another power in the apocalyptic battle, in opposition to the spirit of the world (2:12; cf. Eph. 2:2) and the spiritual rulers of this age. Could it be, then, that Paul sees preaching (undertaking in the power of the Spirit) as an affront to the powers? He certainly believes that Satan is the chief opponent to his ministry (1 Thess. 2:18; 2 Cor. 11:1-15).

The power of cross preaching has already been vindicated by the existence of the Corinthian church, for these believers have experienced a reversal in their own fortunes as a result of the power that accompanies the Christian proclamation: "And this is what some of you used to be. But you were washed, you were sanctified, you were justified in the name of the Lord Jesus Christ and in the Spirit of our God" (6:11; cf. 1 Thess. 1:9; Gal. 3:5; 2 Cor. 12:12).[53] In 1:26-31 Paul invites all believers to consider the meaning of the terms *wise*, *powerful*, and *noble* in a new light. If God has chosen the cross as the means to save the world, then all human modes of perceiving and standards of evaluation have been upended.[54] Paul recalls the Corinthians' past, reminding them of the transformation of their past condition, and highlighting God's mysterious and paradoxical election manifested in their own present condition. The theme of reversal looms large in these passages and reaches its culmination in the quotation of an OT passage: "Let the one who boasts boast in the Lord" (1:31). This passage is likely taken from the Greek version of Hannah's song, a passage missing from its Hebrew counterpart:

> Let not the wise man boast in his wisdom, and let not the powerful man boast in his power, and let not the wealthy man boast in his wealth, but let him who boasts boast in this: to understand and know the Lord and to do justice and righteousness in the midst of the earth. (1 Kgdms 2:10 OG; cf. 1 Sam. 2:10 MT)[55]

Hannah's song praises God's gracious gifts and calls attention to God's reversal and confounding of human expectations. This is the God who has reversed the condition of the Corinthians. And since many of the believers would not have experienced a change in societal status (κατὰ σάρκα) upon their receipt of the gospel, Paul must surely be engaging in a transvaluation of the terms σοφός ("wise"), δυνατός ("powerful"), and εὐγενής ("noble") in 1:26, a transvaluation that is only available to those who have experienced an epistemological transformation. This is necessitated not only by the paradoxical theo-logic of the cross but also by the power that accompanies the preaching of the cross.

---

53. Cf. Barrett, *First Epistle to the Corinthians*, 66: "When Paul preached a divine power gripped his hearers (or some of them; cf. 1:18) and constrained them to penitence and faith; this was the work of the Holy Spirit."

54. Cf. Hays, *First Corinthians*, 30.

55. It is also possible that Paul has Jer. 9:22-23 in mind; but the context of judgment in Jeremiah makes Hannah's prayer more likely. See Hays's discussion, *1 Corinthians*, 33–35.

We are here mainly concerned with the second of these terms, δυνατός ("powerful").[56] If God has reversed the position of the not-powerful to that of powerful, then we will have to interpret this description in light of what Paul has said about the message of the cross, which he labels as the "power of God." In 1:18, Paul equates ὁ λόγος ὁ τοῦ σταυροῦ with δύναμις θεοῦ. A similar point is made in 1:23-24: to the "called"—both Jews and Greeks— Christ is "the power of God and wisdom of God." Since this word of the cross is the power of God, those who have this word are powerful. This recognition is crucial, as we shall see, for in our next section, Paul invites the Corinthians to exercise this power in handing a sexual pervert over to Satan (5:4-5).

Church Discipline: Physical and Spiritual Exclusion (1 Cor. 5:1-13)

First Corinthians 5 deals with the important practice of ecclesial discipline. Paul has received a report[57] of incest in the Corinthian community and, in response, issues a harsh sentence on the man cohabiting with his "father's wife" (5:1).[58] 1 Cor. 4:18-21 provides the crucial segue into 1 Corinthians 5. In 4:18-21, Paul

---

56. A brief word about the transvaluation of the words "wise" and "noble" is in order. Concerning wisdom, Paul has already established that the wisdom of this world is folly before God (1:20). According to the world's mode of perceiving, then, not many of the Corinthians were (and are) wise. But what seems foolish in the eyes of the world is what God has chosen, in order to shame the "wise" of this age (1:27). The same redefinition applies to the terms εὐγενής ("noble"). In 1:3 Paul speaks of God as "our Father." This is a term that denotes adoption as sons of God (cf. Gal. 4:5-7). Believers are therefore born of God, a (re)birth that denotes nobility. One of the distinguishing marks of nobility was wealth and generosity (see LSJ, "εὐγενής," 323). Those of noble birth through their benevolence demonstrated their enormous wealth. Paul, conversely, reminds the Corinthians of their own wealth, not in earthly things, but in things far richer: the Corinthians have been enriched in all things, including word and speech (1:4); and all things belong to the Corinthians (3:21), including the world, life, and death (3:22). Thus, while κατὰ σάρκα the Corinthians may not be of noble origins, yet by being heirs with Christ, all things belong to them.

57. Cf. 1.11; 16.17.

58. The language is likely taken from Lev. 18:7-8, where this specific union is forbidden. For condemnation of this practice in Judaism see Lev. 20:11; Deut. 22:30; 27:20; *Jub.* 33:10–13; 11QT 66.11–12; Philo, *Spec.* 3:12–21; Jos., *Ant.* 3:273–74; *m. Sanh.* 7:4; *m. Ker.* 1:1. It is plausible that the woman is not a member of the Corinthian congregation, since Paul does not issue a judgment on her as well (cf. 5:12). The present active infinitive of the verb ἔχω suggests an ongoing sexual relationship between the man and his stepmother. See Fee, *The First Epistle to the Corinthians,* 200, 278; M. Konradt, *Gericht und Gemeinde: Eine Studie zur Bedeutung und Funktion von Gerichtsaussagen im Rahmen der paulinischen Ekklesiologie und Ethik im 1 Thess und 1 Kor,* BZNW 117 (Berlin: Walter de Gruyter, 2003), 297–98. C. S. de Vos ("Stepmothers, Concubines and the Case of πορνεία in 1 Corinthians 5," *NTS* 44 [1998]: 104–14) has argued for the possibility that the woman may have been the man's father's concubine.

warns those who, presuming that he will not be coming to Corinth, are "puffed up." To these people, Paul announces his imminent visit (4:19) and a test of their "power": "I will come quickly to you, if the Lord wills, and I will know not the word of those who are puffed up, but the power [of those who are puffed up]" (4:19). The kingdom of God, Paul avers, is not a matter of word but of power. The Corinthians have a choice; Paul could either come to them in a loving and gentle "spirit" or with a rod. The contrast between Paul's physical presence and absence is put to the test in this ordeal, for Paul issues the harsh sentence against the immoral man of chapter 5 with the assurance that he will somehow be present with the church (in spirit) when the church disciplines the immoral man. In order to show the Corinthians that the power about which he speaks can be manifested even while he is physically absent, Paul decides to come to this immoral man with a rod (ἐν ῥάβδῳ; 4:21) in the spirit. As the segue into our pericope, the latter reference is crucial for our own reading of this passage, not least because it echoes Ps. 89:32-33 (Ps. 88:33-34 OG).

This psalm recounts God's covenant with David and his descendants. God warns his elect that if they forsake and violate the divine commandments and statutes, he will visit their transgressions (lit. "lawlessness"; ἀνομίας) with a rod (ἐν ῥάβδῳ). But God still holds out his steadfast love and faithfulness to the covenant, even while punishing their iniquity (Ps. 89:32-33).[59] This point is crucial, for Paul himself, being the apostle and representative of God,[60] will come down on this man's iniquity with a rod (ἐν ῥάβδῳ);[61] yet he leaves open the possibility of the man's salvation (5:5).

First Corinthians 5 is a notorious *crux interpretum* in the Corinthian correspondence. As a result, we can expect a rich profusion of solutions to be offered for the many thorny exegetical issues raised in this chapter: (1) How are we to understand Paul's order for the immoral man to be handed over to Satan? What does Paul mean by destruction of the flesh? (2) Whose salvation is at stake in 5:5; is it the immoral man, the community, or the πνεῦμα? Whose πνεῦμα is to be saved; is it the spirit of the man or the Spirit of God that indwells the body of Christ? (3) Is this sentence to be carried out for all cases of sexual immorality and of the list of vices in 5:9-10 within the body of Christ? In the next section we critically evaluate the solutions scholars have offered to each of these questions. We will then proceed to offer our own interpretation of

Against this view, see A. Lindemann, *Der erste Korintherbrief*, HNT 9/1 (Tübingen: Mohr Siebeck, 2000), 124.

59. Cf. 2 Sam. 7:14-15.

60. See K. H. Rengstorf, "ἀπόστολος," in *TDNT* 1:407–47.

61. This is the only occurrence of this word in the Pauline corpus.

this passage, drawing on the book of Job as a helpful key to understanding this passage.

PROPOSED SOLUTIONS

(1) Some scholars argue that "handing over to Satan" is a death sentence; Paul expects his sentence to result in the man's death.[62] Scholars who hold to the death interpretation often point to Ananias's and Sapphira's death in Acts 5:1-10, the death Paul mentions in 1 Cor. 11:30-32 occurring within the Corinthian community as a result of their aberrant observance of the Lord's Supper, curse and expulsion pronouncements in Qumran texts,[63] and curse formulae in magical papyri.[64] In an essay entitled "A Critique of the 'Curse/Death' Interpretation of 1 Corinthians 5:1-8," James T. South has provided compelling refutations of the death interpretation, even if his own proposed solutions fail to convince.[65]

South notes that the Greek and Jewish curse formulae are not genuine parallels to 1 Cor. 5:5: not only are all the Greek magical texts at least a century later than Paul, but in none of the Greek magical texts is a person handed over to Satan. In addition, the magical documents are not communal documents.[66] Concerning the Qumran formulae, South concludes that the evidence is inconclusive.[67] We may note that those outside the community of

---

62. See, for example, Tertullian, *On Modesty* 13–14; E. Käsemann, "Sentences of Holy Law in the NT," in *New Testament Questions of Today* (Philadelphia: Fortress Press, 1969 [1957]), 66–81; R. Kempthorne, "Incest in the Body of Christ," *NTS* 14 (1968): 569–70; H. Conzelmann, *1 Corinthians*, 97; Barrett, 126–27; Bultmann, *Theology of the New Testament*, 1:233; V. G. Shillington, "Atonement Texture in 1 Corinthians 5:5," *JSNT* 71 (1998): 39. G. Forkman speaks of death in "both the physical and ethic-religious meaning" (*The Limits of the Religious Community: Expulsion from the Religious Community within the Qumran Sect, within Rabbinic Judaism, and within Primitive Christianity* [Lund: CWK Gleerup, 1972], 146); and S. D. MacArthur speaks of "a slow death which involves physical suffering" ("'Spirit' in Pauline Usage: 1 Corinthians 5.5," in *Studia Biblica* 3, ed. E. A. Livingstone, JSNTSup 3 [Sheffield: JSOT Press, 1978], 251).

63. See, e.g., 1QS 2:5–6; 2:12–18; CD 7:21–8.3. See C. J. Roetzel, *Judgement in the Community: A Study of the Relationship between Eschatology and Ecclesiology in Paul* (Leiden: Brill, 1972), 112–25.

64. Cf. *PGM* 4:1247, 5:70–95, 5:174–80, 5:185–210, 5.335–36. See A. Deissmann, *Light from the Ancient East* (London: Hodder & Stoughton, 1927 [1911]), 302; A. Y. Collins, "The Function of 'Excommunication' in Paul," *HTR* 73 (1980): 255–56.

65. J. T. South, "A Critique of the 'Curse/Death' Interpretation of 1 Corinthians 5.1-8," *NTS* 39 (1993): 539–61; Cf. South, *Disciplinary Practices in Pauline Texts* (Lewiston, NY: Mellen Biblical Press, 1992), 23–88.

66. South, "Critique," 545–46.

67. South, "Critique," 546.

the sons of light are to be destroyed by Belial (CD 7.21–8.3), and this would, therefore, by definition apply to those expelled from the elect community.[68] This destruction is eschatological, however; it will occur on the "day of God's visitation." 1 Cor. 5:5, in contrast, does not posit eschatological death or destruction of the incestuous man, but rather eschatological salvation. Finally, as South notes, Acts 5:1-11 and 1 Cor. 11:30 are also not genuine parallels. None of these deaths are due to Satan's agency; instead, the Spirit or divine agency may be involved in both deaths.

The most recent detailed study of 1 Corinthians 5 attempts to recover the curse/death interpretation. David Raymond Smith surveys a wide range of ancient Jewish and Greco-Roman curse (or "binding") traditions and situates 1 Corinthians 5 within the wider context of cursing in Paul's cultural milieu.[69] While acknowledging the weaknesses of previous curse/death interpretations, Smith argues that Paul's words in 1 Cor. 5:5 bear a "conceptual resonance" with the wider common language of cursing in his cultural milieu. Most, if not all, of the arguments presented in Smith's work will be dealt with directly or indirectly in the course of our own treatment of this passage. For now, we note that at best Smith's arguments do establish that 1 Cor. 5:5 envisions some form of physical affliction and exclusion, but not necessarily death. Smith, for example, points to the phrase γυνή πατρός as establishing a biblical context of cursing and "destruction" (that is, death) in Deuteronomy and Leviticus.[70] The Deuteronomy and Leviticus background to 1 Corinthians 5 cannot be denied. As a number of commentators have noted, for example, the six sins Paul lists in 1 Cor. 5:11 correlate with six passages in Deuteronomy that call for the death penalty, followed by the formula of exclusion that Paul quotes in 1 Cor. 5:13: "So you shall drive out the evil person from among you."[71] Nonetheless, as William Horbury has shown, commandments for execution were widely interpreted in the Second Temple period as implying exclusion and expulsion

68. Thus, South's argument against the Qumran evidence could be a bit more nuanced. For example, he seems to deny the connection between Belial and Satan ("Critique," 546). In Qumran and Second Temple Jewish literature, however, Belial and Mastema are often designations for the leader of demonic angels. Thus, it is not farfetched to see Satan and Belial as equivalent figures. See our discussion below.

69. D. R. Smith, *"Hand This Man Over to Satan": Curse, Exclusion and Salvation in 1 Corinthians 5*, LNTS 386 (London: T&T Clark, 2008).

70. See Smith, *Hand This Man Over*, 123–34.

71. Cf. Deut. 13:1-5; 17:2-7; 19:16-20; 21:18-21; 22:21-30; 24:7. See B. Campbell, "Flesh and Spirit in 1 Cor 5:5: An Exercise in Rhetorical Criticism of the NT," *JETS* 36 (1993): 339n31; P. Ellingworth and H. Hatton, *A Translators Guide on Paul's First Letter to the Corinthians* (London: United Bible Societies, 1985), 105; and especially B. Rosner, *Paul, Scripture and Ethics: A Study of 1 Corinthians 5–7* (Leiden: Brill, 1994), 69.

from the community.[72] Indeed, in light of the Deuteronomy background to 1 Corinthians 5, if death is meant in 1 Cor. 5:5, then it is difficult to see why others in the Corinthian congregation who indulge in, for example, sexual immorality (cf. 1 Cor. 6:9-20; Deut. 22:13-30) and idolatry (cf. 1 Cor. 10:19-22; Deut. 13:1-5; 17:2-7) should escape a death curse. Herein lies a major weakness in Smith's position and other studies on this passage: a failure to establish the uniqueness of the man's case in 1 Corinthians 5. We will develop this thought in subsequent sections.

Smith also notes "resonances" between 1 Cor. 5:5, 1 Tim. 1:20, and Job 2:6.[73] These "resonances," however, do not establish death as the fate of the incestuous man at Corinth. In both 1 Tim. 1:20 and Job 2:6 "handing over to Satan" involves some form of physical affliction that does *not* result in death, but rather produces transformation in the afflicted person. We will argue this position in detail later. Finally, we should also note that the evidence from 1 Cor. 11:30-34, which Smith points to, might seem to support a curse/death interpretation of 1 Corinthians 5. But this seems to us specious reasoning. 1 Corinthians 11 is a case of judgment inflicted directly by God.[74] More specifically, it concerns irreverent contact with the dangerous presence of God; and this evokes OT images of God's holiness and the danger that God's holiness poses to those who fail to handle it with care.[75] This must be distinguished from "handing over to Satan."

Against the curse/death interpretation, we may note in addition to the above that Paul never describes death anywhere as a "destruction of the flesh";[76] and, as we shall argue below, Paul's mode of dealing with deviant believers elsewhere (specifically 2 Cor. 2:1-11; Gal. 6:1; and 2 Thess. 3:14-15) does not fit with the death interpretation. In the end, the biggest challenge to the curse/death interpretation of this passage is how to account for the soteriological purpose for the πνεῦμα expressed in 5:5.[77] Indeed, as Matthias Konradt notes, Paul's soteriology rules out the possibility of ascribing atoning significance to the death of the incestuous man: "Sühnende Kraft hat allein der Tod Jesu."[78]

---

72. See W. Horbury, "Extirpation and Excommunication," *VT* 35 (1985): 13–38.

73. See Smith, *Hand This Man Over*, 146–50.

74. We note in passing that a novel reading of 1 Cor. 11:30-34 has been suggested by S. W. Henderson in her study of the social dimension of this passage. Henderson notes that death in 1 Cor. 11.30 could be the natural consequence of leaving some in the community hungry and weak. See Henderson, "'If Anyone Hungers . . . ': An Integrated Reading of 1 Cor 11.17-34," *NTS* 48 (2002) 195–208, esp. 206n42.

75. See, e.g., Num. 4:17-20; 1 Sam. 6:6-7; 2 Sam. 6:19-21.

76. Fee, *First Epistle to the Corinthians*, 211.

77. Cf. Fee, *First Epistle to the Corinthians*, 210; Konradt, *Gericht und Gemeinde*, 315–317.

The latter objection forces us to detect that some notion of repentance or transformation is implied in Paul's sentence in 1 Cor. 5:5.[79] That is why the alternative position that views Paul's sentence as referring to some form of physical suffering,[80] with remedial purpose, seems more plausible.[81] This is the position we adopt in this essay, and we will later argue for this position using the book of Job.

(2) Some scholars argue that the "spirit" of 1 Cor. 5:5 is not the "spirit" of the incestuous man but the Holy Spirit who resides within the community.[82] While this view is correct to draw attention to the fact that πνεῦμα in 5:5 is not preceded by the pronoun αὐτοῦ, it still fails to take seriously the soteriological significance of the verb σῴζω in Paul. Claims such as, "If they [the community] have defiled the Spirit by, for example, sexual sins, the Spirit will be lost to the community and they [the community] will be excluded from the kingdom of God,"[83] or "By removing the one immoral member from the community the membership keeps the Spirit of Christ, while the Spirit is effectively taken from the immoral man,"[84] are unsuccessful attempts to circumvent the setbacks confronting this view. It is perhaps significant that this view quickly elides the salvation of the "Spirit" into salvation of "the community," and thereby collapses

78. Konradt, *Gericht und Gemeinde*, 316.

79. Cf. Fee, *First Epistle to the Corinthians*, 213; South, "Critique," 546; C. Wolff, *Der erste Brief des Paulus an die Korinther*, THKNT 7 (Leipzig: Evangelische Verlagsanstalt, 1996), 104–5; Hays, *First Corinthians*, 86; Konradt, *Gericht und Gemeinde*, 317.

80. See, for example, J. B. Lightfoot, *Notes on the Epistles of St Paul from Unpublished Commentaries* (London: Macmillan, 1895), 204; G. W. H. Lampe, "Church Discipline and Interpretation of the Epistle to the Corinthians," in *Christian History and Interpretation: Studies Presented to John Knox*, ed. W. R. Farmer, C. F. D. Moule, and R. R. Niebuhr (Cambridge: Cambridge University Press, 1967), 337–61.

81. While Smith discusses briefly two proponents (one patristic and one contemporary) of a physical suffering and exclusion reading of 1 Corinthians 5 (see Smith, *Hand This Man Over*, 29–33), he fails to engage extensively with this position, since his main target throughout seems to be proponents of an *exclusion alone* reading of this passage, a position that he attributes to a desire to establish a contemporary application of this passage for today's church (see Smith, *Hand This Man Over*, 38–56).

82. This view was first proposed by Tertullian, *On Modesty* 13; also Ambrosiaster, *Commentary on Paul's Epistles*. See also Lindemann, *Der erste Korintherbrief*, 128. Cf. D. B. Martin (*The Corinthian Body* [New Haven: Yale University Press, 1995], 174), who argues that the spirit to be saved is both the spirit of the man and that of the church, and the flesh to be destroyed is both that of the man and that of the church.

83. A. Y. Collins, "Function," 260; so also R. F. Collins, *First Corinthians*, 213: "He directs the community to excise the fleshly individual—so characterized by reason of his incestuous behavior—from its midst so that the community might live under the power of the Spirit and be preserved for the day of the Lord."

84. Shillington, "Atonement Texture," 35.

the distinction between the two entities. In the final analysis, this position stumbles on the very fact that the Spirit, as God's own Spirit (1 Cor. 2:12) and the sign of believers' adoption as "sons" with Christ (Rom. 8:14-17; Gal. 4:6), never requires salvation in Paul.

The view that "flesh" and "spirit" in 1 Cor. 5:5 denotes Paul's typical contrast between these two terms also needs to be evaluated. According to this view, by putting the man out of the believing community, Paul's desire was for the destruction of the fleshly or carnal nature in the man (or the church[85]) to be destroyed.[86] This position expands our semantic range beyond anthropological categories and acknowledges the view, present in early Judaism and Christianity, that Satan can at times serve God's purpose.[87] Nonetheless, if "flesh" in 1 Cor. 5:5 refers to the fleshly or carnal nature, then this passage contradicts everything Paul has to say about the fleshly nature elsewhere. In Paul, Satan is never the agent through whom the fleshly nature is overcome. It is actually the reverse: Satan seeks to entice and revive the fleshly desires. That is why Paul refers to Satan as the "tempter" (ὁ πειράζων) in 1 Thess. 3:5; and only two chapters after our pericope, Paul admonishes married couples not to deprive each other of sex, so that Satan will not tempt (πειράζω) them (1 Cor. 7:5). On the contrary, it is the Holy Spirit who aids believers in their struggle to curb the desires of the flesh (Romans 7-8; Galatians 5-6). Thus, it is exegetically unsupportable and theologically unwarranted to posit Satan as the agent of destruction of the incestuous man's fleshly desires.[88] Paul's own characterization of the man's transgression shows that he does not expect those outside the body of Christ to have control over their fleshly nature: "Actually,

---

85. Campbell, "Flesh and Spirit," 340–41.

86. A. Y. Collins, "Function," 259; South, "Critique," 544–45; 552–53; Fee, *First Epistle to the Corinthians*, 213; R. F. Collins, *First Corinthians*, 212; J. Cambier, "La Chair et l'Espirit en 1 Cor v. 5," *NTS* 15 (1968–69): 221–32; N. G. Joy, "Is the Body Really to Be Destroyed? (1 Corinthians 5:5)," *BT* 39 (1988): 429–36; A. C. Thiselton, "The Meaning of ΣΑΡΞ in 1 Corinthians 5.5: A Fresh Approach in the Light of Logical and Semantic Factors," *SJT* 26 (1973): 204–28; Thiselton, *First Epistle to the Corinthians*, 395–98; L. Vander Broek, "Discipline and Community: Another Look at 1 Corinthians 5," *RefR* 48 (1994): 5; V. C. Pfizner, "Purified Community—Purified Sinner: Expulsion from the Community according to Matt 18:15-18 and 1 Cor 5:1-5," *ABR* (1982): 46–47.

87. That Satan can on occasion serve God's purpose does not mean that Satan is not God's enemy. T. C. G. Thornton ("Satan—God's Agent for Punishing," *ExpTim* 83 [1972]: 151–52), therefore, overstates his case.

88. Thus, 2 Cor. 12:7 is inapplicable to this argument (contra South, "Critique," 560). 2 Cor. 12:7 is applicable to 1 Cor. 5:5 only if Paul's "thorn" in 2 Cor. 12:7 is a reference to some physical ailment (though this position is contested) *and* "flesh" in 1 Cor. 5:5 refers to the man's physical flesh, not ethical flesh.

sexual immorality is reported among you, and of a kind that is not condoned[89] *even* among the gentiles" (5:1). *Not even* gentiles condone *porneia* of this kind, which means, in essence, that gentiles *do* condone certain kinds of *porneia*, while all forms of *porneia* are forbidden in the body of Christ (cf. 5:9-11). In addition, Paul's statement to the Corinthians that to shun the sexually immoral, covetous, idolaters, slanderers, drunkards, and robbers *of the world* would mean having to escape the world entirely (5:10) tells us all we need to know about what Paul thinks of moral standards outside the body of Christ. Thus, it seems absurd, to say the least, to suggest that Paul, who views the Holy Spirit given to the body of Christ as the believer's aid in the battle against the impulses of the flesh, would put an incestuous man *outside* the church to learn to control his fleshly nature.

(3) We turn now to our final question—whether handing over to Satan is a sentence to be carried out in each case of immorality (including the vice list in 5:9-10) in the church. Paul had previously written to the Corinthians not to associate with certain immoral persons (5:9-10). The Corinthians (mis)understood Paul to be saying that they should not associate with *all* immoral persons. Paul, therefore, clarifies his position in the present letter by emphasizing that the "judgment" about which he speaks applies only to someone who is called believer (lit. "brother") and yet lives in immorality (5:11). Believers are within their place to judge those within the body of Christ; but God will judge those on the outside (5:12). Thus, the "brothers" and "sisters" who practice sexual immorality, covetousness, idolatry, slander, drunkenness, or robbery must be excluded from the fellowship of believers (5:11). As previously noted, the vices are likely taken from a list of offenses in Deuteronomy that call for the death penalty. And since some of these offenses were already present in the Corinthian community (e.g., 6:7-8; 6:9-20; 10:18-22; 11:21), it is highly unlikely that Paul would recommend that every believer caught in one of these sins be handed over to Satan.[90]

The sentence Paul wants the church to mete out to this offender is extremely severe and goes beyond mere exclusion (though the sentence involves exclusion [5:2, 13]). Thus, contrary to a number of commentaries on this passage,[91] Paul is not dealing with mere exclusion or excommunication per se.[92] Paul could have phrased his demand in a number of ways if he wanted the

---

89. The verb must be supplied here. On our word choice here, see the discussion below.

90. Cf. Gal. 6:1; 2 Thess. 3:14-15.

91. See, for example, South, "Critique," 544, 553–55; Fee, *First Epistle to the Corinthians*, 208–209; S. K. Kistemaker, " 'Deliver This Man to Satan' (1 Cor 5:5): A Case Study in Church Discipline," *MSJ* 3 (1992): 41–42; Campbell, "Flesh and Spirit," 332n8; J. M. Gundry Volf, *Paul & Perseverance: Staying In*

congregation to merely expel this man from its fellowship. For example, Paul could have written:

> As for the man who is incestuous, after admonishing him once or twice, have nothing more to do with him. (Titus 3:10; adapted)[93]

The above proposal could have been accomplished without the context of worship, without Paul being present in spirit, and without the power of Jesus Christ.[94] Thus, the practice to be carried out is first of all a *community practice* and can only be accomplished with the *power of Jesus*.[95] A correct interpretation of this passage must, as a result, go beyond mere expulsion in attempting to account for the nature of the punishment. It must also account for why this particular man receives such a severe sentence. In short, there is a causal thread between the man's actions and his severe sentence that must be established for a correct interpretation.

Paul's harsh sentence cannot be explained simply by appeal to the gross nature of the offense, one that supposedly "does not occur"[96] even among the gentiles (5:1). As evidence from Tacitus (*Ann.* 6:19), Martial (*Epigrammata* 4:16), and Dio Cassius (*Roman History* 58:22) shows, cases of incest are well documented among gentiles, though they were unlawful and unacceptable.[97] Thus, if this was simply a case of human weakness on the part of the offender,

---

and Falling Away (Louisville: Westminster/John Knox, 1991 [1990]), 117–18; Robertson and Plummer, *First Epistle to the Corinthians*, 99.

92. So also MacArthur, " 'Spirit' in Pauline Usage," 249–50; Lampe, "Church Discipline," 352; Smith, *Hand This Man Over*, 55–56.

93. Cf. 1 Tim. 5:20.

94. Pace Kistemaker, "Deliver This Man to Satan," 41: "Handing someone over to Satan is akin to the prescription Jesus gave his disciples: treat an unrepentant sinner as a pagan or a tax collector (Matt 18:17)."

95. Cf. Ambrosiaster, *Commentary on Paul's Epistles*, who notes correctly that something more than common consent is being demanded from the community in the expulsion of the man; and G. Harris, "The Beginnings of Church Discipline: 1 Corinthians 5," *NTS* 37 (1991): 16–18. Consequently, nothing could be farther from the truth than J. D. M. Derrett's thesis that Paul intends the Corinthians to hand over the incestuous man to civil authorities for his execution ("'Handing Over to Satan': An Explanation of 1 Cor. 5:1-7," *Revue internationale des droits de l'antiquité* 26 [1979]: 11–30).

96. It may be inaccurate to supply a verb of nonexistence here, as is found in a number of translations and commentaries (see, e.g., NIV; NRSV; NASB; Wolff, *Der erste Brief des Paulus an die Korinther*, 98; E. Fascher, *Der erster Brief des Paulus an die Korinther*, 1st ed., THKNT 7/1 [Berlin: Evangelische Verlagsanstalt, 1975], 1:155; Lindemann, *Der erste Korintherbrief*, 120; J. Murphy-O'Connor, "1 Corinthians 5:3-5," in *Keys to First Corinthians: Revisiting Major Issues* [Oxford: Oxford University Press, 2009], 12).

or indifference on the part of the church, one would expect Paul's response to be admonishment, as is found in Gal. 6:1 (cf. 1 Corinthians 8–10; 2 Thess. 3:14-15; Titus 3:10; Matt. 18:15-17). The connection between the man's deeds and Paul's decrying of the church's lackadaisical response is significant, for it is likely that this man's deeds were an ostentatious display of depravity that also received theological justification from the perpetrator.[98] As Paul tells us, the man was performing his deeds "in the name of the Lord Jesus" (τὸν οὕτως τοῦτο κατεργασάμενον ἐν τῷ ὀνόματι τοῦ κυρίου Ἰησοῦ; 5:3-4). The phrase ἐν τῷ ὀνόματι τοῦ κυρίου Ἰησοῦ could be taken as modifying the verb συναχθέντων ("When you are assembled in the name of the Lord Jesus");[99] or the verb κέκρικα ("I have already pronounced judgment in the name of the Lord Jesus").[100] The word order, however, rules out the first option, since elsewhere in Paul the same prepositional phrase follows the verb it modifies (cf. 1 Cor. 6:11; 2 Thess. 3:6; Col. 3:17). And since in its occurrences in Paul the phrase is never far removed from the verb,[101] the second option is weakened, if not entirely eliminated. Thus, with a number of commentators,[102] we take the prepositional phrase with the verb immediately preceding it, κατεργάζομαι. This seems to us the more natural reading of the text. This reading not only dovetails well with the general tenor of the letter to the Corinthians, but it also helps us to account adequately for Paul's harsh sentence. J. Murphy-O'Connor has argued persuasively that the situation addressed in 1 Corinthians 5 was viewed by Paul as representative of the arrogance and boasting that characterized the Corinthian community (see 5:2; 5:6; cf. 3:21; 4:6, 7, 18-19; 6:12; 8:1; 10:23).[103] The Corinthians thought themselves to be in possession of a wisdom and knowledge that permitted them to do whatever they pleased

97. For further discussion, see A. D. Clarke, *Secular and Christian Leadership in Corinth: A Socio-Historical and Exegetical Study of 1 Corinthians 1-6* (Leiden: Brill, 1993), 74–88.

98. Cf. A. Y. Collins, "Function," 253: "Paul's response is more understandable if the illicit relationship was put forward, not only as a legitimate, but even as a commendable act of Christian freedom."

99. So, e.g., NIV; JB; NASB; NEB; NET; REB; LUTH; J. Weiß, *Der erste Korintherbrief*, 9th ed., KEK 5 (Göttingen: Vandenhoeck & Ruprecht, 1910), 127; Lightfoot, *Notes on the Epistles*, 204; Barrett, *First Epistle to the Corinthians*, 124; South, *Disciplinary Practices*, 35.

100. So, e.g., RSV; NRSV; NAB; NLT; Fee, *First Epistle to the Corinthians*, 207–08; Konradt, *Gericht und Gemeinde*, 311–12.

101. See Murphy-O'Connor, "1 Corinthians 5:3-5," 11–19, esp. 12.

102. See, e.g., E. Pagels, *The Gnostic Paul: Gnostic Exegesis of the Pauline Letters* (Philadelphia: Fortress Press, 1975), 64; W. Schrage, *Der erste Brief an die Korinther*, EKKNT 7/1 (Zürich: Benziger Verlag, 1991), 1:372; Lindemann, *Der erste Korintherbrief*, 125–26; Murphy-O'Connor, "1 Corinthians 5:3-5," 11–19; A. Y. Collins, "Function," 253; Hays, *First Corinthians*, 84.

103. Murphy-O'Connor, "1 Corinthians 5:3-5," 12.

(cf. 6:12-20). Murphy-O'Connor writes: "This overweening confidence in their own rightness was born of the sense of difference from others, which was rooted in the fact that they had been baptized in the name of Jesus (cf. 1:13)."[104] Given such an outlook it is not hard to see the man giving theological justification to his incestuous relationship on the basis of his freedom in Christ (cf. 6:12).

In short, through his deplorable actions, the man seized the freedom to persist in his lifestyle as occasion to perpetrate a false gospel. The man, in essence, had become a false teacher.[105] Paul's severe reprimand of this man, then, is consistent with how he treats false teachers in his letters.[106] Earlier in the Letter to the Corinthians, Paul identifies the community as God's temple (3:16) and asseverates that God will destroy anyone who destroys the temple of God (3:17). The context suggests that Paul is referring to those who harm the church through false teaching and divisiveness. The same applies to the incestuous man in 1 Corinthians 5: by justifying his sinful deeds as a theological practice, the man's actions have become analogous to the messengers of Satan masquerading as angels of light (2 Cor. 11:1-15).[107] Consequently, when this man is handed over to Satan, *with the power of Jesus*, it will reveal whose side he truly is on. It is also important to note that in the only other example of persons being handed over to Satan in the early church, 1 Tim. 1:20, the culprits are propagating false teaching. In 1 Tim. 1:20, we catch a glimpse of how one of our earliest interpreters of Paul sought to apply Paul's enigmatic phrase. The author hands Hymenaeus and Alexander over to Satan (παρέδωκα τῷ σατανᾷ) so that they will learn not to blaspheme. Persons who were handed over to Satan were those who had the capacity to spread their corrosive views within the body of Christ.

The incestuous man's influence,[108] if unchecked, will spread like cancer through the body of Christ.[109] He, therefore, needs to be unmasked quickly

---

104. Ibid.

105. Schrage is, therefore, on the right track when he claims that Paul confronts a "provokativ-ideologischen Akt" (*Der erste Brief an die Korinther*, 1:372), though he does not develop his argument persuasively.

106. Cf. Gal 1:8; 5:10; 2 Cor 11:1-15; Phil 3:2.

107. Cf. 1 John 2:18; 4:1.

108. Clarke, *Secular and Christian Leadership*, 74–88, has argued for the possibility that the incestuous man may have been of high social standing within the community; so also J. K. Chow, *Patronage and Power: A Study of Social Networks in Corinth*, JSNTSup 75 (Sheffield: Sheffield Academic Press, 1992), 130–41. If this hypothesis is correct, it may provide some explanation for the urgency of Paul's call, since this man would command even greater influence.

109. A brief word about Shillington's thesis is in order. Shillington argues that the scapegoat ritual of Leviticus 16, where the scapegoat is handed over to Azazel on the Day of Atonement, informs Paul's

before he corrodes the church, like yeast working through a batch of dough (5:6).[110] With such a one in the body of Christ, there is no room for boasting (5:6); when tolerating such behavior, the church has no grounds to take pride in its spiritual achievements. As a matter of fact, this is where the church ends up when it begins to focus on, and take pride in, its spirituality, arcane knowledge, and spiritual gifts (4:6-18; 8:1; 13:4; 14:12).[111]

Having shown the uniqueness of this man's case and the difficulties inherent in the various proposals for this passage, how do we make sense of this pericope? What do we make of the man's fate? In the following section, we turn to the book of Job, which is echoed in this pericope, as a helpful key to shed further light on this enigmatic Pauline passage. Our own interpretation may not eradicate all the problems this text presents, but we hope to add another dimension to the discussion.

JOB AS INTERPRETIVE KEY

Paul alludes to the book of Job throughout his letters.[112] He offers direct quotations from Job in Rom. 11:35 (Job 41:11) and 1 Cor. 3:19 (Job 5:12-13). 1 Corinthians also contains at least four allusions to Job: 1 Cor. 1:20 (Job 12:17); 1 Cor. 1:24 (Job 12:13); 1 Cor. 2:10 (Job 11:7); 1 Cor. 4:4 (Job 27:6). Thus, if we can detect a strong echo of Job 2:4-6 in 1 Cor. 5:5,[113] we may be on safe grounds to look to Job as a possible background for our interpretation of 1 Corinthians 5. The concepts are similar and the verbal resemblances are stronger than any of the parallels often adduced for 1 Cor. 5:5, despite some

dynamistic sentence of 1 Cor. 5:5 (Shillington, "Atonement Texture," 29–50). The incestuous man becomes the sin-bearing victim who bears away the sins of the community. There are many problems with this thesis. It should suffice, however, to note that Paul never transfers the sins of the community to the incestuous man. The sin in view is not that of the community but that of the man. If there is any potential transfer that might take place it is the sinful influence of the one man that has the potential to spread to the community, not the other way around. In addition, in order to find some parallel between the goats of Leviticus 16 and the ritually unclean incestuous man of 1 Corinthians 5, Shillington avers: "Goats were desert dwelling animals, already impure even before they entered the sacred precincts" (45). It is significant that Shillington cites no evidence for this claim. Goats are not included in the impure animals lists of Leviticus 11 and Deuteronomy 14. Moreover, according to the Torah (see Leviticus 11), mammals that both ruminate and have cloven hooves are kosher. This will include goats.

110. See Gal. 5:9, where Paul again uses the same yeast proverb in a context in which he is arguing against the spread of false teaching.

111. Cf. Pfizner, "Purified Community," 41.

112. Cf. 1 Thess. 5:8 (Job 2:9); 5:22 (Job 1:1; 1:8); 2 Thess. 2:8 (Job 4:9); Gal. 6:7 (Job 4:8); Phil. 1:19 (Job 13:16); 2 Cor. 4:6 (Job 37:15); Rom. 1:20 (Job 12:7-9); Rom. 8:34 (Job 34:29); Rom. 9:20 (Job 9:12); Rom. 11:33 (Job 5:9); Rom .11:33 (Job 9:10); Rom. 11:34 (Job 15:18).

113. Cf. Job 1:12; 19:25-27.

divergences. A closer examination of Paul's anthropological terms may account for the divergences in anthropological terminology.

Both texts are worth quoting at this point:

ὑπολαβὼν δὲ <u>ὁ διάβολος</u>[114] εἶπεν <u>τῷ κυρίῳ</u>
δέρμα ὑπὲρ δέρματος
ὅσα ὑπάρχει ἀνθρώπῳ ὑπὲρ τῆς ψυχῆς αὐτοῦ ἐκτείσει
οὐ μὴν δὲ ἀλλὰ ἀποστείλας τὴν χεῖρά σου ἅψαι τῶν ὀστῶν
αὐτοῦ καὶ <u>τῶν σαρκῶν</u> αὐτοῦ
εἰ μὴν εἰς πρόσωπόν σε εὐλογήσει[115]εἶπεν δὲ <u>ὁ κύριος</u> τῷ διαβόλῳ
Ἰδοὺ <u>παραδίδωμί</u> σοι αὐτόν
μόνον τὴν ψυχὴν αὐτοῦ διαφύλαξον. (Job 2:4-6)[116]

<u>παραδοῦναι</u> τὸν τοιοῦτον <u>τῷ σατανᾷ</u> εἰς ὄλεθρον <u>τῆς σαρκός</u>
ἵνα τὸ πνεῦμα σωθῇ ἐν τῇ ἡμέρᾳ <u>τοῦ κυρίου</u>. (1 Cor. 5:5)[117]

In both Job 2 and 1 Corinthians 5, a man is handed over (παραδίδωμι) to Satan. The OG translates the Hebrew הַשָּׂטָן ("The *satan*") with ὁ διάβολος. In the NT, διάβολος and σατανᾶς are synonyms for the devil.[118] Paul, however, never uses the term διάβολος; his preferred term is σατανᾶς.[119]

The anthropological terms used in the two texts present a challenge, though not an insurmountable one. In Job, God permits Satan to afflict Job's ὀστέον καὶ σάρξ (bone and flesh [MT בָּשָׂר וּ עֶצֶם]; cf. 2:7), but Job's ψυχή (MT נֶפֶשׁ) is off limits.[120] Paul relatively seldom uses ψυχή in his letters.[121]

---

114. Hebrew = הַשָּׂטָן ("the *satan*").

115. Hebrew euphemism בָּרַךְ.

116. "Then the Slanderer carried on and said to the Lord, 'Skin for skin; whatever a man has he will give in payment for his life. However, stretch forth your hand and touch his bones and his flesh; surely, he will curse you to your face.' Then the Lord said to the Slanderer, "Behold, I am handing him over to you; only guard his life."

117. "Hand this man over to Satan for the destruction of his flesh, in order that the spirit might be saved in the day of the Lord."

118. Cf., for example, Matt. 4:10-11, where both terms are used.

119. Rom. 16:20; 1 Cor. 7:5; 2 Cor. 2:11; 2 Cor. 11:14; 2 Cor. 12:7; 1 Thess. 2:18; 2 Thess. 2:9.

120. It is probable that the OG translator of Job holds to an anthropology in which the ψυχή could represent either life in general or the inner, invisible aspect of a person, while the σάρξ represents the outer, material aspects of a person. This is confirmed by the wording of such passages as Job 7:15, 9:21, 27:4—passages that bear almost no resemblance to their MT counterparts. Thus, one could read Satan's own words as a desire to afflict Job's outer person (ὀστέον καὶ σάρξ [bone and flesh]; cf. Job 2:7). God, therefore, gives Satan permission to afflict Job's flesh and bones, but he is commanded to guard carefully Job's ψυχή. Ψυχή here, and almost always elsewhere in the LXX and OG, translates the Hebrew נֶפֶשׁ.

Paul never places ψυχή in proximity to σάρξ, and he never contrasts ψυχή with σάρξ.[122] His preferred pair is σάρξ and πνεῦμα.[123] On one occasion he contrasts ψυχή with πνεῦμα (1 Cor. 15:45), and this contrast may also be implied in the antithesis between the cognate terms ψυχικός and πνευματικός (1 Cor. 2:14; 15:44; 15:46; cf. James 3:15; Jude 19). ψυχικός is also synonymous in Paul with two cognates of σάρξ, σάρκινος and σαρκικός, words also often contrasted with πνευματικός (1 Cor. 3:1-3; 9:11; 2 Cor. 1:12; 3:3; 10:4; Rom. 7:14; 15:27). Thus, if the author of 1 Peter, for example, can set σαρκικός in opposition to ψυχή (1 Pet. 2:11), such a move would be extremely unlikely for Paul, because Paul seems to regard the ψυχή as being very close to the σάρξ.

These observations may explain the verbal divergences between Paul and the OG translation of Job. If Paul's wording in 1 Cor. 5:5 is based on OG Job, it should come as no surprise that Paul would move away from the OG translator's pair of σάρξ and ψυχή to his own preferred pair of σάρξ and πνεῦμα.[124] When σάρξ and πνεῦμα stand together in Paul, they are often theological pairs denoting different human orientations toward God.[125] However, in Col. 2:5 Paul provides a σάρξ-πνεῦμα contrast that has anthropological emphasis. It is perhaps also significant to note that Paul uses σάρξ to refer to human and animal physical bodies in passages such as 1 Cor. 15:39 and 1 Cor. 15:50. Finally, in 1 Cor. 2:11 Paul speaks of the human πνεῦμα.[126]

It seems, therefore, plausible that Paul has Job in mind when he formulates 1 Cor. 5:5. If there are divergences in vocabulary, and if these divergences seem to stand in tension with Paul's general anthropology,[127] it is the result of

Since the ψυχή and σάρξ may represent the inner and outer person, respectively, for the OG translator of Job—it is at least possible that Paul read the OG Job this way—then ψυχή and σάρξ could be viewed as diametrically different components of the human being for the translator. If Paul understood the verse this way, it may help explain Paul's deviation from the OG translator. See our discussion below.

121. The term appears only twelve times in the authentic Pauline letters (counting Colossians). Two of the instances are taken over from OT quotations (Rom. 11:3; 1 Cor. 15:45). The terms πνεῦμα and σάρξ are, however, ubiquitous in the Pauline letters.

122. When ψυχή is used, it can carry the connotation of "being" or "life" (cf. Rom. 2:9; 11:3; 13:1; 16:4; 1 Cor. 15:45; 2 Cor. 12:15; Phil. 2:30; Col. 3:23; 1 Thess. 2:8); it has the sense of "mind" in Phil. 1:27, and in 1 Thess. 5:23 it is included in a list with spirit and body (σῶμα).

123. See, e.g., Gal. 5:16-18; 6:8; Rom. 7:14—8.17. Cf. Gal. 2:20; 2 Cor. 10:3.

124. The possibility that Paul goes directly from the Hebrew OT to the Greek in some instances must also be left open.

125. Cf. Rom. 8:4-10; Gal. 5:17-19; 6:8.

126. See also 2 Cor. 7:1; 1 Thess. 5:23.

127. What our brief outline of Paul's anthropological terms and 1 Cor. 5:5 may suggest is that we may need to exercise some caution in our attempts to reduce each of Paul's anthropological terms to single concepts. For a discussion of Paul's anthropology, see R. Jewett, *Paul's Anthropological Terms: A Study of*

Paul's desire to conform the basic form of his OT text into his own preferred terminology, while still retaining an echo of his source. And if Paul has the book of Job in mind, the point of contact is not between the sexually immoral man and Job;[128] rather, the points of contact lie in the role Satan plays in both 1 Corinthians 5 and Job, and the role God plays in Job, which is assumed by Paul and the body of Christ in 1 Corinthians. It should come as no surprise to the attentive listener that Paul (together with the church) assumes the role God plays in Job, for in the segue into this pericope (1 Cor. 4:21)—which we have argued echoes Ps. 89:32-33—Paul has already assumed God's rod of chastisement. Thus, in both Job and 1 Corinthians, God, or a representative of God, hands a person over (παραδίδωμι) to Satan for the affliction of his physical flesh.

When we first encounter Satan in Job, we are given a hint that he may have attempted previously to gain access to Job's life.[129] But this has been unsuccessful since, in his words, "[God has] put a fence, on every side, around [Job] and his house and all that he has" (Job 1:10). For Satan to get to Job, God must remove this protective hedge, though God still places limits on Satan's power. God gives Satan permission to afflict Job's flesh and bones, but Satan can go no further.

In 1 Corinthians 5, the sexually immoral man is also enjoying a protective hedge by being a member of the body of Christ. Paul's own argument presupposes this: he orders the man to be handed over to Satan and in an equivalent command also orders that the sexually immoral person be put out of their fellowship (5:13). In other words, the only way that Satan can have access

---

Their Use in Conflict Settings (Leiden: Brill, 1971); G. H. van Kooten, *Paul's Anthropology in Context: The Image of God, Assimilation to God, and Tripartite Man in Ancient Judaism, Ancient Philosophy and Early Christianity*, WUNT (Tübingen: Mohr Siebeck, 2008); M. Mitchell, *Paul, the Corinthians, and the Birth of Christian Hermeneutics* (Cambridge: Cambridge University Press, 2010), 38–57.

128. The charge that Paul could not have Job in mind because Job deals with a righteous and blameless man while 1 Corinthians 5 deals with an immoral man should be taken seriously, though, in our view, this charge should not be permitted to have the last word by virtue of the fact that Paul deems all humans to be under the power of sin (see, e.g., Rom. 3:9-18; 3:20; 3:21-24; 3:27-30). Thus, it seems plausible to posit that Paul would not have put Job in any special category. I am grateful to John Barclay for this insight.

129. It is indeed the case that a distinction needs to be made between the *satan*, a (benign?) member of the heavenly court in the OT (cf. Job 1–2; Zech. 3:1-5), and Satan, an evil archenemy of God and the elect in later Jewish and Christian literature. But since this modern distinction was insignificant to Paul, we have kept Satan in our treatment of the figure in Job. We have also argued elsewhere that the *satan* in Job is not as benign as this modern distinction often supposes; see our article, "'The *satan*' in Light of the Creation Theology of Job," *HBT* 34 (2012): 19–34.

to this man is if the protective hedge the man is enjoying is removed.[130] Christ has rescued believers from the present evil age (Gal. 1:4), but those who are outside the body of Christ are ruled by the god of this age (cf. 2 Cor. 4:4; Gal. 1:4).[131] Participation in the body of Christ ensures some protection from the evil powers of this age.

This insight finds further confirmation in Paul's allusion to the Passover in 1 Cor. 5:8: "Cleanse out the old yeast that you may be a new batch of dough—just as you really are unleavened; for Christ our Passover has been sacrificed." Paul introduces the Passover as the occasion to purge all leaven, a symbol of all that is unclean and pollutes. This image provides an explanation for Paul's call for the immoral man's expulsion.

Yet our discussion of the limits of Satan's power recalls another important aspect of the Passover. The Passover was instituted to commemorate the passing over of the houses of the Israelites in Egypt, when the angel of death came to strike down the firstborn of the Egyptians (Exod. 12:26-27). All the Israelites who marked their doors with the blood of the lamb were protected from the angel of death. The reverse is also true: those Israelites who did not distinguish themselves with the mark of blood would have suffered the same fate as the Egyptians. Inherent in the Passover celebration, then, is the conviction that members of the community of the elect do enjoy God's protection from the destructive powers of evil. The blood of the lamb marked the Israelites out as a community under God's protection.[132] In the same way, believers, having been bought with a price—the precious blood of Christ (cf. 1 Cor. 1:30; 6:20; 7:23; 1 Pet. 1:18-19; Rev. 5:9)—are under God's protection from the power of Satan. Thus, this immoral member will need to be thrust out of the body of Christ before Satan can have full access to his flesh.

It is important for us to qualify the protection believers enjoy from the powers of evil, since the protection is not absolute. This point not only picks up an important theme that runs through Paul's letters—that the total destruction of the powers belongs to the end (cf. 1 Cor. 15:24-25; Rom. 8:22-23)—but it also helps to make sense of the urgency with which Paul treats this case. The powers are actively operating in the world; and if their devices are not quickly unmasked, they can gain entry into the church. While members of the body of Christ may enjoy some protection from the powers, believers have

---

130. Cf. Theodoret of Cyrus, *Commentary on the First Epistle to the Corinthians* 193 (PG 82:262): "We are taught by this that the devil invades those who are separated from the body of the church because he finds them deprived of grace"; translation in ACCS 7:47.

131. Cf. 1 John 5:19; Eph. 2:1-2.

132. Hays, *First Corinthians*, 83.

to be vigilant in this ongoing struggle with the powers, for the powers are continually working to gain entry into the body of Christ.[133] Here 2 Cor. 2:5-11 provides a very instructive parallel to our pericope, not only because it reflects the remedial purpose behind the church's discipline of offenders but also because Satan emerges as a factor in the church's handling of the offender.

In 2 Cor. 2:1-11, Paul recalls a painful visit made to Corinth that occasioned a painful letter (2 Cor. 2:3-4). A member of the Corinthian church has committed a grave offense. The identity of the offender and the nature of the offense are matters of speculation.[134] What can be said with certainty is that Paul made calls for the punishment of this offender, which the Corinthian church eventually heeded (2 Cor. 2:6). In 2 Cor. 2:1-11, Paul appeals for forgiveness of, and reconciliation with, the one who caused both him and the church much grief. It is within this other context of church discipline that Paul again introduces Satan, just as he had done previously in 1 Corinthians 5: "But if you have forgiven anyone, I also have. And what I have forgiven—if I have forgiven anything—I have done so in the presence of Christ (ἐν προσώπῳ Χριστοῦ) for your sake, in order that Satan might not take advantage of us; for we are not ignorant of his schemes" (2:10-11). The key to understanding Satan's role in this passage may lie in the phrase ἐν προσώπῳ Χριστοῦ. While this phrase could mean "in the person of Christ," or "as the representative of Christ" (REB; NEB),[135] the reference to Satan suggests that a Semitism of the Hebrew לפני, "in the presence of Christ," is preferable. The phrase echoes the tradition of Satan as the accuser of the elect before God, which we have already encountered in Job (cf. Job 1:6-9; Zech. 3:1-2). This OT tradition is developed further in Second Temple Jewish literature and the Dead Sea Scrolls, where Mastema (משטמה)—likely a variation of שטן[136]—and his cohorts accuse humanity before God.[137] Paul echoes this tradition in the letter to the Romans: "Who will bring accusations against God's elect? God does the acquitting; who is to render a verdict of guilt?" (Rom. 8:33-34).[138] It is probable that this is the

---

133. Cf. Eph. 6:10-13; 1 Pet. 5:8.

134. There is a long tradition of identifying the offender in 2 Corinthians 2 with the incestuous man of 1 Corinthians 5, though this is unlikely. For a discussion of the various positions, see V. P. Furnish, *II Corinthians*, AB 32A (Garden City, NY: Doubleday, 1984), 160–68.

135. See BDAG, "πρόσωπον," 887–88.

136. Cf. *Jub.* 10:7–9, where Mastema is explicitly identified as Satan. See J. W. van Henten, "Mastemah משטמה," in *Dictionary of Deities and Demons in the Bible*, ed. K. van der Toorn, B. Becking, P.W. van der Horst (Leiden: Brill, 1999), 553–54.

137. See *Jub.* 17:16; 48:15–18; *1 En.* 40 :9. Cf. CD 16 :3–6; 4Q225 2 :2 :13.

138. Cf. *1 En.* 41:9.

tradition Paul has in mind in 2 Cor. 2:10-11 when he connects Satan with forgiveness "in the presence of Christ."

According to this tradition, Satan is able to bring accusation before God against the elect upon discovery of some perceived transgression on the part of the elect. In Second Temple Jewish literature, Satan is often barred by angels from bringing accusations.[139] However, in Paul's own appropriation of this tradition, it is Christ Jesus, seated at the right hand of God, who intercedes for believers against the one who might bring accusations (Rom. 8:33-34). Thus, in 2 Cor. 2:10, when Paul forgives in the presence of Christ, he is in essence calling on the believer's intercessor as a witness[140] to his actions, and thus arms Christ—the defense attorney, to use a modern analogy—with evidence to counter Satan's charges.[141]

Within the worldview described here, *how believers live their lives matters, for Satan uses perceived transgressions of believers as an opportunity to gain access beyond the limits God has set for him.* This is precisely Satan's scheme; and Paul is not ignorant of this scheme against the Corinthian body. If the Corinthians do not forgive and become reconciled with the repentant brother, Satan will exploit the situation.[142] Satan seeks to "take advantage of" (πλεονεκτηθῶμεν, 2 Cor. 2:11)[143] the church. In the OG of Hab. 2:9 and Ezek. 22:27 the verb πλεονεκτέω translates the Hebrew בצע, which denotes an "unlawful gain."[144] Paul declares that Satan will attempt to use the unmerciful stance of the church as a means to claim more than his due with the church and afflict the Corinthian body.[145] This insight suggests that if the church demonstrates an unmerciful stance in their dealing with the incestuous man—that is, by dealing with him in a way that leaves no room for repentance and reconciliation—then Satan will attempt to take more than his due with the community.

The above discussion may also provide us with a reason for why Paul wants the Corinthians to expel the incestuous man from their midst: Satan will seek to gain access into the community if this transgression is not purged. While the body of Christ may be providing a protective hedge around this immoral

---

139. See, for example, *Jub.* 48:15–19; *1 En.* 40:9.

140. So also C. K. Barrett, *A Commentary on the Second Epistle to the Corinthians*, HNTC (New York: Harper and Row, 1973), 93.

141. Cf. 2 Cor. 1:23, where Paul calls on God as a witness.

142. Margaret Thrall, *The Second Epistle to the Corinthians*, 2 vols., ICC (London: T & T Clark, 1994), 1:181.

143. G. Delling, " πλεονέκτης," *TDNT* 6:267–74.

144. See BDB, "בצע."

145. In the words of the author of Ephesians, "Do not give the Devil a foothold" (Eph. 4:27).

person, it is also the very presence of this immorality within the body that, if unchecked, would eventually give Satan access to the body. The church, therefore, ought to be mourning[146] this man's deeds, rather than boasting of their newly discovered wisdom (5:2). The immoral man needs to be thrown out of the body (5:13). Paul is not as concerned with the evildoers outside the body of Christ, since Satan already has access to these people: those outside the believing community are governed by the wisdom of this age and ruled by the god of this age (2 Cor. 4:4). It is the body of Christ that Satan wants access to, and as long as there are unrepentant transgressors—who also give theological justification to their deplorable deeds—within the body, Satan will find his way into the body. That is why immorality within the body needs to be unmasked quickly and expelled, for it will damage not only the immoral person but also the body of Christ: Satan must be prohibited from gaining access into the body of Christ by means of the corrupting influence of an unrepentant immoral member. In short, in order to prevent Satan from taking more than his due with the body of Christ, the believing community has a responsibility to purge corrosive sins from its midst and to do so graciously, leaving room for repentance and reconciliation.

Nonetheless, as noted previously, Paul is not demanding mere excommunication in 1 Corinthians 5. A letter of expulsion would not achieve the result Paul desires. Neither would a delegation sent to inform the man that he could not return to the church achieve this result. Paul's claim that the kingdom of God is not a matter of speech (4:20) rules out these possibilities. The kingdom of God is a matter of power (4:20); that is why the "power of our Lord Jesus" (5:4) must be present in order for the Corinthian community to be able to carry out this practice. The community's action is a spiritual practice that results in spiritual exclusion, one that places a person spiritually outside the body of Christ. A comparison with Paul's own physical absence is apt. While Paul is physically absent from Corinth, he will actually be present at Corinth in spirit (5:3) when this practice is carried out.[147] In contrast, when

---

146. B. Rosner's argument that Paul urges the Corinthian community to mourn because God holds the whole community responsible for the sin of the incestuous man is not entirely convincing; see Rosner, "'ΟΥΧΙ ΜΑΛΛΟΝ ΕΠΕΝΘΗΣΑΤΕ': Corporate Responsibility in 1 Corinthians 5," *NTS* 38 (1992): 470–473. Paul thinks the Corinthians are implicated in their indifference to the incestuous man's presence in the community. But this is a far cry from imputing corporate guilt to the community.

147. Contra Barrett, *First Epistle to the Corinthians*, 124 ("[Paul] will make his contribution, as the Corinthians reflect on what they remember of his convictions, character, and ways, and on what they know of his mind in the present matter") and G. A. Cole, "1 Cor 5:4 '... with my spirit,'" *ExpTim* 98 (1987): 205 ("Paul's presence at Corinth in 1 Cor 5:4 could have taken the form of an authoritative verbal one, located in his written judgment"), this is more than mere psychological and epistolary presence.

this spiritual practice is effectively carried out, even if this incestuous man may make his way to the gathering of the church on occasion, as long as he remains unrepentant, he is spiritually excluded from the body. Unlike what Paul has to say about his actual presence in 5:3, then, should this man remain unrepentant after the community's action, even if he should find himself physically present with the church, he will be absent in the spirit. Yet for the sake of protecting the body from Satan's schemes, and in order to prevent this man's influence from spreading like yeast, this practice must also include physical expulsion from the church. All this is difficult for the modern mind to grasp; but we need to remember that Paul was not writing for twenty-first-century rationalists.

As discussed earlier, a number of scholars understand the phrase "hand over to Satan for the destruction of the flesh" to mean death.[148] But 2 Cor. 2:5-11, as a parallel incident of the church's dealing with a wayward member, shows that Paul is not calling for the incestuous man's death.[149] The allusions to Ps. 89:32-33 and Job 2 also establish Paul's demand as a call for some sort of physical suffering, in hopes that the man will repent and return to the church. God still holds out his love and steadfastness to the covenant amidst punishment in Ps. 89:32-33, and Job's suffering results in a change in Job: Job's suffering leads to penitence and Job acquires a new vision of the cosmos (cf. Job 42:6).[150] This interpretation receives further support from 1 Tim. 1:20, where Hymenaeus

What Paul means here may be difficult for us to grasp, but Paul believed he would be present when the church gathered to carry out the sentence. Thus, the phrase ὡς παρὼν (5:3) should not be translated as "as if/though present" (NIV; RSV; NRSV; NASB; etc.); there is almost nothing in favor of this translation. Paul has already judged the man as one who is actually present; so, correctly, G. G. Findlay, "St. Paul's First Epistle to the Corinthians," in *The Expositor's Greek Testament*, ed. W. R. Nicoll (Grand Rapids: Eerdmans 1961 [orig. 1900]), 808.

148. The major challenge this camp may raise against the argument presented here has to do with Paul's use of the word ὄλεθρος; for the word often carries the strong meaning of death or annihilation. In 2 Thess. 1:9, however, Paul contrasts ὄλεθρος αἰώνιος—which he describes as exclusion from the glorious presence of God—with eternal life. Ὄλεθρος in this (eschatological) context cannot mean death or annihilation (see Abraham J. Malherbe, *The Letters to the Thessalonians*, AB 32B [New York: Doubleday, 2000], 402), but rather an eternal life of affliction that is the opposite of an eternal life of glory. Paul is, therefore, capable of using the same term to describe the physical affliction that will come upon an offender as a result of his being excluded from the body of Christ. Paul's hope is that the affliction suffered will save the man from ὄλεθρος αἰώνιος. Ultimately, as we hope to have shown, the cumulative evidence of Job 2:4-6, 1 Tim. 1:20, 2 Cor. 2:5-11, and Ps. 89:32-33 point in the direction of physical suffering leading to repentance.

149. Cf. Gal. 6:1; 2 Thess. 3:14-15.

150. The NRSV translates Job 42:6 as "Therefore I despise myself, and repent in dust and ashes." We have argued elsewhere that a better translation, in light of the logic of the book of Job, might be: "Therefore I recant and adopt a different opinion concerning dust and ashes"; see our "'The *satan*' in

and Alexander are "handed over to Satan" in hopes of achieving a change in their character. Handing over to Satan, therefore, also has a remedial purpose for the author of 1 Timothy. Our own analysis of 1 Corinthians 5 confirms the author of 1 Timothy's interpretation of this sentence in Paul. Paul's hope is that the incestuous man's physical affliction will result in a change in him and an eventual return to the community of believers.[151]

Was this severe discipline by Paul and the Corinthian church successful, and did the incestuous man repent of his deeds? We have no way of verifying what was the outcome of the church's discipline on the incestuous man. But if this discipline achieved its intended purpose, we can easily imagine Paul penning these words to the man:

> But even if I caused you sorrow by my censure, I do not regret it. Even if I did regret it—for I see that my censure hurt you, if only for a little while—now I rejoice, not because you were made sorry, but because your sorrow led you to repentance. For you became sorrowful as God intended and so were not harmed in any way by us. *Godly sorrow brings repentance that leads to salvation.* (2 Cor. 7:8-10; adapted)[152]

CONCLUSION

In this chapter we have focused on two practices, cross-centered preaching and church discipline. As we argued in part 1 of this study, practices are narrative dependent; Christian practices point to a story about God's dealing with his creation. In order to set the world right, God sent his only Son into the world; and Christ's appearance in the world ushered in a new age, with the result that the old age (or the present form of this world) is passing away. The story

Light of the Creation Theology of Job," 19–34. Both translations, nonetheless, capture the transformation in Job, which is the result of his suffering and encounter with God.

151. Cf. Konradt, *Gericht und Gemeinde*, 320–21. Konradt argues for a similar position: that the physical afflictions suffered at the hands of Satan would eventually bring about a change in the incestuous man. Thus, his dismissal of Job in his treatment of this passage (*Gericht und Gemeinde*, 317) is quite unfortunate. We hope to have shown that if one is to arrive at an interpretation of 1 Cor. 5:5 that sees Satan's physical afflictions leading to transformation in the incestuous man, then the strong echoes with Job and 1 Tim. 1:20 will need to be taken very seriously and developed. We may also note in passing that the interpretation presented here finds an instructive parallel in the rabbinic concept of atonement by suffering, especially in the rabbinic teaching that affliction leads a person to examine his/her ways, which in turn engenders repentance and an earnest seeking after God (see, e.g., R. Akiba's reflection on Manasseh in *Mek. Bahodesh* 10).

152. Cf. 2 Tim. 2:25-26.

of Christ's encounter with the guardians of the old age—the principalities and powers—is well entrenched in Christian tradition. From the temptation of Jesus (Matt. 4:1-11; Luke 4:1-13) to the devil's influence on Judas to betray Jesus (Luke 22:3-6; John 13:21-30), which sets in motion the sufferings and death of Jesus, early Christians saw powers of evil at work in the world and in opposition to Jesus' ministry. The powers' opposition to Jesus reaches its climax on the cross, where Christ's death is said to have been an encounter between demonic forces and forces of good (cf. Mark 15:24-41). In Paul's complex theology, it was "the rulers of this age" who crucified the Lord of glory (1 Cor. 2:8). Thus, to preach the message of the cross is to be swept into the cosmic battle that began with Christ's apocalyptic invasion of the world. For Paul, then, such preaching cannot be undertaken with worldly wisdom, but must be undertaken in the power of the Holy Spirit.

In addition, since for Paul the powers pervade all aspects of existence, he sought to create a Christian *habitus* that will guide the ecclesial community's practices. He wanted the early believers to discern the work of the powers in their midst and to take action before the powers took more than their due with the community. The community, therefore, had to learn how to deal with deviant members. The incorrigible perverts needed to be put out of the community, in hopes that Satan's affliction might lead to their repentance and eventual salvation. Their continued presence within the body made the community vulnerable to Satan's attacks. Those who repented of their misdeeds needed to be welcomed back into the body, lest Satan takes more than his due with the community. In either case, the cultivation of a Christian *habitus* creates an acute sensitivity to the insidious work of the powers. And what all these go to show is that, for Paul, Christian life and practice cannot be separated from the reality of cosmic powers.

6

Bondage Under the Elements: Galatians

Right from the beginning of the letter to the Galatians, Paul gives the reader a hint of the theme (or conviction) that will undergird his arguments in the rest of the letter. Paul says in 1:4 that Jesus "gave himself for our sins, in order that he might deliver us from the present evil age" (τοῦ δόντος ἑαυτὸν ὑπὲρ τῶν ἁμαρτιῶν ἡμῶν ὅπως ἐξέληται ἡμᾶς ἐκ τοῦ αἰῶνος τοῦ ἐνεστῶτος πονηροῦ). This theme reflects the apocalyptic belief that humans are subject to cosmic powers beyond their control, and that it takes a higher power to rescue humans from these cosmic powers.[1] For Paul, the present age is evil and its (legal and ritual) elements are enslaving. It is only through participation in Christ that a person can be rescued from this evil age.

There are practices that are characteristic of this present age that Paul wants the believers at Galatia to reject, for to submit to these practices is to become subject to enslaving powers that rule the present evil age (4:1-10). It is, therefore, not surprising that the concept of "freedom" features prominently in Paul's Letter to the Galatians (cf. 1:4; 3:13; 3:28; 4:5; 4:22-31; 5:1; 5:13); the deliverance of Christ from the present evil age has brought freedom. In Galatians 2, Paul speaks of "false brothers" who had sneaked into his private meeting with reputable leaders (2:1-5). Paul maintains that the false brothers had arrived stealthily at the private meeting, and that these false brothers came to monitor activities. Paul characterizes the surveillance activity of the false brothers as an attempt "to spy out our freedom which we have in Christ Jesus" (κατασκοπῆσαι τὴν ἐλευθερίαν ἡμῶν ἣν ἔχομεν ἐν Χριστῷ Ἰησοῦ; 2:4). This concept of freedom is vital for our understanding of practices of power at Galatia. Christ has rescued believers from the present evil age (1:4), with its enslaving powers. Those who are in Christ, therefore, have freedom. For Paul, then, to submit to certain practices would be to take on the yoke of slavery

---

1. Cf. J. L. Martyn, *Galatians: A New Translation with Introduction and Commentary*, AB 33A (New Haven: Yale University Press, 1997), 23.

(cf. 5:1; 5:13).[2] Thus, in this chapter, we shall see that practices of power in the letter to the Galatians are activities that belong to the passing age, submission to which exposes believers and unbelievers to the cosmic powers that enslave those who participate in these activities.

This is the central message of Gal. 4:1-11, a pericope that some scholars have deemed as the theological center of the entire letter.[3] In this pericope Paul makes the astonishing claim that there is a link between life under the Law and life under the στοιχεῖα ("the elements"). This chapter will attempt to provide a solution to this puzzle. The argument put forth in Gal. 4:1-11 is a continuation of the argument begun in Galatians 3.[4] Thus, we begin our discussion with Galatians 3 in the next section, before turning our attention to Gal. 4. We hope to show how Paul's statements about the institution of the Law in Gal. 3:19 may provide the key to unlocking the connection between the Law and the elements. It is the main contention of this chapter that what links the Law and the elements for Paul is his discovery, in retrospect, that both the Law and the elements can be co-opted by higher powers.

THE INSTITUTION OF THE LAW (GALATIANS 3)

Galatians 3 begins the application of Paul's rebuke of Peter at Antioch (2:11-21) to events at Galatia.[5] At Antioch, Peter and others (including Barnabas) had been swayed by missionaries to separate themselves from gentiles at meals (2:12-13). A parallel situation is taking place at Galatia, where the gentiles are being forced by missionaries to adopt certain Jewish practices. Paul's rebuke of Peter, then, serves as the gateway into addressing the developments at Galatia. The thrust of Paul's argument to Peter, which applies equally to the Galatians' present situation, is that God's gracious act to set right (δικαιόω)[6] all that has

---

2. Cf. 4:22-31, where Paul uses the adjective, "free," five times. Cf. also 3:13; 3:28; 4:5.

3. See, for example, Martyn: "The sentence comprising [ch. 4] vv 3-5 is nothing less than the theological center of the entire letter" (*Galatians*, 388); Martinus de Boer: "[Gal. 4:1-7] is probably the central theological passage of [Paul's] letter to the Galatians" ("The Meaning of the Phrase τὰ στοιχεῖα τοῦ κόσμου in Galatians," *NTS* 53 [2007]: 204-24).

4. A number of scholars have also noted this fact. Cf., e.g., E. P. Sanders, *Paul, the Law, and the Jewish People* (Minneapolis: Fortress Press, 1983), 65-70; D. Campbell, *Deliverance of God: An Apocalyptic Rereading of Justification in Paul* (Grand Rapids: Eerdmans, 2009), 885.

5. There is debate on where to terminate Paul's address to Peter. A number of commentators and translations end Paul's speech at 2:14 and treat 2:15-21 as separate from events at Antioch (cf. NRSV). We favor the position that Paul's address to Peter extends into vv. 15-21 (cf. NIV).

6. On this meaning of δικαιόω, see Martyn's commentary, *Galatians*. Martyn consistently translates the verb as "rectify" and the noun (δικαιοσύνη) as "rectification." Cf. R. B. Hays, "Justification," *ABD* 3:1129-33.

gone wrong is not achieved through the Law but through Christ's life, death, and resurrection.[7] This is the argument Paul seeks to make in the entire letter, and in chapter 3, he formulates this argument using the story of Abraham. It is probable that by pointing to Abraham's own circumcision and his circumcising of his entire household in Gen. 17:23-27, the missionaries at Galatia pointed to Abraham as a model for observance of the Law. But drawing on his reading of the Abraham story, Paul observes that Abraham was declared righteous in Gen. 15:6 *prior to* his circumcision; Abraham's righteousness was on the basis of his faith, not works of the Law. Thus, as Paul's argument goes, the true "sons" of Abraham (Gal. 3:6-7) are those "from faith" (ἐκ πίστεως), and these are marked for the promise of the Holy Spirit (3:14). This argument will find its culmination in 4:6-7, when all believers (male and female; cf. 3:28) are made into "sons" of God upon receipt of the Spirit of God's "Son" (cf. 3:5). Paul asserts that the promise was spoken to Abraham 430 years before the Law (3:17). This promise is the covenant that God established with Abraham and his "seed" ("who is Christ"; 3:16) on the basis of faith, and this established covenant cannot be nullified by the Law that enters the scene centuries later. Since the Law is not based on faith, believers in Christ are "heirs" (κληρονόμοι) according to the promise (3:29; cf. 4:1, 7). The "inheritance" (ἡ κληρονομία), then, does not depend on the Law (3:18), but on the promise.

Having advanced an argument in 3:15-18 that almost undercuts the usefulness of the Law, Paul is forced to address the question of the significance of the Law: "Why, then, the Law?" (3:19). The Law, according to Paul, "was added" (προσετέθη) for the sake of transgressions, having been instituted through angels by a mediator, until the seed to whom the promise was made should come (3:19). The Law was added, presumably as a supplement to the promise; but to what purpose? Interpretations differ on how τῶν παραβάσεων χάριν should be understood. The (improper) preposition χάριν could either be causal ("because of transgressions," that is, to restrain transgressions)[8] or telic ("in order to stimulate or provoke transgressions").[9] Paul's choice of the

---

7. To delve into the subjective/objective genitive debate of Paul's πιστίς Χριστοῦ construction would go well beyond the scope of this chapter. Suffice it to say that we favor the subjective genitive interpretation. See Hays, *The Faith of Jesus Christ: The Narrative Substructure of Galatians 3:1–4:11*, 2nd ed. (Grand Rapid: Eerdmans, 2002 [orig. 1983]).

8. So F. Sieffert, *Der Brief an die Galater*, KEK 7, 8th ed. (Göttingen: Vandenhoeck & Ruprecht, 1894), 223; Hays, "The Letter to the Galatians" in *The New Interpreter's Bible*, vol. 11 (Nashville: Abingdon, 2000), 266–67.

9. So Betz, *Galatians*, Hermeneia (Philadelphia: Fortress Press, 1979), 163–67; F. F. Bruce, *The Epistle to the Galatians*, NIGTC (Grand Rapids: Eerdmans, 1982), 181–82; Martyn, *Galatians*, 352–55. Cf. Rom 4:15; 5:20-21.

noun παράβασις ("transgression") could imply the latter, since transgression is possible only after the Law has already been established.[10] Nonetheless, as we shall see shortly, the metaphor of the Law as a παιδαγωγός (3:24-25) makes such a reading implausible; this analogy suggests strongly that the Law was instituted to restrain transgressions. In any case, Paul has declared the temporality of the Law, since the Law fulfilled its function until the coming of Christ (3:25; 4:7).

Within the immediate context the passive verb προσετέθη may be a reference to the angels; but it is likely best to interpret the verb as a divine passive (cf. 3:16), making God ultimately responsible for the addition of the Law. According to Paul, the Law was instituted (διαταγείς)[11] δι' ἀγγέλων. The preposition διά could either be understood as causal ("by angels") or instrumental ("through angels"). The natural grammar favors the latter and, as we shall see, evidence from Second Temple Jewish literature also favors the latter. It is highly plausible that Paul is here drawing on (and transforming) Jewish tradition that associated the giving of the Law with angels. According to Deut. 33:2,

> The LORD came from Sinai; He dawned from Seir upon them; He shone forth from Mount Paran; and with him were myriads of holy ones, from his right אשדת to them.

The LXX translator rendered the obscure Hebrew word אשדת ("lightning"; "fiery law") as ἄγγελοι, giving the final line as

> ἐκ δεξιῶν αὐτοῦ ἄγγελοι μετ' αὐτοῦ
> from his right hand angels with him.

This text is what may have engendered myriad traditions that highlighted the surpassing glory of the Law by pointing to the angelic role in its inception.[12] In Acts 7:53 Stephen castigates the Jews for not obeying the Law that was ordained through the angels. And in Heb. 2:2-3, ὁ λόγος seems a likely reference to the Sinaitic Law spoken through the angels ("For if the word [ὁ λόγος] spoken through the angels was sure, and every transgression and disobedience received a just recompense, how can we escape if we neglect so great a salvation?").[13]

---

10. Martyn, *Galatians*, 354-55.

11. Cf. Plato, *Laws* 932a; Hesiod, *Works and Days*, 276.

12. See, for example, Josephus, *Ant.* 15:136; *T. Dan* 6:2; Philo, *Somn.* 1:140-44; *Apoc. Mos.* 1; *Pesiq. Rab.* 21:7-10.

Paul echoes this tradition of angelic participation in the giving of the Law at Sinai. Nonetheless, Paul's reference to the role of angels in the genesis of the Law is unlike his Jewish contemporaries, for Paul does not invoke angelic participation to show the surpassing glory of the Law. On the contrary, Paul speaks of angelic participation in the inception of the Law to show that the Law is mediated and to hint at the reality that the Law can fall into the hands of higher powers. We shall argue the latter point in detail in later sections.

Angelic role in the institution of the Law, in light of Paul's argument in Galatians, presents another conundrum: Did the angels institute the Law on God's behalf at Sinai or were they acting alone in God's absence?[14] This may depend on how one interprets the enigmatic statement of 3:20:[15] ὁ δὲ μεσίτης ἑνὸς οὐκ ἔστιν ὁ δὲ θεὸς εἷς ἐστιν. N. T. Wright has provided a stimulating interpretation of 3:20 that reads ἑνός, "of one," as a reference to the "one" family of the "one" God, the single seed promised to Abraham in 3:15-18.[16] According to this reading, the point of 3:20 is that Moses is not the mediator through whom the one family is brought into being, since Moses brought a revelation to one race only, Israel. But since God is one, God desires one family, not different families composed of Jews and gentiles. This interpretation is ingenious but not entirely convincing. First, it does not adequately account for Paul's perceived connection between being under the στοιχεῖα and being under the Law, for it fails to wrestle with the reality of bondage that Paul perceives as linking life under the two entities (3:22-25; 4:1-11). In Wright's reading, the connection between the two entities is that the Law becomes like a local or tribal deity, that is, the στοιχεῖα.[17] In our detailed analysis below of the term, we will show that the στοιχεῖα must not be equated with deities. Second, Wright's argument presupposes that the mention of angels must be confined to 3:19, with no connection to 3:20.[18] This view is exegetically unwarranted,

13. See L. T. Johnson, *Hebrews: A Commentary*, NTL (Louisville: Westminster John Knox, 2006), 86–89. Contra L. H. Silberman, who thinks the angels in this verse are the "prophets" of 1:1 ("Prophets/Angels: LXX and Qumran Psalm 151 and the Epistle to the Hebrews," in *Standing before God: Studies on Prayer in Scriptures in Tradition with Essays (FS J. M. Oestereicher)*, ed. A. Finkel and L. Frizzell [New York: KTAV, 1981], 91–101).

14. Cf. H. Hübner, *Das Gesetz bei Paulus*, FRLANT 119 (Göttingen: Vandenhoeck & Ruprecht, 1978).

15. Ernest De Witt Burton mentions a nineteenth-century study (Fricke, *Das exegetische Problem Gal. 3:20*, 1879) that counts about three hundred different interpretations of this verse; Burton, *A Critical and Exegetical Commentary on the Epistle to the Galatians*, ICC (Edinburgh: T & T Clark, 1921), 191.

16. N. T. Wright, *The Climax of the Covenant: Christ and the Law in Pauline Theology* (Minneapolis: Fortress Press, 1991), 157–74. So also Hays, "Letter to the Galatians," 267–68 (with some qualification).

17. Wright, *Climax*, 170.

however. Whatever one makes of Gal. 3:19-20, it must account for the fact that contrary to God's direct word spoken to Abraham, the Law came to Israel through intermediaries.

Thus, J. Louis Martyn's interpretation seems to move in the right direction, though he overcooks his position. According to Martyn, 3:20 must be translated as "Now a mediator does not represent one person (a singular party), but God is the one," implying that Moses, the mediator of the Sinaitic Law, was not representing God, "the Lord [who] is one" (Deut. 6:4). Rather, at Sinai Moses was conveying the Law on behalf of a group of angels acting in God's absence.[19] This interpretation is possible; yet it seems to us difficult to maintain in the light of the allusion to Deut 33:2 LXX: the angels, according to this OT reference, were "with him [that is, with God]." Indeed, Second Temple Jewish literature contains evidence of angelic mediation or institution (*on God's behalf*) of the Law in general or the two main practices in dispute at Galatia in particular, which Paul labels as "works of the Law":[20] circumcision and calendrical observances.[21] A few examples will suffice.

In *1 Enoch*, Enoch receives heavenly knowledge about the secrets of the times and signs associated with the celestial bodies (cf. 1 *En.* 1:2; 2:1–3; 3:1; 4:1; 5:1–4), which he is ordered to pass on to the generations of the world (1 *En.* 82:1–2). This knowledge is mediated by angels who are working for God:

> True is the matter of the exact computation of that which has been recorded; for Uriel—whom the Lord of all the creation of the world has ordered for me (in order to explain) the host of heaven—has revealed to me and breathed over me concerning the luminaries, the months, the festivals, the years, and the days. He has the power in the heaven both day and night so that he may cause the light to shine over the people—sun, moon, and stars, and all the principalities of the heaven which revolve in their (respective) circuits. These are

---

18. Ibid., 172.

19. So Martyn, *Galatians*, 352–70.

20. On "works of the Law" as specific practices of Jewish ethnic distinctiveness, see J. D. G. Dunn, "The New Perspective on Paul" and "Works of the Law and the Curse of the Law (Gal. iii. 10-14)," in *Jesus, Paul and the Law: Studies in Mark and Galatians* (Louisville: Westminster/John Knox, 1990), 183–214, 215–41.

21. While table regulations were an issue at Antioch, there is nothing in Galatians to suggest that this was also the case at Galatia. It is very likely that Paul would have addressed table regulations directly if these were also at issue in Galatia.

the orders of the stars which set in their (respective) places, seasons, festivals, and months (1 *En.* 82:7–10; cf. 75:3).[22]

The angel of God passes down heavenly knowledge on the divinely instituted festivals and sacred days and the appointed times for these holy days and festivities.

The book of Jubilees also presents the angelic role in the transmission of "works of the Law." The author of Jubilees relates an account of a detailed revelation to Moses by an angel of the presence.[23] The words of the angel are spoken to Moses during his forty-day stay on Mount Sinai (Exod. 24:18), when Moses went up to receive the tablets of the Law and the commandments. The angel first receives the tablets of the Law (*Jub.* 1:29) and, in an extended revelation, the angel delivers to Moses the tablets containing the history of creation and Israel, including laws concerning circumcision and Jewish calendrical observances. Having narrated to Moses the story of Abraham's circumcision and the circumcision of Abraham's entire household, the angel commands Moses thus:

> This law is for all the eternal generations and there is no circumcising of days and there is no passing a single day beyond the eight days because it is an eternal ordinance ordained and written in the heavenly tablets. And anyone who is born whose own flesh is not circumcised on the eighth day is not from the sons of the covenant which the Lord made for Abraham since (he is) from the children of destruction. And there is therefore no sign upon him so that he might belong to the Lord because (he is destined) to be destroyed and annihilated from the earth and to be uprooted from the earth because he has broken the covenant of the Lord our God. (*Jub.* 15:25–26)[24]

22. Quotations are taken from E. Isaac's translation in *OTP* 1:5–89.

23. The angel of the presence is not a circumlocution for God, because according to *Jubilees*, the angels of the presence are the first kind of angels created (*Jub.* 2:2–3). The roles assigned to the angel of the presence rather speaks to God's indirect contact with the world, since the angel of presence assumes roles often attributed to God in Genesis and Exodus (cf. *Jub.* 6:19, 22; 12:22; 30:12; 48:4; 48:13). According to Jubilees, then, God acts through *mediators*. See J. C. VanderKam, "The Angel of the Presence in the Book of Jubilees," *DSD* 7 (2000): 378–393, esp. 390–93.

24. Quotations are taken from O. S. Wintermute's translation in *OTP* 2:35–142. Cf. J. Vanderkam's translation in *The Book of Jubilees: A Critical Text*, 2 vols., Corpus Scriptorum Christianorum Orientalium, 510–11, Scriptores Aethiopici, 87–88 (Louvain: Peeters, 1989).

Jubilees is not content with informing the reader that the reason every Israelite male must be circumcised is because of God's covenant with Abraham requiring that Abraham and his seed be circumcised for eternity (*Jub.* 15:11–16); the angel of presence also informs Moses that all males in Israel must be circumcised because the angels of the presence also underwent circumcision on the day of creation (15:27). The theological and historical implications of the last point are beyond the parameters of this chapter, but it should suffice to note here evidence of a tradition that an angel stood behind the delivering of the law concerning circumcision to Moses, and that the work of this angel is not opposed to God.

The angel also stresses to Moses the importance of faithful observance of certain special times. After narrating to Moses Israel's escape from Egypt, the angel commands Moses to remember the appointed time of the Passover celebration:

> And you, remember this day all the days of your life and observe it from year to year all the days of your life, once per year on its day according to all of its law and you will not delay (one) day from (its) day according to all of its law and you will not delay (one) day from (its) day or from (one) month to (another) month. (*Jub.* 49:7)

The angel also reminds Moses to command the Israelites to observe the feast of unleavened bread (*Jub.* 49:22) and the Sabbath (*Jubilees* 50). What is curious about the laws pertaining to the Sabbath is that the angel takes full responsibility for the institution of certain special times in relation to the Sabbath:

> And after this law I made you know the days of the Sabbaths in the wilderness of Sin which is between Elim and Sinai. . . . On account of this I ordained for you the weeks of years, and the years, and the jubilees (as) forty-nine jubilees from the days of Adam until this day and one week and two years. (*Jub.* 50:1–4)

The angel of presence assumes responsibility for the institution of certain special days. Thus, we not only have here evidence of the angel mediating the Law to Moses, but also instituting certain special days related to the Law.

Important is the recognition that all these angels behind either the institution or mediation of the Law or works of the Law were working on God's behalf and not against God's purpose. Crucially, this shows that angelic powers can stand behind the Law.[25] Yet Paul's ambivalent treatment of angels throughout his letters requires us to take this knowledge a step further. Paul knows of good angels (2 Thess. 1:7; Gal. 1:8; cf. Gal. 4:14) and he knows of evil angels (2 Cor. 11:14; 12:7; cf. Rom. 8:38). Still, in the majority of Paul's mention of angels, the angels seem to occupy a morally neutral position (cf. 1 Cor. 4:9; 6:3; 11:10; 13:1; Col. 2:18 [?]). This is significant, because it suggests that for Paul angels are not necessarily inherently good or evil; what is important is how humans experience their work. Thus, while the angelic powers who stood behind the inauguration of the Law may have been working on God's behalf, the question for Paul is how the work of angelic powers behind the Law is being experienced by him and his contemporaries. In this regard, Paul's experience of the way the Law was functioning meant for him that the angelic powers who had gotten hold of the Law were not working on God's behalf: the Law was causing division in the body of Christ (2:11-21), it was subjecting some to enslaving demands (4:1-11), and it was causing some to be excluded from God's inheritance promised to the gentiles in Abraham (3:8). In other words, the Law was reproducing the very issues it was meant to address; the Law, which was supposed to liberate God's people from bondage, had become oppressive. The Law, then, had fallen victim to higher powers who were using the Law to produce outcomes contrary to the Law's aims (Gal. 5:17).[26] We have already encountered a similar argument in Romans, even if the polemical nature of Galatians does not permit Paul to give a judicious articulation of this view.[27] In Romans, "Sin" is the higher power that co-opts the Law and uses the Law to produce outcomes contrary to the Law's aims (cf. Romans 7).[28]

It is in light of this co-opting of the Law by angelic powers whose work is experienced as oppressive that the rest of Galatians 3 must be understood. In 3:22 Paul speaks of the written text (which is mediated, unlike the promises spoken directly by God to Abraham and to his seed [3:15-16]) as "locking up" (συγκλείω) everything under sin. All believers were confined under the power of the Law (3:23-25; cf. 3:10-14) until the arrival of faith. The image of imprisonment under the Law looks forward to the image of being under guardians and household managers (ὑπὸ ἐπιτρόπους καὶ οἰκονόμους) in 4:1-2.

25. To miss this crucial point would be to fail to grasp what Paul is doing in Galatians and elsewhere.

26. On this interpretation of Gal 5:17, see Martyn, *Galatians*, 536–40.

27. Cf. Sanders, *Paul and Palestinian Judaism* (Philadelphia: Fortress Press, 1977), 550: "In the heat of the argument Paul does say worse things . . . about the law [Gal. 3:19], but the soberer reflection evident in Romans, as well as what he says about the law in Phil. 3 and elsewhere, shows the thrust of his argument."

28. See our chapter on Romans for a full discussion. See also P. W. Meyer, "The Worm at the Core of the Apple," in *The Word in This World: Essays in New Testament Exegesis and Theology* (Louisville: Westminster John Knox, 2004), 57–77.

Before faith came (cf. 3:26; 4:7) being ὑπὸ νόμον was like being ὑπὸ παιδαγωγόν. A παιδαγωγός was a trusted slave employed in Greek and Roman families to keep charge of a boy from about age six to sixteen, monitoring his outward behavior and tending to the child whenever the child left the house, for example, to attend school.[29] In Paul's argument, the παιδαγωγός serves a similar function in Galatians 3 to that of the ἐπίτροποι and οἰκονόμοι in Gal 4: both supervise minors and both are compared to the Law.[30] The supervisory nature of these agents need not necessarily be oppressive. For example, evidence abounds on the important (and honorable) custodial functions of the παιδαγωγός, whose job it was to supervise the child's conduct and help nurture the child to become a productive citizen as an adult.[31] Aristotle, for example, writes: "Just as it is necessary for a child to live according to the direction of the *paidagogos* (κατὰ τὸ πρόσταγμα τοῦ παιδαγωγοῦ), so the appetitive element must live according to the rational principle" (*Eth. nic.* 3:12:8). The παιδαγωγός was viewed as necessary to restrain the passions of childhood. Paul's analogy of the παιδαγωγός, therefore, makes the view that the Law was added to produce transgressions implausible.[32]

But the παιδαγωγός was also infamous for inflicting harsh punishment.[33] Alciphron, for example, records an incident in which the boisterous Charicles was severely beaten on his back and face with a crooked staff by his παιδαγωγός, Smicrines, who also dragged the boy off like a lowly slave (Alciphron, *Epistle*, 3:7:3–4). The gang of servants who followed Smicrines, at his nod, severely flogged the ward's friends as well and dragged them off to prison. Thus, in his study of the παιδαγωγός in ancient art and literature, N. H. Young observes that the figure is often depicted as carrying a crooked staff and sometimes a strap, handy instruments for disciplining the disobedient.[34]

---

29. Burton, *Galatians*, 200. For recent discussions of the παιδαγωγός in Galatians and for much of the primary evidence, see R. N. Longenecker, "The Pedagogical Nature of the Law in Galatians," *JETS* 25 (1985): 53–61; D. J. Lull, "'The Law Was Our Pedagogue': A Study in Galatians 3:19-25," *JBL* 105 (1986): 481–98; N. H. Young, "*Paidagogos*: The Social Setting of a Pauline Metaphor," *NovT* 29 (1987): 150–76; Young, "The Figure of the *Paidagogos* in Art and Literature," *BA* 53 (1990): 80–86; A. T. Hanson, "The Origin of the Paul's Use of ΠΑΙΔΑΓΩΓΟΣ for the Law," *JSNT* 34 (1988): 71–76; T. D. Gordon, "A Note on ΠΑΙΔΑΓΩΓΟΣ in Galatians 3.24-25," *NTS* 35 (1989): 150–54.

30. See de Boer, "Meaning," 211.

31. See, e.g., Plato, *Resp.* 467D, *Lysis* 208C, *Leg.* 7:808D–E; Xenophon, *Lac.* 3:1; Dio Chrysostom, *Ven.* 114; Plutarch, *Mor.* 830B; Epictetus, *Diatr.* 1:11.22–23.

32. So also Lull, "The Law Was Our Pedagogue," 482.

33. See, e.g., Philo, *Flacc.* 14–15, *Migr.* 115–16; Plutarch, *Mor.* 37D; 73A–B.

34. Young, "The Figure of the *Paidagogos* in Art and Literature," 83–84. Young's conclusions about the word's use in Gal 3:24-25 are different from ours, however.

Whether or not one chooses to emphasize the custodial or protective functions of the παιδαγωγός, it seems to us almost impossible to eliminate the notion of oppression from Paul's discussion of this figure and the Law in Galatians 3–4 for a number of reasons: language of "freedom" pervades the letter, as noted in our introduction; the immediate context of the discussion of the παιδαγωγός places this analogy alongside other metaphors of imprisonment ("locked up" [3:22, 23]; "confined" [3:23]);[35] God sent Jesus to *rescue* those under the Law (4:4-6; cf. 1:4); and, most importantly, Paul equates being under the Law with being under the *stoicheia* (4:1-11). Thus, just as the παιδαγωγός can be experienced as oppressive through his vigorous punishments, the Law's mediation through angels means that the Law can have oppressive functions when hostile angelic powers take hold of the Law and use it against God's purpose.

In our view, this helps to illuminate why Paul can assign the power of both the Law and the elements to the present evil age to which humanity is held in bondage, and from which Christ has rescued believers (1:4; 4:1-7). In chapter 4, Paul continues the argument put forth in chapter 3 by arguing that

being under the *stoicheia* = being under the Law.

So far, we have attempted to shed light on the latter half of the equation by showing how for Paul the Law has become oppressive. In the next section, we will show how the elements can be said to be enslaving. As we hope to show, the analogy between the Law and the *stoicheia* is possible because Paul recognizes that just as hostile angelic powers can co-opt the Law, so also angelic powers can co-opt the elements (3:19; 4:1-7). In 4:8-11 Paul will extend the parallel thought in reverse order: just as angelic powers stand behind the elements, so also angelic powers can stand behind Jewish calendrical observances. In the next section, we deal with this argument in detail. It must be remembered throughout that all of this is retrospective for Paul; Paul is able to equate the Law and the elements by looking back through Christ.

Life Under the Elements and the Law (Galatians 4)

Paul begins his argument in Galatians 4 by employing an analogy from legal custom regarding inheritance to convey the point he wants to make. When the heir of the household is a child, he[36] is under guardians (ὑπο ἐπιτρόπους) and household managers (ὑπο οἰκονόμους). In this position the heir is no different

---

35. So Campbell, *Deliverance of God*, 867, 883–86.

than a slave. Beneath this picture is a gruesome reality of life before the arrival of Christ: "So it is also with us: when we were children (νήπιοι), we were enslaved under τὰ στοιχεῖα τοῦ κόσμου" (4:3). The *stoicheia*, then, carry out the same functions as that of the guardians and household managers.[37] Before Christ, though believers were heirs, they were no different from slaves, being enslaved under the *stoicheia*. Even though Paul describes believers as children (νήπιοι; 4:3) before their adoption as "sons" (4:5-6), Paul's analogy breaks down[38] when he introduces the concept of τὸ πλήρωμα τοῦ κρόνου ("the fullness of time") in 4:4. The emphasis now shifts from the concept of childhood and eventual maturity to the appointed time set by the father,[39] when God invades the world through the manifestation of his Son. Paul's introduction of the concept of adoption (4:5) is also a break away from his analogy, since the picture he paints presumes a child who is heir from birth. Thus, while the example concerns the movement of a child—whose condition is similar to slavery, but only in *appearance*—from the age of minority to the age of maturity, the *reality* Paul portrays, speaking retrospectively, concerns a movement from a condition of slavery (of all humanity) to adoption as sons.[40]

That Paul uses the first person plural ("we") in reference to the *stoicheia* (4:3) has led to some improbable exegesis for those who wish to exempt Judaism from enslavement to the *stoicheia*.[41] But that Paul includes *all* humanity in this enslavement is confirmed by v 5, where Paul sets up the other half of his equation: God sent his Son "in order to redeem *those* under the Law, in order

36. Galatians 3:28 shows that the inheritance includes females as well; but for the sake of Paul's argument —one that is built on believers being adopted as "sons" and, thus, receiving the Spirit of God's "Son"—we retain Paul's masculine pronouns in this discussion.

37. The plural ἐπίτροποι καὶ οἰκονόμοι serves as a parallel to the plural τὰ στοιχεῖα, since it is not likely that one child would be placed under several supervisors. As Martyn has noted, the combination of these two words is "without linguistic parallel" (*Galatians*, 387). Betz has discovered evidence suggesting that an οἰκονόμος was at times put in charge of slaves (*Galatians*, 204). Paul's inclusion of οἰκονόμος may, therefore, serve to underscore the point he wants to make about the slave-like condition of this child. Cf. de Boer, "Meaning," 210.

38. Cf. Martyn, *Galatians*, 386: "Paul paints the picture solely for the sake of the use he will make of it, thus allowing himself both freedom in shaping the picture itself and freedom to close with a development that goes beyond it."

39. Roman law indicates that the age of maturity of the boy was fixed by the state, not the boy's father. See Betz, *Galatians*, 204. Betz, however, finds evidence from the provinces wherein the testator sets the date of maturity. Thus, according to Betz, "This would imply that Paul was influenced more by legal practice in the provinces than by the standards of Roman law" (ibid.). It also possible, as we have already noted—and Betz also acknowledges this possibility—that Paul allows himself freedom to make his analogy conform to the reality he seeks to paint.

40. Cf. de Boer, "Meaning," 210.

that *we* might receive adoption as sons" (4:5, emphasis mine). In this verse, Paul subsumes the recipients of Christ's redemptive work under the condition ὑπὸ νόμον. Thus, to be able to set up Paul's equation correctly, one would have to recognize the flow of Paul's argument:

> The targets of Christ's redemptive work = ὑπο τὰ στοιχεῖα τοῦ κόσμου (4:3)
> The recipients of Christ's redemptive work = ὑπὸ νόμον (4:5).

Indeed, *there is no difference* between the targets of Christ's redemptive work and the recipients of Christ's redemptive work. Thus, the logical conclusion of Paul's argument is:

> ὑπο τὰ στοιχεῖα τοῦ κόσμου = ὑπὸ νόμον.

Paul has in essence argued that being under the Law is in some way equivalent to being under the *stoicheia*! Another way to restate Paul's argument is that prior to Christ, the condition of all humanity (both Jews and gentiles) was enslavement to the elements. But Christ has come to redeem all (both Jews and gentiles) who are under the Law. Thus, *being under* the elements is in some way equivalent to *being under* the Law.[42] Since Paul sets up an equation where ὑπο τὰ στοιχεῖα τοῦ κόσμου is equivalent to ὑπὸ νόμον, the reverse of this argument is implied, though Paul will not make the reverse argument until 4:8-11.

As a result of God's invasion of the world through Christ, believers are no longer slaves, but sons, heirs (κληρονόμοι) through God, having received the Spirit of God's Son in their hearts (4:6-7). Since the Galatians have been liberated from slavery, it is all the more shocking to Paul that they would adopt practices that would again place them under the yoke of slavery. The force of Paul's argument is felt when we recognize that the Galatians would not have seen their adopting of Jewish practices as a return to their former way of life, from which Christ had rescued them. It is at this point that Paul introduces our above equation in reverse order:

---

41. See, for example, L. Gaston, *Paul and the Torah* (Vancouver: University of British Colombia, 1987), 74–75; A. J. Bandstra, *The Law and the Elements of the World* (Kampen: J. H. Kok, 1964), 59–68. Cf. Augustine, *Exp. Gal.* 1 (PL 35:2126).

42. Against those who equate the *stoicheia* with the Law, Paul's argument does not equate these entities but the conditions under these entities. Cf. de Boer, "Meaning," 215.

Formerly when you did not know God, you were enslaved to that which by nature are not gods. But now, knowing God, or rather being known by God, how come you are turning again to the weak and impotent[43] *stoicheia*? Do you desire to be enslaved by them again (4:8–9)?

If in 4:1-7 Paul's argument establishes that being under the *stoicheia* prior to the coming of Christ was no different from being under the Law, in 4:8-11 Paul sets up the same argument in reverse order:

Taking up works of the Law = being enslaved again to the *stoicheia*
ὑπὸ νόμον = ὑπο τὰ στοιχεῖα τοῦ κόσμου.

The argument in 4:8-11 is the same as 4:1-7, but in reverse form. Paul's point is that for the Galatians to take up Jewish works of the Law is to reconvert (ἐπιστρέφετε πάλιν) to their former way of life.[44] In 4:10 Paul mentions the Galatians' adopting of calendrical observances as comparable to being under the *stoicheia*. There is debate as to whether these calendrical observances refer to Jewish[45] or pagan[46] special days or both[47] Jewish and pagan observances. The flow of Paul's argument, however, demands that these calendrical observances refer to Jewish special days, such as Sabbath and Day of Atonement (ἡμέρας), new moon (μῆνας), Passover and Tabernacles (καιρούς), and weeks of years and New Year's Day (ἐνιαυτούς).[48]

The point is to see that Paul continues in 4:8-11 with the same argument put forth in 4:1-7. Paul has already made being under the *stoicheia* tantamount to being under the Law (4:3-5). As we have shown above, the "we" in 4:3

43. That is, dependent on others. For this meaning of πτωχὰ, see BDAG, 896; Martyn, *Galatians*, 411.

44. Cf. Hays, "The Letter to the Galatians," 287: "The action that the Galatians are contemplating would be a conversion in reverse."

45. See Burton, *Galatians*, 233–34; J. D. G. Dunn, *The Epistle to the Galatians*, BNTC (Peabody, MA: Hendrickson, 1993), 227–28; R. N. Longenecker, *Galatians*, WBC 41 (Dallas: Word, 1990), 182; Bruce, *Galatians*, 205–7; R. Y. Fung, *The Epistle to the Galatians*, NICNT (Grand Rapids: Eerdmans, 1988), 193.

46. See T. W. Martin, "Pagan and Judeo-Christian Time-Keeping Schemes in Gal 4:10 and Col 2:16," *NTS* 42 (1996): 105–19.

47. See de Boer, "Meaning," 217; J. M. G. Barclay, *Obeying the Truth: A Study of Paul's Ethics in Galatians* (Edinburgh: T & T Clark, 1988), 63–64; Betz, *Galatians*, 218; Ragnar Bring, *Commentary on Galatians* (Philadelphia: Muhlenberg, 1961), 190.

48. For biblical references to Paul's vocabulary as a reference to Jewish calendrical observances, see Burton, *Galatians*, 233–34. Paul's general description may be an allusion to the Genesis creation story (cf. Gen. 1:14). See Martyn, *Galatians*, 416–18; Hays, "Letter to the Galatians," 288.

refs to both Jews and gentiles because the "we" in 4:5 refers to both Jews and gentiles. Thus, 4:1-7 makes general statements about both Jews and gentiles prior to the arrival of Christ. But then Paul abruptly shifts the attention solely to the gentiles in 4:8, employing the second person plural to remind them of their former lives from which they had been delivered. Having been known by God, these gentile believers had been delivered from that which by nature are not gods, the weak and impotent *stoicheia*. Paul's reference, then, to the enslavement of the Galatians to the *stoicheia* might strike the Galatians as odd, if they had in fact fully abandoned their past. The Galatians would agree with Paul about their former life, but will be shocked to hear Paul say there is not much difference between their current adoption of certain practices and their former life. For Paul's argument to work and retain its force, the flow of the argument, which has established an equivalence between being under the *stoicheia* and being under the Law in 4:1-7, must make a similar move in 4:8-11, in reverse direction: accepting Jewish works of the Law is the same as being under the *stoicheia*.[49] This argument is confirmed by 4:11: "I fear for you, lest somehow I have toiled among you in vain (εἰκῇ)." The only other time the word εἰκῇ is used in Galatians is in 3:4, where Paul argues that to accept the works of the Law means the Galatians have suffered in vain. The logic of 4:1-11, as we have attempted to lay out here, then, fits with the overall purpose of Galatians, a forceful argument against gentiles adopting Jewish works of the Law as a means for inclusion into the community of the elect (cf. 2:6-9; 3:1-5; 5:2-5; 6:12-13). In 4:1-11 Paul seeks to show the Galatians that to accept the works of the Law is to return to the place where they were before they accepted the gospel of Jesus Christ.

The crux of interpretation for Gal. 4:1-11 is how to understand the identity of τὰ στοιχεῖα τοῦ κόσμου, an expression that has puzzled interpreters for centuries.[50] In the ensuing discussion we treat this expression in detail, since a correct interpretation of the expression is crucial for understanding Paul's argument. We present the various proposals offered for how to understand the expression, showing the strengths and weaknesses of each proposal. We

---

49. The present middle indicative, παρατηρεῖσθε, suggests that the Galatians have already begun following Jewish special times (cf. 5:7). Pace de Boer, who takes this as a conative present, "you (want to) observe" ("Meaning," 214). The context of the letter suggests that the Galatians had not yet adopted all the works of the Law, but some (cf. 5:3). Circumcision was still pending (5:1-3). It is likely, as Burton has suggested, that the missionaries began by asking the Galatians to accept only part of the Law (*Galatians*, 233). Circumcision was next for the missionaries, having secured calendrical observances.

50. We will not concern ourselves in this chapter with the use of the same expression in Col. 2:8, 20. We will discuss these verses in our chapter on Colossians.

contend that the expression should be understood as the four basic elements of the cosmos, which are co-opted by higher powers in idolatrous worship. Thus, the co-opting of the Law by higher powers allows Paul to equate life under the Law and the elements.

THE IDENTITY OF THE *STOICHEIA TOU KOSMOU*

Interpretations of the *stoicheia* generally revolve around the four meanings listed in the second English edition of Walter Bauer's *Lexicon*, BAGD:[51]

> 1. *elements (of learning), fundamental principles*
> 2. *elemental substances*, the basic *elements* from which everything in the natural world is made, and of which it is composed . . . The four elements of the world (earth, air, fire, water)
> 3. the *elemental spirits* which the syncretistic religious tendencies of later antiquity associated with the physical elements
> 4. *heavenly bodies*

The third English edition, BDAG, alternatively, groups the definitions of BAGD under two broad headings:[52]

> 1. basic components of something, *elements*—
>> 1.1 of substances underlying the natural world, the basic elements from which everything in the world is made, and of which it is composed
>> 1.2 of basic components of celestial constellations, *heavenly bodies*
>> 1.3 of things that constitute learning, *fundamental principles*
> 2. transcendent powers that are in control over events in this world, *elements, elemental spirits*

The formal definitions from BAGD are retained, but definitions 1, 2, and 4 have been grouped together under one semantic field in BDAG.[53] This decision may be explained by the fact that the word στοιχεῖον probably derives from the word στοῖχος, which means a "series," a "row," or a "line." The verbal form, στοιχέω, means "to go in a line or row" or "to be in line with."[54] Thus, A. J. Bandstra may be correct to note that the word has a basic formal meaning of

---

51. BAGD, 769.
52. BDAG, 946.
53. Cf. de Boer, "Meaning," 205–8.
54. See D. Delling, "στοιχεῖον", *TDNT* 7:670–87.

"inherent component"; but this basic idea was given specific meanings when applied to a variety of contexts, while still retaining its basic idea.[55] The English word, "element," therefore, aptly captures this concept, for this word can have a variety of meanings (for example, an aspect of something abstract; chemical elements; mathematical member of a set; weather conditions; elements of the Eucharist, and so on).

In our discussion we follow the list in BAGD, since this is the list routinely cited by scholars.[56] We address each of these four meanings in increasing order of plausibility for reading Gal. 4:1-11.

STOICHEIA AS ELEMENTARY TEACHINGS

The word could mean "rudimentary or fundamental principles." This is certainly the meaning implied by Aristotle in *Politics* 1309b16, when he speaks of the principle according to which one ensures that the section desirous of the constitution is stronger in numbers than the section not desirous of it; this principle Aristotle labels as μέγιστον στοιχεῖον ("supreme elementary principle"). Plato also speaks of a "fundamental assumption" in *Laws* 7.790C. So also Xenophon, speaking to Aristippus, suggests that τροφῆς ὥσπερ ἀπὸ τῶν στοιχεέων ("elementary principles of food"; *Mem.* 2:1:1) is a good starting place for educating youths about self-control. The same concept may be implied in Philo's contrast of things elementary to things concrete and perfected in *Her.* 209.[57] In Heb. 5:12 the author, commenting on the spiritual lethargy of his audience, laments that they have not yet attained spiritual maturity: "For though by this time you ought to be teachers, you need someone to teach you again the elementary principles [τὰ στοιχεῖα τῆς ἀρχῆς] of God's oracles." The author of

---

55. Bandstra, *Law and the Elements*, 31–45. Bandstra's work contains very useful discussions of the patristic evidence on *stoicheia*.

56. Other proposed meanings for the *stoicheia* in Galatians include "the Law," "the flesh," "sin," and "death." See, for example, Bandstra, *Law and the Elements*, 61–67; Blinzler, "Lexikalisches zu dem Terminus τὰ στοιχεῖα τοῦ κόσμου bei Paulus," in *Studiorum Paulinorum Congressus Interntionalis Catholicus (1961)*, AnBib 1718 (Rome: Pontifical Biblical Institute, 1963), 442–43; Fung, *Galatians*, 181–90; R. Bring, "Der Mittler und das Gesetz: Eine Studie zu Gal. 3:20," *KD* 12 (1966): 292–309; P. Vielhauer, "Gesetzesdienst und Stoicheiadienst im Galaterbrief," in *Rechtfertigung: Festscrift für Ernst Käsemann zum 70 Geburtstag*, ed. J. Friedrich, W. Pöhlmann, and P. Stuhlmacher (Tübingen: Mohr, 1976), 543–55. In 4 Macc. 12:13 and 2 Macc. 7:22 the *stoicheia* are the basic constituents (elements) of the human body.

57. In *Opif.* 126 the elements are the vowels of grammar; they are seven in number, demonstrating the power of the number seven.

Hebrews compares the *stoicheia* to milk for infants, contrasting that with solid food for the mature.

Some scholars have argued that this meaning of *stoicheia*—"elementary principles"—best fits the context of Gal. 4:1-11.[58] According to this interpretation, the period of spiritual minority (4:1-2) consists of required regulations and observances fundamental to both Jewish and pagan religions, which are impotent to give life, and Paul is urging his readers not to return to this period of spiritual immaturity.

There are problems, however, with this interpretation. First, this position requires some notion of growth to maturity from a childhood state. But, as the context clearly suggests, a notion of growth destroys the punctiliar sense of Paul's argument concerning God's in-breaking redemption at the "appointed time" (4:2, 4-5). After Paul says, "When we were children" (4:3), he proceeds to flesh out this statement with "we were slaves" (4:3), not "we were immature." The slavery condition cannot be outgrown.[59] In addition, the "elementary teachings" interpretation at times posits that being under the *stoicheia* in 4:1-5 refers only to pre-Christian Jewish life, while the reference in 4:6-11 is only to gentiles.[60] This dichotomy is unwarranted, however. Paul's use of the first person plural in 4:3 locates all humanity (both Jews and gentiles) under the power of the *stoicheia* before the arrival of Christ. Lastly, also problematic for this interpretation is Paul's characterization of the *stoicheia* as τοῖς φύσει μὴ οὖσιν θεοῖς ("that which by nature are not gods"; 4:8) and ἀσθενῆ καὶ πτωχὰ ("weak and beggarly"; 4:9). As we shall see below, this characterization represents standard Jewish opinion that when pagans worship idols, they are in actuality worshiping the elements.

---

58. Those who argue this position include patristic exegetes, Clement of Alexandria, *Strom.* 1:11:50 (PG 9:749); *Strom.* 6:8:62 (PG 9:284); *Strom.* 6:15:117 (PG 9:341); Origen, *Comm. Matt.* 10:9–10 (PG 10:10); Jerome, *Com. Gal.* (PL 26:371A–D); Tertullian, *Marc.* 5:4:1 (PL 2:475–76); 5:19:7 (PL 2:520–22). For modern interpreters, see J. B. Lightfoot, *Saint Paul's Epistle to the Galatians: A Revised Text with Introduction, Notes, and Dissertations* (London: Macmillan, 1887), 167; Burton, *Galatians*, 517; Delling, "στοιχεῖον", 685; W. Carr, *Angels and Principalities: The Background Meaning and Development of the Pauline Phrase Hai Archai kai hai Exousiai*, SNTSMS 42 (Cambridge: Cambridge University Press, 1981), 75–76; W. Wink, *Naming the Powers: The Language of the Powers in the New Testament* (Philadelphia: Fortress Press, 1984), 67–72; Linda Belleville, " 'Under Law': Structural Analysis and the Pauline Concept of Law in Galatians 3:21–4:11," *JSNT* 26 (1986): 64–69; D. R. Moore-Crispin, "Galatians 4:1-9: The Use and Abuse of Parallels," *EvQ* 60 (1989): 203–23; Longenecker, *Galatians*, 165–66; D. R. Bundrick, "TA STOICHEIA TOU KOSMOU (Gal 4:3)," *JETS* 34 (1991): 353–64; F. J. Matera, *Galatians*, Sacra Pagina 9 (Collegeville, MN: Liturgical Press, 1992): 149–50.

59. Cf. Martyn, *Galatians*, 389.

60. See, for example, Belleville, "'Under Law,'" 68–69.

In sum, although the meaning of *stoicheia* as "elementary principles" is attested at the time of Paul, it does not provide us with the best option for understanding Paul's argument in Gal. 4:1–11.

STOICHEIA AS HEAVENLY BODIES

As noted in BDAG, the concept of *stoicheia* as constituent elements of something may be extended to include the basic components of celestial constellations, that is, "heavenly bodies." These heavenly bodies were sometimes viewed as demonic forces. When this meaning is applied to Galatians, it might help to explain Paul's reference to calendrical observances in 4:10, which may include the religious observances of the Galatians, under the influence of the stars.[61]

The evidence for *stoicheia* as heavenly bodies, however, reflects a post–first-century development (see Justin, *2 Apol.* 5:2; Theophilus, *Autol.* 2:35). The pre-Pauline evidence (Wisd. of Sol. 13 and Jewish apocalyptic literature) adduced in favor of this position is dubious. In Wisd. of Sol. 13:1–9 the author names fire, wind, water, stars and the luminaries of heaven. A surface reading might suggest that the celestial bodies were reckoned with the *stoicheia*. But this is uncertain since the word *stoicheia* is not used in Wisd. of Sol. 13:1–9. It is more likely, however, that the author expands the list of the four basic elements (7:17; 19:18) to include the heavenly luminaries.[62] Philo, for example, lists the four elements of earth, water, air, and fire, and then proceeds to distinguish the sun, the moon, and the other stars and planets as "the perfect things made of them [that is, the elements]" (*Contempl.* 5).[63]

In addition, Jewish apocalyptic literature on occasion depicts the stars as personal forces who will be held accountable on the day of judgment for their actions. For example, in *1 En.* 21:1–6 Enoch sees a vision of seven stars bound together and burning in a desolate place. These seven, according to Uriel, "are among the stars of heaven which have transgressed the commandments of the Lord and are bound in this place until the completion of ten million years, (according) to the number of their sins." While this verse could be interpreted to mean that the stars are personal forces (with will and intellect), it is more

61. According to Tertullian, Paul is arguing against those who hold this position (*Marc.* 5:4:1 [PL 2:475–6]). For patristic exegetes who themselves supported this interpretation, see Chrysostom, *Homilies on Colossians* 6 (Col. 2:8); *Commentary on Galatians* 4 (4:3); Augustine, *Exp. Gal.* 1 (PL 35:2126–30).

62. Cf. Martyn, *Galatians*, 398: "The claim that no pre-Pauline text includes the stars among the elements can be literally maintained even in the face of Wisdom 13."

63. Translations are taken from *The Works of Philo: Complete and Unabridged*, trans. C. D. Yonge (Peabody, Mass.: Hendrickson Publishers, 2008).

likely that this verse is a reference to a disruption in the natural order and movements of the luminaries. According to the author, God has set the patterns, movements, and cycles within the natural order. These seven stars, then, have strayed from their natural course and, as a result, have violated the order that God has set in place. That this interpretation might be in view is hinted in *1 En.* 2:1–3:

> Examine all the activit(ies which take place) in the sky and how they do not alter their ways, (and examine) the luminaries in heaven, how each one of them rises and sets; each one is systematic according to its respective season; and they do not divert from their appointed order. And look at the earth and turn in your mind concerning the action which is taking place in her from the beginning to the end: how all the work of God as being manifested does not change. And behold the summer and the winter, how the whole earth is filled with water and clouds and dew; and he causes rain to rest upon her.

Thus, it is highly plausible that the transgression of the seven stars consists in their deviating from the systematic order of the luminaries appointed by God. These stars may either have "gained upon" or "fallen behind" their fixed positions (*1 En.* 74:12; cf. *Pss. Sol.* 18:10–12; *T. Naph.* 3:1–5; Sir. 16:26–28).

In sum, there is no clear evidence during or prior to the time of Paul of authors who viewed the heavenly bodies as personal forces or equate *stoicheia* with the heavenly bodies, and this lack of evidence is a setback for the attempt to apply this meaning to Galatians 4. While the lateness of the lexicographical evidence by itself should not rule out any interpretation (since late attestation does not necessarily imply late use), it is the case, nonetheless, that if there is a way to make sense of Paul's argument in light of earlier evidence, then there is no need to endorse this interpretation.

STOICHEIA AS ELEMENTAL SPIRITS

The difference between this position and the previous position is at times difficult to discern, since this position comes out of the syncretistic religious tendency to associate spirits with the astral bodies and physical elements;[64]

---

64. Thus, Hans Dieter Betz, for example, speaks of "demonic entities of cosmic proportions and astral powers which were hostile towards man" (*Galatians*, 205). So also C. J. Kurapati: "It is found legitimate to interpret the phrase [*stoicheia tou kosmou*] as elemental and/or astral spirits which kept both Jews and the Gentiles alike under their tyranny" ("Spiritual Bondage and Christian Freedom According to Paul" [Ph.D. Dissertation; Princeton Theological Seminary, 1976], 55; cf. 66–69).

thus, the expression "elemental" or "elementary" spirits. Paul, according to this position, views the *stoicheia* as demonic spirits who hold humans—both Jews and gentiles—in bondage prior to, and outside of, Christ. This is by far the most common interpretation of the *stoicheia* in Galatians 4, and it helps to make sense of the enslaving function that Paul attributes to the *stoicheia*.[65]

Our earliest evidence for associating spirits with astral bodies comes from the *Testament of Solomon* (c. second to third century CE). [66] In *T. Sol.* 8:2 the seven spirits who appear before Solomon identify themselves as "heavenly bodies" (cf. *T. Sol.* 15:5; 18:1–2). In addition, it is very likely that in *2 En.* 12:1, 15:1 and 16:7 the elements are spirits. *2 En.* 12:1 describes the solar elements as spirits ("And I looked and saw flying spirits, the solar elements, called phoenixes and khalkedras, strange and wonderful");[67] and these very solar elements are said to burst into song in 15:1.[68] A step from viewing the *stoicheia* as astral spirits is to

---

65. Augustine's position leaves room for this interpretation, *Exp Gal.* 1 (PL 35:2126–30) (see Bandstra's discussion of Augustine, *Law and the Elements*, 10–12). Modern interpreters reach a range of nuanced conclusions, see O. Everling, *Die paulinische Angelologie und Dämonologie: Ein biblisch-theologischer Versuch* (Göttingen: Vandenhoeck & Ruprecht, 1888), 66–76; E. Y. Hincks, "The Meaning of the Phrase τὰ στοιχεῖα τοῦ κόσμου in Gal. 4.3 and Col. 2.8," *JBL* 15, no. 1 (1896): 183–92; M. Dibelius, *Die Geisterwelt im Glauben des Paulus* (Göttingen: Vandenhoeck & Ruprecht, 1909), 78–85; W. Grundmann, *Der Begriff der Kraft in der neutestamentlichen Gedankenwelt*, BWANT 4:8 (Stuttgart: Kohlhammer, 1932), 48–49; Bo Reicke, "The Law and This World according to Paul: Some Thoughts Concerning Gal 4:1-11," *JBL* 70, no. 4 (1951): 259–76; W. Bousset and H. Gressmann, *Die Religion des Judentums im späthellenistichen Zeitalter*, 3d ed., HNT 21 (Tübingen: Mohr, 1966), 323; P. L. Hammer, "Element (Elemental Spirit)," in *IDB* 2:82; H. Schlier, *Der Brief an die Galater*, 12th ed. KEK 7 (Gottingen: Vandenhoeck & Ruprecht, 1962), 190–91; Schlier, *Principalities and Powers in the New Testament* (New York: Herder and Herder, 1961), 23–24; Sanders, *Paul and Palestinian Judaism*, 554–55; G. Howard, *Paul: Crisis in Galatia*, SNTSMS 35 (Cambridge: Cambridge University Press, 1979), 76–82; Bruce, *Galatians*, 204; C. B. Cousar, *Galatians*, Interpretation (Louisville: John Knox Press, 1982), 92–93; H. Hubner, "Paulusforschung seit 1945: Ein Kritischer Literaturbericht," *ANRW* 2:25:4 (1987), 2691–94; E. Krentz, *Galatians, Philippians, Philemon, 1 Thessalonians*, ACNT (Minneapolis: Augsburg, 1985), 59–60; C. K. Barrett, *Freedom and Obligation* (Philadelphia: Westminster, 1985), 39; J. Rohde, *Der Brief des Paulus an die Galater*, THKNT 9 (Berlin: Evangelische Verlagsanstalt; 1989), 131; J. C. Becker, *Paul the Apostle to the Gentiles* (Louisville: Westminster John Knox, 1993), 269–70.

66. On the dating of *T. Sol.*, see discussions in D. Sperber, "Some Rabbinic Themes in Magical Papyri," *JSJ* 16 (1983): 93–108; P. S. Alexander, "Incantations and Books of Magic," in E. Schürer, *The History of the Jewish People in the Age of Jesus Christ (175 B.C.E.–A.D. 135): A New English Version*, rev. and ed. G. Vermes, F. Millar, and M. Goodman, vol. 3, part 1 (Edinburgh: T & T Clark, 1986), 342–79; P. Schäfer, "Jewish Magic Literature in Late Antiquity and Early Middle Ages," *JJS* 41 (1990): 75–91.

67. Translation by F. I. Anderson, in *OTP* 1:91–221.

68. See also *Theodotus* 55.

link them to spirits, or demons, in general, comparable to Paul's usage of ἀρχαὶ καὶ αἱ ἐξουσίαι elsewhere (cf. Col. 2:10-15).[69]

All the evidence for *stoicheia* as astral spirits is also post–first century, however. In order to circumvent this problem, Clinton Arnold has framed the argument in terms of "traditions" going back to the first century that make use of *stoicheia* as supernatural powers.[70] The assumption, which is a valid one, is that late-second or third-century MSS do preserve traditions that go back to the first century or before. Arnold, in addition to the evidence from *T. Sol.* and *2 En.*, points to Greek magical papyri, which often connect *stoicheia* with stars and/or star spirits or gods. In addition, a fourth-century papyrus calls the astral decans that rule every 10 degrees of the zodiac στοιχεῖα τοῦ κόσμου (*PGM* 39:18–21).[71] Arnold's conclusion is that "in the context of magic and astrology, even in Jewish and early Christian circles the term *stoicheia* was indeed used of personalized spiritual forces that have significant influence over the affairs of day-to-day existence."[72]

Arnold's flexible approach toward lexical data must be applauded. Nonetheless, we still cannot overlook the fact that early evidence for *stoicheia* as elementary spirits or demonic powers remains very tenuous; and Arnold's dating of magical texts is a bit too random.[73] As noted above, late attestation by itself is not enough to rule out any interpretation if that interpretation best fits the context in Paul. However, if one can make a case for interpreting the *stoicheia* in Paul as the four basic elements, a meaning that is unequivocally contemporary to Paul—and I think this can be done—then, as with the "heavenly bodies" interpretation, there is no need to endorse the "elementary spirits" or "demonic powers" interpretation of the *stoicheia*. More importantly, however, a crucial exegetical distinction needs to be made between *association*

---

69. See L. E. Scheu, *Die "Weltelemente" beim Apostel Paulus (Gal. 4,3.9 und Kol 2,8.20)*, Universitas Catholica Americae 37 (Washington: Catholic University of America Press, 1933); In-gyu Hong, *The Law in Galatians* (JSNTSup 81; Sheffield: JSOT Press, 1993), 165; C. Arnold, "Returning to the Domain of the Powers: Stoicheia as Evil Spirits in Galatians 4:3, 9," *NovT* 38 (1996): 55–76.

70. Arnold, "Returning to the Domain," 56–59; see also Arnold, *The Colossian Syncretism: The Interface between Christianity and Folk Belief at Colossae*, WUNT 77 (Tübingen: Mohr Siebeck, 1995).

71. For the Greek and English magical texts, see K. Preisendanz, *Papyri Graecae Magicae: Die Griechiscen Zauberpapyri*, 2 vols, 2d rev. ed. by A. Heinrichs (Stuttgart: Teubner, 1973–74); H. D. Betz, ed., *The Greek Magical Papyri in Translation*, vol. 1 (Chicago: University of Chicago Press, 1986).

72. Arnold, *Colossian Syncretism*, 171.

73. See Guy Williams's critique of Arnold in *The Spirit World in the Letters of Paul the Apostle: A Critical Examination of the Role of Spiritual Beings in the Authentic Pauline Epistles*, FRLANT (Göttingen: Vandenhoeck & Ruprecht, 2009), 164–65.

and *equation*. There is a difference between associating the *stoicheia* with higher powers and making the *stoicheia* the powers themselves.[74] As we hope to show, Paul's argument in Galatians is built on association of the *stoicheia* with higher powers, not an equation of the *stoicheia* with higher powers.

STOICHEIA AS FOUR BASIC ELEMENTS FROM WWHICH THE WORLD WAS COMPOSED

The predominant usage of τὰ στοιχεῖα in literature prior to and contemporary with the NT is to refer to the basic elements from which the world is composed: air, water, fire, and earth.[75] The author of Wisdom of Solomon refers in a number of places to the basic elements from which the universe was composed (Wisd. of Sol. 7:17; 13:1–9; 19:18–22). So also Philo, who often refers to the four elements from which the world was fashioned (*Opif.* 131; *Her.* 197; 209; 226; *Contempl.* 3–5; *Mos.* 1:96). This meaning of the *stoicheia* is also implied in 2 Pet. 3:10-12, which speaks of the dissolution of the elements on the day of the Lord. The same meaning is also attested in the postapostolic period (e.g., Justin, *Dial.* 62:2; *Diogn.* 8:2; Hermas, *Vis.* 3:13).[76]

This is the most widely attested usage of τὰ στοιχεῖα in the time of the NT. Our interpretation of Paul's use of the term in Gal. 4:1-11 must, therefore, at least begin with the four basic elements.[77] Worth noting also is the fact that Paul is not the only Jew to connect the four elements in some way with the Sinaitic Law. The author of *4 Ezra* mentions the four elements at the giving of the Law at Mt. Sinai:

> And your glory passed through the four gates of fire and earthquake and wind and ice, to give the Law to the descendants of Jacob, and your commandment to the posterity of Israel. (*4 Ezra* 3:19)[78]

---

74. Cf. Belleville, "'Under Law,'" 66.

75. On occasion one also encounters ether in place of fire, since the two are routinely connected. See Delling, "στοιχεῖον", 674.

76. See also Clement of Alexandria, *Protrepticus* 5:65 (PG 8:168–69).

77. Relatively few interpreters argue for this meaning in Galatians 4. See R. DeMaris, "Element, Elemental Spirit," in *ABD* 2:445; D. Rusam, "Neue Belege zu den στοιχεῖα τοῦ κόσμου," *ZNW* 83 (1992): 119–25; E. Schweizer, "Slaves of the Elements and Worshipers of Angels: Gal 4:3, 9 and Col 2:8, 18, 20," *JBL* 107 (1988): 455–68; F. Thielmann, *From Plight to Solution*, NovTSup 61 (Leiden: Brill, 1989), 80–83; Martyn, *Galatians*, 393–406; de Boer, "Meaning," 204–24.

78. Translation by Bruce. M. Metzger, in *OTP* 1:517–59.

Thus, Paul is not unique in connecting the Law with the four elements, although, as we shall see, Paul's invocation of the elements in relation to the Law is distinct from that of the author of *4 Ezra*.

To say merely that the *stoicheia* are the four elements does not settle the puzzle of interpretation, however. We have to see how the meaning of τὰ στοιχεῖα as the four physical elements of the universe fits into the argumentative and historical context of Paul's letter to the Galatians. In what follows, I consider two possibilities for interpreting Paul's argument in light of the four basic elements: *the four elements as angelic powers* and *the four elements as the idols of the pagan religion of the Galatians*.[79] We will argue for the latter.

First, it is possible that *the four elements are angelic powers*. That our starting point must be the four elements does not necessarily rule out a demonic interpretation of the *stoicheia*. One could still maintain that by *stoicheia* Paul meant the angelic powers that rule in the present evil age. But if our starting point for interpretation is the four basic elements, then this view must find evidence that equates one or more of the four elements with angelic powers. There is some evidence that one might adduce. For example, according to *4 Ezra* 8:20–22 God's word turns the angels into wind and fire: "O Lord . . . before whom the hosts of angels stand trembling and at whose command they are changed into wind and fire, whose word is sure and whose utterances are certain." The concept here is that some of the traditional elements are formed from angels; and it is a concept that one encounters elsewhere in early Jewish and Christian literature. The author of Hebrews also invokes this concept. In seeking to draw a contrast between the transitory nature of angels and the eternal nature of the Son, the author quotes Ps. 104:4, a psalm that portrays God's use of the winds and flames as messengers: "Concerning the angels he says, "He [is the one who] makes his angels winds, and his servants flames of fire" (Heb. 1:7; cf. Ps. 104:4). We might even add a very obscure passage from *1 En*. 60:19, where the reservoir of the mist (wind?) *is* an angel.[80]

So the view that the *stoicheia* could be angelic powers is still a possibility, even in the face of limiting the identity of the *stoicheia* to the four basic elements. However, it is not clear how to classify the elements that are formed from angels. Do these angels still retain their personal character after their transformation into one of the elements? In other words, do the elements

---

79. These categories are not meant to be exhaustive.

80. Cf. M. Knibb, who follows a couple of MSS that read, "And in its storehouse is an angel" (*The Ethiopic Book of Enoch: A New Edition in the Light of the Aramaic Dead Sea Fragments* [Oxford: Clarendon Press, 1978], 146–47).

formed from angels retain their intellect and will like the angels? Are the elements that are formed from angels similar to or distinct from all other elements? If so, then how do we classify these particular elements? On these puzzling questions, our texts leave us with no answers. If the elements formed from angels do retain their personal character, then they will fit with a demonic interpretation of the *stoicheia*. But without much evidence, this is very hard to say. Therefore, while the demonic interpretation of the *stoicheia* might better account for Paul's claim that the Galatians are being held in bondage by the *stoicheia*, the evidence leaves us with more confusion than answers.

More importantly, however, even if we had evidence to suggest that these particular elements formed from angels do retain their personal character, a demonic interpretation—that is, one that *equates* the *stoicheia* with angelic powers—does not fit with the logic of Paul's argument in Galatians; for this view would have Paul equate being under an impersonal entity (the Law) with being under personal entities (demonic beings). As we hope to show, this parallel destroys the logic of Paul's argument. In short, it is primarily on exegetical grounds that the interpretation that equates the *stoicheia* with demonic powers is to be rejected as an interpretation of Galatians 4.

Second, it is plausible that the *stoicheia* are *the idols of the pagan religion of the Galatians*. In our view, J. Louis Martyn has given the most sophisticated interpretation of the *stoicheia* as the four elements to date.[81] Martyn's position rightly assumes the four physical elements as the starting point for interpreting the *stoicheia* in Galatians; but Martyn presses beyond this meaning for Paul. Martyn argues that before the arrival of the Teachers[82] in Galatia, the Galatians would have been in touch with some philosophical tradition that speculated that the elements of earth, air, fire, and water constituted the universe's foundation. Citing evidence from Jewish sources that adopted the elements in apologetics toward gentiles (Wisd. of Sol. 13:1–5), and Jewish apologists who referenced Abraham's understanding of the elements (Philo *Abr.* 69–70; Josephus *Ant.* 1:155–156), Martyn argues that the Teachers preached a message concerning ascent from the elements (the stars included) to God, offering Abraham as the quintessential paradigm of this ascent. Abraham, according to the Teachers, is the paradigmatic proselyte who "is said to have made the journey to the knowledge of God by an astrological contemplation of the elements, being the first to observe the holy feasts at the correct times (e.g., *Jubilees* 16)."[83]

81. See Martyn, *Galatians*, 393–406; cf. Martyn, *Theological Issues in the Letters of Paul* (Nashville: Abingdon Press, 1997), 125–40.

82. For this term as description of Paul's opponents in Galatia, see Martyn, *Theological Issues*, 7–24.

Thus, according to the Teachers' message, by making the ascent from the contemplation of the elements to God, the Gentile believers had become true, Law-observant descendants of Abraham. When Paul writes to the Galatians, he argues that prior to the Christ-event all humanity, including Jews under the Law, were enslaved under the elements *of the cosmos*. The cosmos of which Paul speaks is the cosmos that consisted of pairs of opposites (cf. Gal. 6:14-15): circumcision and uncircumcision; Law and not-Law; Jew and Gentile. The precedent for linking cosmos and the term "elements" with pairs of opposites can be found in Philo (cf. *Deo* 107-49). Martyn argues that thinkers in Paul's time, such as Ben Sira and the author of Wisdom, "would have agreed with the traditional statement: The elements of the cosmos *are* pairs of opposites."[84] Paul, however, drawing from this tradition, engages in a "transformation of language" by announcing the apocalypse of Christ as the liberation from enslaving pairs of opposites: Jew/Gentile; slave/free; male/female (Gal. 3:28; cf. Gal. 6:14-15; 4:3, 8-9). In sum, Paul adopts the ancient equation of the elements of the cosmos with archaic pairs of opposites to interpret the religious impact of Christ's apocalypse. In Christ, the elements of religious distinction find their termination.

Martyn's ingenious interpretation is not without problems, however. Crucial for Martyn's interpretation is the view that the key to unlocking *Paul's* meaning, in distinction from that of the Teachers at Galatia, is the descriptive phrase τοῦ κόσμου. But even a casual glance reveals that Paul does not repeat this descriptive phrase after the first mention of *stoicheia*. Thus, it is not clear why Paul dropped τοῦ κόσμου in the only other time he uses στοιχεῖα in Galatians (4:9), if he intended this description of the *stoicheia* to be the key to his meaning. The full expression is not unique to Paul. Philo, for example, writes, "There are four elements of which the world consists, namely, earth, water, air, and, fire . . . the elements of the world (τὰ στοιχεῖα τοῦ κόσμου)" (*Aet.* 107-9).[85] As Josef Blinzler and Dietrich Rusam have convincingly shown, by the end of the first century, the full phrase had become a standard expression for the four physical elements.[86] Thus, if Paul meant to deviate from the standard meaning of the full expression, then it is difficult to see why he did not state this much

---

83. Martyn, *Galatians*, 400.

84. Ibid., 404; emphasis in the original.

85. Cf. Aristotle, *Metaphysics* 986b.

86. See Blinzler, "Lexikalisches," 429-44; Rusam, "Neue Belege," 119-25. Rusam notes only one exception for the full phrase, a late-second-century CE document in which Sextus Empiricus attributes to the Pythagoreans the view that numbers were τὰ στοιχεῖα τοῦ κόσμου (*Pyr.* 3:152). See also Schweizer, "Slaves of the Elements," 455-68.

clearer.[87] That Paul omits τοῦ κόσμου in 4:9 may be a signal to the reader that he wishes to lay primary emphasis on τὰ στοιχεῖα.[88]

Second, because Martyn distinguishes between how the Teachers used the full expression and how Paul meant it, his reconstruction of the Teachers' views must presuppose that the Galatians had not fully abandoned their association with the *stoicheia* at the time of the Teachers' arrival, a situation that the Teachers sought to exploit. According to Martyn, the Teachers said to the Galatians:

> The presence of idols in the temples of your former religion shows that you Gentiles ignorantly reverenced the elements as though they were gods. More tragic still, Paul did nothing really to terminate your ill-informed relation to the elements. . . . You are to ascend from the foolish and idolatrous worship of the elements themselves to the knowledge of the true God who created them, celebrating the holy times ordained by him in his Law, and doing so at the junctures fixed by the activity of his servants, the astral elements.[89]

This view, however, cannot be maintained in light of the evidence and logic of Gal. 4:1-11. Paul's logic is that by turning to the Law the Galatians are in essence *reconverting* (ἐπιστρέφετε πάλιν) to their former way; this argument demands that the Galatians had terminated completely their former association with the *stoicheia* (cf. 1:6-9; 5:7).[90]

In addition to Martyn's treatment of the *stoicheia*, we may also make mention of Martinus de Boer's work, which is the most recent detailed treatment of the *stoicheia* in Galatians.[91] De Boer also begins with the four physical elements of the universe as the starting point for his interpretation of the *stoicheia* in Galatians, but argues that the phrase must be read in some other or additional way to make sense of its context in Galatians.[92] De Boer argues that τὰ στοιχεῖα is a metonymy for the religious beliefs and practices of the Galatians prior to their becoming believers, in particular calendrical

---

87. Martyn's claim that "Paul apparently assumes that the Galatian congregations will listen to the whole of the epistle several times and with extreme care" (*Galatians*, 404–5) does not eliminate this problem.

88. A point also noted by Carr, *Angels and Principalities*, 72.

89. Martyn, *Galatians*, 399–400.

90. A point rightly noted by de Boer ("Meaning," 216n51; 215n49).

91. Ibid., 204–24.

92. Ibid., 207–8.

observances. He arrives at this conclusion from the assumption that worship of the *stoicheia* by the Galatians must bear some resemblance, either conceptually or functionally, to the observance of the Law. This de Boer finds in Paul's reference to calendrical observances (4:10): the worship of the *stoicheia*, just like observances of the Law, involves calendrical observances.[93]

De Boer's argument not only supposes that Paul's reference to calendrical observances in 4:10 includes both Jewish and pagan calendrical observances, but also that Paul elects to use the term *stoicheia* because the Jewish observances are similar in kind to the pagan calendrical observances. From our analysis of this passage above, both of these assumptions are not without problems; at the very least they undercut the force of Paul's argument. As noted previously, the force of Paul's argument is felt if the reference to calendrical observances in 4:10 is a reference to Jewish holy times, adoption of which bore no resemblance to the pagan past of the Galatians. Another way of stating this is that prior to Paul's argument in Galatians, the Galatians would have had no way of connecting their Law observances with their past veneration of the στοιχεῖα.

The biggest weakness of previous "basic elements" readings of the *stoicheia* (such as Martyn's and de Boer's) is a failure to account adequately for the *bondage* to the elements about which Paul speaks. This suggests that a correct interpretation of the *stoicheia* must somehow incorporate higher demonic powers into the understanding of the *stoicheia* as basic elements. This is what we are going to attempt to do in the remainder of this chapter. In short, is there a way to interpret τὰ στοιχεῖα as the four basic elements while also maintaining the logic and flow of Paul's argument that to be ὑπὸ νόμον is tantamount to being ὑπὸ τὰ στοιχεῖα? There is enough evidence both in biblical and extra-biblical sources to answer our question in the affirmative.[94] The position we argue in the next section is a modified version of the "elementary spirits" interpretation. Our position does not equate the στοιχεῖα with the spirits, but rather with the four elements, while acknowledging that there are spiritual powers who co-opt the elements. In our view, this is the best way to make sense of Paul's argument, one which equates being under the Law with being under the elements. We will draw on our discussion of Paul's statements about the

---

93. Ibid., 216–17. This point was also made by Sanders, *Paul, the Law, and the Jewish People*, 69. Cf. John Chrysostom, *Hom. Gal.*, ch. 4 (PG 61:657); Ambrosiaster, *Comm. in Ep. ad Gal.* (PL 17:350); T. C. G. Thornton, "Jewish New Moon Festivals, Galatians 4:3-11 and Colossians 2:16," *JTS* 40, no. 1 (1989): 99–100.

94. Pace James Scott, *Adoption as Sons of God*, WUNT 2:48 (Tubingen: Mohr, 1992), 159–60: "neither this [meaning of τὰ στοιχεῖα as four physical elements] nor any other interpretation of τὰ στοιχεῖα τοῦ κόσμου seems to satisfy the context."

institution of the Law to show that the point of contact between the Law and the elements is that both entities can be co-opted by higher powers.[95]

POINT OF CONTACT BETWEEN THE LAW AND THE ELEMENTS

We are now in a position to address the issue we posed at the beginning of this chapter: How is Paul able to connect life under the Law with life under the στοιχεῖα? The key lies in paying close attention to the description of the στοιχεῖα Paul gives us: they are "that which are by nature not gods" (4:8) and "weak and impotent" (4:9). These characterizations fit with the standard Jewish view that when gentiles worship idols they are in fact worshiping the elements. Of particular importance are two passages from Philo and Wisdom of Solomon that express this view. Both of these passages are worth quoting at length. We begin with Philo:

> With whom, however, who is there of those who [sic] profess piety that we can possibly compare? Can we compare those who honor the elements, earth, water, air, and fire? to whom the different nations have given different names, calling fire Hephaestus, I imagine because of its kindling, and the air Hera, I imagine because of its being raised up, and raised aloft to a great height, and water Poseidon, probably because of its being drinkable, and the earth Demeter, because it appears to be the mother of all plants and of all animals. But these names are the inventions of sophists: but the elements are inanimate matter, and immovable by any power of their own, being subject to the operator on them to receive from him every kind of shape or distinctive quality which he chooses to give them. But what shall we say of those men who worship the perfect things made of them, the sun, the moon, and the other stars, planets, fixed stars, or the whole heaven, or the universal world? And yet even they do not owe their existence to themselves, but to some creator whose knowledge has been perfect, both in mind and degree. (Philo, *Contempl.* 3–5)

The author of Wisdom of Solomon sounds a similar tone against the idolatrous worship of the elements:

---

95. Cf. Reicke ("The Law and This World," 262), who points to Gal. 3:19 as key to interpreting the *stoicheia*. But as will be seen below, our position is radically different from Reicke's, since Reicke identifies the *stoicheia* with the angels of 3:19. Our assertion that Paul's argument is built on association, not identification, undermines Reicke's position.

> For all human beings who were ignorant of God were foolish by nature, and from the good things that are seen they were unable to know the one who is, nor, though paying attention to his works, did they recognize the craftsman, but either fire or wind or swift air or the circle of the stars or the turbulent water of the luminaries of heaven they thought to be gods that rule the world. If it was through delight in their beauty that they took these things to be gods, let them know how much better than these is their Sovereign Lord, for the first author of beauty created them. And if they were amazed at their power and working, let them perceive from them how much more powerful is the one who formed them. (Wisd. of Sol. 13:1–4)[96]

Crucial for our ability to establish the link between the Law and the elements is to recognize that these Jewish polemical texts against idolatry must be subjected to a mirror reading, a move which most scholars have failed to make. One cannot underestimate the distorting tendencies of such polemic against pagan worship, concerted efforts to paint pagan religion in the worst possible light in order to demonstrate the superior nature of Judaism (or Christianity).[97] To this end, we must observe that it is an immense caricature of pagan worship to say that those who engage in idolatry are merely worshiping natural elements.[98] On the contrary, idol worship is foremost a partaking in the numinous power behind the natural elements. Thus, Jewish and Christian polemic against idolatry seems ambivalent, often vacillating between mocking idols as lifeless matter and acknowledging that lively powers stand behind the physical elements.[99]

In a parody of idolatry, Second Isaiah paints a picture of a practice that is so deplorable in nature that those who engage in it are severely lacking in judgment:

> All who make idols are futile, and the things they desire do not profit; their witnesses neither see nor know, that they may be put to shame. Who fashions a god or casts an image to no profit?

---

96. Translation by Michael A. Knibb in the NETS.

97. It is also possible that Jewish and Christian apologists wholly misunderstood pagan religion. But as the discussion below shows, there is enough reason to reject this view.

98. See J. D. Levenson, "Is There a Counterpart in the Hebrew Bible to New Testament Antisemitism," *JETS* 22 (1985): 242–60; J. Marcus, "Idolatry in the New Testament," *Interpretation* (2006): 152–64.

99. Cf. Deut. 32:17; 2 Kgs. 19:16-19; Pss. 96:5; 106:37; 115:4-8; Isa. 37:17-20; *1 En.* 99:7; *T. Sol.* 26:7; *Jub.* 12:1–5; 22:17.

Behold, all his companions shall be put to shame, for the craftsmen are mere humans; let them all assemble, let them stand forth, let them be terrified, let them be put to shame together. The craftsman shapes iron into a tool and works over the coals; he shapes it with hammers, and forges it with his strong arm; he becomes hungry and his strength fails, he drinks no water and becomes weary. The craftsman shapes wood, stretches a line, he outlines it out with a pencil; he works it with planes, and marks it with a compass; he makes it into the figure of a man, with the beauty of a man, to sit in a house. He cuts down cedars; or he chooses a holm tree or an oak and lets it grow strong among the trees of the forest; he plants a cedar and the rain makes it grow. Then it becomes fuel for a man; he takes a part of it and warms himself, he kindles a fire and bakes bread; also he makes a god and worships it, he makes it a graven image and falls down before it. Half of it he burns in the fire; over the half he eats flesh, he roasts meat and is satisfied; also he warms himself and says, "Aha, I am warm, I have seen the fire!" And the rest of it he makes into a god, his idol; and falls down to it and worships it; he prays to it and says, "Deliver me, for you are my god!" (Isa. 44:9-17)

Second Isaiah's biting sarcasm is glaring, but is the portrait he paints accurate? Indeed, as H. W. F. Saggs has noted, the implication "that a tree-trunk might pass immediately from sculptor to worshipper" is one that Second Isaiah himself probably knew to be false.[100] The assumption that underlies such parody of idolatry is misguided, for those who worshiped idols participated in higher powers that were not limited to material objects. Other Jewish and Christian texts, notwithstanding the parodies, did acknowledge this numinous reality, and therefore attributed idolatry to the work of demons (see, e.g., Deut. 32:17; Ps. 106:37; *Jub.* 22:17; *1 En.* 99:7; *T. Sol.* 26:7). Indeed, in response to immense caricatures of pagan religion (by especially Christians), the fourth-century Greek rhetorician Libanius, after describing the statue of Asclepius in Beroea, remarked strongly: "No one was so shameless that he would dare to say that the sacrifices were offered to the statue" (*Oratio* 30:22–23).[101]

In short, we encounter two distinct early Jewish and Christian stances toward idolatry: one that ridicules idols as nothing and idolatry as ludicrous, and

---

100. H. W. F. Saggs, *The Encounter with the Divine in Mesopotamia and Israel* (London: Athlone Press, 1978), 191n38.

101. Translation in E. J. Edelstein and L. Edelstein, *Asclepius: A Collection and Interpretation of the Testimonies* (Baltimore: John Hopkins Press, 1945), 350. Cf. Plutarch, *Mor.* 379c.

another that acknowledges the presence of higher powers behind the idols.[102] In this respect, *T. Sol.* 4:6–7 is quite telling, for in this Jewish Christian polemical text against idolatry, the mockery of idolatry is made from the viewpoint of the demon behind the inanimate matter. A demon by the name of Onoskelis mocks humans who worship her star. According to this demon, humans deceive themselves by thinking they will be beneficiaries of her benevolence by seriously worshiping her. Onoskelis says, "I grant little to those who seriously worship me" (*T. Sol.* 4:7).[103] In this text we find the two stances toward idolatry combined, for amidst the mockery of idolatry is the implicit acknowledgment of a demon behind the worship of the inanimate matter. And this may suggest that *these two stances toward idolatry are inseparable.* When Second Isaiah, for example, parodies pagan religion, it is doubtful that he himself believes that the gods of pagan religion can be identified with material objects; rather, his parody is meant to neutralize the threat these gods pose to faithful worship of YHWH,[104] which in turn suggests a numinous reality behind the idols. That the two stances concerning idolatry are inseparable is confirmed by the fact one may encounter both stances in the same author (e.g., *Jub.* 12:1–5; 22:7; Chrysostom, *Hom. 1 Cor. 20.2* [PG 61:163]).

The latter point is crucial, for in Paul's writings we encounter both of the Jewish stances toward idolatry discussed above,[105] suggesting that Paul regarded the two stances as inseparable. We have deferred a discussion of the issue of food offered to idols in 1 Corinthians 8–10 until this point.[106] Paul's address of this issue helps shed further light on our discussion thus far. Paul, in responding to

102. The two stances presented here are by no means exhaustive; but, as we shall see below, they are the most pertinent to our understanding of Gal. 4:1-11.

103. Translation by D. C. Duling in *OTP* 1:935–87.

104. See J. D. Levenson, "Yehezkel Kaufmann and Mythology," *Conservative Judaism* 36 (1982): 36–43.

105. Cf. R. Horsley, "Gnosis in Corinth: 1 Corinthians 8.1-6," *NTS* 27 (1980): 32–51.

106. We cannot address in detail here all the issues surrounding 1 Cor 8–10. But see the discussions in N. Walter, "Christusglaube und Heidnische Religiosität in Paulinischen Gemeinden," *NTS* 25 (1979): 425–36; J. Murphy-O'Connor, "Freedom or Ghetto (1 Cor. viii, 1-13; x, 23 – xi, 1)," *RB* 85 (1978): 543–74; W. L. Willis, *Idol Meat in Corinth: The Pauline Argument in 1 Corinthians 8 and 10*, SBLDS 68 (Chico: Scholars Press, 1985); C. K. Barrett, "Things Sacrificed to Idols," in *Essays on Paul* (London: SPCK, 1982), 40–59; G. D. Fee, "Εἰδωλόθυτα Once Again: An Interpolation of 1 Corinthians 8–10," *Bib* 61 (1980): 172–97; B. N. Fisk, "Eating Meat Offered to Idols: Corinthian Behavior and Pauline Response in 1 Corinthians 8–10 (A Response to Gordon Fee)," *TJ* 10 (1989): 49–70; P. D. Gooch, *Dangerous Food: 1 Corinthians 8–10 in Its Context*, SCJ 5 (Waterloo: Wilfred Laurier University Press, 1993); G. W. Dawes, "The Danger of Idolatry: First Corinthians 8:7-13," *CBQ* 58 (1996): 82–98; A. T. Cheung, *Idol Food in Corinth: Jewish Background and Pauline Legacy*, JSNTSup 176 (Sheffield: Academic Press, 1999); J. Smit, *"About the Idol Offerings": Rhetoric, Social Context and Theology of Paul's Discourse in First Corinthians*

the Corinthians' question concerning food offered to idols, agrees in principle with the "knowledgeable" (τὸν ἔχοντα γνῶσιν; 8:10)[107] that "'an idol is nothing in the world' and that 'there is no God but one'" (8:4). The "knowledgeable" faction in the congregation held the view that because an idol has no reality,[108] believers should not be concerned about potential dangers in their exposure to idol temples and festivals—the implication being that believers can participate in pagan sacrificial meals. Paul, while agreeing in principle with the claim that an idol is nothing, nonetheless detects that an oversimplification of this view could have dangerous outcomes for the former pagans. The problem at Corinth is that the "knowledgeable" are of the (wrong) perception that the Jewish stance toward idolatry that ridicules idols as nothing can exist in isolation from the other stance that views idolatry as the work of demons.[109] Paul knows that these views are inseparable (cf. 10:19-20). He, thus, pushes beyond the claim that an idol is nothing in the world to acknowledge that "even though there may be so-called gods whether in heaven or on earth—just as there are many gods and many lords—yet for us there is one God, the Father, from whom are all things and in whom we exist, and one Lord, Jesus Christ, through whom are all things and through whom we exist" (8:5-6). In other words, the God of Israel is not one god among many, for the pagan deities do not belong on the same ontological plane as God. Yet the "so-called" gods of paganism cannot simply be dismissed as nonexistent and therefore irrelevant.[110] To do so would be to put oneself in harm's way. This is the theological conviction that undergirds Paul's detailed dealing with the subject of food offered to idols.[111]

8:1—11:1, BETL 27 (Leuven: Peeters, 2000); D. E. Garland, "The Dispute Over Food Sacrificed to Idols (1 Cor 8:1—11:1)," *PRSt* 30 (2003): 173–97.

107. The oft-encountered distinction between the "strong" and "weak" in analyses of 1 Corinthians 8–10 must be rejected as importing terms and concerns from Romans 14–15 into 1 Corinthians. Paul never uses the term "strong" in 1 Corinthians 8–10.

108. We may not be in a position to speculate about the origin of this view among the Corinthian gentiles, but considering the widespread attestation of this view in Judaism (cf., e.g., 2 Kgs. 19:16-19; Pss. 96:5; 115:4-8; Isa. 37:17-20), it may not be far-fetched to suggest that the these gentiles may have acquired this view from Jewish missionaries at Corinth. It is also possible that Paul may have shared this view as part of his proclamation during one of his visits to Corinth (cf. 1 Cor. 12:2; Gal. 4:8-9; 1 Thess. 1:9).

109. Cf. 8:2: "If anyone thinks he knows something, he does not yet know as he ought to know."

110. So Wright, *Climax of the Covenant*, 128.

111. We agree with Gordon Fee that a distinction needs to be made between Paul's address to the question concerning eating sacrificial meals at idol temples (1 Cor 8:1—10:22), which Paul explicitly forbids, and eating idol food in general, that is, food sold in the *macellum* (10:23—11:1), which is ultimately a matter of indifference for Paul, except if the food is explicitly identified as previously

Paul deals with this issue from two aspects: the social aspect and the theological aspect.[112] At the social level, Paul argues that love must govern the Corinthians' conduct (8:1-3). Believers must renounce their rights to participate in sacrificial meals, because it would cause their fellow believers to fall (8:7-13).[113] The former pagans had their own *habitus*;[114] they "were accustomed" (8:7) to partaking in sacrificial meals in honor of a number of deities. None of these gods demanded exclusivity.[115] Thus, for the "knowledgeable" to continue to participate in sacrificial meals in light of their acquired knowledge that "an idol is nothing in the world" would cause those not having this knowledge (8:7) to do likewise and to assume, in effect, that the God of their new faith is just one god among many—but this in itself is a return to idolatry. Because their participation in sacrificial meals will have grave repercussions for their fellow believers, Paul argues that every believer must refuse to participate in sacrificial meals. At the theological level, Paul argues that "the knowledgeable" only know in part (8:2), for the view that an idol is nothing in the world cannot be divorced from the reality of demonic powers behind the practice. Believers cannot partake in sacrificial meals, because the gods of the pagan pantheon do exist; they are demons in disguise. Partaking in temple meals, then, is a practice of power that would expose believers to the demonic powers behind the idols. Contrary to the pagans' former customs, the God of Israel demands exclusivity; and believers' exclusive allegiance to the one God and one Lord precludes them from partaking in meals offered to other lords and other gods (8:4-6; 10:1-22).

In sum, Paul evinces both Jewish perspectives toward idolatry. On the one hand, Paul can agree with the view that that an idol is "nothing" in the world (1 Cor. 8:4); that is, an idol is lifeless, nonexistent, and impotent. The pagans in Corinth were once influenced and led astray by "mute idols" (1 Cor. 12:2). In keeping with Jewish condemnation of idolatry (Rom. 2:1-2), he can paint idolatry as a vain, misguided worship that foolishly honors the creature (human-made images or animals) rather than the Creator (Rom. 1:18-23). But, on the

---

sacrificed to an idol. See Fee, *The First Epistle to the Corinthians*, NICNT (Grand Rapids: Eerdmans, 1987), 357–63.

112. A helpful classification noted in J. Smit, "'Do Not Be Idolaters': Paul's Rhetoric in First Corinthians 10:1-22," *NovT* 39 (1997): 40–53. In the ensuing discussion we adopt Smit's distinction between the social and theological aspects of Paul's argument.

113. In 1 Cor. 9:1-27 Paul uses his own renunciation of his apostolic rights as a model for this teaching.

114. See part 1 of this study for further discussion.

115. Walter, "Christusglaube und Heidnische Religiosität," 429–30; Willis, *Idol Meat in Corinth*, 213.

other hand, Paul warns believers against food sacrificed to idols, because those who sacrifice to idols in fact sacrifice to the demons behind the idols (1 Cor. 10:19-20). Paul, nonetheless, recognizes that these two views are inseparable: what makes humans subject to impotent and dumb idols is the existence of higher powers behind the lifeless objects.

Turning our attention back to Galatians, we recognize that both of the Jewish stances toward idolatry are also combined in Gal. 4:1-11. On the one hand, the *stoicheia* are "that which are by nature not gods" (4:8); they are "weak and impotent" (4:9). But, on the other hand, the *stoicheia* are powerful enough to hold humans in bondage (4:3). And this is possible because behind the lifeless elements stand powerful forces that have co-opted the elements and enslaved those who participate in worship of the elements.

Throughout early Jewish and Christian literature, one encounters the view that God has set an angel over one or more of the four basic elements of the universe.[116] In *1 En.* 60:19–23, angels have been appointed for the correct regulation of the wind, rain, and earth:

> When the rain-wind becomes activated in its reservoir, the angels come and open the reservoir and let it out; and when it is sprayed over the whole earth, it becomes united with the water which is upon the earth; and whensoever it unites with (other waters; it unites) with the water upon the earth which is for the use of those who dwell on the earth, for it is nourishment for the earth (sent) from the Most High in heaven. So in this manner there is a measuring system for the rain given to the angels. (*1 En.* 60:21–23; cf. 60:19–20)

These angels are responsible for opening the reservoirs of winds and rain, releasing the appropriate measures in due seasons. Their work also ensures that the earth is nurtured and sustained. In the same way, four angels are set over the four winds in Rev. 7:1; the angel introduced in Rev. 14:18 is said to possess the authority over fire, and in Rev. 16:5 the angel who speaks is described as ἀγγέλου τῶν ὑδάτων ("the angel of the waters"). In addition, 2 *En.* 4:2 and 5:1 also mention the tradition of angels being set over water, and in *T. Ab.* 13:11 the archangel Purouel is said to possess authority over fire.

A fragmentary passage from Philo is worth quoting at this point. Philo, as we have seen earlier, understands the elements as inanimate matter. In another

---

116. Cf. Hilary of Poitiers, who also recognizes that angels have power over the elements (*Tract. Ps.* 61:2; 67:9). According to Jerome, many regard the elements as the angels set over the four elements (*Comm. Gal.* [PL 26:371A–D]).

passage from a fragment of his commentary on Genesis, however, Philo has this to say about the elements:

> Some of my teachers who knew the doctrines of the nature of philosophers have said that the (six) elements are earth and water, air and fire, love and hate. In the same manner, however, the prophet (Isaiah), when he speaks of the four lower wings of the seraphim—the ones that serve to cover the face and the feet—means symbolically to refer to *the hidden powers of the (first) four elements* (τῶν τεττάρον στοιχείων ἀποκρύφους δυνάμεις)." (*Deo* 127–31; emphasis mine)[117]

Whatever one makes of what Philo means by ἀποκρύφους δυνάμεις ("hidden powers"),[118] here is an explicit acknowledgement of a hidden potent force behind the inanimate matter.[119]

As with traditions concerning the Law, the traditions about angelic governance of the elements presuppose that the angels are working on God's behalf. Nonetheless, for Paul and other early Jews and Christians, when pagans worship these elements in order to participate in the numinous power behind the elements, the powers have deflected worship from the one true God and can, therefore, no longer be said to be working on God's behalf. The elements have been co-opted by higher powers whose work is enslaving.

When the evidence from Gal. 3:19-25 and Second Temple Jewish literature about the angelic mediation of the works of the Law are combined with a mirror reading of Jewish polemic against worship of the elements, it is safe to say that in Gal. 4:1-11 Paul is able to set up an equation that links two impersonal entities of Law and elements by means of hidden powers that can co-opt these entities. Herein lies the point of contact between the Law and the elements: *behind these benign impersonal entities of Law and physical elements stand higher powers who co-opt these entities in order to produce outcomes that are*

117. Passage taken from F. Siegert's reconstructed Greek text, *Philon von Alexandrien: Über die Gottesbezeichnung "wohltätig verzehendes Feuer" (De Deo)* (Tübingen: Mohr Siebeck, 1988), 30–31. (I have adopted Martyn's translation, *Galatians*, 405).

118. Cf. Siegert, *Philon*, 131.

119. Cf. Philo, *Abr.* 68–88. Philo acknowledges that there is an invisible power behind the heavenly luminaries; but for Philo, to the extent that these luminaries stay their ordained course, the invisible power is God himself. There are times, for Philo, when God employs subordinate powers to carry out a particular task, which is opposite to God's bestowing of gifts. The subordinate powers help to preserve the transcendence of God for Philo (cf. *Sacr.* 59–60; *Spec.* 1:41–50) and to guard God against evil, "so that he [God] might be looked upon as the cause of good only, and of no evil whatever antecedently" (*Abr.* 143; cf. *Cher.* 51–52).

oppressive. This helps to account for how both the Law and the elements can be spoken of as weak and impotent and yet also sufficiently powerful to enslave humanity.

Indeed, if our contention that the angels of Gal. 3:19 were working on God's behalf is correct, then another point of contact between the Law and the elements is that both are part of God's good creation. The Law is good and holy (cf. Rom. 7:12), for it stems from God's hand. So also is creation as it left God's hands (cf. Gen. 1:31). Nonetheless, the fact that pagans worship the elements show that something has gone wrong in the created order; higher powers who have fallen out of fellowship with the Creator have co-opted certain aspects of creation and in the process have deflected worship from the Creator. This point is articulated explicitly in Colossians, which is the subject of the next chapter. The powers behind the elements cannot be said to be serving their God-intended purpose, for by deflecting worship from the Creator, they have become demonic. The same can be said of the Law. The Law is good and holy, for it was instituted through angels working on God's behalf. Yet when Paul assesses the way the Law is currently functioning—driving a wedge between Jew and Gentile, increasing dissension within the community, and producing outcomes contrary to what the Law was intended to achieve—Paul detects that certain hostile powers have taken hold of the Law and are using it against God's will. Paul, looking backwards through the prism of Christ, detects that something has gone wrong in creation and with God's good Law. And in the heated polemic of Galatians, Paul has set out to demonstrate how these two phenomena are related.

Conclusion

In this chapter we have argued that Paul equates life under the Law and life under the elements, because both the Law and the elements can be co-opted by higher powers. The gentiles had their own *habitus* prior to their conversion. This *habitus* included frequenting idol temples, behind which Paul detects demonic powers. These powers had co-opted the elements and enslaved those who participated in the worship of the elements. Paul also discerns that higher powers can stand behind the Law; this is clear enough from the Law's inception (Gal. 3:19). Yet the Law has become oppressive for Gentile believers, who are being forced to take on the "works of the Law." The Law has become divisive (2:11-13), erecting a wall of separation between Jew and Gentile against God's purpose in Christ to create a unified people (3:28). Higher powers, then, are using the Law against God's purpose. To this end, Paul detects a point of contact between the demand for gentiles to take on works of the Law and the worship of the elements: higher powers are using these entities against God's intended purpose to enslave humans. In all this, however, we have to emphasize the retrospective nature of Paul's thinking. As Sanders observes, Paul moves from solution to plight not from plight to solution;[120] thus, the equivalence of life under the elements and life under the Law is apparent to Paul only in light of Christ.

Now that faith has come, believers are no longer subject to the oppressive requirements of the Law and the elements. A new source of power has arrived on the scene and is made available to believers: God has sent the Spirit of his Son into the hearts of believers, crying out "Abba Father" (4:6). It is only by means of the victory of the cross that believers are able to participate in victory over the powers that seek to co-opt the elements and the Law. In his death and resurrection, Christ enjoyed victory over the powers of this age. Therefore, by receiving Christ's Spirit, believers also participate in the victory of the cross (5:24). The Spirit of God's Son is the power that stands behind the community of believers as the community battles with the desires of the flesh (Gal. 5:16). The Spirit directs the community and forms the character of the community. This formation creates a Christian *habitus* that will guide the community's practices. When the Spirit guides the Christian community, the community will discern the hostile powers behind worship of the elements and will be governed by a new law, the law of Christ (6:2). This new law can be summed up in a single sentence: "Love your neighbor as yourself" (5:14). The love of which Paul speaks is not only grounded in but also finds its full realization in the divine reality: God's Son gave himself for our sins in order that he might redeem all who are under the Law and the *stoicheia* from the present evil age, so that all may receive adoption as "sons" (1:3-4; 4:4-5; cf. 2:20).[121] And when this self-giving love serves as the paradigm for the community's practices together with the Spirit's guidance, there will no longer be Jew nor Greek, slave nor free, male and female, for all will be *one* in Christ (3:28).

120. See Sanders, *Paul, the Law, and the Jewish People*, 68. See also Campbell, *Deliverance of God*, 883–86.

121. See Hays, "Christology and Ethics in Galatians: The Law of Christ," *CBQ* 49 (1987): 268–90.

7

Rescue from the Power of Darkness: Colossians

The author[1] of Colossians addresses his letter to a congregation that is on the verge of being led captive by an invading "philosophy" (2:8). Some teachers had prescribed a strict regimen of ascetical practices (2:16-23) and on the basis of this called into question the inclusion of others within the body of God's people (2:16, 18).[2] The invading teaching that the author assails seems to have both Jewish and non-Jewish elements. On the one hand, references to the στοιχεῖα τοῦ κόσμου (2:8, 20) and principalities and powers (2:10) suggest a pagan element to the teaching. Col. 1:27, for instance, seems to presuppose a "gentile" audience. On the other hand, references to circumcision (2:11), festivals, new moons, and Sabbaths (2:16) are evocative of a Jewish dimension to the invading teaching. These details, taken together, are perhaps an indication that the congregation was a mixed group, comprising both Jews and gentiles (cf. Acts 19:10)—in the author's own words, "circumcised and uncircumcised" (3:11).[3] Colossae was located in the valley of the Lycus River, which flowed through southwestern Phrygia and into its confluence with the Meander River. Together with Laodicea and Hierapolis (cf. Col. 4:13) these three formed the cities of the Lycus Valley.

---

1. We defer the question of authorship until the end of our detailed study. See the end of this chapter for a discussion of authorship.

2. Morna Hooker has argued that the author saw no threat at Colossae and, thus, only issued general warnings with no specific target in sight (Hooker, "Were There False Teachers in Colossae?", in *Christ and Spirit in the New Testament: Studies in Honour of C.F.D. Moule*, ed. B. Lindars and S.S. Smalley [Cambridge: Cambridge University Press, 1990], 121–34). This argument, while it is to be commended for cautioning against exaggerating the scale of the battle, swings the pendulum too far in the other direction.

3. At the very least we may infer from the letter that the mostly gentile congregation interacted with Jews in the region.

When the Lycus Valley came under the rule of the Seleucid kings of Antioch after the death of Alexander the Great (c. 323 BCE), Antiochus III (c. 223–187 BCE) settled vital centers of Phrygia and Lydia with two thousand Jewish families from Babylonia to help stabilize the region (Josephus, *Ant.* 12:3:4). The political changes in the ensuing years that saw the Lycus Valley become the Roman province of Asia did not much affect the Jewish population in the region.[4] In 62 BCE the proconsul of Asia, Lucius Valerius Flaccus, ordered the seizure of the proceeds from the annual half-shekel tax that the Jews from Asia—like all other Jews—were sending to Jerusalem for the upkeep of the temple (Cicero, *Flac.* 67–68). According to Cicero one hundred pounds of gold were impounded at Apamea and about twenty pounds were seized at Laodicea, the centers of collection. This suggests a significant Jewish population in Phrygia.[5] We are, thus, on safe grounds affirming a Jewish element to the invading teaching at Colossae. Nonetheless, the non-Jewish elements should neither be obliterated nor subsumed under the Jewish elements, since not all features in the letter are explicable within an entirely Jewish framework. This will become more apparent in the ensuing discussion below. For now we can safely note that the position the author of Colossians attacks grew out of the diverse pagan and Jewish religious matrix of the region and, as a result, was composed of both pagan and Jewish ideas and practices.

While the author does not launch his attack on the invading teaching at Colossae until chapter 2, the Christ hymn of chapter 1 (1:15-20)[6] lays the foundation for the assault on the invading teaching in chapter 2. The Christ

---

4. See F. F. Bruce, "Colossian Problems Part 1: Jews and Christians in the Lycus Valley," *BSac* 141 (1984): 3–15.

5. Cf. A. J. Marshal, "Flaccus and the Jews in Asia (*Pro Flacco* 28.67–69)," *Phoenix* 29 (1975): 139–54.

6. Colossians 1:15-20 stands out from its surrounding context. The surrounding context, for example, contains numerous participle verb forms, while Col. 1:15-20 contains only one (εἰρηνοποιήσας [1:20b]; cf. vv. 3-8, 9-14, and vv. 21-23). (See our discussion below on the participial clause of 1:20b). In addition, the personal pronouns referring to the readers and/or writer and first- or second-person verbs in the surrounding context drop out of Col. 1:15-20 (see D. G. Moo, *The Letters to the Colossians and to Philemon*, PNTC [Grand Rapids: Eerdmans, 2008], 108). Finally, this brief section contains a number of Pauline *hapax legomena*: ὁρατός; θρόνος; κυριότης; πρωτεύω; κατοικέω; ἀποκαταλλάσσω; εἰρηνοποιέω. (In addition to the words that only occur in Col. 1:15-20, we have also included in this list words that show up only in both Col. 1:15-20 and Ephesians, since it is highly plausible that Ephesians was dependent on Colossians). Thus, it is likely that Col. 1:15-20 is a piece of traditional liturgical material quoted by the author. It is also possible that this liturgical material was composed by the author himself. But the unique style and vocabulary weakens this position. As we shall argue at the end of this chapter, if Paul is the author of Colossians, then the theme of reconciliation of the powers presented in Col. 1:15-20 makes it unlikely that Col. 1:15-20 is a piece of elevated Pauline prose.

hymn is the launchpad of the author's arguments. The strategic placement of the hymn at the beginning of the letter—the letter moves from the greetings (1:1-2) to intercession and thanksgiving (1:3-11), which passes into an introduction to the hymn (1:12-14) and the hymn itself (1:15-20)—makes this hymn central to the author's purpose. It is our contention that the entire letter may be an extended reflection on the implications of confessing this hymn for the life of the Colossian believers. The author presents the hymn to the believers before refuting false claims (2:8-23) and drawing out the implication of their confession for Christian ethical living (3:1-4:6). By quoting the hymn at the beginning of the letter, the author offers the believers at Colossae an authoritative statement of truth to which these believers have given their assent and then proceeds to draw out the implications of confessing this hymn in order to refute false claims that have made their way into the Colossian church. In what follows, therefore, we begin with a detailed study of the background, setting, and structure of the Colossian hymn and proceed next to flesh out the implication of the hymn's setting and structure for our understanding of practices of power in the letter to the Colossians. In the letter to the Colossians we encounter worship of the στοιχεῖα as a practice of power that exposes devotees to the powers of darkness who have deflected worship from the one, true Creator, and baptism as the practice of power that transfers believers from the realm of darkness to the kingdom of Christ.

The Colossian Hymn: Background and Setting

The hymn[7] of Col. 1:15-20 presents a theology of the cosmic Christ, whose death, resurrection, and role in the creation and sustenance of the created order have exalted him ruler and Savior over all that exists. There are disagreements on whether the author of the letter and the author of the hymn are one and the same, though a majority of scholars view Col. 1:15-20 as an early Christian hymn or hymn-like composition with some redactions by the author

---

7. Some have questioned whether Col. 1:15-20 should be called a hymn. It certainly does not correspond to established Hebrew or Greek hymns. Cf. J. C. O'Neill, "The Source of Christology in Colossians," *NTS* 26 (1979): 87–100; J. F. Balchin, "Colossians 1:15-20: An Early Christian Hymn? The Arguments from Style," *VE* 15 (1985): 65–69; S. M. Baugh, "The Poetic Form of Col 1:15-20," *WTJ* 47 (1995): 227–44. The question of what to call it is a moot point; these verses may have been part of an early Christian hymn (cf. Col. 3:16) or confession (more on this later). We can, however, recognize that its rhythmical prose and strophic arrangement make it poetic, and we may, thus, label it as "hymnic." Cf. J. M. G Barclay, *Colossians and Philemon*, NTG (Sheffield: Sheffield Academic Press, 1997), 56–63. For the sake of simplicity, we refer to the Col. 1:15-20 piece as a hymn throughout this chapter, though the reader should imagine quotation marks around the term ("hymn") each time it is used in this chapter.

of Colossians. The question of authorship cannot be taken up at this point, since most attempts to establish whether the hymn was pre–Pauline or a Pauline composition tend to assume Pauline authorship of Colossians and then proceed to compare the vocabulary and concepts of the hymn with that of the non-disputed Pauline letters.[8] We have not assumed Pauline authorship in our study and can, therefore, return to the question of authorship only at the end of this chapter, after a detailed study of the material in its own right. Thus, at this point we provisionally accept the position that Col. 1:15-20 was an early Christian hymn that the author of Colossians includes in his epistle and redacts to hone his own message to the congregation. The real test is whether we can demonstrate this through a careful investigation of the structure of the hymn. We will take this up in the next section.

Scholars are also divided on the issue of the Jewish or non-Jewish tradition that forms the ideological background to the hymn. The main contenders are a form of Gnosticism and Jewish wisdom tradition. A number of scholars connect this hymn with Gnosticism, especially the theme of gnostic redeemer-myth.[9] According to Ernst Käsemann, the pristine hymn was a pre-Christian, gnostic myth.[10] This myth was later Christianized by redactions and incorporated into the church's baptismal liturgy.[11] The hypothesis of gnostic influence on first-century Christianity, which hails from pre-1950 German scholarship, has since fallen on hard times and has been largely discredited. The hypothesis can be defended only by digging up evidence from the second century and later and imposing it on first-century tendencies of thought. There is no evidence of the existence of a gnostic *Urmensch-Erlöser* in the times preceding, or contemporary with, first-century Christianity.[12] Some, therefore, prefer to speak of "incipient-Gnosticism" or "Gnosis"[13]—a recognition that some of the concepts and terms encountered in second-century Gnosticism were "in the air" in the first century,

---

8. See, e.g., L. R. Helyer, "Colossians 1:15-20: Pre-Pauline or Pauline?" *JETS* 26 (1983): 167–79; P. Benoit, "L'Hymne Christologique de Col 1.15-20," in *Christianity, Judaism and Other Greco-Roman Cults: Studies for Morton Smith at Sixty*, ed. J. Neusner (Leiden: Brill, 1975), 226–63; P. Ellingworth, "Colossians i. 15-20 and Its Context," *ExpTim* 73 (1961–62): 252–53.

9. See, e.g., R. S. Barbour, "Salvation and Cosmology: The Setting of the Epistle to the Colossians," *SJT* 20 (1967): 257–71; J. H. Burtness, "All the Fullness," *Dialog* 3 (1964): 257–63; F. B. Craddock, "'All Things in Him': A Critical Note on Col. I. 15-20," *NTS* 12 (1965): 78–80; R. Bultmann, *Theology of the New Testament* (Waco, TX: Baylor University Press, 2007 [orig. 1951–5]), 1:175–80.

10. E. Käsemann, "A Primitive Christian Baptismal Liturgy," in *Essays on New Testament Themes* (Philadelphia: Fortress Press, 1982 [orig. 1964]), 149–68.

11. Käsemann believes that 1:12-14 is a Christian liturgical introduction to the pre-Christian hymn; and that τῆς ἐκκλησίας (1:18) and διὰ τοῦ αἵματος τοῦ σταυροῦ αὐτοῦ (1:20) are both Christian interpolations into the hymn.

although inchoate.[14] This is also a recognition that Christianity and Gnosticism arose out of the same matrix and, thus, shared some of the same motifs and terms, without having to posit dependence or influence. J. Fossum, for example, relates the concept of Christ as the "image of the invisible God" to gnostic (and Jewish) mystical hypostatization of the divine image in Gen. 1:26.[15] Fossum's study shows the influence of Judaism on Gnosticism at its inception and the existence of Jewish-gnostic speculations about creation that were close to the claims made about Christ in the Colossian hymn.[16]

The vast majority of scholars, however, look to the OT and Jewish wisdom tradition as the background to the motifs and vocabulary of the hymn.[17] C. F. Burney contends that Col. 1:15-18 is a Pauline midrashic commentary on the first word in Gen 1:1, בראשית, based on the presentation of Wisdom in Prov. 8:22-31.[18] Burney insists that πρωτότοκος πάσης κτίσεως (Col. 1:15) is a direct reference to Prov. 8:22; and that Paul moves from applying ראשית in Prov. 8:22 to Christ to a development of the same term as used in the creation account of Genesis. Paul, according to Burney, gives three interpretations of the Hebrew preposition ב: "in" ("in him were created all things"); "by" ("all things were created through him"); "into" ("all things were created into him," that is, as its goal). The substantive ראשית is then offered four explanations: "beginning" (Christ is before all things); "sum total" (all things are summed up in Christ); "head" (Christ is the head of the church); "firstfruits" (Christ is the firstfruits of

---

12. See C. Colpe, *Die religionsgeschichtliche Schule: Darstellung und Kritik ihres Bildes vom gnostichen Erlösermythus*, FRLANT 78 (Göttingen: Vandenhoeck & Ruprecht, 1961); E. M. Yamauchi, *Pre-Christian Gnosticism: A Survey of the Proposed Evidences*, 1st ed. (Grand Rapids: Eerdmans, 1973).

13. See R. Yates, "Colossians and Gnosis," *JSNT* 27 (1986): 49–68.

14. See R. McL. Wilson, "Slippery Words: II. Gnosis, Gnostic, Gnosticism," *ExpTim* 89 (1978): 296–301.

15. J. Fossum, "Colossians 1.15-18a in the Light of Jewish Mysticism and Gnosticism," *NTS* 35 (1989): 183–201.

16. See Barclay, *Colossians and Philemon*, 65–66.

17. The literature is vast; in addition to Burney, Mann, Wright and Beasley-Murray's studies in the ensuing discussion, see, e.g., C. F. D. Moule, *The Epistles of Paul the Apostle to the Colossians and to Philemon*, CGTC (Cambridge: Cambridge University Press, 1957), 59; P. T. O'Brien, *Colossians, Philemon*, WBC 44 (Waco, TX: Word Books, 1982), 32–57; F. F. Bruce, "Colossian Problems Part 2: The 'Christ Hymn' of Colossians 1:15-20," *BSac* 141 (1984): 99–111; L. R. Helyer, "Cosmic Christology and Col 1:15-20," *JETS* 37 (1994): 235–46; J. Behr, "Colossians 1:13-20: A Chiastic Reading," *SVTQ* 40 (1996): 247–64; J. S. Lamp, "Wisdom in Col 1:15-20: Contribution and Significance," *JETS* 41 (1998): 45–53; O'Neill, "Source of Christology in Colossians," 87–100. For a survey, see Helyer, "Recent Research on Col 1:15-20," *Grace Theological Journal* 12 (1992): 51–67.

18. C. F. Burney, "Christ as the ΑΡΧΗ of Creation," *JTS* 27 (1926): 160–77.

the dead).[19] For Burney, then, the main aim of the hymn is to show that in all senses Christ fulfills all of the meanings of בראשית.[20]

Burney's work has garnered support in the studies of F. Manns[21] and N. T. Wright,[22] both of whom acknowledge their indebtedness to Burney and extend his findings further.[23] Wright, for example, argues for the poem to be situated within the matrix of both Jewish wisdom tradition and the entire Jewish monotheistic worldview. He observes that Burney overlooks ἀρχή, which is the most obvious translation of ראשית (cf. LXX Gen. 1:1; Prov. 8:22-31). According to Wright, just as in Jewish monotheistic traditions creation reaches its climax in the election of Israel, so also in Col. 1:15-20 the celebration of creation climaxes in the creation of a new people through the resurrection of Jesus. Wright also observes that Burney fails to draw the link between εἰκὼν in Col. 1:15a and Gen. 1:26 (and Wisd. of Sol. 7:26), which highlights the creation of humans. Wright asserts that Israel is the creator's true humanity and this vocation of Israel becomes focused on the Messiah. In sum, according to Wright, when these modifications are added to Burney's proposal, we detect in the Colossian hymn a celebration of creational and covenantal monotheism.[24] We also note P. Beasley-Murray's study, which locates the hymn within Christian interpretation of several OT passages.[25] Beasley-Murray finds that Gen. 1:26-28, with its themes of "image" and "dominion," dovetails well with the focus of the Colossian hymn. In addition, ὅτι ἐν αὐτῷ εὐδόκησεν πᾶν τὸ πλήρωμα κατοικῆσαι is best understood in light of passages such as Ps. 67 (68):17 OG, where the temple is described as the dwelling place of God: εὐδόκησεν ὁ θεὸς κατοικεῖν ἐν αὐτῷ (that is, Mount Zion). In the Colossian hymn Christ is assigned the role of the Jerusalem temple.[26] In the end, while Beasley-Murray acknowledges the influence of Jewish speculation about Wisdom and Adam on the formation of this hymn, he also asserts that the driving force behind the hymn is the Christian confession of Jesus as Lord.[27]

19. Ibid., 174–76.

20. Ibid., 175.

21. F. Manns, "Col. 1, 15-20: Midrash Chrétien de Gen. 1, 1," *RevScRel* 53 (1979): 100–10.

22. N. T. Wright, "Poetry and Theology in Colossians 1.15-20," *NTS* 36 (1990): 444–68.

23. So also W. D. Davies, *Paul and Rabbinic Judaism* (Mifflintown, Pa: Sigler, 1998 [orig. 1948]): 150–52, who finds in Burney's study an example of rabbinic material in Paul.

24. Wright, "Poetry and Theology," 458.

25. P. Beasley-Murray, "Colossians 1:15-20: An Early Christian Hymn Celebrating the Lordship of Christ," in *Pauline Studies: Essays Presented to Professor F. F. Bruce on his 70th Birthday*, ed. D. A. Hagner and M. J. Harris (Grand Rapids: Eerdmans, 1980), 169–83.

26. Ibid., 177.

27. Ibid., 179.

The above parallels do not prove that these traditions or speculations were the source of the Colossian hymn. At best, we may conclude that the hymn echoes Jewish wisdom motifs and protognostic themes, or that Jewish wisdom motifs and protognostic themes provide close analogies to the Colossian hymn. Nonetheless, as noted by Bruce Vawter, "[The hymn] is not explained wholly by either of them and in part it is in conflict with both of them."[28] For example, the hymn affirms the goodness of the created order—as God's own handiwork in Christ, while Gnosticism saw the created order as inherently flawed and sought to escape it. In addition, in Jewish wisdom literature, Wisdom is never said to be the image of God; Wisdom is described as the image of God's perfect goodness (Wisd. of. Sol. 7:26).[29] Wisdom is also the personification of a divine attribute or the Torah. For the early Christians, however, as witnessed in the Colossian hymn, Christ was not personified; Christ was a person, the incarnate God on earth.[30] The hymn, then, without a perfect home in Jewish wisdom tradition or early protognostic thought, must be understood as a poetic reflection on the church's experience of the risen Christ.

The hymn may have had its origins in the liturgy of the early church. Some of the themes celebrated in the hymn may have had wider circulation in first-century Christian circles, as attested by Heb. 1:2-3, John 1:1-5, Rev. 1:5, 3:14.[31] Most scholars, therefore, agree that this hymn was part of an early Christian liturgy. But the setting of this liturgy is uncertain. E. Lohmeyer posited a setting of the Lord's Supper for this hymn, according to which Paul extends to Christ in Col. 1:13-20 a cosmic redeemer motif with origins in the Jewish ritual for the Day of Atonement.[32] Echoes of the Lord's Supper are thin at best, however; and there are no direct allusions to the Lord's Supper in the entire letter.[33] Käsemann has proposed a baptismal setting for the hymn. He points to the formulation τοῦ υἱοῦ τῆς ἀγάπης αὐτοῦ (1:13), which he sees as a paraphrase of the words spoken to Jesus at his baptism (Mark 1:11), and baptismal motifs, such as deliverance from darkness and translation into Christ's kingdom and

---

28. B. Vawter, "The Colossians Hymn and the Principle of Redaction," *CBQ* 33 (1971): 62–81.

29. See Fossum, "Colossians 1.15-18a," 187. For parallels in Wisdom tradition, see Prov. 8:22-31; Wisd. of Sol. 1:7, 7:22–27, 8:1, 8:12–14, 9:9; Bar. 3:38; Sir. 1:4, 24:4–11, 43:26. See also Philo, *Leg.* 1:43; *QG* 2:118, 4.97; *Virt.* 62; *Ebr.* 30–31; *Her.* 189, 199; *Fug.* 109, 112. Discussion in Lamp, "Wisdom in Col 1:15-20," 50–53.

30. Cf. Bruce, "The 'Christ Hymn' of Colossians 1:15-20," 101.

31. The parallels from Rev 3:14 are intriguing for the fact that the Loadicean church addressed in the Apocalypse was also situated in the Lycus Valley.

32. E. Lohmeyer, *Die Briefe an die Kolosser und an Philemon*, 12 Aufl. (Göttingen: Vandenhoeck & Ruprecht, 1961), 40–68.

33. Cf. Käsemann, "Primitive Christian Baptismal Liturgy," 44.

forgiveness of sins.[34] Käsemann's view assumes that the Christianized hymn begins at v. 12;[35] in fact, he draws all his baptismal imagery from 1:12-14. It is difficult to regard 1:12-14 as part of the hymn, however.[36] The shift from the personal references to the Colossian believers in 1:12-14 to the absence of direct references in 1:15-20 makes it unlikely that vv. 12-14 were part of the hymn. In addition, most of the themes sounded in 1:12-14 are picked up again in 1:21-23 after the citation of the hymn. We are, therefore, inclined to view 1:12-14 as stemming from the author's own hand. Thus, despite the allusions to baptism in other parts of the letter (e.g., 2:11-13; 3:1), we cannot be confident about the baptismal setting of the hymn, though this remains an attractive possibility. All we might be able to say with confidence is that the hymn was used in early Christian worship or instruction. That the author chooses to quote this hymn at the beginning of the letter may, therefore, reveal a plan to begin with an authoritative tradition that the believers have already professed or regularly profess. By reminding them of their own confession, the author is able to proceed to show the believers what this profession means for their daily lives and practices.

In what follows we hope to defend the latter claim through a close examination of the structure of the Colossian hymn. We lay out the structure of the hymn and hope to show that the original hymn reveals a chiastic structure with a few redactions by the author of Colossians. It is our contention that these redactions provide an important window into what the author is doing in the rest of the letter, especially as it relates to the principalities and powers. We cannot be confident in our ability to entirely reconstruct the original hymn; parts of it may be lost to us. But enough of the hymn remains (with its strophic patterns and thematic peculiarities) for us to attempt this reconstruction and draw some inferences. This we will attempt in the next section.

THE STRUCTURE OF THE HYMN

J. M. Robinson has provided a detailed study of the structure of the Colossian hymn.[37] Robinson investigates the liturgical features of the hymn, the parallels between the strophes, and divergences in style in order to detect possible redactions. The result is a balanced hymnic composition with two even parts

---

34. Ibid., 44–45.

35. See ibid., 153–54. See also Lohmeyer, *Die Kolosser und an Philemon*, 40–68; J. Behr, "Colossians 1:13-20: A Chiastic Reading," 247–49.

36. On the possible background of 1:12-14, see G. S. Shogren, "Presently Entering the Kingdom of Christ: The Background and Purpose of Col 1:12-14," *JETS* 31 (1988): 173–80.

37. J. M. Robinson, "A Formal Analysis of Colossians 1 15-20," *JBL* 76 (1957): 270–87.

that deal equally with cosmic and soteriological concerns. Nonetheless, as some commentators have pointed out,[38] the balance detected by Robinson is more superficial than substantive. For example, when Robinson places the strophes side by side, ὅς ἐστιν εἰκὼν τοῦ θεοῦ τοῦ ἀοράτου finds a correspondence in ὅς ἐστιν ἀρχή;[39] and the correspondence to ὅτι ἐν αὐτῷ ἐκτίσθη τὰ πάντα ἐν τοῖς οὐρανοῖς καὶ ἐπὶ τῆς γῆς in 1:16 is ὅτι ἐν αὐτῷ εὐδόκησεν πᾶν τὸ πλήρωμα κατοικῆσαι in 1:19, with τὰ πάντα and πᾶν τὸ πλήρωμα providing the crucial link between these lines. Despite the repetitions of formulas and catchwords, when the parallels are probed the correspondence between them are merely verbal, not substantive.

If, as we have argued in the previous section, the hymn had its origin in the liturgy of the church, then content would be a more decisive factor in shaping the hymn than strophic or metric symmetry.[40] Demands of content would have played as crucial a role in the formation of this hymn as demands for structural symmetry. Thus, while attempts to structure this hymn based on strophic patterns and metric balance are fruitful, our starting point for excavating the hymn must be the content or themes of the hymn, since verbal parallels are not necessarily a reliable index to conceptual foundations. In what follows, then, we attempt to delineate the structure of the hymn based on its content. We have bracketed lines that we believe to be redactional on the part of the author of Colossians.

> A ὅς ἐστιν εἰκὼν τοῦ θεοῦ τοῦ ἀοράτου
> B πρωτότοκος πάσης κτίσεως
> C ὅτι ἐν αὐτῷ ἐκτίσθη τὰ πάντα
>   a ἐν τοῖς οὐρανοῖς
>   b καὶ ἐπὶ τῆς γῆς
>   b´ τὰ ὁρατὰ
>   a´ καὶ τὰ ἀόρατα
>   b´ εἴτε θρόνοι εἴτε κυριότητες
>   a´ εἴτε ἀρχαὶ εἴτε ἐξουσίαι
> C´ τὰ πάντα δι᾽ αὐτοῦ καὶ εἰς αὐτὸν ἔκτισται
> B´ καὶ αὐτός ἐστιν πρὸ πάντων
> C´ καὶ τὰ πάντα ἐν αὐτῷ συνέστηκεν

38. See, e.g., N. Kehl, *Der Christushymnus im Kolosserbrief: eine motivgeschichtliche Untersuchung, zu Kol. 1, 12–20* (Stuttgart: Katholisches Bibelwerk, 1967): 40–50.

39. Robinson notes that both εἰκὼν and ἀρχή are designations of the Logos in Philo (Robinson, "Formal Analysis," 275–76).

40. A point also noted by Vawter, "The Colossians Hymn and the Principle of Redaction," 70–71.

[D <u>καὶ αὐτός ἐστιν ἡ κεφαλὴ τοῦ σώματος τῆς ἐκκλησίας</u>]
Β΄ ὅς ἐστιν ἀρχή
    πρωτότοκος ἐκ τῶν νεκρῶν
    ἵνα γένηται ἐν πᾶσιν αὐτὸς πρωτεύων
Α΄ ὅτι ἐν αὐτῷ εὐδόκησεν πᾶν τὸ πλήρωμα κατοικῆσαι
    καὶ δι᾽αὐτοῦ ἀποκαταλλάξαι τὰ πάντα εἰς αὐτόν
[Ε <u>εἰρηνοποιήσας διὰ τοῦ αἵματος τοῦ σταυροῦ αὐτοῦ δι᾽αὐτοῦ</u>]
    b εἴτε τὰ ἐπὶ τῆς γῆς
    a εἴτε τὰ ἐν τοῖς οὐρανοῖς

The hymn consists of two strophes (1:15-17 and 1:18-20),[41] both signaled by the phrase ὅς ἐστιν. The first strophe begins with the assertion that Christ is the image of the invisible God (1:15) and the second strophe returns to the relationship between God and Christ in 1:19-20. We have, thus, marked as A the lines expressing the theme of the relationship between God and Christ in the hymn. The theme of the priority of Christ is the distinguishing mark of the lines we have designated as B in the hymn. These lines are held together mostly by the preposition or prefix πρό (cf. πρωτότοκος; πρὸ πάντων; πρωτεύων).[42] The lines we have marked as C highlight the sphere of Christ: Christ as the sphere within which creation comes into being and exists. These lines place prepositions such as ἐν, διά, and εἰς before Christ (cf. ἐν αὐτῷ; δι᾽ αὐτοῦ; εἰς αὐτὸν).

Lines D and E are additions to the hymn by the author. Both of these lines can be eliminated without losing the structural flow of the hymn. The two strophes of the hymn (1:15-17 and 1:18b-20) contain three lines each that are introduced by the relative pronoun ὅς and the conjunctions ὅτι and καὶ. These introductory words establish a pattern of ὅς, ὅτι, καὶ clauses in both strophes of the hymn:

---

41. Some scholars break the hymn into more divisions. Some see in this hymn three stanzas, two main strophes with a middle verse as a connecting stanza; see, e.g., R. P. Martin, *Colossians and Philemon*, NCB (Grand Rapids: Eerdmans, 1973): 55–57; E. Schweizer, "The Church as the Missionary Body of Christ," *NTS* 8 (1961): 1–11; Schweizer, *The Letter to the Colossians* (Minneapolis: Augsburg, 1982 [orig. 1976]): 53–88; Schweizer, "Col 1:15-20," *RevExp* 87 (1990): 97–104; Beasley-Murray, "An Early Christian Hymn," 169–83. Others opt for an essentially bipartite structure; see, e.g., Robinson, "Formal Analysis," 270–87; Ellingworth, "Colossians i.15-20 and Its Context," 252–53. C. Masson, for his part, detects five strophes of four lines each; Masson, *L'Épître de saint Paul aux Colossiens*, CNT 10 (Neuchâtel: Delachaux, 1950): 97–107.

42. The only exception to this rule is the use of ἀρχή in 1:18; but ἀρχή also denotes the priority of Christ. Its use with πρωτεύων in 1:18 conveys the idea that Christ has set a precedence for others to follow.

ὅς ἐστιν εἰκὼν (1:15)
ὅτι ἐν αὐτῷ (1:16)
καὶ αὐτός ἐστιν (1:17)
ὅς ἐστιν ἀρχή (1:18)
ὅτι ἐν αὐτῷ (1:19)
καὶ δι᾽ αὐτοῦ (1:20)

Line D disrupts the ὅς, ὅτι, καὶ pattern of both strophes by introducing an additional καὶ line at the end of the first strophe (καὶ αὐτός ἐστιν ἡ κεφαλὴ τοῦ σώματος τῆς ἐκκλησίας). Line D also introduces the theme of the church into a hymn that has so far had a cosmic referent and, thereby, disrupts the consistent cosmological orientation of the hymn. In 1:24 the author will repeat the claim that the church is Christ's body: ὑπὲρ τοῦ σώματος αὐτοῦ ὅ ἐστιν ἡ ἐκκλησία. We cannot endorse here the oft-encountered view that the author only inserts "the church" into this line, and, thereby, reinterprets the original hymn, which viewed Christ as the head of the cosmic body.[43] As N. Kehl has insightfully pointed out, if the original hymn viewed σώματος as the cosmos of which Christ is the head, then it is difficult to see how the cosmos still requires reconciliation through Christ.[44] Kehl, however, insists that the entire line was part of the original hymn, a position difficult to maintain in the face of the objections we have raised. It seems to us less demanding to the imagination to regard all of line D as the author's addition to the original hymn.

Line E must also be regarded as an addition by the author of Colossians; it is an expansion of the theme of reconciliation introduced in the second strophe of the hymn. The poem flows smoothly from καὶ δι᾽ αὐτοῦ ἀποκαταλλάξαι τὰ πάντα εἰς αὐτόν to εἴτε τὰ ἐπὶ τῆς γῆς εἴτε τὰ ἐν τοῖς οὐρανοῖς. The insertion of εἰρηνοποιήσας διὰ τοῦ αἵματος τοῦ σταυροῦ αὐτοῦ δι᾽ αὐτοῦ[45] into this stanza situates the site of reconciliation at the cross and, thereby, introduces the theme of the cross into a strophe whose main concern is the resurrection.[46] In

---

43. See, e.g., E. Schweizer, *The Church as the Body of Christ* (Atlanta: John Knox, 1964), 65; Käsemann, "Primitive Christian Baptismal Liturgy," 151–53; Martin, *Colossians and Philemon*, 59; Fossum, "Colossians 1.15-18a," 197. Against this position, see Beasley-Murray, "An Early Christian Hymn," 180, who notes that ancient writers often drew a contrast between the cosmic body and the divine soul (cf. Plato, *Timaeus* 34–36; *Philebus* 30; Cleanthes, *Hymn to Zeus*, fragment 537; Alexander Aphrodisiensis, *De Mixtone* 12:609) or between the cosmic body and the divine reason (cf. Xenophon, *Memorabilia Socratis* 1:4; 9:14; Aristotle, *De Anima* 1:5), not between the head and the body.

44. Kehl, *Christushymnus*, 39–45.

45. The awkward phrase δι᾽ αὐτοῦ is not contained in B D* F G I L. It is strongly attested, however, in P⁴⁶ ℵ A C D¹. It is likely that a scribe deliberately omitted the phrase because of the ambiguity it creates.

46. This addition is analogous to the addition of θανάτου δὲ σταυροῦ to the Christ hymn of Phil 2:8.

addition, the form of line E is unlike anything encountered in the entire hymn; the participial style finds formal parallels in the author's explication of the second strophe of the hymn in 2:13-15 (especially, 2:13c; 2:14a; 2:14c; 2:15a; 2:15c).[47]

It is our contention that both of these additions to the hymn are crucial for understanding the aims of the author in Colossians. These redactional passages must be given serious consideration in their own right, for they witness to the manner in which the author of Colossians proceeds to unfold his own theology in the rest of the letter. The additions to the hymn attune readers to the author's own thoughts and aims, a claim that we hope to unpack later in this chapter.

Finally, it is important not to split the phrases θρόνοι εἴτε κυριότητες and ἀρχαὶ εἴτε ἐξουσίαι, because the phrase ἀρχαὶ καὶ ἐξουσίαι occurs in complete form in the rest of the letter (2:10; 2:15) and elsewhere in the NT (Eph. 1:21, 3:10, 6:12; 1 Cor. 15:24).[48] When these phrases are kept complete, the result is an inner chiastic structure in 1:16: abb′a′b′a′. We will discuss the implications of this inner structure in the next section.

When lines D and E are set aside (for the moment[49]), the original hymn[50] reveals the following structure: ABC{abb′a′b′a′}C′B′C′B′A′{ba}. The overarching structure is ABCC′B′C′B′A′, and this larger structure finds confirmation in the fact that the inner structure in 1:16 exhibits the pattern abbaba, which parallels the BCCBCB structure of the larger poem. In short, as we see it, attention to both the content and strophic patterns of the hymn reveals the following overarching and inner structures of the Colossian hymn:

ABCC′B′C′B′A′
{abb′a′b′a′}{ba}

The implications of this structure will be unpacked in the next section.

THE MESSAGE OF THE HYMN'S STRUCTURE

A number of important points, germane to our topic, can be gleaned from the hymnic structure we detected in the previous section. It is important to point these out before investigating in detail the author's additions to the hymn.

First, the abb′a′b′a′ inner structure in 1:16 that mirrors the BCC′B′C′B′ pattern of the overarching structure of the hymn suggests that the "thrones" and

47. See Robinson, "Formal Analysis," 284.

48. Cf. Titus 3:1.

49. As noted, these lines cannot be discarded without losing crucial aspects of the author's theology.

50. That is, the original hymn as has been handed down to us. It is possible that elements of the hymn have been eliminated. But we have enough of the hymn left to be able to investigate it as it stands.

"lordships" be viewed as earthly, visible authorities, while the "principalities" and "powers" refers to invisible, heavenly powers:

a ἐν τοῖς οὐρανοῖς
b καὶ ἐπὶ τῆς γῆς
b΄ τὰ ὁρατὰ
a΄ καὶ τὰ ἀόρατα
b΄ εἴτε θρόνοι εἴτε κυριότητες
a΄ εἴτε ἀρχαὶ εἴτε ἐξουσίαι

The terms θρόνοι and κυριότητες hail from political terminology of the period. The word θρόνος refers to the seat upon which a person of high honor sits, and it is used in Greek literature, the OG, and the NT as a reference to kings and their royal power (e.g., Herodotus, *Hist.* 1:14:3; Xenophon, *Cyr.* 6:1:6; Gen. 41:40; Exod. 11:5, 12:29; Judg. 3:20; 1 Sam. 2:8; 2 Sam. 3:10, 7:13, 16; 1 Kgs. 1:13, 17; Luke. 1:32, 52; Acts 2:30).[51] Similarly, while κυριότης can denote cosmic supernatural powers,[52] it may also refer to human rulers (e.g., Memnon, *Hist.* [*FGH* 434 fgm 1:4:6]).[53] Contrary to common opinion, then, according to the hymn's structure, these terms are to be taken as a reference to earthly rulers, not supernatural rulers. And their combination with the invisible, heavenly powers (ἀρχαί, ἐξουσίαι) presents us with a comprehensive vision of reality; Christ's lordship penetrates all spheres of the cosmos—earthly and heavenly.

Second, the larger ABCC΄B΄C΄B΄A΄ pattern reveals what it means for Christ to be the image of God. In this structure, the claim that Christ is the image of the invisible God (ὅς ἐστιν εἰκὼν τοῦ θεοῦ τοῦ ἀοράτου; 1:15) comes full circle in the confession that in Christ all the πλήρωμα ("fullness") was pleased to dwell (ὅτι ἐν αὐτῷ εὐδόκησεν πᾶν τὸ πλήρωμα κατοικῆσαι; 1:19). The subject of the verb εὐδόκησεν (1:19) is most likely πᾶν τὸ πλήρωμα, not Christ, since ἐν αὐτῷ is a reference to Christ. The word πλήρωμα shows up in the Valentinian gnostic system as a technical term for the totality of the thirty aeons or supernatural forces that served as a link between the immaterial, uncreated God and the material, created world.[54] It would be anachronistic, however, to suggest that the hymn is drawing on this gnostic concept, since

51. The term is also used for the throne of God (Ps. 9:4, 7; 11:4; 45:6; 47:8; Isa. 66:1; Matt. 5:34, 23:22; Acts 7:49; Rev. 1:4, 3:21; 20:11); of Christ (Heb. 1:8; Rev 3:21); of the elders (Rev. 4:4, 11:16); of the twelve apostles (Matt. 19:28; Luke 22:30; Rev. 20:14); and of Satan (Rev. 2:13).

52. Cf. *1 En* 61:10; *2 En* 20; *T. Sol.* 8:6.

53. In 2 Pet. 2:10 and Jude 8 the term seems to denote the glory of God that false teachers have rejected or despised.

54. Cf. Hippolytus, *Haer.* 6.29; Epiphanius, *Pan.* 31:10:13, 31:13:6, 31:16:1.

evidence of the early (or widespread) use of the word as a technical term is lacking.[55] It is much more likely that the Valentinians were dependent on Colossians and Ephesians[56] for their appropriation of the term.[57] The word is very common in both the OT and NT, where it is used in a variety of nontechnical senses often to denote the contents of the land, including human inhabitants (that is, the "fullness" of the earth and sea or "totality" of population), or the fullness of eschatological consummation.[58] Thus, as noted by C. F. D. Moule, one would need to have strong evidence to cause one to look to an external source for its primary meaning.[59]

Col. 1:19 corresponds almost exactly to Ps. 67:17 (OG): εὐδόκησεν ὁ θεὸς κατοικεῖν ἐν αὐτῷ. If the hymn has this psalm in mind,[60] whereby Christ replaces the holy temple, then πλήρωμα may be a periphrasis for ὁ θεός ("God").[61] This is certainly how the author of Colossians understands this sentence of the hymn. When the author inserts the line εἰρηνοποιήσας διὰ τοῦ αἵματος τοῦ σταυροῦ αὐτοῦ δι'αὐτοῦ into the hymn, the masculine participle (εἰρηνοποιήσας) assumes a masculine subject, despite the neuter πᾶν τὸ πλήρωμα. This is confirmed in 2:9, where the author repeats the idea expressed in 1:19 but makes the reference to God explicit: "In him [Christ] all the fullness of the deity dwells bodily" (ἐν αὐτῷ κατοικεῖ πᾶν τὸ πλήρωμα τῆς θεότητος σωματικῶς). Col. 1:19 is best interpreted in light of Col. 2:9 and Ps. 67:17 (OG) and must, therefore, be construed as "in him [Christ] all the fullness [of the deity] was pleased to dwell."[62] God dwelt in Christ in all his fullness.[63] The overarching structure of the hymn, then, explains how Christ can be said

55. Cf. P. D. Overfield, "Pleroma: A Study in Content and Context," *NTS* 25 (1979): 384–96.

56. Cf. Eph. 1:22-23; 3:19; 4:12-13.

57. See G. B. Caird, *Paul's Letters from Prison: In the Revised Standard Version* (Oxford: Oxford University Press, 1976), 180–81.

58. See, e.g., 1 Chron. 16:32; Ps. 23:1 (OG); 88:12 (OG); 95:11 (OG); 97:7 (OG); Jer. 8:16; 47:2 (OG); Ezek. 19:7; 30:12; Rom. 11:12, 25; Gal. 4:4.

59. Moule, *Colossians and Philemon*, 166.

60. It may not be sheer coincidence that the author of Ephesians quotes Ps. 67:18 (OG) after expressing the idea of the unity of the Godhead (Eph. 4:4-7) and expands on this verse, including in his interpretation the notion of the πληρώματος τοῦ χριστοῦ (4:13).

61. Cf. Caird, *Paul's Letters from Prison*, 181.

62. The RSV and NRSV are therefore correct to insert the words "of God" into 1:19, even though these words are not present in the Greek text. In light of the above discussion, according to the sense of the main clause in 1:19 δι'αὐτοῦ in 1:20 must refer to Christ (cf. 1:22) and εἰς αὐτόν in 1:20 must refer to God, even if taken in a reflexive sense as expressing εἰς ἑαυτόν. So also J. B. Lightfoot, *Saint Paul's Epistles to the Colossians and to Philemon: A Revised Text with Introductions, Notes, and Dissertations* (London: Macmillan, 1904 [orig. 1875]), 158. The masculine εἰς αὐτόν in 1:20 could also imply that the hymn itself intends for πλήρωμα to stand for a masculine. See Moule, *Colossians and Ephesians*, 70–71.

to be the visible image of the invisible God: in Christ God in all his fullness was pleased to dwell. According to the structure of the hymn we have set out in this chapter, *as the image of God*, Christ has made the invisible God visible to humanity, because in Christ the fullness of the deity dwells. Christ is the visible embodiment of the invisible God, for in Christ God has manifested his being and nature.[64]

The OT presentation of the divine image is instructive for our understanding of Colossians. We first encounter the concept of "the image of God" in Gen. 1:26-27:

> Then God said, "Let us make man in our image (בצלמנו; κατ᾽εἰκόνα ἡμετέραν LXX), according to our likeness (כדמותנו; καθ᾽ὁμοίωσιν LXX); and let them have dominion over the fish of the sea, and over the birds of the air, and over the cattle, and over all the earth, and over every creeping thing that creeps upon the earth." So God created man in his own image (בצלמו), in the image of God (בצלם אלהים; κατ᾽εἰκόνα θεοῦ LXX) he created him; male and female he created them. (Gen. 1:26-27)

According to the creation account humans were created in the "image" of God, according to God's "likeness." In the book of Genesis the words צלם ("image") and דמות ("likeness") are so intertwined that they appear to be synonymous and seem to be interchangeable.[65] In Gen. 5:3, for example, both terms are used in reverse order to Gen. 1:26 to describe Seth's relationship to Adam. Thus, in Gen. 5:1 the LXX translates the word דמות ("likeness") with εἰκών, the common Greek word for "image":

> In the day when God created man, he made him in the likeness of God (בדמות אלהים; κατ᾽εἰκόνα θεοῦ LXX). (Gen. 5:1)

---

63. The notion that the fullness of the Godhead dwells in the body of Christ may not be far from John's claim that "the Word became flesh" (John 1:14); for the Word, who "was God" (John 1:1), made the invisible Father visible in the incarnation (John 1:18; 14:9). Cf. A. C. Cotter, "The Divinity of Jesus Christ in Saint Paul," *CBQ* 7 (1945): 259–89, esp. 264–65; cf. Wright, "Poetry and Theology," 459–64.

64. Cf. Bruce, "The 'Christ Hymn' of Colossians 1:15-20," 101–8; D. Tripp, "ΚΑΤΟΙΚΗΣΑΙ, ΚΑΤΟΙΚΕΙ (Colossians 1:19, 2:9): Christology, or Soteriology Also?" *ExpTim* 116 (2004): 78–79.

65. An excavation at Tell Fekheriyeh in Syria in 1979 produced a ninth-century BCE statue with an inscription of Aramaic cognate equivalents of both terms (צלם and דמות) as synonymous terms designating the statue. See A. R. Millard and P. Bordreuil, "A Statue from Syria with Assyrian and Aramaic Inscriptions," *BA* 45 (1982): 135–41.

Most modern scholars agree that the syntax of Gen. 1:26-28 in the context of Gen. 1:1—2:3 presents a functional, purpose-oriented understanding of the *imago Dei*: being made in the image of God, humans are to exercise control in creation on God's behalf.[66] It is also becoming an accepted view among modern scholars that the OT democratization of the divine image served as ideological critique to the view propagated in Ancient Mesopotamian or Egyptian literature that only the king or the Pharaoh was made in the image of God.[67] J. Richard Middleton, for example, has written a compelling book in which he argues that, read contextually in its historical background, the *imago Dei* of Gen. 1:26-27 serves as a polemic against ancient Near Eastern notions of humanity and kingship, and, by extension, against the use of such notions to justify an oppressive social order.[68] Drawing on widely recognized connections between Mesopotamia and the primeval history (Genesis 1–11)—such as parallels between Genesis 1 and Babylonian literature, especially *Enuma Elish*—Middleton argues that within the Mesopotamian worldview, the *imago Dei* legitimated the social hierarchy, one in which the lower classes served the gods precisely by serving the king, who was made in the image of the gods. The *imago Dei*, then, in the Genesis narrative, served as ideological critique intended to subvert an oppressive social system by democratizing the ancient Near Eastern royal ideology.

But the OT presentation of the divine image did not only serve to undermine ANE monarchic propaganda. Important for our purpose is the recognition that the OT concept of the divine image also served as a polemic against pagan idolatry, which was condemned for confining the divine presence to lifeless "images." This is made all the more likely, when we notice that the term צלם ("image") is a common Hebrew term for idols (Num. 33.52; 2 Kgs.

---

66. See, e.g., I. Hart, "Genesis 1:1—2:3 As Prologue to the Book of Genesis," *TynBul* 46 (1995): 315–36, at 317–24; R. Davidson, *Genesis 1–11*, 3d ed. CBC (Cambridge: Cambridge University Press, 1980), 25; G. M. Landes, "Creation and Liberation," *USQR* 33 (1978): 79–89; D. J. A. Clines, "The Image of God in Man," *TynBul* 19 (1968): 53–103; D. T. Asselin, "The Notion of Dominion in Gen 1–3," *CBQ* 16 (1954): 277–94. The divine function of ruling creation embedded in the concept of the *imago Dei* is predicated of Christ in the Colossian hymn through the titles attributed to Christ. The titles that denote priority ("firstborn," "beginning," or "ruler") also celebrate the supreme position of Christ over the created order. (So also "head").

67. See P. Bird, *Missing Persons and Mistaken Identities: Women and Gender in Ancient Israel* (Minneapolis: Fortress Press, 1997), 134–38.

68. J. Richard Middleton, *The Liberating Image: The Imago Dei in Genesis 1* (Grand Rapids: Baker, 2005). See also M. G. Brett, *Genesis: Procreation and the Politics of Identity* (New York: Routledge, 2000), 24–48.

11:18; 1 Chron. 13:17; Ezek. 7:20, 16:17, 23:14; Amos 5:26).[69] The OT prophets derided pagan nations for limiting the divine presence to mere representations. The prophet Isaiah, for instance, berates the nations for idolatry because God has no "likeness" (דמות):

> To whom then will you liken (דמה) God, or what likeness (דמות) compare with him? The idol? (Isa. 40:18-19)

From the prophet's perspective, the divine presence cannot be represented by a lifeless, motionless object—"an image that will not move" (Isa. 40:20). According to A. Schüle, the development of the concept of humans as (living) bearers of the "image of God" was contemporaneous with prophets like Second Isaiah and Ezekiel, who spoke with contempt of idols:

> It is remarkable that very much at the same time when prophets like Deutero-Isaiah and Ezekiel poured scorn on the idols, the idea of the "Image of God" was very much alive in another strand of biblical tradition that is probably contemporaneous with these prophets: according to the priestly telling of creation in Gen 1,1-2,4a it is not lifeless matter, not a man-made statue, but humans as living beings that are envisioned to be indeed the true image of God. It is important to see these different approaches as part of the same time and of the same historical discourse.[70]

The "image of God" discourse became a polemic against the idolatry of the nations surrounding Israel. Against the ancient Near Eastern cults, which located the divine presence in the shape of images, the OT declares that it is not lifeless objects, but living beings that bear the divine image.

This OT anti-idolatrous presentation of the divine image is instructive for understanding certain aspects of the letter to the Colossians, for the author of Colossians presents Christ—the image of the invisible God; the dwelling of the fullness of the deity—as a polemic against the στοιχεῖα τοῦ κόσμου. In Col. 2:8-9, the philosophy that is "according to" the στοιχεῖα τοῦ κόσμου is contrasted with that which is "according to" Christ. The στοιχεῖα are

---

69. Cf. W. Kaiser Jr., who argues that צלם means "carved or hewn statue or copy"; Kaiser Jr., *Towards an Old Testament Theology* (Grand Rapids: Zondervan, 1978), 76. See also G. H. van Kooten, *Paul's Anthropology in Context: The Image of God, Assimilation to God, and Tripartite Man in Ancient Judaism, Ancient Philosophy and Early Christianity*, WUNT (Tübingen: Mohr Siebeck, 2008), 3-4.

70. A. Schüle, "Made in the 'Image of God': The Concepts of Divine Images in Gen 1-3," *ZAW* 117 (2005): 1-20, on 9.

characterized by a philosophy and *empty* deceit (according to the author) that involves *human* tradition (2:8). The antithesis of the στοιχεῖα τοῦ κόσμου is Christ (2:9): in Christ dwells the *fullness* of the *deity* bodily—as such, in contrast to the human origin of the philosophy, the gospel of Christ is a spiritual wisdom of divine origin (cf. 1:9; 2:2-3), and to encounter Christ through the preaching of this gospel is to encounter God. In Christ believers are being brought to "fullness"—in contrast to the emptiness that characterizes the human traditions associated with the στοιχεῖα. And, finally, Christ is the head of all principalities and powers—which is to say that whatever the στοιχεῖα may be or whatever stands behind the στοιχεῖα, Christ is immeasurably superior to them. The placement of the στοιχεῖα in proximity to the ἀρχή καὶ ἐξουσία suggests that the στοιχεῖα and the principalities and powers are somehow related. It may be unwise, however, to equate the στοιχεῖα with the principalities and powers.[71] We have argued this position fully in our chapter on Galatians. Here we only summarize the important aspects of our findings that are germane to our discussion. The reader is encouraged to consult our chapter on Galatians for most of the evidence on the στοιχεῖα.

The common usage of τὰ στοιχεῖα in the time prior to and contemporary with the NT was to refer to the four basic elements of air, water, fire, and earth, from which the universe was believed to be composed.[72] By the end of the first century, the full expression, τὰ στοιχεῖα τοῦ κόσμου, had become a fixed way of referring to the four elements.[73] This should, therefore, be the starting point of discussion when the full expression is used in the NT, and Colossians is no exception (cf. Col. 2:8; 2:20). We noted in our chapter on Galatians that Jewish authors often caricatured pagan religion as mere worship of the natural elements.[74] Nonetheless, as we argued, it is not the natural elements per se that pagans worshiped; rather those who worshiped the elements discerned a higher power behind the elements and participated in the numinous power behind the elements.[75] This is confirmed in the belief that angelic powers had been set

71. Pace G. Bornkamm, "The Heresy of Colossians," in *Conflict at Colossae: A Problem in the Interpretation of Early Christianity, Illustrated by Selected Modern Studies*, ed. F. O. Francis and W. A. Meeks (Missoula, Mont.: Society of Biblical Literature, 1973), 123–45, at 123–24.

72. Cf. Wisd. of Sol. 7:17; 13:1–9; 19:18–22; Philo, *Opif.* 131; *Her.* 197; 209; 226; *Contempl.* 3–5; *Mos.* 1:96; 2 Pet. 3:10-12.

73. See J. Blinzler, "Lexikalisches zu dem Terminus τὰ στοιχεῖα τοῦ κόσμου bei Paulus," in *Studiorum Paulinorum Congressus Interntionalis Catholicus (1961)*, AnBib 1718 (Rome: Pontifical Biblical Institute, 1963), 429–44; D. Rusam, "Neue Belege zu den στοιχεῖα τοῦ κόσμου," *ZNW* 83 (1992): 119–25.

74. Cf. 2 Kgs. 19:16-19; Ps. 96:5; Ps. 106:37; 115:4-8; Isa. 37:17-20; Philo, *Contempl.* 3–5; Wis. of Sol.13:1–4.

over one or more of the four basic elements.[76] Higher powers were believed to stand behind the elements, and when these powers deflected worship from the one true God and creator to creation, then in the view of early Jewish and Christian writers these powers were no longer functioning as God's emissaries and were to be regarded as demonic (cf. Deut. 32:17; *1 En.* 99:7; *T. Sol.* 26:7; 1 Cor. 10:20). Thus, when the author of Colossians admonishes believers against the "philosophy" which is "according to the elements of the cosmos" (κατὰ τὰ στοιχεῖα τοῦ κόσμου) and "not according to Christ" (οὐ κατὰ Χριστόν), and warns them against being "made captives" (συλαγωγέω) by this philosophy (2:8), we are to hear these words as a recognition that the powers behind the elements pose a threat to the lordship of Christ by deflecting worship from Christ. And by co-opting the elements and deflecting worship from Christ, these powers can no longer be said to be on God's side. They must be classed with the powers of darkness (2:13). Thus, by submitting to the στοιχεῖα τοῦ κόσμου believers risk exposing themselves to dark powers and being "made captives" by these powers. As in the letters to the Galatians and Corinthians, we encounter in Colossians idolatry as a practice of power that exposes humans to forces of darkness.

When the Colossian hymn speaks of "all things" needing to be reconciled to God in Christ (1:20), we catch a glimpse of why even material creation needs to be reconciled to God: higher powers have co-opted certain aspects of the created order and in the process have deflected worship from the Creator. To this end, Brian Walsh is certainly on the right track by insisting on reading Col. 2:8-23 as an address to idolatry, even though, in his own words, the "text does not spell out the problem so explicitly in terms of idolatry."[77] Walsh observes that "Paul's" rhetoric against the Colossian philosophy mirrors the OT rhetoric against idolatry. For example,

> While Hos 5:4 insists that idolatry carries a spirituality that makes repentance and the knowledge of God impossible, Col 2:8 describes this as a captivating philosophy, closing down options for a full-

---

75. We may detect some of this caricaturing of pagan worship taking place in Col. 2:20-23. The rules concerning what may not be touched or tasted depict those under bondage to the elements as investing ordinary materials ("things destined to perish with use" [2:22]) with religious significance. This can hardly reflect an accurate picture of pagan worship, for it does not acknowledge the numinous power behind the objects. Some Jewish texts, however, do acknowledge powerful forces behind idolatry. Cf. Deut. 32:17; *1 En.* 99:7; *T. Sol.* 26:7.

76. See, e.g., *1 En.* 60:19-23; *2 En.* 4:2; 5:1; Rev. 7:1; 14:18; 16:5; *T. Ab.* 13:11.

77. B. Walsh, "Late/Post Modernity and Idolatry: A Contextual Reading of Colossians 2:8—3:4," *ExAud* 15 (1999): 1-17, on 8.

orbed discipleship. Paul's depiction of this philosophy as empty deceit (2:8), a shadow without substance (2:17) that has a mere appearance of wisdom (2:23), clearly echoes earlier biblical judgement on idolatry as worthless, vanity, and nothingness (Isa 44:9; Jer 2:4; Pss 97:7, 115:4-7, 135:15-18). And while the prophets love to remind idolaters that their idols are constructed by humans (Isa 2:8, 41:6-7, 44:11; Jer 10:1-9; Hos 8:4, 6, 13:2; Hab 2:18; Ps 115:4), the apostle repeatedly claims that this philosophy is a human tradition (2:8), a human way of thinking (2:18) that imposes human commands and teachings (2:20).[78]

Walsh's observation confusingly conflates the pagan and Jewish (e.g., 2:16-18) elements in the position the author of Colossians is attacking. Nonetheless, on his reading of Col. 2:8 in terms of idolatry, his hunch is correct. We have already shown this through our own treatment of the στοιχεῖα τοῦ κόσμου and the OT anti-idolatrous appropriation of the divine image.

For the author of Colossians, Christ is the response to the στοιχεῖα τοῦ κόσμου. In Christ dwells the fullness of the deity; and because the fullness of the deity dwells in Christ, Christ has filled the deep chasm between God and humans and between the heavenly realm and the earthly realm. No longer do the former pagans need to go through some lifeless image to access the deity behind the image. Christ, as the image of the invisible God, makes God himself present to the world.[79] In this argument, the author of Colossians stands within a long history of OT tradition that argued that the divine presence was not contained in lifeless images but in living beings,[80] which for the author of Colossians is Christ.

In short, the structure of the Colossian hymn has immense implications for how we understand certain aspects of the letter. The overarching structure of the hymn together with the OT treatment of the divine image point to the following results: the OT anti-idolatrous presentation of the divine image finds an instructive parallel in the way the author of Colossians draws on his understanding of Christ as the image of God to combat the στοιχεῖα τοῦ κόσμου. Christ is the image of the invisible God, for in him dwells the fullness of the deity bodily. By his resurrection (1:18), Christ has ushered in the new creation and new humanity, which is embodied in the community of believers.

78. Ibid., 9.

79. Cf. Irenaeus, *Haer.* 4:4:2; 4:6:6.

80. Cf. Theodoret of Cyrus, *Interpretation of the Letter to the Colossians* (PG 82:597bc–598bc); Gregory of Nazianzus, *Orations* 30:20.

And when believers conform to Christ, they will themselves be transformed into the image of the Creator (Col. 3:10).[81]

AUTHOR'S REDACTION OF THE HYMN

We now turn our attention to the implications of the important additions to the hymn for our understanding of the letter and the principalities and powers. In our study of the structure of the hymn, we argued that the author has added two lines to the original Christian hymn: καὶ αὐτός ἐστιν ἡ κεφαλὴ τοῦ σώματος τῆς ἐκκλησίας and εἰρηνοποιήσας διὰ τοῦ αἵματος τοῦ σταυροῦ αὐτοῦ δι'αὐτοῦ. It is our contention that these additions are paradigmatic for how the author proceeds to unpack his own theology in the rest of the letter. In what follows we hope to demonstrate this assertion as it relates to the principalities and powers.

FROM COSMIC TO LOCAL

In 1:18, the author inserts a line that claims that the church is Christ's body and that Christ is the head of this body: καὶ αὐτός ἐστιν ἡ κεφαλὴ τοῦ σώματος τῆς ἐκκλησίας. Up until the point of insertion, the hymn has an unbroken cosmological focus. By inserting this line at this point, the author reveals a tendency that will be encountered later in the letter as he lays out his own theology to the Colossians: moving from the larger cosmic drama to specific, local application. By inserting a line about the church, the author narrows the cosmic drama to the local arena. This is a move that we will see the author making in the rest the letter; the author narrows themes and events of cosmic dimensions to specific application in the life of the church or believers, thereby implying that the cosmic drama has ecclesiological implications. Whatever is happening on the cosmic stage can also be conceived of in terms of the church's own experiences and encounters. Two examples of this move are germane to our topic: (1) the author applies the cosmic reconciliation stated in the hymn (1:20) to the Colossian believers in 1:21-23; and (2) the author connects believers' stripping of the fleshly nature (2:11-12; cf. 3:9) to Christ's divesting himself of the powers in 2:15.

(1) RECONCILIATION OF THE POWERS AND BELIEVERS

In 1:21-23 the author of Colossians shifts the focus of reconciliation from the cosmic drama to the human social order by applying the theme of cosmic reconciliation to the Colossian believers. The Greek verb ἀποκαταλλάσσω

---

81. Cf. D. H. Johnson, "The Image of God in Colossians," *Didaskalia* 3, no. 2 (1992) 9–15.

("to reconcile") occurs in the NT only in Col. 1:20 and 1:22 and the expansion of these passages in Eph. 2:16.[82] That the word is not attested in literature prior to the NT suggests that the author of Colossians has adopted the word straight from the hymn and is expanding on the thought expressed in the hymn. If the hymn speaks of God's intention to reconcile all things to himself through Christ, according to the author, this cosmic reconciliation hoped for in the hymn has already begun, for it has been realized in the life of the Colossian believers. Believers who were once "alienated" from God and were "enemies" of God have been reconciled to God through the death of Christ. They have personally experienced what is spoken of in the hymn, for Christ has presented them holy and blameless before God (1:22); they now live a life that is in conformity to the gospel preached to them (1:23), and have full access to God's presence. Believers are living in the new creation; the eschatological reality that would encompass all creatures has already been inaugurated in the church.

This hermeneutical application of the theme of reconciliation expressed in the hymn indicates that the author envisions the cosmic reconciliation professed in the hymn as something akin to the present lot of believers:[83] "*You also* (καὶ ὑμᾶς) were formerly alienated and enemies in your mind, in your evil works; but now he has reconciled you in the body of his flesh through his death to present you holy and faultless and blameless before him" (1:21-22). God will "make peace" with "all things"—on earth and in the heavens (1:20),[84] all that are presently "alienated" from God and "enemies" of God—including the principalities and powers. This suggests that a disruption has occurred in the created order. All things were created in Christ (1:16) and creation as it left the hands of the Creator was very good (cf. Gen. 1:31). The powers, then, were once a part of God's good creation; they were once on God's side. But they have become estranged from God and whatever fellowship or relationship they had with God is now disordered. It is not clear when and how the powers strayed from God.[85] What the author knows—and in keeping with other early Christian

---

82. Cf. 2 Cor. 5:18-20; Rom. 5:1-11; 11:15.

83. This point is crucial for our understanding of the reconciliation of the powers.

84. It is likely that the stress on both Christ's humanity and divinity in the letter stems from the recognition that both the divine and human are essential to achieve the reunion between the two separate worlds, divine and human. Cf. Athanasius, *Orations Against the Arians* 3:26:31 (NPNF2 4:410); Chrysostom, *Homilies on Colossians* 3 (NPNF1 13:272); Cyril of Jerusalem, *Catechetical Lectures* 13.33; Gregory of Nyssa, *Against Eunomius* 12:4 (NPNF2 5:241); Ephrem the Syrian, *Commentary on Tatian's Diatessaron* 14.

85. Some have attributed the cause of the disruption to "sin." See, e.g., H. Bavinck, *Reformed Dogmatics*, vol. 3: *Sin and Salvation in Christ*, ed. John Bolt (Grand Rapids: Baker Academic, 2006), 472; G. L. Shultz Jr., "The Reconciliation of All Things in Christ," *BSac* 167 (2010): 442–59, esp. 450–51.

and Jewish writers—is that some aspects of the created order have been co-opted by higher powers who have in the process deflected worship from the Creator. This for the author of Colossians is prima facie evidence that something has gone wrong within the created order. The powers can no longer be said to be God's messengers; they have strayed and will, therefore, need to be restored and reunited with their Creator.

We have argued that εἰρηνοποιήσας διὰ τοῦ αἵματος τοῦ σταυροῦ αὐτοῦ δι᾽ αὐτοῦ is the author's addition to the hymn to flesh out further the meaning of reconciliation and locate the cross as the site of inauguration of this reconciliation. The author of Colossians envisions a time when God will "make peace" with the principalities and powers through Christ. This concept of reconciliation of the powers is a theological conundrum, and commentators have, as a result, been reluctant to extend the reconciliation expressed in Colossians to the principalities and powers. One way to circumvent the problem has been to limit the scope of τὰ πάντα ("all things") in 1:20. It has been suggested, for example, that "all things" only pertains to human beings, since it is humans who have exchanged God's glory for images.[86] This view, however, overstates the human role in the fallenness of the created order and ignores the cosmic dimension of the disruption within creation. In addition, 1:16 strongly establishes that the scope of τὰ πάντα is much more comprehensive and cannot be limited to the human world alone; according to 1:16, "all things" must at the very least include the principalities and powers.[87]

Another attempt to escape the problem is the tendency to draw a distinction between the nature of the reconciliation envisioned for believers and that envisioned for the powers. Commentators tend to speak of "pacification" of the spiritual powers, whereby the peace effected by the cross is imposed on the powers.[88] The powers do not willingly surrender to Christ's lordship but are forced to do so by Christ's power, which is mightier than their own. This view, however, hardly fits the description of "making peace"; rather it fits more

This may be more a reading of Romans 5–8 into Colossians than careful attention to the message of Colossians. The cause of the disruption is not stated in Colossians.

86. See, e.g., Kehl, *Christushymnus*, 163–65; I. H. Marshall, "The Meaning of Reconciliation," in *Unity and Diversity in the New Testament: Essays in Honor of George E. Ladd*, ed. R. A. Guelich (Grand Rapids: Eerdmans, 1978), 117–32, esp. 126–27.

87. So also Origen, *On First Principles* 4:4:3. Cf. D. J. Moo, *The Letters to the Colossians and to Philemon*, The Pillar NT Commentary (Grand Rapids: Eerdmans, 2008), 134; R. A. Peterson, " 'To Reconcile to Himself all Things': Colossians 1:20," *Presbyterion* 36 (2010): 37–46.

88. See, e.g., F. F. Bruce, "Colossian Problems Part 4: Christ as Conqueror and Reconciler *BSac* 141 (1984): 291–302; Bruce, "The 'Christ Hymn' of Colossians 1:15-20," 109–10; Shultz, "Reconciliation of All Things," 452–58.

the description of "bringing order." In this case, the powers cannot be said to have been reconciled, for if they are brought to "order" against their will, the powers will gladly rebel again when the opportunity presents itself. And this can only with great difficulty be made to conform to the picture envisioned in Colossians. The picture envisioned is that all things come to recognize Christ as their creator and Lord and willingly surrender to his rulership. The purpose of reconciliation is to draw all things back to God and to recognize and worship Christ as Lord of all. Such acknowledgment and worship cannot be forced.

Also, if as we have argued the author moves from the cosmic to the local in applying the reconciliation of the powers to the believers, then the reconciliation of the powers must mirror that experienced by believers. The attempts, therefore, to make a distinction between believers and the powers may be theologically expedient, but it is exegetically unwarranted. Colossians makes a daring claim concerning the powers that is encountered nowhere else in the Pauline corpus: because the powers were created in Christ and were originally a part of God's good creation, the powers, who are now alienated from God and enemies of God, will be restored by means of reconciliation through Christ.

(2) BAPTISM AND CHRIST'S ENCOUNTER WITH THE POWERS AT THE CROSS

The dominion of darkness is the lot of the world apart from Christ. The powers still operate in the world and are still capable of causing great damage in the world. That is why believers need to be "transferred" into a new realm (1:13). In this new setting believers are not under the dominion of the powers of darkness and the powers cannot interfere with believers' relationship to God (1:21-23; 2:13-15).[89] The transfer into the kingdom of Christ takes place in baptism, the event in which one of the main footholds of the powers of darkness—the fleshly nature (τοῦ σώματος τῆς σαρκός; cf. 2:18)—is stripped (ἀπέκδυσις) and buried (2:11-12; cf. 3:9). The fleshly nature[90] belongs to the old world order that is fading with the arrival of Christ's kingdom, the world order ruled by the powers of darkness and from which believers have been rescued (1:12-14). To be transferred into the kingdom of God's Son (1:13) means leaving the fleshly nature behind with the old age. It is in baptism that believers are stripped of their old nature and existence and are transferred into a new sphere with a new nature (2:11-12; 3:5-10).[91] The author portrays baptism as a kind of spiritual circumcision performed by Christ (τῇ περιτομῇ τοῦ Χριστοῦ);[92] baptism is a

---

89. Cf. Rom 8:31-39. See Caird, *Paul's Letters from Prison*, 173.

90. Cf. Käsemann, "Primitive Christian Baptismal Liturgy," 162: "The Adamic body tyrannized over by the demonic rulers of this aeon. The strength of the cosmic powers collapses with the collapse of their form of existence."

circumcision made without hands (περιτομῇ ἀχειροποιήτῳ), in which not a part of the physical body is taken off but the fleshly nature of the believer is put off (2:11-12).[93] Conversely, the uncircumcision of the fleshly nature (τῇ ἀκροβυστίᾳ τῆς σαρκὸς) is a state of alienation from God (2:13). In baptism, believers are moved from this state of alienation to a state of reconciliation with God. Baptism is the practice of power that transfers believers from the sphere of darkness to the sphere of light. In this new setting the life of believers is "hid with Christ in God" (3:3), beyond the reach of the powers. To cast off the fleshly nature also means putting off the practices of the old existence (3:9): sexual immorality, impurity, lust, evil desires, idolatry, anger, rage, malice, slander, filthy, lies (3:5, 8). The practices that issue from the new person include compassion, kindness, humility, gentleness, patience, forbearance, forgiveness, and love (3:12-14).

As we have argued in previous chapters, the story of Christ's encounter with the powers on the cross undergirds Christian baptism as a practice of power—an activity that rescues believers from the powers of darkness. The author of Colossians connects believers' experience in baptism with Christ's own experience with the powers on the cross (2:14-15) and thereby shows how believers' own experience in baptism is grounded in the experience of Christ at the cross.[94] He does this by electing to use the same root of the word used to describe believers' shedding of the old nature in baptism (2:11; 3:9) for Christ's encounter with the powers—ἀπεκδύομαι (2:15). The word occurs only in Colossians in the entire biblical corpus. Thus, our understanding of the word

---

91. Cf. Caird, *Paul's Letters from Prison*, 192: "[In baptism] the old nature dies, to be replaced by the new manhood of the risen Lord. Thus, the baptized person no longer lives in that old order over which the principalities and powers hold sway, nor does he owe them any continuing allegiance."

92. So also Chrysostom, *Homilies on Colossians* 6 (*NPNF1* 13:285).

93. Despite the parallel in 1:22, τοῦ σώματος τῆς σαρκός in 2:11 must have believers as its subject, not Christ, since it lacks the possessive pronoun αὐτοῦ present in 1:22. The notion that Christ strips off his physical body at his death (see, e.g., C. A. A. Scott, *Christianity according to St. Paul* [Cambridge: Cambridge University Press, 1927], 36) smacks of Gnosticism (cf. *Gos. Truth* 19:35–21:6) and would be in conflict with the antignostic theology the author has presented so far, especially by taking over a hymn that celebrates the goodness of creation. It must, therefore, be rejected. The fleshly nature that believers put off must not be equated with their physical bodies, whose putting off at baptism would imply physical death for all believers. See Caird, *Paul's Letters from Prison*, 194: "The sphere in which the world-rulers exercise their authority is not the physical universe, as contrasted with some disembodied, spiritual existence, but the old world order corrupted by sin, as contrasted with the world which God has designed and is bringing into being through the reconciling power of Christ."

94. Cf. Ambrose, *Concerning Repentance* 2:2:9 (*NPNF2* 10:346): "This, too, is plain, that in him who is baptized the Son of God is crucified, for our flesh could not eliminate sin unless it were crucified in Jesus Christ."

in the context of 2:14-15 must be consistent with its use in 2:11 and 3:9. In both 2:11 and 3:9 it has the sense of "putting off" the fleshly nature or old person that belongs with the old world order. Thus, it may be inaccurate to translate the same word in the context of 2:14-15 as "disarm," which would mean that "God or Christ disarmed the principalities and powers." The author's selection of the word for 2:15 is deliberate and is in keeping with his tendency to move from the larger cosmic drama to local application. His use of the word intends to signal a connection between Christ's encounter with the powers at the cross and the reality accomplished for believers in the event of baptism. To this effect, Christ does not "disarm" the powers in the cross per se—the powers are still potent and continue to do damage in the world. Rather, Christ "divests himself of" the sphere of the powers' dominion in the cross (cf. 1:12-13). In his resurrection Christ entered his own kingdom (1:13), the domain where his sovereignty is unqualified.[95] And it is Christ's divesting himself of the powers that is reenacted in the lives of the believers during baptism, when believers, stripped naked before the baptismal water, divest themselves of the fleshly nature that belongs to the old world order governed by the principalities and powers. Baptism reenacts an already-accomplished reality achieved through the cross of Christ; believers are transferred from the domain of the powers to the kingdom of Christ. Conforming to Christ's template, believers die and are buried with Christ and are raised to life into full possession of their new lot in Christ.

In the baptismal water believers are washed—a reflection of their cleansing from sin. According to the author, while believers were dead in their transgressions, God raised them to life with Christ (in baptism) by forgiving them all their sins (2:13; cf. 1:14). At the cross, God or Christ wiped away the χειρόγραφον that was against the believers, set it aside from their midst, and nailed it to the cross (2:14). Col 2:14-15 is a notorious *crux interpretum*.[96] Is God the subject of the verbs throughout these verses or is Christ the subject? What is the cheirographon? Some commentators are inclined to view God as the subject throughout 2:14-15, because they see a change of subject from God in 2:13 to Christ in 2:14-15 as harsh and unwarranted. This, however, creates considerable exegetical difficulties that render these verses almost unintelligible. Some of the difficulties may be eliminated when Christ is made the subject of some of the verbs, if not all the verbs, in 2:14-15. As the one who was nailed to the cross and

---

95. Even though the hymn celebrates the universal lordship of Christ, this is an eschatological hope and an objective reality only for believers, who know that despite the fact that the powers can still do a great deal of damage in the world, they are subject to Christ and will one day come to acknowledge Christ as Lord. Cf. 1 Cor. 15:24-28.

96. Virtually every word in these verses is subject to dispute.

confronted the powers on the cross, Christ seems to be the more natural subject of the verbs ἐξαλείφω and αἴρω in 2:14. In 2:15 also it is best to regard Christ as the subject, since the verb ἀπεκδυσάμενος is in the middle voice and should therefore be reflexive. As we have argued in this section, in light of the author's use of the same verb in his baptismal reflection to represent believers' shedding of the old nature belonging to the old world order that is under influence of the powers (3:9; 2:11-12), Christ should be viewed as the proper subject of this verb: in his death and resurrection, Christ "divested himself of" the domain of the principalities and powers and was transferred into his own kingdom of light (1:12-13). As we shall also see shortly, Christ should also be taken as the subject of verb θριαμβεύω; it is Christ who "triumphs" over the principalities and powers in the cross, not God. Nowhere in the NT is God's confrontation with the powers at the cross recounted.

Even if we are to accept Christ as the subject of the verbs in 2:14-15, it is still not entirely clear how τὸ χειρόγραφον τοῖς δόγμασιν ὃ ἦν ὑπεναντίον ἡμῖν should be understood. The word *cheirographon* literally means "handwriting." It refers to a handwritten document that serves as a certificate of indebtedness, signed by the debtor.[97] Proposals for understanding the cheirographon in Colossians include an IOU, the Mosaic Law, or Christ himself. The view that the cheirographon is an IOU posits that it is a certificate of debt autographed by mankind to God.[98] This view has in its favor the fact that it fits with the ancient usage of the word, though it is not clear how all humanity came to acknowledge its debt to God. The view that the cheirographon is the Mosaic Law[99] has the ability to account for the distinctively Jewish elements of the letter within the context in which the word appears. But this view has to be nuanced, since it is hard to see how the entire Law may be set aside and nailed to the cross. The third option regards the cheirographon as Christ himself. This view derives from Jean Daniélou's discovery of a Jewish-Christian exegesis of Col. 2:14 in *Odes Sol.* 23:5-9 and *Gos. Truth* 19:35–20:25, in which the Heavenly Book[100] is identified

---

97. See Tob. 5:3; 9:5. Cf. Philem. 1:19.

98. See, e.g., Chrysostom, *Homilies on Colossians* 6 (*NPNF1* 13:286); Chrysostom, *Baptismal Instructions* 3:21 (*ACW* 31:63); Ambrose, *Jos.* 4:19 (FC 65:201); Moule, *Colossians and Philemon*, 97–99; Barclay, *Colossians and Philemon*, 83.

99. See, e.g., Theodore of Mopsuestia, *Commentary on Colossians* (*Theodori episcopi Mopsuesteni* 1:290); Severian of Gabala, *Pauline Commentary from the Greek Church* (NTAbh 15:323-24); Caird, *Paul's Letters from Prison*, 195; Wright, *The Epistles of Paul to the Colossians and to Philemon*, TNTC (Grand Rapids: Eerdmans, 1986), 110–14.

100. Cf. Rev. 5:1-3.

with Christ.[101] Blanchette has carried this view further by arguing that the cheirographon of Col 2:14 represents Christ himself.[102] Against this view, it is difficult to see how Christ may be said to have been "against us" (ὑπεναντίον ἡμῖν). How could the cheirographon be set aside by being nailed to the cross if it represents Christ? And how could Christ, being against us and being set aside on the cross, be the same one to achieve redemption and reconciliation for the world on the cross?

In our view, while none of the above interpretations of the cheirographon is complete to stand on its own and bear the full weight of the meaning of the term, each view contains an element of truth and, as such, none should be entirely dismissed. Some aspect of each of these three interpretations must be incorporated—though in a highly qualified sense—since any specific background for the use of the term in Christian literature is lacking.[103] It is best, nonetheless, to begin with the understanding of the cheirographon as the Mosaic Law, since the overall context in which the word appears seems to point in this direction.[104] In the discussion leading up to the mention of the cheirographon, the author reinterprets Christian baptism in terms of circumcision (2:11-13); and the discussion of the cheirographon (2:14-15) immediately leads into warnings against festivals, new moons, and Sabbaths (2:16). Thus, cheirographon as the Mosaic Law suits well the overall context, which is rife with allusions to Judaism. In addition, the Mosaic Law is said to have been "written" by Moses in Deut. 31:9, and in Exod. 31:18 the Law of the covenant is said to have been "written" with the finger of God. Neither case fits perfectly with the idea of cheirographon as signed by the debtor; nonetheless, both passages fit with the fundamental definition of cheirographon as "handwriting."[105]

The use of the phrase τὸ χειρόγραφον τοῖς δόγμασιν ὃ ἦν ὑπεναντίον ἡμῖν within the context of 2:14-15 suggests, however, that it may be too simplistic to say that cheirographon represents the entire Mosaic Law. This

---

101. See J. Daniélou, *The Theology of Jewish Christianity*, vol. 1 of *The Development of Christian Doctrine before the Council of Nicaea* (London: Darton, Longman and Todd, 1964), 192–204. On the Heavenly Book, see L. Koep, *Das himmlische Buch in Antike und Christentum: Eine religionsgeschichtliche Untersuchung zur altchristlichen Bildersprache* (Bonn: Peter Hanstein, 1952).

102. O. Blanchette, "Does the Cheirographon of Col 2,14 Represent Christ Himself?," *CBQ* 23 (1961): 306–12.

103. This is also a caution against pushing the metaphor to the limit; it breaks down.

104. The author of Ephesians seems to have understood the cheirographon as the Law (Eph. 2:15).

105. The term δόγματα is used as a reference to the Law in Philo, *Leg* 1.55; *Gig.* 52; Josephus, *C. Ap.* 1.42; *3 Macc.* 1:3.

view has to be nuanced in light of the principalities and powers. It may be best to view the cheirographon as *the Mosaic Law in the hands of the powers*. There seems to be an echo in Col. 2:14-15 of the Jewish tradition concerning accusing angels, chief among whom is Satan, "the accuser" (cf. Job 1:6-9; Zech. 3:1-2;[106] *Jub.* 17:16; 48:15-18; *1 En.* 40:9; Rev. 12:10. Cf. CD 16:3–6; 4Q225 2:2:13). The work of these angels is predicated on the assumption of the existence of a divine, natural Law and a sense of cosmic "justice." These angels, on the basis of human transgression of the divine Law, accuse humans before God with the aim of getting the just Judge to punish humans for their transgressions.[107] In many of these references, gentiles are presumed to be under a similar sentence, since the Jewish Law was often viewed as corresponding to the divine natural Law.[108] When the divine Law falls into the hands of the powers the result is a blind execution of "justice" that is merely punitive in nature. The powers use the legal requirements of the Law against humanity.[109] It is this Law—co-opted by the powers—that Christ raises up high on the cross, from the midst

---

106. Lightfoot sees in the metaphor of Christ divesting himself of the powers the vision concerning Joshua the high priest in Zech 3:1-5, who, having been accused by Satan, divests himself of his filthy garments and is clothed with festal apparel (*Saint Paul's Epistles to the Colossians and to Philemon*, 189).

107. We have argued in our treatment of 1 Corinthians 5 that a similar tradition underlies Paul's question in Rom 8:33, "Who will bring accusations against God's elect?"

108. Cf. *T. Naph.* 3:2–5: "Sun, moon and stars do not alter their order; thus you should not alter the Law of God by the disorder of your actions. The gentiles, because they wandered astray and forsook the Lord, have changed the order, and have devoted themselves to stones and sticks, patterning themselves after wandering spirits. But you, my children, shall not be like that: in the firmament, in the earth, and in the sea, in all the products of his workmanship discern the Lord who made all things, so that you do not become like Sodom, which departed from the order of nature" (H. C. Kee's translation in *OTP* 1:812). Cf. Rom. 2:14-16. This is where the definition of cheirographon as an IOU may be incorporated. Cf. Moule, *Colossians and Philemon*, 97: "The bond in question here is signed by men's consciences: for a Jew, it is his acceptance of the revealed Law of God as an obligation to abide by; for the Gentile, it is a corresponding recognition of obligation to what he knows of the will of God."

109. In G. Steindorf's published Akhmimic manuscript of the *Apocalypse of Elijah* (c. third century CE), the accusing angels write down all the sins of mankind in the heavenly book, labeled here as "cheirographon" (*Apokalypse des Elias* 4:1–20 in G. Steindorff, *Die Apokalypse der Elias, eine unbekannte Apokalypse, und Bruchstücke der Sophonias-Apokalypse*, TUGAL 17 [Leipzig: J. C. Hinrichs, 1899], 38–43). This document cannot be used as evidence for the cheirographon as a heavenly book in Col. 2:14—as some have erroneously argued (see, e.g., H. Weiss, "The Law in the Epistle to the Colossians," *CBQ* 34 (1972): 294–314, esp. 302, 310)—since it is late and has been Christianized. What is important to note is that the existence of a heavenly book to record wrongdoing is contingent upon the existence of the Law; there is no heavenly record without the Law. This point is made clearly in *Jub.* 30:21–23, where the angel says to Moses: "All of these words I have written for you, and I have commanded you to speak to the children of Israel that they might not commit sin or transgress the ordinances or break the covenant which was ordained for them so that they might do it and be written down as friends. But if they

of believers (αὐτὸ ἦρκεν τοῦ μέσου), and nails to the cross (προσηλώσας αὐτὸ τῷ σταυρῷ). And in the process of lifting the co-opted Law high upon the cross where it was highly visible, Christ exposed the principalities and powers as enemies of both God and humanity: in the cross, Christ exposed the powers who know of no other form of "justice" but blind retributive "justice" as not being on God's side, for God graciously forgives transgressions (2:13). When the divine Law falls into the hands of the powers, the result is a strict nomism with no margin of error, which inevitably results in disastrous consequences. "In it" (ἐν αὐτῷ), that is, in the cross, Christ made evident in his own body what had become wrong with God's good Law: the Law in the hands of the powers brings about the execution of one who knew no sin. In the blatantly public event of the crucifixion, Christ exposed the principalities and powers and made a public spectacle of them. The cross, then, became the site of a stunning revelation; for it was in this event that Christ uncovered how the exercise of the powers' authority had become demonic.[110] The cross, rather than standing as a symbol of scorn and disgrace for the Christian Messiah, was, paradoxically, the place where Christ subjected the powers to ridicule and shame by blowing off their cover. In this revelation, Christ "triumphed" (θριαμβεύω)[111] over the powers, like a victorious Roman emperor leading his conquered enemies in triumphal procession (2:15).[112]

RECONCILIATION AS "MAKING PEACE"

As we have already argued, the second addition the author makes to the hymn is εἰρηνοποιήσας διὰ τοῦ αἵματος τοῦ σταυροῦ αὐτοῦ δι'αὐτοῦ. This addition is the author's explication of what is latent in the expression καὶ δι'αὐτοῦ ἀποκαταλλάξαι τὰ πάντα εἰς αὐτόν . . . εἴτε τὰ ἐπὶ τῆς γῆς εἴτε τὰ ἐν τοῖς οὐρανοῖς. The author locates the inauguration of reconciliation in a historical event—the crucifixion of Christ. This theme of reconciliation

transgress and act in all the ways of defilement, they will be recorded in the heavenly tablets as enemies" (O. S. Wintermute's translation in *OTP* 2:113–14). Cf. *Mart. Ascen. Isa.* 9:22–23.

110. On our reading of 2:14–15, what is in view here is not so much *defeat* of the powers per se, but the *unmasking* of the powers. The theme of defeat of the powers on the cross should not be pressed too far, since defeat of the powers on the cross is incongruent with their ultimate reconciliation (1:20) and the acknowledgement of the still-potent "power of darkness" from which believers have been rescued (1:13). Perhaps the different depictions of the powers can be made to fit if we regard the unmasking of the powers as their defeat.

111. On the verb θριαμβεύω, see L. Williamson, Jr., "Led in Triumph: Paul's Use of *Thriambeuo*," *Int* 22 (1968): 317–32.

112. On the Roman triumphal procession, see H. S. Versnel, *Triumphus: An Inquiry into the Origin, Development and Meaning of the Roman Triumph* (Leiden: Brill, 1970).

presupposes a rupture in the created order; the creation that was made in and for Christ has fallen out of fellowship with the Creator. All things, therefore, need to be reconciled with God through Christ. The author understands this reconciliation as "making peace"; it is a restoration of the disrupted fellowship that all creation enjoyed with God. This reconciliation accomplished through the cross of Christ is comprehensive; it extends beyond human creatures to "all things" (τὰ πάντα)—either on earth or in heaven, including the principalities and powers (1:16, 20). Some scholars have argued that the principalities and powers should not be seen as hostile forces, but rather as part of the angelic host of Christ's own victory parade. Wesley Carr argues that principalities and powers are part of Christ's angelic entourage who celebrate his glorification in heaven; they are good angels.[113] They were created by Christ and have always been his. At the cross they join together in celebration of Christ's splendor: "This glorification of Christ is achieved by the public recognition of him by the angels of heaven."[114] Carr's argument is followed by Roy Yates, who argues that since those who were led in triumph in a Roman victory parade were not defeated captives, the principalities and powers cannot be hostile spirit-powers, but part of the angelic hosts celebrating the fruits of victory.[115] Yates notes that ἐδειγμάτισεν ἐν παρρησίᾳ means "to display in public boldly," without necessarily carrying connotations of shame.[116]

This latter view is unlikely, however, since the only other use of the rare verb δειγματίζω in the NT (Matt. 1:19) carries connotations of public disgrace.[117] In addition, the theme of cosmic reconciliation sounded in the Colossian hymn and expounded by the author in the verses immediately following the hymn deals a decisive blow to the argument that the principalities and powers are good angelic hosts of God. Our own reading has suggested that—even if we would allow that the co-opting powers of the elements and the Law were originally God's messengers—the theme of reconciliation implies that a disruption has occurred within the created order, and certain aspects of the created order, including the principalities and powers, can no longer be viewed as existing in unbroken fellowship with God. The cross, as the site of

---

113. W. Carr, *Angels and Principalities: The Background Meaning and Development of the Pauline Phrase Hai Archai kai hai Exousiai*, SNTSMS 42 (Cambridge: Cambridge University Press, 1981), 47–85, esp. 63–64.

114. Carr, *Angels and Principalities*, 64.

115. R. Yates, "Colossians 2:15: Christ Triumphant," *NTS* 37 (1991): 573–91, esp. 579–80.

116. Yates, "Christ Triumphant," 580.

117. The verb does not occur in the OG.

revelation, exposed the principalities and powers as powers of darkness (1:13) whose exercise of authority has become demonic.

In addition, we have argued that the author's application of the theme of cosmic reconciliation to the Colossian believers (1:20-23) suggests that the author sees a correlation between the reconciliation of the powers and the kind enjoyed by believers. This argument poses a problem for the thesis that the principalities and powers are good angels. If believers were once "alienated" from God and were "enemies" of God (1:21) and, therefore, had to be reconciled through Christ, then the principalities and powers will need to be reconciled because they are presently alienated and enemies of God.

WORSHIP TO/BY THE ANGELS

The author of Colossians associates the false teaching at Colossae with angelic worship in 2:18. It is not clear whether the author intends by the phrase θρησκείᾳ τῶν ἀγγέλων "worship offered to angels" (objective genitive) or "worship offered by the angels" (subjective genitive). Most scholars writing prior to the publication of Fred O. Francis's study in 1963[118] took the phrase to be an objective genitive, denoting a literal worship offered to angels at Colossae.[119] According to this position, such worship led to a diminishing of the person and role of Christ. Francis, however, broke new ground in the debate by arguing that the phrase should be taken as a subjective genitive, as a description of what visionaries witnessed upon entering the heavenly realm in mystical ascents. The visionaries "entered" (ἐμβατεύω)[120] the heavenly realm to witness angels worshiping God in heaven and joined the angels in their liturgy (cf. 2

---

118. F. O. Francis, "Humility and Angel Worship in Col. 2:18," reprinted in Francis and Meeks, *Conflict at Colossae*, 163-95.

119. See, e.g., Lightfoot, *Saint Paul's Epistles to the Colossians and to Philemon*, 194–96; T. K. Abbott, *A Critical and Exegetical Commentary on the Epistles to the Ephesians and to the Colossians*, ICC (New York: C. Scribner's Sons, 1897), 268. So also, Schweizer, *Letter to the Colossians*, 159–60. Cf. Origen, *Against Celsus* 5:8; Theodoret of Cyrus, *Interpretation of the Letter to the Colossians* (PG 82:613ab–614ab), who reports that this practice persisted for a long time in Phrygia and Pisidia, prompting the gathering of a synod at Loadicea in Phrygia to place a ban on the invocation of angels (see canon 35 of the Council of Loadicea).

120. Based on the discovery of the verb ἐμβατεύω in some second-century CE inscriptions from the temple of Apollo at Claros in the province of Asia (cf. W. M. Ramsay, "Sketches in the Religious Antiquities of Asia Minor (Plates I–IV)," *ABSA* 18 [1911–12]: 37–79), M. Dibelius argued that, since this word was a technical term for initiation in mystery religions, the Colossian "error" was a form of syncretistic mystery practice (Dibelius, "The Isis Initiation in Apuleius and Related Initiatory Rites," in Francis and Meeks, *Conflict at Colossae*, 61–121; cf. Francis, "The Background of Embateuein (Col 2:18) in Legal Papyri and Oracle Inscriptions," in Francis and Meeks, *Conflict at Colossae*, 197–207). Dibelius,

En. 20:1–5; *3 En.* 1:6–12; *T. Job* 48–50; *Apoc. Ab.* 17; *Mart. Ascen. Isa.* 7:32–37; 8:16–17; 9:27–29; 4Q400–405). Diet, drink, strict observance of festivals, new moon, Sabbaths, and ταπεινοφροσύνη[121] in 2:16-18 represent the rigorous asceticism that were regarded as necessary preparation for the mystical ascents and reception of visions (cf. Dan. 9:3; 10:2-14; *4 Ezra* 5:13; 6:31; 12:51–13:1; *2 Bar.* 12:5–13:2; Herm. *Vis.* 3:10:6; Herm. *Sim.* 5:3:7; *Apoc. Ab.* 9:6–7).[122] Gershom Scholem has shown that such fascination with the angelic realm and mystical ascents was current in Judaism before and after the destruction of the temple.[123] Thus, a number of scholars have followed Francis in understanding θρησκείᾳ τῶν ἀγγέλων as a subjective genitive.[124]

While we agree that Jewish mystical ascent is the practice the author of Colossians has as his target, we cannot entirely eliminate the objective genitive understanding of the phrase for two reasons. First, the evidence Francis presents for taking the phrase as a subjective genitive in Col 2:18 is tenuous at best, since in his examples the term θρησκεία is used in a genitive relation with humans ("Ιουδαίων"; *4 Macc.* 5:7; Josephus, *Ant.* 12:5:4).[125] As Clinton Arnold has correctly observed in his detailed survey of the usage of the term, when θρησκεία is used with the genitive case in relation to supernatural beings or typical objects of worship (such as an idol) the genitive expression is always the object of the noun θρησκεία (e.g., Josephus, *Ant.* 1:13:1; Philo, *Spec.* 1:315;

---

however, overemphasized the pagan character of the cult—if any such thing ever existed at Colossae—and downplayed any Jewish influence.

121. Cf. 3:12, where the author includes the same word in a list of Christian virtues.

122. Cf. C. Rowland, *The Open Heaven: A Study of Apocalyptic in Judaism and Early Christianity* (London: SPCK, 1982), 228–29; Rowland, "Apocalyptic Visions and the Exaltation of Christ in the Letter to the Colossians," *JSNT* 19 (1983), 73–83. Rowland's attempt to apply ταπεινοφροσύνη to the activities performed by the angels in heaven cannot be judged a success. The term is clearly used for human activities or virtue in Col. 2:23, 3:12 and its occurrences in early Christian texts (cf. Acts 20:19; Phil. 2:3; 1 Pet. 5:5; Eph. 4:2; Herm. *Vis.* 3:10:6; Herm. *Sim.* 5:3:7). In addition, there is no evidence that the Colossian teachers were attempting to imitate the behavior of angels, and the evidence Rowland draws from Qumran seems inapplicable to his case.

123. See G. Scholem, *Major Trends in Jewish Mysticism* (New York: Schocken, 1961 [orig. 1954]); Scholem, *Jewish Gnosticism, Merkabah Mysticism and Talmudic Tradition* (New York: Jewish Theological Seminary of America, 1965 [orig. 1960]). Cf. N. Kehl, "Erniedrigung und Erhöhung in Qumran und Kolossä," *ZKT* 91 (1969): 364–94.

124. See, e.g., C. A. Evans, "The Colossian Mystics," *Bib* 63 (1982): 188–205; Rowland, "Apocalyptic Visions and the Exaltation of Christ," 73–83; R. Yates, "'The Worship of Angels (Col 2:18),'" *ExpTim* 97 (1985): 12–15; J. D. Dunn, "The Colossian Philosophy: A Confident Jewish Apologia," *Bib* 76 (1995): 153–81.

125. See also Josephus, *Ant.*, 16:4:3; *J.W.* 2:10:4.

Wisd. of Sol. 14:27).[126] Second, the subjective genitive reading fails to account adequately for the clause that carries θρησκείᾳ τῶν ἀγγέλων further, καὶ οὐ κρατῶν τήν κεφαλήν ("and not holding fast to the head"). Proponents of the subjective genitive reading tend to attenuate the force of this clause by giving the clause an ecclesiological referent. For example, Francis argues that the clause means "being at variance with the church" and this deviance "calls into question [the errorists'] faithfulness to church authority and tradition."[127] So also Craig Evans, who argues that the clause implies that "the errorists are not functioning properly in the church, the body of Christ, of which all believers are members and over whom Christ is the 'head.'"[128] These interpretations, however, are too weak to capture the force of the author's statement. By augmenting the phrase about angelic worship with a statement about Christ, the author wishes to underscore the fact that the practice in view is detracting from *Christ*. That the form of the practice somehow demotes Christ is the reason for the author's objection to the practice. Indeed, by shifting the focus of the clause καὶ οὐ κρατῶν τήν κεφαλήν from Christology to ecclesiology, these modern authors are making precisely the sort of move that the author of Colossians is denouncing.

In sum, the possibility that actual worship was offered to the angels in this practice at Colossae cannot be easily dismissed.[129] Nonetheless, it is not improbable that the author, by referring to this mystical practice as worship directed to angels, has chosen to portray the practice in extreme terms and emotive language in order to deter the believers from this practice. Accordingly, the author's portrayal of his opponents, while credible,[130] would not be entirely accurate. His opponents would certainly have resented his description as a misrepresentation of their practice.[131] The author, however, does not think he is resorting to slanderous or inflammatory language to

126. C. Arnold, *The Colossian Syncretism: The Interface between Christianity and FolkBelief at Colossae*, WUNT 77 (Tübingen: Mohr Siebeck, 1995), 90–95.

127. Francis, "The Christological Argument of Colossians," in *God's Christ and His People: Studies in Honour of Nils Alstrup Dahl*, ed. J. Jervell and W. A. Meeks (Oslo: Universitetsforlaget, 1977), 192–208, on 202, 204.

128. Evans, "Colossian Mystics," 199.

129. So Bruce, "Colossian Problems Part 3: The Colossian Heresy," *BSac* 141 (1984): 195–208, on 204. The counterargument that worship of angels could not be in view because it was foreign to Judaism is faulty. The prohibitions against angelic worship in Christian and Jewish literature (cf. Rev. 19:10; 22:8-9; *Mart. Ascen. Isa.* 7:21; *Apoc. Zeph.* 6:15; Philo, *Fug.* 212; *Somn.* 1:238 *b. Hul.* 40a; *b. 'Abod. Zar.* 42b; *a. Ber.* 9:13a; *Mek. Yitro* 10) at the very least suggest that some were prone to straying in this direction.

130. There has to be some credibility if the author is not to undermine his own position as unfair and libelous.

characterize their mystical ascents as angelic worship; he thinks he has grounds for his characterization, because in his view those who participate in this practice are not "holding fast to the head"—not to mention the fact that they are also puffed up by their fleshly "minds"[132] (2:18-19). The author feels justified in characterizing the nature of this practice at Colossae as angelic worship, because, in his view, it detracts from the lordship of Christ. The way the false teachers are undertaking their mystical ascents is tantamount to angelic worship, for it deflects worship from the one who is due worship—Christ.

If some form of Jewish mysticism characterized by rigorous asceticism is in view in 2:16-19, then 2:20-23 makes perfect sense, since the gentiles' former religion also included rigorous ascetism and regulations (cf. 2:8). This rigor of devotion urged self-discipline: "Do not touch, do not taste, do not handle" (2:20).[133] It is, therefore, likely that the former pagans were attracted to the Jewish mystical practices because of their pronounced asceticism, rigorous devotion, and self-discipline. This is one of the points of contact the author detects between worship of the elements and the mystical ascents. The author detects that both are characterized by rigorous human tradition.[134] One can, therefore, perceive a looming danger of the gentiles assimilating their pagan past and the now proclaimed ascetic requirements of their newfound religion.[135]

131. It is the major weakness of H. Van Broekhoven's study of the social profiles of the author and his rivals that he proceeds from the assumption that the author's portrayal of his opponents is fair and accurate. See Broekhoven, "The Social Profiles in the Colossian Debate," *JSNT* 66 (1977): 73–90, esp. 80.

132. In our view this statement is strong indication that ἃ ἑόρακεν ἐμβατεύων (2:18) must denote the detailed parsing of the visions witnessed by the visionaries. In 2 Macc. 2:30 the verb ἐμβατεύω is used in the sense of "investigating closely" or "going into details" (cf. Philo, *Plant.* 80). Thus, the visionaries "go into details" concerning what they have seen in their heavenly ascents. Contrast Paul's recounting of his heavenly ascent in 2 Cor. 12:1-9: Paul does not mention any rigorous ascetic preparation; he notes that humans are not permitted to speculate about the things witnessed in the heavenly ascents; and he warns against the danger of boasting that such experiences may engender.

133. Severian of Gabala, *Pauline Commentary from the Greek Church* (NTAbh 15:324–26), is one of the few patristic exegetes to have noticed a change here from Jewish elements of the teaching to pagan practices. We have already noted that there may be a slight mischaracterization of pagan practices in 2:20. Pagan practices should not be viewed as a mere obsession with transient materials in rules concerning what may not be touched or eaten, as the author suggests. Behind these restrictions lies a fear of contact with objects that were deemed to be sacred because of their link to a spiritual power. These objects of devotion were assigned sacred significance because those who deemed them to be consecrated had detected the presence of higher powers behind them.

134. The author uses the root δόγμα to characterize both the χειρόγραφον and worship of the elements (2:14; 2:20); cf. 2:8.

135. T. K. Abbott has suggested that the Colossian "error" could have stemmed from the Colossians holding such a high transcendent view of God that God was deemed to be unapproachable; thus, angelic

Thus, the author had to remind the believers that they had already died to the elements of the cosmos in baptism, and dying to the elements means an end to all rigorous ordinances in religion (2:20). To submit to the rigorous demands of the mystical practices is tantamount to returning to the state of bondage under the elements from which believers had been delivered.

CONCLUDING REMARKS AND AUTHORSHIP

Colossians presents a comprehensive vision of reality, at whose center is Christ. Christ is the mystery of all reality, the key to the universe. In Christ dwells the fullness of the deity bodily; and, as a result, Christ has made the invisible God present to the world. He was before all things and all things were created in him and continue to hold together in him. In Colossians, Christ is the core of all reality; the entire created order finds its meaning and integrity in Christ. And, as such, even the ultimate destiny of the principalities and powers (reconciliation with God) is locked up in Christ. The principalities and powers were also part of God's good creation, having been created in Christ and for Christ.

Yet a rupture has occurred within the created order, such that the principalities and powers can no longer be said to be on God's side. The powers have co-opted certain aspects of material creation and in the process have deflected worship from Christ. And because the powers have deflected worship from Christ they are to be regarded as powers of darkness (cf. 1:14). The former gentiles had their own *habitus*, and this involved frequenting idol temples and participating in idol worship. In idolatry, worshipers sought access to the numinous power behind the elements. The author of Colossians sought to create a Christian *habitus*, one that would govern the gentile Christians' practices. For the author, to access the powers behind the elements is to expose oneself to powers that align themselves against Christ in the cosmic battle.

In the cross, Christ exposed the powers as not being on God's side; he revealed in his own body how the powers can co-opt the Law: the Law in the hands of the powers can result in the crucifixion of one who knew no sin. This story of Christ's encounter with the powers on the cross undergirds a Christian practice that engages the powers: baptism. While the powers still continue to

mediation was needed to approach God (*Epistles to the Ephesians and to the Colossians*, 268). So also Chrysostom, *Homilies on Colossians* 7 (NPNF1 13:288); Severian of Gabala, *Pauline Commentary from the Greek Church* (NTAbh 15:325). If Abbott and these patristic exegetes are correct, then another point of contact between the worship of the elements and the mystical ascents would be the attempt to access a supreme power through some intermediary. The author of Colossians's claim that in Christ dwells the fullness of the deity would be an apt response to these practices: to encounter Christ is to encounter the person of the deity enthroned in heaven.

do a great deal of damage in the world, believers have been transferred from the realm of their dominion to the kingdom of Christ in baptism. In baptism, believers are buried with Christ and raised to a new life with Christ in God (3:1-4). During baptism, believers put off the sinful nature—a site of death (2:13) and a sphere of the powers' influence—in participation in Christ's own escape from the domain of the powers (2:15). Practices of power in the Letter to the Colossians are practices that either leave humans vulnerable to the powers of darkness (worship of the elements) or protect believers from the powers (baptism).

Does this theology of the powers in Colossians corroborate our study of the powers in the nondisputed letters of Paul, or has the theology of the powers moved too far from Paul, so that Colossians' theology of the powers must be added to evidence against Pauline authorship of the letter? In what follows we briefly note some key similarities and differences.

SIMILARITIES

There are numerous similarities between the presentation of the powers in Colossians and what we have encountered in the nondisputed letters of Paul. Highlighting a few of the important convergences is in order. First, our interpretation of the cheirographon is consistent with our treatment of 1 Cor. 2:6-8, where "the rulers of this age" are said to have crucified the Lord of glory; and it supplements well Paul's argument in Romans 7 about Sin co-opting the Law. Paul believed that behind Christ's death stood larger cosmic forces who operated behind the human administrators. Paul does not attribute much significance to the human authorities, because they are not the main actors on the cosmic stage. There were higher powers on the scene at Christ's crucifixion, and it is these powers that Paul identifies. In addition, Paul's problem with the Law is that it is impotent in the face of higher powers who co-opt the Law and use it to produce outcomes contrary to the Law's aims. In Romans 7 Sin co-opts the Law and uses the Law to produce outcomes that are contrary to the religious self's wishes and the Law's intended purpose. In Colossians the Law in the hands of the powers results in the crucifixion of one who knew no sin and a blind "justice" against humanity that is mainly retributive. We have also encountered a similar argument in our treatment of Galatians, where we argued that by creating divisions in the body of Christ and placing oppressive demands on Gentile believers, the Law had fallen into the hands of higher powers who were using it against God's purpose of bringing freedom to believers and creating a unified people in Christ.

Also, we observe that the presentation of the *stoicheia* in Colossians is analogous to their presentation in Galatians and seems to confirm our reading of Galatians.[136] Paul's argument in Galatians is that to submit to certain Jewish practices of the Law is tantamount to returning to the state of bondage under the elements. So also the author of Colossians argues that to submit to the rigorous demands of certain Jewish practices is equivalent to their former life of bondage under the elements. Finally, the recognition that the elements have been co-opted by higher powers and thus some aspects of material creation are in need of reconciliation is not far from Paul's view that creation has been subject to bondage of corruption and is awaiting redemption (Rom. 8:19-22).[137]

DIFFERENCES

In Col. 2:15 Christ's "triumph" over the powers is an already accomplished fact that took place on the cross. In 1 Cor. 15:24-25, however, the subjugation of the powers is reserved for the eschaton. This difference should not be overstated, however. We have already observed that what is in view in Col. 2:14-15 is not so much a defeat of the powers, but rather an unmasking of the powers. In the cross, Christ exposes the powers as hostile forces. Herein lies their "defeat," if we may call it such. In addition, in the nondisputed letters Paul presents the church as the locus of Christ's presence and the place where the principalities and powers have no dominion, even if their ultimate defeat will be revealed in the future.[138] Incorporation into the body of Christ through baptism provides protection against the powers, though this protection is not ultimate. A similar concept is presented in Colossians, where believers are said to have been rescued from the power of darkness and transferred into the kingdom of Christ (1:13-14) and are still urged to continue firm and established in the faith (1:23).

---

136. Cf. Dunn, "Colossian Philosophy," 169: "[In Gal 4,3 and 9 the phrase στοιχεῖα τοῦ κόσμου] is clearly linked into the Jewish law, understood itself as a kind of power set in charge over Israel like a slave-custodian or guardian (Gal 3,23-25; 4,1-3.9-10), and given 'through angels' (3:19). The close association of the thought here [Colossians] with talk of Jewish festivals (Col 2,16; cf. Gal 4,10) and 'angel worship' (Col 2,18) strongly suggests that we are moving in the same realm of thought and association as with the same phrase in Galatians."

137. We may also add to the above arguments that, if our argument on the author's redaction is correct, then the inclusion of Line E into the hymn fits with Paul's emphasis of the cross; and it is analogous to the (hypothetical) Pauline addition of "even death on a cross" to the Christ hymn of Philippians (2:8). The cross is absolutely central to Paul's theology. For Paul, God's action in the world can be summed up in the event of the cross. See L. Morris, *The Cross in the New Testament* (Grand Rapids: Eerdmans, 1965), 181.

138. See our chapters on Corinthians and Romans.

We encounter the tension between the already and not yet so characteristic of NT eschatology.[139]

The biggest difference we encounter between the treatment of the powers in Colossians and the nondisputed letters has to do with the notion of reconciliation of the principalities and powers, which is directly connected with the view that all the powers were created in and for Christ. Nowhere in the nondisputed letters of Paul do we encounter the idea that all the powers were created in Christ and, thus, will ultimately be reconciled (brought to "peace") with God through Christ.[140] As noted in our chapter on Romans, Sin and Death as personified powers in Romans 5–8 rule out this possibility. According to Romans, Sin entered the cosmos as a result of Adam's transgression and Sin's entrance brought Death with it. These powers are not God's creation. In addition, in the authentic letters, the ultimate destiny of the powers is defeat or destruction (cf. 1 Cor. 2:6; 15:24-25; Rom. 16:20), not reconciliation as we encounter in Colossians.

If Colossians is authentic, then the above observations would represent enormous shifts in Paul's view concerning the powers. G. B. Caird has, therefore, suggested that Paul changed his views concerning the powers over time.[141] Caird observes that Paul experienced the impartial intervention of Roman justice before Gallio and other Roman officials in the latter stages of his life, leading Paul to a deep appreciation of Roman law, which in turn shifted his view concerning the powers. Caird writes,

> This mellowing of Paul's attitude towards Rome[142] goes some little way to explain another change which took place in his thinking at about the same time. In his earlier writings Paul accepted the apocalyptic outlook, which did not look beyond the defeat of those spiritual powers which were at enmity with God. They belonged to the present age, and with the passing of the present age they too would pass away. But in his imprisonment epistles he has begun to

139. See R. B. Hays, "Operation Evil Power: If Christ Has Truly Defeated the Powers of Satan on the Cross (Col 2:15), Why Do the Powers of Evil Effectively Operate in the World?" *Christianity Today* 48 (2004): 74.

140. While 2 Cor. 5:18-20 also speaks of reconciliation, it is unlikely that "the world" (κόσμος) in 2 Cor. 5:19 has the same comprehensive scope as "all things" in Col. 1:16, 20, since the verse goes on to say that God is "not counting their (αὐτῶν) transgressions against them (αὐτοῖς)." Human beings are in view in 2 Cor. 5:19. Rom. 3:6 shows that Paul can use κόσμος for human beings.

141. G. B. Caird, *Principalities and Powers: A Study in Pauline Theology* (Eugene, OR:Wipf and Stock, 2003 [orig. 1956]), 26–30; Caird, *Paul's Letters from Prison*, 181–82.

142. Here Caird has Rom. 13:1-5 in mind.

entertain the hope that even the powers may be brought within the scope of God's redemption.[143]

Caird's view raises the question of dating and chronology of the Pauline letters. In Caird's chronology, Romans precedes Colossians.[144] But if with Caird we are to assume Pauline authorship of Colossians, then it is more likely that Colossians was written around the time of Philemon (cf. Col. 4:7-17; Philem. 23-24), a letter probably written earlier than Romans from Ephesus or Caesarea (cf. Philem. 22). More importantly, in light of Rom. 16:20, it is not apparent that the view that Paul changes his mind concerning the powers can be maintained; in Rom. 16:20 Satan is soon to be "crushed" under the feet of believers.

One possible approach is to posit that the Colossian hymn has in mind only the *Geisterwelt*, not the personification of abstract nouns as powers, such as Sin and Death.[145] The author of the Colossian hymn is not presenting a view of the powers that is as comprehensive as we encounter in Paul's letters. Another possible approach is to let the tension between the destruction and reconciliation of the powers stand, though this raises the question of the extent to which the author of Colossians, whether Paul or a close associate of Paul, shared the theology of the hymn he quotes at the beginning of the letter (Col. 1:15-20), where the theme of reconciliation of the powers is first featured. On the one hand, it is difficult to imagine an author quoting and building on a theology that stood in tension with his own. The author seems to be in basic agreement with the theology of the hymn even if he finds the need to modify aspects of the hymn. On the other hand, if, as we have suggested, the hymn was part of an early Christian liturgy,[146] then the author may have selected the hymn because it was something most of his readers would have been familiar with. The citation of the hymn was not haphazard; it was supposed to have an effect on the audience, if they had, indeed, professed the message of the hymn. It was a calculated move to strike a chord in the hearts of those who had confessed its message as the sacramental liturgy that was relevant in affirming their new identity. The hymn would, then, be the meeting point between the author and his audience: the author cites the hymn to establish common ground with his audience and next proceeds to show the implications of their confession for their Christian life. The result may be that the author has allowed the hymn to dictate the parameters of his discussion and his argument, since the hymn

---

143. Caird, *Principalities and Powers*, 27.

144. See Caird, *Paul's Letters from Prison*, 2–6.

145. See the next chapter for further discussion.

146. Cf., e.g., 2:9-15, which applies the second strophe of the hymn to baptism.

was authoritative in the community to which the letter was addressed. We, therefore, have grounds to draw a parallel here between the author's citation of the hymn in Colossians and Paul's quotation of early Christian confessions in his nondisputed letters that stand in tension with his own teachings. In Rom. 1:3-4, for example, Paul quotes an early christological creed that associates Christ's sonship with the moment of the resurrection. Within the Pauline corpus, however, we encounter statements that posit divine sonship prior to the resurrection (cf. Rom. 5:10; 8:3, 29, 32; 1 Cor. 1:9; 15:28; 2 Cor. 1:19; Gal. 1:16; 2:20; 4:4; 1 Thess. 1:10).[147]

It seems almost unavoidable that these similarities and differences will be assessed and weighed differently by various scholars. Cumulatively, there are more convergences than divergences, though it is not clear how each should be weighed and whether the divergences require us positing a different author. In our view, the evidence for pseudonymity is inconclusive. And until decisive evidence can be mounted for the non-Pauline authorship of Colossians, we have reason to read this letter with centuries of tradition that viewed the letter as stemming from Paul's own hand.

---

147. Cf. B. Byrne, *"Sons of God—"Seed of Abraham": A Study of the Idea of the Sonship of God of All Christians in Paul against the Jewish Background*, AnBib 83 (Rome: Biblical Institute Press, 1979), 197–206.

8

Summary: What are the Powers for Paul?

Having discussed practices of power in the Pauline congregations, we are now in a position to address the question of what the powers are for Paul. Our detailed treatment of the Pauline letters leads us to acknowledge upfront the extreme hermeneutical difficulty in accounting for Paul's principalities and powers. Paul's theology of the powers defies our usual categories. Paul's terminology and conception of the powers includes the *Geisterwelt*, which consists of spiritual entities with intellect and will. These entities operate on a cosmic scale but also directly influence events on the earthly stage. Chief of these is Satan (σατανᾶς),[1] who bears the full weight of the title ὁ θεὸς τοῦ αἰῶνος τούτου ("the god of this age"; 2 Cor. 4:4). Because Satan belongs to *this age*, he is aligned on the other side of the battlefront against God and Christ. Satan and his minions constitute οἱ ἄρχοντες τοῦ αἰῶνος τούτου ("the rulers of this age"; 1 Cor. 2:6, 8); and these opposing forces were the main actors in the larger cosmic drama at the crucifixion of Jesus (1 Cor. 2:8). Since Satan belongs to this age and opposes God's purposes, Satan works to hinder Paul's own mission (1 Thess. 2:18) and schemes to find his way into the church in order to disrupt the church (2 Cor. 2:11). The church, therefore, has to be vigilant, for even apostles within the church could be advancing Satan's agenda (2 Cor. 11:1-15). The vigilance of believers extends beyond the church to their own personal lives, for Satan seeks to tempt believers by appealing to their fleshly desires (1 Cor. 7:5). As a result, Satan also bears the title of "the tempter" (1 Thess. 3:5). Nonetheless, despite Satan's governance of this age, God's absolute sovereignty is never impugned. This is demonstrated by God's ability to use even Satan to bring about good outcomes (1 Cor. 5:5; 2 Cor. 12:7). Before

---

1. Cf. G. Aulen, *Christus Victor: An Historical Study of the Three Main Types of the Idea of Atonement,* trans. A. G. Hebert (New York: Macmillan, 1951), 66-73.

the Parousia, Satan will usher in the lawless one who will oppose everything associated with God (2 Thess. 2:1-11); but, in the end, God will crush Satan under the feet of believers (Rom. 16:20).

The *Geisterwelt* also includes angels and demons. Satan has his angels (2 Cor. 12:7) and he is able to transform himself into an angel of light (2 Cor. 11:14).[2] Angels (ἄγγελοι) receive an ambiguous presentation in the Pauline letters. 2 Cor. 11:14 and 2 Cor. 12:7 assume the existence of evil angels. This may explain why Paul includes angels in his list of "powers" that seek to separate believers from the love of Christ (Rom. 8:38). But there are also good angels who are part of the heavenly court. These are the mighty angels of Christ or angels of God (2 Thess. 1:7; Gal. 1:8; cf. Gal. 4:14; Gal. 3:19 [?]).[3] On many other occasions, however, angels seem to be morally neutral in Paul (cf. 1 Cor. 4:9; 6:3; 11:10; 13:1; Gal. 3:19 [?]; Col. 2:18 [?]). In contrast to his presentation of angels, Paul speaks of demons (δαιμόνια) in purely negative terms. As the driving force behind idolatry, demons are antithetical to God and Christ (1 Cor. 10:20-21).

As argued in our chapters on Galatians and Colossians, Paul's use of the expression τὰ στοιχεῖα τοῦ κόσμου ("the elements of the world"; Gal. 4:3, 9; Col. 2:8, 20) is intimately connected to his understanding of idolatry. It is not clear in Paul how the angels and demons are related. We can only note that just as Paul associates some angels with Satan (2 Cor. 12:7; 2 Cor. 11:14), he also associates idolatry with Beliar (Βελιάρ)—likely another name for Satan (2 Cor. 6:14—7:1).[4] The term Beliar may be a variant of Belial, who is portrayed

---

2. This is the closest reference in Paul to the theme of Satan as a fallen angel. Paul does not show any interest in speculations about the origin of Satan. In the Qumran documents, the commander of the evil forces, Belial, is variously referred to as the Angel of Darkness (1QS 3:20-21), the Prince of the realm of Darkness (1QM 17:5-6; cf. the Prince of Light [1QS 3:20-21]); and the Spirit of Deceit (1QS 4:9).

3. Cf. "angel of light" (2 Cor 11:14).

4. Some scholars view 2 Cor. 6:14—7:1 as a non-Pauline fragment; see, e.g., J. A. Fitzmeyer, "Qumran and the Interpolated Paragraph in 2 Cor. 6:1-7:1," *CBQ* 23 (1961): 271–80; K. G. Kuhn, "Les rouleaux de cuivre de Qumran," *RB* 61 (1954): 193–205; H. D. Betz, "2 Cor 6:14—7:1: An Anti-Pauline Fragment?" *JBL* 42 (1973): 88–108. For a convincing argument for the integrity and authenticity of this pericope, see G. D. Fee, "II Corinthians VI.4—VII.1 and Food Offered to Idols," *NTS* 23 (1977)- 140–161. Fee points to the fact that the quantity of *hapaxes* in this pericope is not an unusual feature in Paul. Paul in other places introduces a sudden influx of *hapax legomena* (e.g. 1 Cor. 4:7-13; 2 Cor. 6:3-10). In addition, Fee questions whether noun forms of verbs used in other places by an author should be considered *hapax legomena* (μετοχή, cf. μετέχω in 1 Cor. 9:10, 12; 10:12, 17; μολυσμοῦ, cf. μολύνω in 1 Cor. 8:7). He notes that the verbal counterparts of συμφώνησις and συγκατάθεσις are NT words, and Paul has a penchant for using συν-compounds that are NT *hapax legomena*. Finally, since ἑτεροζυγοῦντες is similar to the Pauline compound σύζυγος (Phil. 4:3), and since παντοκράτωρ is found in the LXX, we are left

in Jewish literature as a Satan-like figure.[5] Important for our purposes is the fact that in *T. Dan* 1:7–3:6 Beliar is also referred to as Satan. The use of the term in 2 Cor. 6:14—7:1, then, indirectly links Satan with the demons, since Paul sees idolatry as the locus of demons (1 Cor. 10:20-21).

Paul is not interested in the names and ranks of these entities.[6] This is because for Paul they all represent the same phenomena: custodians of this passing age who are aligned on the opposite side of the battle line against God and Christ, and deflection of worship from the one true Creator. Together all these form the many so-called gods and lords in the world (1 Cor. 8:5-6). We cannot deny the reality and concreteness of the entities that inhabit the *Geisterwelt* for Paul. Paul presents these entities in a way that suggests that he knows of their real existence.

Paul also personifies abstract concepts as powers. The Flesh, Death, and Sin are at times personified in Paul as demonic forces confronting humanity. The Flesh can be spoken of as a powerful sphere of influence; it is a sphere that imposes its will on those who walk in it. As long as humans live in the Flesh, they will bear fruit that leads to death (cf. Rom. 7:5; Rom. 8:5-6, 8:9, 8:12-13; Gal. 5:19-24). In order to escape the Flesh, believers must be hidden in Christ (Rom. 8:1) or walk in the Spirit (Rom. 8:1-13; Gal. 5:16-17). Death is also spoken of as a tyrant power that controls human life. Adam's transgression unleashed Death, which in turn "ruled" from the time of Adam to the time

with one true *hapax legomenon* in this periocope: Βελιάρ. Fee correctly perceives that 2 Cor. 6:14—7:1 is directly related to 1 Cor. 8–10. In both passages, Paul prohibits believers from partaking at tables in idol temples because there are demonic forces behind the idols. In addition to Fee's arguments we add that 2 Cor. 6:14—7:1 also has conceptual and linguistic affinities with passages in 2 Corinthians where Paul deals with spiritual forces. By partaking in tables at idol temples the Corinthians risk giving grounds to the Devil to take more than his due with the believing community (cf. 2:10-11). In addition, in 4:4-6 the "god of this age" has blinded the νοήματα of the ἄπιστοι, preventing the φωτισμὸν of the gospel of glory from shining in their hearts, and, as a result, leaving them in darkness – unlike believers whose God causes light to shine out of darkness (ἐκ σκότους φῶς λάμψει). Similarly, in 6:14—7:1 the ἄπιστοι belong to the realm of σκότος, which is ruled by Beliar. Believers, however, belong to the realm of φῶς, which is under the lordship of Christ. Thus, this pericope cannot be viewed as alien to 2 Corinthians.

5. The common term *Belial* occurs in early Jewish literature as the name of the leader of the evil angels or evil spirits (cf. CD 5:18; 12:2; 1QS 1:18; 1:23–4; 2:4–5, 18–19; 1QM 1:1, 5, 13, 15; 13:11). The less common variant form of the name used by Paul (Beliar) is attested in *Jub.* 1:20; 15:33; *T. Reu.* 4:8, 11; *T. Levi* 18:12; *T. Jud.* 25:3; *T. Dan* 5:10–11; *T. Benj.* 6:1; 7:1. In these passages, Beliar is the prince of the demonic forces.

6. So also C. E. Arnold, *Powers of Darkness: Principalities and Powers in Paul's Letters* (Downer's Grove, IL: Intervarsity Press, 1992), 98–99. Second Temple Jewish literature goes into great detail about the names, origins, functions, and ranks of these entities (cf. *Jub.* 2:1–4; *1 En.* 6:1–8; 7:1–6; 8:1–4; 9:1–11; 10:1–22).

of Moses (Rom. 5:14; 5:17). Death is included in the list of "powers" seeking to sever believers from the love of God in Christ (Rom. 8:38); and in 1 Cor. 15:24-26, Death is the last enemy of Christ that will be destroyed together with every principality and authority and power. Finally, Sin is a tyrant power who "rules" in the world (Rom. 5:12-21). Sin is a slave master who rewards its slaves with a wage of death (Rom. 6:12-23). Sin co-opts the Law into producing results contrary to the Law's aims and "deceives" the religious self into carrying out deeds contrary to the self's wishes (Romans 7).

An extremely difficult hermeneutical question is what to make of Paul's personification of abstract nouns as powers. In his study of the use of metaphor in Christian theology, Colin Gunton argues against the tendency to view metaphor as merely a term of art and secondary for expressing truth.[7] Noting the obstacles presented by modern empiricist accounts of the world, Gunton observes that there is "increasing awareness that what have been called modern ways of thought are not definitive, final or in any way adequate to the variety and richness of the world with which we have to do."[8] Human language develops in the course of human interaction with the world, and metaphor gives expression to this extension of human language. Gunton contends that metaphor is not an abuse of language; metaphor opens windows into reality for those who employ it. Metaphor involves the use of a word or words in new or unusual contexts in human speech ("transference"[9]) to bring to expression truth about the way the world is. For Gunton, "the truth of a claim about the world does not depend upon whether it is expressed in literal or metaphorical terms, but upon whether language of whatever kind expresses human interaction with reality successfully (truthfully) or not."[10] Metaphor is a way of speaking about the real world; metaphor allows us to understand not the whole of some reality, but parts of it, leaving room for openness and mystery, speech and silence.

We will show below how such an approach to metaphor may be helpful for understanding Paul's literary personifications.[11] For now, we note that

---

7. C. Gunton, *The Actuality of Atonement: A Study of Metaphor, Rationality and the Christian Tradition* (Grand Rapids: Eerdmans, 1989). See also P. Ricoeur, *The Rule of Metaphor: Multi-Disciplinary Studies of the Creation of Meaning in Language* (Toronto: University of Toronto Press, 1981 [orig. 1975]); Ricoeur, "Biblical Hermeneutics," *Semeia* 4 (1975): 29–148.

8. Gunton, *Actuality of Atonement*, 53.

9. See Aristotle, *Poetics* 1457b, 7–8.

10. Gunton, *Actuality of Atonement*, 35.

11. For an application of Gunton's study to personified righteousness in Rom 6 and 9–10, see D. J. Southall, *Rediscovering Righteousness in Romans: Personified Dikaiosyne within Metaphoric and Narratorial Settings*, WUNT 240 (Tübingen: Mohr Siebeck, 2008).

Gunton's attempt to apply his own findings to the "language of demons" cannot be deemed a success.[12] According to Gunton, the NT texts dealing with the language of demons "present us not with superhuman hypostases trotting about the world, but with the metaphorical characterisation of moral and cosmic realities which would otherwise defy expression."[13] Here Gunton collapses the treatment of the *Geisterwelt* in the NT into Paul's literary personifications of abstract concepts as powers, particularly the Law.[14] It is important to preserve this distinction, however. Satan, angels, and demons are not metaphors for Paul. In this respect, we will have to agree with Troels Engsberg-Pedersen that for Paul angels, demons, and Satan were "wholly real and existent . . . These were real beings, most probably at home in the heavenly sphere (possibly in its sublunary part), but also directly influential in the earthly sphere on and in human beings in particular."[15] Where Gunton's approach may be helpful is not in its application to Paul's *Geisterwelt* (contrary to his own methodology),[16] but rather in its application to Paul's literary personifications.[17]

It is unlikely that by personifying abstract concepts, Paul presents a hypostatization of these abstract nouns, as some have argued.[18] In other words, Paul is not attributing "some kind of independent being to that which might otherwise have been thought of as a characteristic or action of another being."[19] Rather, Paul personifies these abstract nouns by endowing them with will and intellect. Nonetheless—and drawing from Gunton's study of

---

12. See Gunton's chapter entitled "The Battlefield and the Demons" (*Actuality of Atonement*, 53–82).

13. Ibid., 66.

14. Gunton is dependent on the structural interpretations of the powers, specifically the work of G. B. Caird. See Caird, *The Language and Imagery of the Bible* (Philadelphia: Westminster, 1980) 242; Caird, *Principalities and Powers: A Study in Pauline Theology* (Eugene, OR: Wipf and Stock, 2003 [orig. 1956]).

15. T. Engberg-Pedersen, *Cosmology and Self in the Apostle Paul* (Oxford: Oxford University Press, 2010), 93.

16. Even though Gunton sees his approach as an attempt to distinguish myth from metaphor and to steer a middle course between "a naively supernaturalist view of the demonic and a reductionist one" (*Actuality of Atonement*, 66), statements such as "The language of possession by demonic forces . . . is used to express the helplessness of human agents in the face of psychological, social and cosmic forces in various combinations," and "The language of the demonic . . . is language which enables us to bring to expression the fact of the subjection of human moral agents to forces they are unable to control" (*Actuality of Atonement*, 70, 73) smack of Bultmannian demythologizing.

17. On personification, see J. J. Paxson, *The Poetics of Personification* (Cambridge: Cambridge University Press, 1994).

18. See, e.g., T. Laato, *Paul and Judaism: An Anthropological Approach* (Atlanta: Scholars Press, 1995), 75; M. Dibelius *Die Geisterwelt im Glauben des Paulus* (Göttingen: Vandenhoeck & Ruprecht, 1909), 122.

19. Definition of "hypostatization" in J. Barr, "Hypostatization of Linguistic Phenomena in Modern Literary Theory," *JSS* 7 (1962): 85-94, on 93.

metaphor—personification should be viewed not as mere literary ornament, but as a way of expressing truth about the mysterious nature of our world.[20] One way in which this can be seen in Paul is the way in which Paul's personification sometimes works at "fixing reference" or intimating reference.[21] For example, when Paul speaks of Sin seizing the opportunity afforded by the commandment to "deceive" the religious self in order to produce death (Rom. 7:7-11), he echoes the serpent's deceiving of Eve in the Garden of Eden (Gen. 3:13; cf. 2 Cor. 11:3, 14). Here, as we noted in our chapter on Romans, personified Sin stands for the serpent or Satan. Personification becomes a way of speaking about Satan, a way of unmasking Satan's activities in the world. Concerning the process of fixing reference by means of metaphor, Gunton writes:

> If we fix the meaning of something metaphorically—by referring to the cross as a sacrifice or a part of the anatomy as muscle—we do two things. First, we use a word which points to part of the world in such a way that we can begin to talk and think about it. Second, in the process we enable the meaning of the language to change as it is adapted to those features of the world which we hope it will help us to understand.[22]

It is our contention that such a way of viewing metaphoric language is instructive for understanding Paul's use of personified nouns as powers: the personifications enable Paul to give language to concrete happenings in the world—what has happened and what is happening—for which humans struggle to find the appropriate language. We may also acknowledge that Paul's personification does not always have a fixed reference—or at least, on most occasions, it is difficult to see an ontological referent or to identify the identity of the personified actant.[23] Yet even here we cannot deny that Paul's language

20. On the relationship between metaphor and personification, see Ricoeur, *Rule of Metaphor*, 59-60: "Personification . . . in turning an inanimate, non-sentient, abstract, or ideal entity into a living and feeling being, into a person, reminds us of the metaphorical transfer from the inanimate to the animate. It is true that personification does not take place only through metaphor but also by metonymy and synecdoche. But what distinguishes personification by means of metaphor and metaphor properly speaking, except the extension of the verbal unity?"

21. See Gunton, *Actuality of Atonement*, 40–47.

22. Ibid., 44.

23. Paxson develops extensive categories of personification (*Poetics of Personification*, 42; emphases original): (1) *substantialization, materialization, hypostasization*, or the figural translation of any noncorporeal quantity into a physical, corporeal one; (2) *anthropomorphism*, or the figural translation of any nonhuman quantity into a character that has human *form*; (3) *personification (prosopopeia)*, or the

goes beyond *mere* figure of speech; for it seeks to convey a truth about the way our world is—a world which is often characterized by mystery, a world in which certain occurrences transcend human articulation.

We may be tempted to see in this move Paul's break with his Jewish contemporaries. In his study of Paul's principalities and powers, Chris Forbes argues that Paul's presentation of the powers (which include pure abstractions, literary personifications, and actual personal spiritual beings) is rooted in Greek thinking, particularly the Middle Platonism expressed in Philo and Plutarch.[24] According to Forbes, the nearest parallels to Paul's conceptual framework on the powers are not to be found in Jewish apocalyptic but in Middle Platonic cosmological thinking. Throughout this study we have shown that Paul's conception and language of the powers is very much at home in Jewish literature and apocalypticism. Here we only note that the one aspect of Paul's presentation of the powers that is often pointed to as evidence of Paul's break with his Jewish contemporaries and predecessors (that is, Paul's personification of abstract concepts as powers)[25] also finds precedents in Paul's Jewish heritage.[26] Take, for example, the Essene doctrine on the two spirits (1QS 3:15–4:26). According to this doctrine, God has appointed two spirits for humans in which they may walk: the spirits of truth and injustice (ועולה רוחות האמת), also called the spirits of light and darkness (רוחות אור וחושך). Those controlled by the spirits of truth or light have an upright character and perform deeds of righteousness; but those ruled by the spirits of injustice or darkness are perverse in their ways. Overseeing each of these spirits are the Prince of Light and the

---

figural translation of any nonhuman quantity into a sentient human capable of thought and language, possessing *voice* and *face*. This is a helpful taxonomy, in that it may alert us to the range of taxonomic possibilities when evaluating Paul's personifications.

24. C. Forbes, "Paul's Principalities and Powers: Demythologizing Apocalyptic?" *JSNT* 82 (2001): 61–88; Forbes, "Pauline Demonology and/or Cosmology? Principalities, Powers, and the Elements of the World in Their Hellenistic Context," *JSNT* 85 (2002): 51–73.

25. See, for example, Wink (*Naming the Powers: The Language of the Powers in the New Testament* [Philadelphia: Fortress Press, 1984], 104) and Berkhof (*Christ and the Powers* [Scottdale, PA: Herald, 1977; orig. 1953], 23), who see in this a discontinuity between Paul and his Jewish contemporaries.

26. Commenting on J. C. Beker's assertion that in apocalyptic thinking "human agents, historical entities, and natural phenomena" viewed as "dominated and pervaded by transcendent spiritual forces" and that "such mythological personification abounds in the New Testament" (Beker, *Paul the Apostle* [Philadelphia: Fortress Press, 1980], 189–92), Forbes writes: "True, but not in apocalyptic literature; there the demonic forces are not merely 'personified.' They are conceived of as fully personal. They have names and ranks, and are personal characters rather than personified abstractions like Sin and Death" (Forbes, "Paul's Principalities and Powers," 84). The ensuing discussion will show that such an assumption is misleading.

Angel of Darkness. The nature of all humans is ruled by these two spirits, and all deeds are determined by each person's portion in the two spirits:

כיא אל שמן
בד בבד עד קץ אחרון ויתן איבת
עולם בין מפלגותם תועבת אמת עלילות עולה
ריב על כולותועבת עולה כול דרכי אמת וקנאת
משפטיהן כיא לוא יחד יתהלכו ואל ברזי שכלו
ובחכמת כבודו נתן קץ להיות עולה ובמועד פקודה
ישמידנה לעד
ואז תצא לנצח אמת תבל כיא
התגוללה בדרכי רשע בממשלת עולה עד
מעד משפט נחרצה

For God has set the spirits in equal measure until the final age, and has put an everlasting enmity between their divisions. Truth abhors the deeds of injustice, and Injustice abhors all the ways of truth. And their strife is fierce in all their judgments, for they do not walk together. God, in the mysteries of His understanding, and in the wisdom of His glory, has set an end for Injustice; and at the appointed time of the visitation He will destroy it forever. Then Truth, which has wallowed in the ways of wickedness during the dominion of Injustice until the time of appointed judgment, shall go out into the world forever. (1QS 4:16–20; my translation)

Important for our purposes are the personifications of Truth and Injustice. The context suggests that Truth is shorthand for the "spirits of Truth" and Injustice is shorthand for the "spirits of Injustice." Also important is the recognition that the phrase, "the dominion of Injustice" (בממשלת עולה), is a periphrasis for a phrase often encountered in the Qumran documents, "the dominion of Belial" (בממשלת בליעל).[27] Injustice is personified as a sphere of influence that controls life and as an evil force that contends the forces of good. What we find here is analogous to Paul's treatment of Sin as a personified power (at least in Rom 7), whereby the personified concept has an intimated reference, for example, the serpent. In Gen 4:7, Sin is said to be lurking at the door desiring to master Cain;[28] and according to Sir 27:10 Sin lies in wait for those who practice

27. See, e.g., 1QS 1:18, 23; 2:19; 1QM 1:15; 13:10; 14:9–10; 18:1; 4Q256 2:3, 7; 4Q290 f1:2.

injustice, like a lion waiting to pounce on a prey. In the latter examples, as in other occurrences of personification in Paul, the literary personification is not necessarily referential. In short, these examples show that Paul's personification of abstract concepts is well at home in ancient Judaism.

In light of the above discussion, the phrase "principalities and powers" aptly captures Paul's language and concept of the powers, for these terms almost always occur in a cluster of terms or in combination with other "powers" terms.[29] In 1 Cor. 15:24-25, all the enemies of Christ destined for destruction in the end are encapsulated in the phrase πᾶσαν ἀρχὴν καὶ πᾶσαν ἐξουσίαν καὶ δύναμιν. Included under this exhaustive list, Death is singled out as the last enemy to be destroyed (1 Cor. 15:26). In Col. 1:16 ἀρχαί and ἐξουσίαι are combined with θρόνοι and κυριότες; and in Col. 2:8-10 ἀρχή and ἐξουσίαι are placed in proximity to τὰ στοιχεῖα τοῦ κόσμου ("the elements of the world").[30] The comprehensive nature of this phrase is best captured in Rom. 8:38-39:

> For I am persuaded that neither death, nor life, nor angels, nor principalities, nor the present, nor the future, nor powers, nor height, nor depth, nor any other creature, will be able to separate us from the love of God in Christ Jesus our Lord.

As we argued in our chapter on Romans, the above list consists of antithetical pairs, establishing a pattern of AB AB AB C AB C: θάνατος (A), ζωή (B); ἄγγελοι (A), ἀρχαὶ (B); ἐνεστῶτα (A), μέλλοντα (B); δυνάμεις (C); ὕψωμα (A), βάθος (B); τις κτίσις ἑτέρα (C). The central location of δυνάμεις ("powers") makes it a comprehensive summary of everything listed before and after it. Thus, *both* literary personifications (Life, Death, Present, Future) *and* spiritual forces (Angels, Principalities, Height, Depth,[31] Any Other Creature) constitute the "powers."

Principalities and powers, then, denote for Paul comprehensive features of reality spanning the whole gamut of existence.[32] The powers permeate all aspects of the cosmos and human existence. In his detailed study of the powers, Forbes responds to K. Ferdinando's claim that "It is indeed difficult to see how

---

28. The relationship between this verse and Romans 5–8 was explored in our chapter on Romans via Ps. 19 (18 OG).

29. Cf. Eph. 1:21; 6:10-12.

30. In Col. 2:15 the phrase is not used in combination with other "powers" terms.

31. Ὕψωμα and βάθος are astronomical terms and may refer here to celestial beings. See our chapter on Romans.

32. So also J. M. G. Barclay, "Why the Roman Empire Was Insignificant to Paul," in *Pauline Churches and Diaspora Jews*, WUNT 275 (Tubingen: Mohr Siebeck, 2011), 383–87.

the New Testament writers could have communicated more clearly than they did that, in their references to Satan, demons and powers, they had in mind personal spirit beings."[33] Forbes demurs: "This is surely the case for Satan and the demons, but not, I think, for the 'powers.'"[34] While this statement may be an attempt to account for the uniqueness of the presentation of the powers in the Pauline corpus, it is misleading in that it gives the impression that Satan and the demons can somehow be detached from the principalities and powers. But why should Satan, demons, and angels be divorced from the powers?[35] The most significant, defining characteristic of the powers is that they belong to "this age" or "this world." It is in the present evil age that the powers exercise dominion; and it is from this present evil age that Christ has come to rescue believers (Gal. 1:4). Sin, Death, and the Flesh—as apocalyptic powers—all belong to the present age and have all been dealt a decisive blow in the cross of Christ; for the cross of Christ has ushered in a new age, so that the present form of "this world" is passing away (1 Cor. 7:31; cf. 1 Corinthians 1–2, 10:11). Thus, when Paul informs us that Satan is the god of this age (2 Cor. 4:4) and together with his minions constitute the rulers of this age (1 Cor. 2:6-8), we are to see them as part of the same phenomenon: opposing powers that line up on the opposite side of God and Christ in the cosmic struggle. That is why all the enemies of Christ (all dominion, authority, and power [1 Cor. 15:24-26]; Satan [Rom. 16:20]) can be spoken of as bound to share the same fate: all will be trampled on.[36] To separate Satan, demons, and angels from the "powers" is to fundamentally misconstrue Paul's complex theology of the powers. Our contention is corroborated by one of the earliest interpreters of Paul—the author of Ephesians. The author of Ephesians does not draw a distinction between the

---

33. K. Ferdinando, "Screwtape Revisited: Demonology Western, African and Biblical," in *The Unseen World: Christian Reflections on Angels, Demons and the Heavenly Realm*, ed. A. N. S. Lane (Carlisle: Paternoster Press, 1996), 108.

34. Forbes, "Paul's Principalities and Powers," 86n89.

35. Forbes tends to couch his argument in the idea of Paul's "preferred way of speaking" ("Paul's Principalities and Powers," 62, 81), which he argues is abstract and impersonal. But how can we make this judgment when Paul's letters are contingent? Statistical data do not bear out the assumption that the terminology Paul prefers is abstract and impersonal. Paul refers to Satan and angels more than any of the other principalities and powers terms: Satan (eight times: Rom. 16:20; 1 Cor. 5:5; 7:5; 2 Cor. 2:11; 11:14; 12:7; 1 Thess. 2:18; 2 Thess. 2:9; cf. 2 Cor. 4:4; 6:15; 1 Thess. 3:5); angel(s) (thirteen times: 1 Thess. 4:16; 2 Thess. 1:7; 1 Cor. 4:9; 6:3; 11:10; 13:1; 2 Cor. 11:14; 12:7; Gal. 1:8; 3:19; 4:24; Rom. 8:38; Col. 2:18; cf. 1 Cor. 10:10); principalities and powers (five times: Rom. 8:38; 1 Cor. 15:24; Col. 1:16; Col. 2:10; Col. 2:15); *stoicheia* (four times: Gal. 4:3; 4:9; Col. 2:8; 2:20).

36. There seems to be an influence of Gen. 3:15 and Ps. 110:1 on both 1 Cor. 15:24-26 and Rom. 16:20 (cf. Psa 91:13).

devil and the principalities and powers; rather, heading his list of the powers is the devil: the devil . . . principalities . . . powers . . . world rulers of this darkness . . . wicked spiritual forces in the heavenly places . . . the evil one (Eph. 6:10-18).

By means of spiritual forces and literary personifications, Paul shows that the powers penetrate all aspects of existence; the powers operate across all levels simultaneously—cosmic, personal, political, social.[37] Personification may also be Paul's way of giving language to that which defies speech, and an acknowledgement of the mystery that often circumscribes human interaction with the world. In this is an implicit acknowledgement of the elusiveness of language for speaking about certain aspects of reality in our world. Personification provides the linguistic accoutrements with the help of which language may be given to the mysterious nature of our world, especially those aspects of human interactions with the world that are unspeakable. In Paul's complex theology, human ability to recognize the powers is compromised (cf. Rom. 1:18—5:21). Because of their all-pervasiveness, they often defy the human capacity of perception; thus, to detect the powers requires an epistemological transformation (cf. 2 Cor. 5:16). If the modern argument against Paul is that his talk about "powers" is mythical, pure hallucination, and lies, Paul's rejoinder is that the powers' ability to "blind" (2 Cor. 4:4) and "deceive" (Rom. 7:11; 2 Thess. 2:9-10) is a warning to each generation that each generation's modes of perception may be equally deceptive. The powers' ability to blind and deceive suggests not only how easy it is to fail to recognize the works of the powers but also how vulnerable even the best of humans are to replicating or furthering the works of the powers. That is why sometimes the powers may, paradoxically, take the form of an apostle in the body of Christ, who causes great harm if she or he is not detected and unmasked (cf. 1 Cor. 5:1-13; 2 Cor. 11:1-15). In our view, Paul's presentation of the *Geisterwelt* and literary personifications is an attempt to capture the all-pervasiveness of the powers and to show that they span the entire gamut of existence, while also acknowledging that "For now we see through a glass dimly.. . . Now we know in part" (1 Cor. 13:12).

In William Shakespeare's play, *Hamlet*, the character Hamlet says to Horatio, who may well be an embodiment of modern rationalism, "There are more things in heaven and earth, Horatio, than are dreamt of in your philosophy" (*Hamlet*, act 1, scene 5). The powers shatter all our modern categories and taxonomies. To refer to the powers as cosmic is to acknowledge the universal scale of their influence—from the cosmic struggle at the crucifixion of Jesus (1 Cor. 2:6-8) to the corruption of the created order (Rom.

---

37. Barclay, "Why the Roman Empire Was Insignificant to Paul," 382.

8:18–39). But this will be an incomplete category, since the powers also affect personal lives—from immorality that plagues individuals (1 Cor. 6:12—7:5) to the death of the entire human race (1 Cor. 15:26; Rom. 5:12—6:23). To say that they are mythical may be an indirect acknowledgment of the test they present to our modern epistemologies and myths, and our own embarrassment at the thought that the modern human has not been able to tame all aspects of reality. That there may exist forces of greater influence that could pose a threat to the modern person's cherished desire for autonomy is too much for the modern person to bear. Paul's complex theology of the powers provides resources for wrestling with the limits of human judgment and the mystery inherent in our vast universe.

To sum up what we have attempted to demonstrate in this project thus far, let us imagine a world two thousand years from now, where the existence of germs is no longer a given in certain regions of the globe. Let us also imagine that some scholars from that future era, who hail from those quarters where belief in the existence of germs hangs in the balance, undertake a study of twenty-first-century understandings of germs. It will be deeply inadequate for these scholars to focus their research solely on what twenty-first-century people "thought" about germs. These scholars would have to study the practices of twenty-first-century persons in light of their perceptions of germs: people wash their hands incessantly; parents disinfect baby bottles after each use; hand sanitizers advertising to kill 99.99 percent of germs are ubiquitous, and so on. And all these are practices conducted by twenty-first-century persons in light of the conviction that a group of insidious living organisms are seeking to invade their bodies. When these future researchers search hard in archives from twenty-first-century zoos to find pictures or videos of germs, they discover none! What their research uncovers, however, is the view that these dangerous organisms are so tiny and so sly that one needs a special set of lenses or equipment to detect them.

The above scenario in essence captures what we have attempted to do with Paul's conception of the principalities and powers by using "practices" as the category with which to understand Paul's powers. For Paul, the powers pervade all aspects of existence and, yet, to detect their work requires an epistemological transformation, since the powers are capable of blinding and deceiving humans (Rom. 7:11; 2 Cor. 4:4).[38] To therefore approach the powers as "myths" would mean attempting to detect the powers without the appropriate lens, that is, the

---

38. We acknowledge that our germ analogy, like all analogies, breaks down when pushed to its logical limit. For example, anyone could discover the appropriate scientific equipment and use it to see the germs. (We are grateful to C. Kavin Rowe for raising this objection). Nonetheless, one would still need

epistemological transformation that the advent of the new age has ushered in (2 Cor. 5:16). To say that the powers are the structures of human existence would be using too limiting a category, since the powers span the whole gamut of existence and operate across all levels simultaneously.[39] The structures of human existence (including human traditions) can be co-opted by the powers (Romans 7; Gal. 4:1-11; Col. 2:14), but the structures are not themselves the powers. To say that the powers are "cosmic" would be to tell only part of the story, since the powers also directly influence personal lives and events on the earthly stage. From the bondage of creation (Rom. 8:18-39; 1 Cor. 10:19-20; Gal. 4:3; Col. 2:8, 20) to social and individual degeneration (1 Cor. 6:12—7:5) and death in the human race (Rom. 5:12—6:23; 1 Cor. 15:26), Paul discerns the work of the powers. To say even that the powers are "spiritual beings" would be to place too much confidence in normal human categories: the powers shatter all our normal categories. In order to grasp the principalities and powers, we will have to acknowledge that they defy human language and reveal to us our limitations. Thus, on occasion, we may have to prayerfully seek careful language (for example, personification) that can do justice not only to the mystery that often circumscribes human interaction with the world, but also our inability to place the powers into predetermined categories.

Yet in order to adequately account for Paul's conception of the powers, we cannot begin by asking what Paul or his contemporaries "thought" or "believed" about the powers. Rather, we have to begin by looking at practices of the Pauline congregations, for the early Christians' conception of the powers is unintelligible without a developed account of their practices. There were certain practices that Paul believed would protect believers from the powers. Other practices, however, according to Paul, would make believers vulnerable to the works of the powers. These "practices of power" include, on one side, baptism (Romans 6), preaching (1 Corinthians 2), ecclesial discipline (1 Cor. 5:1-11) and, on the other side, idolatry and partaking in meals in idol temples (1 Corinthians 8–10; Gal. 4:1-11; Col. 2:6-23).

The Pauline congregations were made up mostly of former pagans. These former pagans had their own *habitus*, habituated dispositions that oriented their activities. For example, the former pagans had been accustomed to practices such as frequenting idol temples and participating in idol-sacrificial meals. For Paul, idolatry represented a deflection of worship from the one Lord and one God. Idols were manifestations of demons (1 Cor. 10:19-20). Thus, for believers

---

to be taught how to use the scientific equipment correctly. Paul's aim is to create a Christian *habitus* so that believers can learn to discern the scheme of the powers.

39. See Barclay, "Why the Roman Empire Was Insignificant to Paul," 363–87.

to continue to frequent idol temples and participate in idol sacrificial meals would be to expose themselves to demons. Paul sought to create a Christian *habitus* among the believers, so that with the help of the Spirit's guidance believers would be able to discern the schemes of the powers among them. The Christian *habitus* would also govern the community's practices. Their own sharing in the body and blood of the Lord Jesus Christ made it impossible for them to partake in the table of other lords and other gods. Their practice of baptism meant that the principalities and powers, powerful though they may be, were dealt a fatal blow in their encounter with Christ on the cross. On the cross, Christ unmasked the powers and divested himself of their domain. When believers undergo baptism they participate in Christ's death, burial, and resurrection and they too are transferred into a new realm where the powers no longer hold sway. It is the story of Christ's encounter with the powers on the cross that undergirds baptism as a practice of power, and to attempt to preach the message of the cross is to be swept into this cosmic battle. While believers may continue to experience the work of the powers, the fate of the powers has already been sealed, for in the end Christ will destroy all dominion, authority, and power (1 Cor. 15:24).

Our hypothetical scenario of forty-first-century scholars studying twenty-first-century conceptions of germs assumes a context in which the existence of germs is no longer taken for granted. In the same way, our study of the powers has so far assumed a context where the notion of the powers is often relegated to primitive myths: Western European and American contexts. But what about those parts of the world where belief in the principalities and powers is very much alive? Our engagement with European and American (male) scholars in part 1 of this study alerted us to the fact that study of the powers, like all other studies, cannot be isolated from context and context-driven questions that are often operative in our judgments. We noted, for example, that Bultmann's "demythologizing" is itself a twentieth-century Western "myth"; and that World War II and the Cold War profoundly influenced Berkhof's structural interpretation of the powers. Thus, in the next (final) chapter of this study we will attempt to show how the powers are interpreted in another context: Africa. We will see how African traditional religious beliefs and practices shape how the powers are interpreted in that context. We will also draw on our findings on practices of power in the Pauline congregations to respond to contextual issues that arise within the African context.

PART III

A Cross-Cultural Perspective

9

The Powers in Cross-Cultural Context: Africa

On a beautiful sunny day in a village in the Ashanti region of Ghana, people have converged to witness the installation of an *obosom* ("god"). A shirtless man with a fiber skirt and amulets around his neck and ankles leaps and dances to the accompaniment of drums, gongs, horns, singing, and clapping. He makes gestures with both hands, to the skies and the ground. The man stops to pour libation. After pouring the gin on the ground, he goes into a trance and utters words that go something like this:

> Onyankopon Tweduampon Kwame, Asase Yaa, etwei ne haha ne nnono, nne Fofie o, na Ta Kwesi ye ri si wo: ye re si wo ama ye anya nkwa, mma ye nya 'wuo, mma y'aso nsi, mma ye kote nso nwu: 'kuro yi 'dekuro nkwa so, mmerante nkwa so, mmawofoo nkwa so, 'kuro yi nkwada nkwa so.
>
> Odum Abena a onyina 'wo no e, mo nyina na ye re fre mo 'ma mo nyina mo aba ama seisei ara ye nyina ye tiri mu asem ye de ahye 'bosom yi mu.
>
> Ye fre wo anadwo, ye fre wo awia, na se ye ka se ebia ye sei ma yen a, ewo se wo ye. Na mmra a ye re hye ama wo 'bosom yi ene se, ye ne ye mma ne ye nana nom, se Ohene bi na ofiri babi aba na ose ore ko 'sa na obe ka kyere wo na se oko ko ko na onni nim a, ese se wo ka kyere yen: se nso se oko na obe di nim a wo ka no nokware. Afei bieku bio, se nnipa na oyare anadwo, ana se awia, ye pagya wo soa na ye bisa se nnipa Asomasi na ore wuo, mmusuo a wo be kyere no mmusu turoro nye nkontampo.
>
> Nne ye 'kuro yi nyina ye mpanyin ne ye nkwadaa nyina ye nyina y'ako apam ye nyina y'aye ko sipe nni ye yem, ye nyina y'aye ko bafua pe se wo Ta Kwesi nne Fofie, nne na ye re si wo: y'afa

215

'guane y'afa akoko, y'afa nsa ye de re be ma wo ama w'atena 'kuro
yi mu afwe 'kuro yi nkwa so. Efiri nne de kopim nne yi wo nguane
ngya yen, efiri nne di kopim nne yi, wo Atanogya, asem biara wo be
ka akyere yen wo ntwa yen akofwie, wo nfa nsuo so ngyina w'anum
so nka asem nso mfa nkyere yen.

Nne Ohene 'bosom ene wo (nne) o, nsamanfo 'bosom ene wo
nne o. Okyena bi na 'Sante 'hene asem aba se ebia me ba Asomasi se
me panyin bi yare na ebia bo mmoden na ko, se osoma 'bofo ma no
ba a na wo re ko, nye se wo re guane agya yen.

Ye nyina y'anum kasa bafua pe.

Supreme God, the Dependable, Kwame,[1] Earth Goddess (Asase
Yaa),[2] Leopard and all beasts and plants of the forest, today is sacred
Friday. And you, Ta Kwesi,[3] we are installing you; we are installing
you, so that we may have life. Do not let us inherit death; do not let
us become deaf; do not let us become impotent. To the chief of this
village, life; to the young men, life; to those who bear children, life;
to the children of this village, life.

You spirits of the tree called Odum Abena[4]—to whom belongs
the silk cotton tree, we call upon you all to come here, so that all the
thoughts in our heads may be placed in this shrine now.

When we call upon you at night, when we call upon you
during daylight, if we say to you "May you do this for us," that is
what you have to do.

And these are the decrees that we—together with our children
and our grandchildren—are instituting for the god of this shrine: if
our king comes from somewhere and says he is going to war, and
he comes to tell you, and if he is going to fight a battle that will end
in defeat, you must tell us; and if his battle will end in victory, you
must communicate that truth as well. And yet again, if disease strikes
a person at night, or in the daytime, if we lift you up and inquire of
you "Is so-and-so passing away?," let the cause of his misfortune that
you identify be definite.

---

1. Kwame is the name given to a male person born on Saturday. It may imply that the sacred day of
this deity falls on a Saturday.

2. Yaa is the name given to a female person born on Thursday. It may imply that the sacred day of this
deity falls on a Thursday.

3. Kwesi is the name given to a male person born on Sunday.

4. Abena is the name given to a female person born on Tuesday.

Today, this entire village, including the elders and the children, all of us have united, we have all become one and there is no dissension among us; we have all united as a single entity and decided that you, Ta Kwesi, on this sacred Friday, be installed today.

We have taken sheep and a fowl, we have taken gin, which we are about to give you so that you may reside in this town and preserve its life. From today and henceforth, do not flee and leave us; from today and henceforth, you fire of Tano, let no word from you to us be misleading; do not fill your mouth with water while addressing us.

Today, you have become a god of the king; you have become a god of our ancestral spirits today. Perhaps on some day in the future the Asante King may come and say, "My child so-and-so, or one of my elders, is sick. Please come with me." Or he may send a messenger to ask you to go with him. In such a case you may go, and we will not think that you are fleeing from us.

These words are spoken by all of us with one accord. (my translation)[5]

The above is my own translation of the account recorded by Captain R. S. Rattray in his study of the Asante tribe of Ghana in 1923. With some modifications today, one could find similar words at any installation of an *obosom* ("god") in a shrine. After these words, animals are slaughtered and their blood made to flow into a pan.

One finds similar practices in African countries south of the Sahara; and such practices provide an important window into the belief systems and epistemological conceptions of Africans.[6] The language used in the installation

5. Twi text in Captain R. S. Rattray, *Ashanti* (Oxford: Clarendon Press, 1923), 147–49. Cf. K. A. Appiah, *In My Father's House: Africa in the Philosophy of Culture* (Oxford: Oxford University Press, 1992), 107–9.

6. To speak of African beliefs is not in any way to deny the immense diversity of the cultures of Africa. Kwame Anthony Appiah, for example, has argued provocatively that because Africa is characterized by total cultural disunity, to engage in any discourse about Africa's cultural unity is to "invent" Africa. In Appiah's scheme a culturally unified Africa is a fallacy. See Appiah, *In My Father's House*, 3–27. While diversity among the various groups of the African continent needs to be acknowledged, we cannot totally obliterate the existence of some unity in culture in sub-Saharan Africa. There exist some underlying commonalities in conceptual framework and practices among the cultures of Africa that cannot be overlooked. Thus, we are in agreement with those scholars who affirm the common features of African culture, while not disregarding the diversity. See, e.g., I. Kopytoff, ed., *The African Frontier: The Reproduction of Traditional African Societies* (Bloomington: Indiana University Press, 1987), 1–86; P.

ceremony presupposes the existence or reality of certain entities. First, it presumes the existence of a Supreme Being called *Onyankopon*,[7] who is praised as dependable (*Tweduampon*), for he is the source of all existence. Second, there are the *abosom* ("gods") or lesser spirits, who are invisible and often manifest themselves in nature (for example, *Asase Yaa* [Earth goddess], *Atanogya* [fire, that is, spirit of Tano],[8] *Odum Abena* [spirit of the Odum Tree]). And third, there are the spirits of the dead ancestors (*nsamanfo*), who are also invisible but are believed to be alive. On this occasion, the god *Ta Kwesi* is being installed in the shrine, and the community—which includes the present generation of elders and children, future generations to come, and ancestors who have passed on—makes a covenant with this god, in hopes that the god will respond to it in times of crises and protect it from misfortune. In this belief system, spiritual forces play a significant role in the lives of people, and that the gods or lesser spirits often manifest themselves in nature also suggests that part of the physical world is animated. These spirits are often invoked for good or for evil.

In cultures all over the continent of Africa, the notion that a Supreme Being (God) created the universe and that disembodied, invisible spirits affect, and often control, the physical world is uncontroversial and need not be rationally defended.[9] After studying about three hundred different peoples in

Curtin, S. Feierman, L. Thompson, and J. Vansina, *African History* (Boston: Little Brown, 1978), 1–24; K. Gyekye, *An Essay on African Philosophical Thought: The Akan Conceptual Scheme*, rev. ed. (Philadelphia: Temple University Press, 1995), 190–210. Gyekye writes: "A painstaking comparative study of African cultures leaves one in no doubt that despite the undoubted cultural diversity arising from Africa's ethnic pluralism, threads of underlying affinity do run through the beliefs, customs, value systems, and sociopolitical institutions and practices of the various African societies" (*African Philosophical Thought*, 192).

7. *Onyankopon* is the common term in the Twi language for "God." Nonetheless, as some scholars have rightly emphasized, it would be wrong to suggest that Africans have simply imported the idea of God from Western belief systems or Christianity into their concept of being. The African notion of God predates the arrival of Christian missionaries on the continent. See E. W. Smith, *The Secret of the African* (London: Student Christian Movement, 1930); E. G. Parrinder, *Religion in Africa* (Baltimore: Penguin Books, 1969), 39.

8. The Tano is a river that runs through the Brong-Ahafo region of Ghana.

9. On the rationality of such beliefs and practices, see Appiah, *In My Father's House*, 107–36. Appiah argues that African traditional religion —with its characteristic belief in the powers of spiritual agents—is in certain respects like modern natural science. Referencing the spirit-installation ceremony, Appiah notes that to ask a spirit to inhabit a shrine means first of all that the people believe that there are spirits. What would be absurd, Appiah contends, would be to posit that this ritual involves anything other than a literal belief in spirits: "The element of the ceremonial is not what is essential; what is essential is the ontology of invisible beings" (Appiah, *In My Father's House*, 112). This belief is neither rationally defended nor rationally attacked. The same is true for belief in the existence of hundreds of thousands of

Africa, John Mbiti discovered that "in all these societies, without a single exception, people have a notion of God as the Supreme Being. This minimal and fundamental idea about God is found in all African societies."[10] He also notes that "myriads of spirits are reported from every African people."[11] Such belief is not only commonplace among the uneducated, or as some would say the un*enlightened*, populace. In her research on African cosmology, Esther Acolatse discovered that the tendency to attribute physical reality to a spiritual world was also held by university students and professors of all disciplines.[12] The practical truth is this: most Africans, whether educated, Christian, or Muslim, retain their worldview that ascribes ontology to invisible beings. Mbiti writes: "Whatever science may do to prove the existence or non-existence of the spirits, one thing is undeniable, namely that for African peoples the spirits are a reality and a reality which must be reckoned with, whether it is a clear, blurred or confused reality."[13] One can even say that this is the prevalent African worldview. And as many African scholars have argued, such belief cannot, and should not, be equated with superstition, for these beliefs are based on experiences and deep reflection.[14] For many in these cultures, the evidence that these spirits do exist is compelling, if not obvious: sick people get better

---

small solar system bodies; for the masses this is not rationally defended, because it is taken to be true. So also in African traditional beliefs, the existence of spirits is uncontroversial. People have acquired these beliefs during their upbringing. But they are not much different from the average person whose thought forms have been shaped by scientific materialism. This is because the overwhelming majority of people in the West, for example, are ignorant about the complex underpinnings of scientific theories. Yet people accept these theories because these are things people have been taught growing up. And until anything happens to shake the foundations of their beliefs, people have little reason to think that it is not true. According to Appiah, the same applies to African traditional beliefs: little has happened in people's lives to alter their belief in spirits. As a matter of fact, "The evidence that spirits exist is obvious: priests go into trance, people get better after application of spiritual remedies, people die regularly from the action of inimical spirits," (Appiah, *In My Father's House*, 118). What we cannot do is to begin by asking such people to assume their beliefs are false or irrational, for they can offer numerous rational arguments in defense of their beliefs. In this regard, then, African traditional religion shares with modern science the purposes of explanation, prediction, and control. See also R. Horton, "African Traditional Religion and Western Science," *Africa* 32, no. 3 (1967): 50–71, 155–87.

10. J. S. Mbiti, *African Religions and Philosophy* (Oxford: Heinemann, 1990), 29.

11. Ibid., 77.

12. E. Acolatse, "Cosmology and Pastoral Diagnoses: A Psycho-Theological Anthropology for Pastoral Counseling in Ghana" (PhD diss., Princeton Theological Seminary, 2002), 68.

13. Mbiti, *African Religions and Philosophy*, 89.

14. See, e.g., Mbiti, *Introduction to African Religion* (London: Heinemann, 1975), 16; E. A. Asamoa, "The Christian Church and African Heritage," *International Review of Mission* 44 (1955): 292–301, esp. 298.

after visits to fetish priests; people die regularly from actions of evil spirits or witchcraft; exorcisms frequently occur in churches; and these exorcisms are often accompanied by the testimonies and transformed lives of the formerly possessed.

The African Puzzle: The Rise of the Charismatic and Pentecostal Movements and the Decline of African Independent Churches

In a context in which the universe is believed to be inhabited by spiritual forces, the NT concept of principalities and powers—interpreted as the invisible world inhabited by hostile spirits—seems to find a natural home.[15] As J. Kwabena Asamoah-Gyadu has observed, "Christians in Africa have found the categories of power, dominion and alleviation of suffering by the power of the Spirit relevant in the general struggle with fears and insecurities within a universe in which supernatural evil is considered hyperactive."[16] Thus, charismatic and Pentecostal churches—movements built on overcoming evil spiritual powers—are flourishing in this context. People find a useful continuity between the emphasis on the spiritual realm in these churches and their inherited traditional religious beliefs. On a visit to one of these churches in Ghana, one might hear songs like:

Me tia obonsam so (2x)
Me hwere ma ko soro me tia obonsam so
Me tia obonsam so (2x)
Me hwere ma ko soro, osoro, osoro metia obonsam so

I have stamped on the Devil
I have leaped to great heights and stamped on the Devil
I have stamped on the Devil

---

15. In a study of Paul's principalities and powers in the African context, Bayo Abijole writes: "St. Paul's theology of Principalities and Powers has great lessons and implications for Christianity in Africa. This is because unlike [the] western world, where supernaturalism had [*sic*] become foreign, the African world is still very similar to the world of first century AD to which Paul addressed his theology. The African world of this century is still dominated by supernatural thoughts of witches, ghosts, spirits, demons and powers which are strongly believed to be against the welfare of man" ("St. Paul's Concept of Principalities and Powers in African Context," *African Theological Journal* 17 [1988]: 118–29, on 127).

16. J. K. Asamoah-Gyadu, "Pulling Down Strongholds: Evangelism, Principalities and Powers and the African Pentecostal Imagination," *International Review of Missions* (2007): 306–16.

I have leaped to greater heights and stamped on the Devil (my translation).

Also:

We conquer Satan
We conquer demons
We conquer principalities
We conquer powers
Shout Halle-Hallelujah (4x).

From televangelists to storefront churches, one cannot miss the prayers of exorcism directed at evil spirits, who are commanded to release people or places from bondage.

Naturally, the downplaying of the spirit realm by historic mission (or mainline) churches has meant that such churches would struggle in this context.[17] Historic mission churches are often viewed as deposits of Western approaches to Christianity—even vestiges of Western colonialism.[18] The Christian faith passed down through these churches is regarded as one that has been shaped by another worldview—that of Western scientific materialism. As the West has advanced technologically, scientific explanations have been put forward for many physical phenomena. Westerners have, therefore, turned away from the invisible world of religion. And it is through this scientific, materialistic worldview that much of Western Christianity is filtered. Theologian Kwame Bediako notes: "By and large, Christian theology in the West made its peace with the Enlightenment. It responded by drawing a line between the secular world and the sacred sphere, as it were, and so established a frontier between the spiritual world on the one hand, and the material world on the other, creating in effect, a dichotomy between them."[19] Nonetheless, as a number of African scholars have noted, the belief in the agency of invisible

---

17. This includes mainline Protestant denominations and Anglican and Roman Catholic churches.

18. A statement by theologians from developing countries meeting in Dar es Salaam in 1976 castigates Western missionaries for their "services to Western imperialism by legitimizing it and accustoming their new adherents to accept compensatory expectations of an eternal reward for terrestrial misfortunes, including colonial exploitation"; cited in S. Torres and V. Fabella, eds., *The Emergent Gospel: Theology from the Underside of History: Papers from the Ecumenical Dialogue of Third World Theologians, Dar es Salaam, August 5–12, 1976* (Maryknoll, NY: Orbis Books, 1978), 266.

19. K. Bediako, "Worship as Vital Participation: Some Personal Reflections on Ministry in the African Church," *Journal of African Christian Thought* 8 (2005): 3–7, on 3.

beings means that most Africans would not fully embrace those theologies, clad in the Western scientific worldview, that are irreconcilable with their beliefs.

In an article written in the mid-twentieth century, Ghanaian theologian and pastor E. A. Asamoa wrestled with the issue of the conflict between what he called the "African heritage" and the Christian faith.[20] With particular attention to his own Ghanaian context, he pointed to African beliefs such as belief in lesser gods, ancestral spirits, witchcraft, and magic and noted that the (missionary) church's attitude toward such beliefs had been dismissive. The church had dismissed witchcraft as mere psychological delusion and trickery and disparaged African belief in the spirit world as "superstition"—"the belief in something that does not exist."[21] Asamoa asseverates:

> Anyone who knows African Christians intimately will know that no amount of denial on the part of the Church will expel belief in supernatural powers from the minds of the African people. What often happens as a result of such denunciation is that a state of conflict is created in the mind of the Christian, and he becomes a hypocrite who in official church circles pretends to give the impression that he does not believe in these things, while in his own private life he resorts to practices which are the results of such beliefs.[22]

Asamoa attributed the denial of the existence of supernatural powers not to Christianity but to Western scientific materialism. In other words, the historic mission churches had become the channels of the worldview of scientific materialism and Western culture in a unique, African context. In consonance with many African scholars, he challenged the notion that African belief in supernatural powers is superstition, since such belief "is not the result of sheer imagination but rather the outcome of direct psychical experience in the supersensible world."[23] According to Asamoa, if the missionary churches were going to be able to penetrate the "African mind" or the "African soul-world," they would have to acknowledge their own European heritage and prejudices and explore unfamiliar fields of knowledge.[24] He called for traditional mission

20. E. A. Asamoa, "The Christian Church and African Heritage," *International Review of Mission* 44 (1955): 292–301.

21. Ibid., 297.

22. Ibid.

23. Ibid., 298. See also John S. Mbiti, *Introduction to African Religion*, 16.

24. Asamoa, "The Christian Church and African Heritage," 300.

churches to take seriously the reality of the spiritual realm and to demonstrate to African Christians that Jesus Christ has triumphed over all other powers.[25]

In a similar vein, while serving as pastor of a church in Nigeria, Osadolor Imasogie noticed that the common reaction of many African Christians in times of crises is to revert back to traditional religious practices. As Imasogie reflected on this baffling reality, he concluded that this was not only the result of some defects in the approach by Christian missionaries, in particular, but deficiencies in the formulation of Christian theology, in general.[26] According to Imasogie, "The observed lack of total commitment of the average African Christian to Christ is due to the lack of 'fit' between Christian theology and African life. This lack of fit is, in turn, due to [the] failure of Western orthodox theologians to take African worldviews into consideration in their theological formulations."[27] Thus, Imasogie argues that, if Christian theology is going to be relevant in Africa, African worldview must be taken into account in theological formulations.[28]

Imasogie proposes three "guidelines" for Christian theology in Africa, guidelines that he feels will help the African Christian to stay totally committed to Christ—even in times of tough crises. First, Imasogie proposes a renewed appreciation of the "efficacy of Christ's power over evil spiritual forces."[29] This proposal recognizes not only that the African worldview is charged with disembodied spirits, but it also perceives that after the Enlightenment the

25. Ibid., 300–1. Cf. Abijole, "St. Paul's Concept of Principalities and Powers in African Context," 127: "African missionaries must lay greater emphasis on [the] victorious show of Christ over powers if their ministry is to be more functional and relevant to African Christians. Soteriology for the African covers the whole sphere of life—body, soul and spirit. The Salvation preached by many western missionaries (who founded Churches in Africa) is salvation of the soul unrelated to man's physical welfare. This is why most mission churches have failed to make much Spiritual impact on their members. It is because of this shortcoming in their evangelical emphasis. Some missionaries even deny the reality of these powers which they regard as superstitious. The other missionaries who partially accepted [sic] the reality of the powers make little or no effort to relate the Gospel message to these problems."

26. O. Imasogie, *Guidelines for Christian Theology in Africa* (Achimota, Ghana: Africa Christian Press, 1983).

27. Ibid., 12.

28. Writing a few years after Imasogie, renowned missiologist Lesslie Newbigin echoed a similar conviction: "If the Gospel is to be understood, if it is to be received as something which communicates truth about the real human situation, if it is, as we say, 'to make some sense,' it has to be communicated in the language of those to whom it is addressed and has to be clothed in symbols which are meaningful to them. It must as we say, 'come alive.' Those to whom it is addressed must be able to say, 'Yes, I see. This is true for my situation'"; Newbigin, *The Gospel in a Pluralist Society* (Grand Rapids: Eerdmans, 1989), 141.

29. Imasogie, *Guidelines for Christian Theology in Africa*, 79.

"rational" Christian theologian is confronted with the challenge of viewing the Biblical accounts of angels, demons, principalities and powers as illusions of an outmoded world. Thus, biblical references to demon possessions and exorcisms, principalities and powers, are often interpreted (especially in the West) as symbols rather than an ontology of spiritual beings. Yet within the African context and worldview, one saturated with belief about spirits, Scripture's accounts of demons and evil spirits are taken literally, not symbolically. Thus, for Imasogie, Christian theology within an African context should demonstrate that "Christ is not only the all-sufficient savior from the power of sin but also the all-sufficient conqueror of demons and deliverer from all fears."[30]

Second, Imasogie proposes a new prominence for the role of the Holy Spirit and the "present mediatory efficacy of the Living Christ."[31] The role of the Holy Spirit cannot be neglected within the African context, for the African finds wholeness in relation to *both* human and spiritual communities. While, because of the "quasi-scientific" worldview of the West, the role of the Holy Spirit still remains on the periphery of Western Christian theology, such cannot be the case in the African context; and this is because Africans seek guidance from spiritual beings through rituals and divinations.

In addition to these two proposals, Imasogie calls for a "new emphasis on the omnipresence of God and the consequent sacramental nature of the universe."[32] Most Africans conceive of God as a transcendent being who is also immanent in creation.[33] Thus, every act or deed is committed in God's presence. A theology of omnipresence within the African context echoes the biblical truth that "Nothing in all creation is hidden from God's sight; everything is uncovered and laid bare before the eyes of him to whom we must give account" (Heb. 4:13).

The proliferation of Pentecostal and charismatic churches on the continent in the last three decades has in some respects affirmed Asamoa's and Imasogie's accounts, though paradoxes remain. Pentecostal and charismatic churches mostly focus on the empowering work of the Holy Spirit, which is demonstrated in ministries of spiritual warfare, exorcisms, and healings. The miraculous manifestations of the Holy Spirit that accompany the ministries of charismatic and Pentecostal churches function as potent evangelizing tools, for they serve as a bridge between Jesus' ministry and traditional religious beliefs.

---

30. Ibid., 80.

31. Ibid., 81.

32. Ibid., 84.

33. This view should not be equated with pantheism. God is believed to be transcendent and, yet, also present to creation and active within creation.

But traditional missionary churches and other non-Pentecostal churches cannot and should not be left out of this account, since these churches are also catching on to this wave, even if their emphasis on the spiritual realm is relatively more measured. In his study of evangelism in Ghanaian churches, Asamoah-Gyadu observes that the lines between Pentecostal and non-Pentecostal forms of Christianity are blurring. This is because many non-Pentecostal churches are also taking a charismatic approach to Christianity that incorporates spiritual warfare, healings, and exorcisms.[34] He observes that "in the last three decades, charismatic renewal movements have emerged strongly within historic mission denominations, and this has changed the face of African Christianity in ways that make strict denominational categorizations tenuous if not contentious."[35] Historic mission churches are routinely making room for pneumatic experiences in their message and forms of worship. And where such emphasis is lacking in these churches, it is commonplace to find members of historic mission churches visiting charismatic prayer and healing camps. Asamoah-Gyadu even notes a paradigm shift in the curriculum at the most prestigious theological institution of Ghana, the Trinity Theological Seminary. He observes that this bastion of theological education had always patterned itself on the Western (mainly European) system of theological education. There has been a shift at the seminary, however, in the last two decades that reflects the changing landscape of Christianity in the country in particular and on the continent as a whole. The curriculum has been expanded to include courses in Pentecostal and charismatic theologies, African and biblical charismaticism, and evangelism and church growth.[36] Christianity in Africa—from the popular level to the coteries of academia—is finding ways to accommodate the African imagination of a spiritually animated universe.

Nonetheless, the rise of Pentecostal and charismatic churches presents a puzzle for understanding African Christianity. On the one hand, it is the case, as we have shown above, that the rise of Pentecostal and charismatic churches in Africa owes much to these churches' ability to relate to African

---

34. Asamoah-Gyadu, "Pulling Down Strongholds," 308–9.

35. Ibid., 308–9. While the above statement aptly captures the changing Christian landscape on the continent, there may be a slight exaggeration in this assertion. Despite the charismatic infusion in historic mission churches, clear patterns of difference emerge. For example, most historic mission churches retain their traditional worship styles (which include hymnody and liturgy) on Sunday mornings. The healing and exorcism services are mostly reserved for annual or biannual "Revivals" or occasional "all-night" Friday services. It is very rare to find a healing or exorcism practice in a traditional mission church on a Sunday morning. We also have to note that some of these traditional mission churches continue to resist the wave of charismatic renewal that is sweeping across the continent.

36. Asamoah-Gyadu, "Pulling Down Strongholds," 313–14.

cosmology. But, on the other hand, charismatic Christianity sets itself in direct opposition to African traditional religion. These churches often hold special deliverance services for members to help them cut off all connections with their family traditions. Thus, the current trends in the Christian landscape present a perplexing puzzle: African Independent Churches (AIC), which were formed independently from missionary churches in an attempt to accommodate traditional religious ideas, are currently on the decline, while the charismatic churches that have no room for African traditional beliefs in their form of Christianity are on the rise. The proliferation of AICs in the 1960s and 1970s has now given way to the Pentecostal wave on the continent.

In the wake of independence from colonial powers, the euphoria of black independence created an atmosphere for the affirmation of African culture and identity. These conditions were fertile grounds for the flourishing of AICs, which mostly sought to endorse African culture against its purported denigration by Western missionaries.[37] A statement by African theologians from the proceedings of a 1965 consultation bespeaks the positive estimation of African culture in the aftermath of African independence:

> We believe that God, the Father of our Lord Jesus Christ, Creator of Heaven and Earth, Lord of History, has been dealing with mankind at all times and in all parts of the world. It is with this conviction that we study the rich heritage of our African peoples, and we have evidence that they know him and worship him. We recognize the radical quality of God's self-revelation in Jesus Christ; and yet it is because of this revelation we can discern what is truly of God in our pre-Christian heritage; this knowledge of God is not totally discontinuous with our previous knowledge of him.[38]

The above statement can be said to capture the spirit of the AICs, but it can no longer be said to be representative of the new face of African Christianity, the charismatic wave that seeks to sever all ties to traditional religions. As Paul Gifford has observed in his detailed study of African Christianity, "Now the growth areas of Christianity [in Africa] are those that demonise African traditions and culture."[39] Statistics of the Ghanaian Christian landscape are quite

---

37. See J. Parratt, *Reinventing Christianity: African Theology Today* (Grand Rapids: Eerdmans, 1995).

38. Cited in K. Dickson and P. Ellingworth, eds., *Biblical Revelation and African Beliefs* (London: Lutterworth, 1969), 16.

39. P. Gifford, *African Christianity: Its Public Role* (Bloomington: Indiana University Press, 1998), 324. Gifford notes that South Africa may be the exception to this rule, since AICs continue to grow in South

telling and may be illustrative of the changing face of Christianity on the continent of Africa. The Ghana Evangelism Committee periodically publishes a survey of churches in the entire country.[40] These surveys are very useful, since they involve actual counting of Christians attending services on Sundays. The survey, taken between 1991 and 1993,[41] showed a 2 percent decline in church attendance in the African Independent Churches between 1987 and 1993 (from 350,805 to 342,912). The Catholic Church also saw a 2 percent decline in this period (from 350,650 to 343,957). The Christian Council, which includes most of the historic mission churches,[42] saw a modest increase of 7 percent (from 491,352 to 525,824). The Pentecostal Council, however, enjoyed an enormous 38 percent increase in this period (from 342,086 to 473,686).[43] These statistics are emblematic of the changing landscape of Christianity on the continent, for as Gifford notes, statistics around the continent give the following impression: "The AICs are in serious difficulty; the mainline churches are static if not decreasing;[44] and substantial growth lies with Pentecostal and 'mission-related' churches."[45]

Africa. But Gifford argues that "the 1980s and 1990s have been for South Africa what the 1950s and 1960s were for Black Africa—years of increasing resistance, struggle, victory and elation" (*African Christianity*, 325).

40. Ghana Evangelism Committee, *National Church Survey, 1993 Update: Facing the Unfinished Task of the Church in Ghana* (Accra: Assemblies of God Literature Centre, 1993).

41. See G.E.C., *National Church Survey*, 16–17.

42. The Christian Council includes the following denominations: A.M.E. Zion; Anglican; Baptist (Convention); Evangelical Lutheran; Evangelical Presbyterian; Mennonite; Methodist; Presbyterian; Salvation Army; Interdenominational; sundry.

43. The survey includes a group of denominations under the heading "Mission Related," which it defines as "Sundry churches and denominations originating from, or, otherwise related to an overseas church or missionary society. No organizational relationship exists between the churches in this group" (G.E.C., *National Church Survey*, 12). These "Mission Related" churches include: Baptist (non-Convention); Churches of Christ; Evangelical Church of Ghana; Good News Churches; New Apostolic Church; United Christian Churches; and sundry. While this group enjoyed the largest growth rate (78 percent), they are also relatively small in number (from 35,370 to 63,008). The Seventh Day Adventists also grew by 15 percent, but their numbers are also relatively few (from 69,318 to 79,499).

44. Gifford's conclusion is drawn relative to the population increase in this period.

45. Gifford, *African Christianity*, 63. On growth of Pentecostals in Nigeria, see R. Marshall, "'God is not a Democrat': Pentecostalism and Democratisation in Nigeria," in *The Christian Churches and the Democratisation of Africa*, ed. P. Gifford (Leiden: Brill, 1995), 239–60.

THE NT LANGUAGE OF THE POWERS AND THE DANGER OF VIOLENCE

The Pentecostal and charismatic churches see their ministries as anchored in the Bible's teachings. They see their work as embodying the NT's witness concerning the principalities and powers. The exorcisms and healings of these ministries are built on Jesus' and the early church's ministries of casting out unclean spirits from the possessed. The Gospels present Jesus' ministry as a clash of two kingdoms: the kingdom of God and the reign of Satan. Jesus ushers in the kingdom of God by releasing persons from bondage to Satan and demons (e.g., Matt. 8:16-17; 12:22-30; Mark 1:21-28; 3:22-27; Luke 4:31-37; 11:14-20). In Acts, the early church's ministry is empowered by the Holy Spirit (Acts 1:8) and is characterized by signs and wonders, including deliverance from evil spirits (e.g., Acts 8:4-8; Acts 19:11-12). A key verse for charismatic churches is Eph. 6:12 (often quoted in the KJV): "For we wrestle not against flesh and blood, but against principalities, against powers, against the rulers of the darkness of this world, against spiritual wickedness in high places." Indeed, while the charismatic renewal on the continent resonates with traditional African religious ideas, as already noted, all such churches set themselves in antithesis to traditional religions and condemn all such practices and worship as demonic. Just as the apostle Paul condemned all the deities ordinarily worshiped in Greco-Roman temples as demons (1 Cor. 8:1-6; 10:19-21), so also these Christian churches condemn the gods of traditional religions as demonic powers.[46] For these Pentecostal and charismatic churches, they are living out the witness of the early church in Acts and being faithful to the language of Scripture concerning the principalities and powers.

Nonetheless, this attempt to live out faithfully every single word of the NT presents a real danger on a continent that has had its fair share of crippling violence (cf. Acts 13:4-12)—from colonization to current ethnic conflicts. The charismatic renewal of Christianity in Africa has created sharp sensitivity to such phenomena as demon possession and witchcraft (sometimes known as evil magic).[47] Charges of demonism are common on the continent.[48] In certain instances, terms like *the devil* and *demons* provide the language with which to articulate the challenges people face in their encounter with modernity or

---

46. The lesser gods of African traditional religion are mostly regarded as spirits created by the Supreme God. They are worshipped as mediators between God and humans; and their mediation preserves God's transcendence. In many African religions these lesser gods are not necessarily opposed to the Supreme God but serve as God's agents.

47. On witchcraft, witches, witch doctors, magic, and medicine men in Africa, see E. Muga, *African Response to Western Christian Religion: A Sociological Analysis of African Separatist Religious and Political Movements in East Africa* (Kampala, Nairobi, Dar es Salaam: East African Literature Bureau, 1975): 70–76.

globalization.[49] In some instances, however, such language is used to brand people, often children and older women, as witches, leading to violent acts perpetrated against them (cf. Acts 13:4-12). In some parts of Africa, children and women charged with witchcraft are mutilated, banished, or, in extreme cases, killed. Witchcraft is viewed as a manifestation of the devil and those charged with having such leanings are viewed as servants of Satan.[50]

As previously noted, while African traditional religious ideas provide an appropriate context for interpreting the NT language of the powers, many Christians in Africa tend to regard their Christian beliefs as directly antithetical to traditional African religions and, thus, often condemn the practices of traditional religions as satanic. Christians are admonished to break any ties with traditional religious practices and symbols. Deliverance services are therefore conducted regularly to "break the yoke" of any family idols or curses; connections to these are believed to pass down misfortune from one generation to another. The condemnations of ties to traditional religions are more pronounced in charismatic and Pentecostal services. Anyone suspected of tapping into the spiritual resources of traditional religions to harm others may be branded a witch and subjected either to exorcism or, in some cases, punishment (cf. Acts 13:4-12). Such discourses are prevalent on the continent; and, on occasion, this may result in conflict or violence against the accused.

Tracy McVeigh, in a report from Nigeria, uncovered a campaign of violence against children fueled by evangelical preachers charging them with witchcraft.[51] According to McVeigh, children named as witches "are burnt, poisoned, slashed, chained to trees, buried alive or simply beaten and chased off into the bush."[52] Deliverance services may be held to exorcise the witchcraft, but, as McVeigh points out, once a child has been branded a witch, even if

48. On the increasing demonizing discourse in different parts of Africa, see D. B. C. O'Brien, "Satan Steps Out from the Shadows: Religion and Politics in Africa," *Africa* 70 (2000): 520–25; R. I. J. Hackett, "Discourses of Demonization in Africa and Beyond," *Diogenes* 50 (2003): 61–75.

49. See B. Meyer, *Translating the Devil: Religion and Modernity among the Ewe in Ghana* (Edinburg: Edinburgh University Press, 1999); A. Apter, "Atinga Revisited: Yoruba Witchcraft and the Cocoa Economy, 1950–1951," in *Modernity and Its Malcontents: Ritual and Power in Postcolonial Africa*, ed. J. Comaroff and J. Comaroff (Chicago: University of Chicago Press, 1993), 111–28.

50. For accounts of beliefs and practices associated with witchcraft in the West African, especially Nigerian, context, see M. Bastian, "'Bloodhounds Who Have No Friends': Witchcraft and Locality in the Nigerian Popular Press," in Comaroff and Comaroff, *Modernity and Its Malcontents*, 129–66.

51. T. McVeigh, "Children Are Targets of Nigerian Witch Hunt," *The Observer* (8 December 2007): 34. Online: http://www.guardian.co.uk/world/2007/dec/09/tracymcveigh.theobserver.

52. Ibid.

her parents want to keep her, she is still in danger of attacks from mobs in the streets.

Some of the stories are personal and deeply heart-wrenching, such as the story of ten year-old Mary Sudnad:

> Mary Sudnad, 10, grimaces as her hair is pulled into corn rows by Agnes, 11, but the scalp just above her forehead is bald and blistered. Mary tells her story fast, in staccato, staring fixedly at the ground.
>
> "My youngest brother died. The pastor told my mother it was because I was a witch. Three men came to my house. I didn't know these men. My mother left the house. Left these men. They beat me." She pushes her fists under her chin to show how her father lay, stretched out on his stomach on the floor of their hut, watching. After the beating there was a trip to the church for a "deliverance."
>
> A day later there was a walk in the bush with her mother. They picked poisonous "asiri" berries that were made into a draught and forced down Mary's throat. If that didn't kill her, her mother warned her, then it would be a barbed-wire hanging. Finally her mother threw boiling water and caustic soda over her head and body, and her father dumped his screaming daughter in a field. Drifting in and out of consciousness, she stayed near the house for a long time before finally slinking off into the bush. Mary was seven. She says she still doesn't feel safe. She says: "My mother doesn't love me." And, finally, a tear streaks down her beautiful face.[53]

Mary was eventually found and taken into the home of good Samaritans Sam and Elizabeth Ikpe-Itauma, who opened their home to abandoned children of misguided witch-hunts. Some journalists report that such stories are becoming common on the continent, and women and children are the primary victims of these cruelties administered in the name of Christianity.[54] We should note that most churches that practice exorcisms do not perpertrate violence against

---

53. Ibid.

54. For similar reports, see L. Igwe, "Witches of Africa," *Independent World Report* 4 (April 2010) n.p. Online: http://www.independentworldreport.com/2010/04/witches-of-africa/; "Witch Hunt: Africa's Hidden War on Women," *The Independent* (12 March 2009). Online: http://www.independent.co.uk/news/world/africa/witch-hunt-africas-hidden-war-on-women-1642907.html; K. Hourfeld, "Churches Involved in Torture, Murder of Thousands of African Children," *LA Times*. Posted on 19 October 2009 at http://www.loonwatch.com/2009/10/churches-involved-in-torture-murder-of-thousands-of-african-children-denounced-as-witches/. Some churches that are involved in witch hunts, however, deny any involvement in violence against women and children. See, for example, M. Oppenheimer, "On a Visit to

the possessed. But the demonizing discourse on the continent ensures that the threat of violence always looms.

PAUL'S PRACTICES OF POWER AS A RESPONSE TO THE AFRICAN CONTEXT

In our survey of African interpretations of the powers it seems that what we encounter in Africa is very distinct from what we encounter in Western approaches to the NT concept of the powers. If there is a tendency in Western scholarship to ignore the powers or relegate the powers to primitive myths, the opposite seems to be the case in Africa: African scholars and Christians take the powers very seriously and interpret the NT powers as speaking to realities in their own experience.[55] Nonetheless, in our view, what we encounter in Africa

the U.S., a Nigerian Witch-Hunter Explains Herself," *The New York Times* (May 22, 2010) p. A11. Online: http://www.nytimes.com/2010/05/22/us/22beliefs.html.

55. A notable exception in Western approaches to the powers can be found in certain American evangelical and charismatic circles. The last four decades (especially the 1980s and 90s) have seen a proliferation of literature on "deliverance" and "spiritual warfare" in some American evangelical and charismatic circles. There may be a number of contributing factors for this. It is possible, as some have noted, that this interest may be due to the rise in occultism and Satanism in American culture. Some have also pointed to popular works on the subject—such as novels by Frank Peretti (*This Present Darkness* [Westchester, IL: Crossway Books, 1986]; *Piercing the Darkness* [Westchester, IL: Crossway Books, 1989]) and M. Scott Peck's *People of the Lie: The Hope for Healing Human Evil* (New York: Touchstone, 1983)—as fueling this interest. (The 1973 movie *The Exorcist* became a Hollywood hit). Others may also point to the exposure of Western scholars and missionaries to the worldviews of other cultures. An interesting study might compare what we encounter in African Christianity with the increasing interest in spiritual warfare among American evangelicals and charismatics. Some examples of works dealing with the subject of deliverance or spiritual warfare in the Western context are D. Basham, *Deliver Us from Evil: A Pastor's Reluctant Encounters with the Powers of Darkness* (Grand Rapids: Chosen Books, 1972); F. Hammond and I. Mae, *Pigs in the Parlor: A Practical Guide to Deliverance* (Kirkwood, MO: Impact Christian Books, 1973); F. MacNutt, *Healing* (Notre Dame, IN: Ave Maria Press, 1974); MacNutt, *Deliverance from Evil Spirits: A Practical Manual* (Grand Rapids: Chosen Books, 1995); K. McAll, *Healing the Family Tree* (London: Sheldon Press, 1982); C. P. Wagner and F. D. Pennoyer, *Wrestling with Dark Angels: Towards a Deeper Understanding of the Supernatural Forces in Spiritual Warfare* (Ventura, CA: Regal Books, 1990); C. P. Wagner, *Engaging the Enemy: How to Fight and Defeat Territorial Spirits* (Ventura, CA: Regal, 1991); N. Anderson, *Victory Over the Darkness: Realizing the Power of Your Identity in Christ* (Ventura, CA: Regal, 1990); E. Murphy, *The Handbook for Spiritual Warfare* (Nashville: Thomas Nelson, 1992); W. C. Viser, *The Darkness among Us* (Nashville: Broadman & Holman, 1994); C. H. Kraft, *Defeating Dark Angels: Breaking Demonic Oppression in the Believer's Life* (Ann Arbor, MI: Vine Books, 1992); C. H. Kraft, T. White, and E. Murphy, eds., *Behind Enemy Lines: An Advanced Guide to Spiritual Warfare* (Ann Arbor: Vine Books, 1994); D. Powlison, *Power Encounters: Reclaiming Spiritual Warfare* (Grand Rapids: Baker, 1995); C. P. Wagner, *Confronting the Powers: How the New Testament Church Experienced the Power of Strategic-Level Spiritual Warfare* (Ventura, CA: Regal, 1996); C. E. Arnold, *Three*

may be overemphasis on the principalities and powers that almost betrays an obsession with the powers. Such an overemphasis on the powers raises some serious questions: Is not what we are witnessing in Africa a syncretism of traditional religions and Christianity? How much of such Christianity is rooted purely in the NT presentation of the powers and how much of this is a mere transference of traditional religious categories to Christianity? One wonders if such overemphasis on the powers is not a direct assimilation of traditional religions into Christianity.[56] For example, it is a well-known fact that in times of extreme crises or misfortune, some Christians visit traditional fetish priests for remedies.

Here Paul's own dealing with former pagans in the Corinthian, Galatian, and Colossian congregations provides helpful resources for thinking about such questions. Paul would regard veneration of traditional gods, idols, and ancestors in the African context as representing the same phenomenon: deflection of worship from Christ. Thus, in agreement with African charismatic and Pentecostal preachers, he would regard such practices as demonic. Returning to shrines and participating in traditional religious festivities, for Paul, would expose believers to demonic powers. Nonetheless, the ways to resist the powers—that is, the practices of power Paul advocates—are not the sort of violent acts perpetrated against the demon possessed. As we saw in our discussion of Colossians, Christ overcomes the powers not through a violent demonstration of his authority but through his suffering death that unmasked the powers as enemies of God (Col. 2:15). In Jesus' death, then, we see Jesus rejecting violence and earthly force as a means to conquer the powers (Cf. Matt. 26:53; John 18:36; 19:10-11). For followers of Jesus, his example invalidates violence and coercion as a means to deal with those accused of witchcraft or demon possession. It is a word that calls the church to resist the temptation

---

Crucial Questions about Spiritual Warfare (Grand Rapids: Baker Books, 1997); A. S. Moreau, *Essentials of Spiritual Warfare: Equipped to Win the Battle* (Wheaton, IL.: Harold Shaw Publishers, 1997); D. Prince, *They Shall Expel Demons: What You Need to Know about Demons—Your Invisible Enemies* (Grand Rapids: Chosen Books, 1998).

56. Behind the above observation is the recognition of the risk with contextualizing the Christian message. Attempts to contextualize the Christian message always run the risk of overriding the gospel itself. The challenge is how to contextualize Christian theology without compromising the Christian message, without communicating an inauthentic gospel. As Newbigin has noted, "If the Gospel is truly to be communicated, the subject in that sentence is as important as the predicate. What comes home to the heart of the hearer must be the real Gospel, and not a product shaped by the mind of the hearer" (Newbigin, *The Gospel in a Pluralist Society*, 141). If the Christian message itself is lost in attempts to make theology relevant to the African culture, there is little gain. Does the Christian message not present a challenge to each generation and to each worldview?

to pursue violence, for, as we shall see shortly, this impulse to violence may itself be a demonic temptation. The church's battle is not waged against human adversaries or human victims but against wicked spiritual forces of darkness. Paul sums this up nicely in 2 Cor. 10:3-4: "For though we walk about in the flesh, we do not wage war according to the flesh, for the weapons of our warfare are not fleshly. Rather, they are powerful in God to demolish strongholds." The author of Ephesians reverberates a similar tone: "For our struggle is not against flesh and blood, but against the rulers, against the authorities, against the world lords of this present darkness, against the spiritual forces of evil in the heavenly realm" (Eph. 6:12). Thus, in the NT's presentation of the powers in general and Paul in particular, we have a vision for the church as an armed force pitted in conflict *not* with flesh and blood but with invisible, spiritual forces; the church wages her battle with prayer (Eph. 6:12-18), proclamation (1 Cor. 2:1-13), and obedient submission of her members as weapons of righteousness (Rom. 6:13).

The church can live in light of the assurance that Christ has dealt a defeating blow to the powers by means of the cross and resurrection. The church can therefore be certain of victory. Consequently, to devote too much time, resources, and energy to witchcraft or even to spiritual warfare is to fail to come to grips with the power of the resurrection, which is the assurance for Christians that the powers will never have the last word against God's people. African Christians cannot (and must not) totally ignore the powers—as is the case in many Western quarters—but they must also not attribute too much significance to the powers in their practices. To attribute too much significance to the powers is to fail to come to grips with the power of our baptism, for in baptism believers are mapped onto Christ's life, death, burial, and resurrection. Participation in Christ's career means that believers have been rescued from the domain of the powers. The powers are still at work in the world, but to affirm our Christian baptism is to live in light of the victory over the powers that took place at the cross, when Christ dealt a fatal blow to the powers, thereby foreshadowing their ultimate destruction (1 Cor. 15:24-26).

In addition, African churches must devote attention to creating a Christian *habitus*, Spirit-led dispositions that will guide the actions of individuals and communities. The cultivation of a Christian *habitus* as a means to engage the powers involves making nurturing and discipleship central to the Christian message and task. Ultimately, it is the creation of a Christian *habitus* that will produce believers who will not seek out (or return to) shrines in times of serious crises.

Furthermore, if we are to affirm with Paul how pervasive and insidious are the schemes of the powers, then the church needs to be on guard lest she herself becomes a base of operations for the powers. According to Paul, the powers have the ability to co-opt God's good Law to produce outcomes contrary to the Law's aims (Rom. 7:9-11). Paul also has something to say about how the powers can deceive the religious self to perform actions whose outcomes, when viewed retrospectively, are contrary to God's purposes (Rom. 7:15-17). The human in Romans 7 under the influence of Sin—personified here as a demonic power—voices a dilemma, which is, as Paul Meyer has shown, "good intention carried out and then surprised and dumbfounded by the evil it has produced, not despair but the same disillusionment so clearly described in [Rom. 7:10]. What should have effected life has produced death."[57] The ability to effect "death" even in the best and most religious of humans speaks to the insidious nature of the powers. In the church's involvement in witch hunts that, in some instances, have resulted in the torture of women and children in Africa, are we not to discern a clear case of God's good word being co-opted by the powers to produce outcomes contrary to its aims; or even an instance of zealous *Christians* being deceived by the powers to perform actions whose outcomes are surprisingly evil?[58] If we are to affirm with Paul the all-pervasive nature of the powers and the powers' ability to blind and deceive even the best and most religious of humans, then we cannot deny that until Christ has ultimately destroyed all dominion, authority, and power, the Christian church must constantly be vigilant, lest she herself becomes a base of operation for the powers.

And, finally, while our study did not encompass the Letter to the Ephesians, our discussion would be incomplete if we did not include prayer as a practice of power in the church's battle against the powers (Eph. 3:14-21; 6:18-20). The church must pray that she might be filled with the knowledge of God's will; that she will be able to discern the work of the powers in the world and in her midst; that she will unmask the powers with the discerning Spirit and authority given her by means of her continued abiding in Christ; and that she will respond to those humans and structures that are being drawn into the ranks of the sons of darkness with love and the hope of redemption.

---

57. P. W. Meyer, "The Worm at the Core of the Apple," in *The Word in This World: Essays in New Testament Exegesis and Theology* (Louisville: Westminster John Knox, 2004), 57–77, on 74.

58. This observation should not be limited to the African context but should also be expanded to include all Christian crusades, inquisitions, attacks on Jews, and the subjugation of all people (for example, blacks, women, homosexuals) in the name of the Bible.

Reference Works

Bauer, W., W. F. Arndt, F. W. Gingrich, and F. W. Danker. *Greek-English Lexicon of the New Testament and Other Early Christian Literature.* 2d ed. Chicago: University of Chicago Press, 1979.

Betz, H. D., ed. *The Greek Magical Papyri in Translation: Including the Demotic Spells.* Chicago: University of Chicago Press, 1986.

Charlesworth, James H., ed. *The Old Testament Pseudepigrapha.* 2 vols. New York: Doubleday, 1983–85.

Danker, F. W., W. Bauer, W. F. Arndt, and F. W. Gingrich. *Greek-English Lexicon of the New Testament and Other Early Christian Literature.* 3d ed. Chicago: University of Chicago Press, 2000.

Jacoby, F. *Die Fragmente der griechischen Historiker.* Leiden: Brill, 1954–64.

Kittel, G., and G. Friedrich, eds. *Theological Dictionary of the New Testament.* Translated by G. W. Bromiley. 10 vols. Grand Rapids: Eerdmans, 1964–1976.

Knibb, M. *The Ethiopic Book of Enoch: A New Edition in the Light of the Aramaic Dead Sea Fragments.* Oxford: Clarendon Press, 1978.

Lauterbach, J. Z., ed. and trans. *Mekilta de-Rabbi Ishmael.* 3 vols. Philadelphia: Jewish Publication Society Press, 1933–35.

Lidell, H. G., and R. Scott, *An Intermediate Greek-English Lexicon: Founded upon the Seventh Edition of Liddell and Scott's Greek-English Lexicon.* Oxford: Clarendon Press, 1900.

Lidell, H. G., R. Scott, H. S. Jones, *A Greek-English Lexicon.* 9th ed. with revised supplement. Oxford: Oxford University Press, 1996.

Oden, T. C., ed. *Ancient Christian Commentary on Scripture.* 28 vols. Downer's Grove, IL: InterVarsity Press, 1998–.

Pietersma, A., and Benjamin G. W., eds. *A New English Translation of the Septuagint: and the Other Greek Translations Traditionally Included Under That Title.* Oxford: Oxford University Press, 2007.

Preisendanz, K. *Papyri Graecae Magicae: Die Griechiscen Zauberpapyri.* 2 vols. 2d. rev. ed. by A. Heinrichs. Stuttgart: Teubner, 1973–74.

Pusey, P. E., ed. *Sancti patris nostri Cyrilli Archiepiscopi Alexandrini in D. Joannis Evangelium: accedunt fragmenta varia necnon tractatus ad Tiberium diaconum duo.* 3 vols. Brussels: Culture et Civilisation, 1965 [orig. 1872].

Vanderkam, J. *The Book of Jubilees: A Critical Text*. Corpus Scriptorum Christianorum Orientalium, 510–11. Scriptores Aethiopici, 87–88. 2 vols. Louvain: Peeters, 1989.

Wallace, D. B. *Greek Grammar beyond the Basics: An Exegetical Syntax of the New Testament*. Grand Rapids: Zondervan, 1996.

Yonge, C. D., trans.. *The Works of Philo: Complete and Unabridged*. Peabody, Mass.: Hendrickson Publishers, 2008.

Bibliography

Abbott, T. K. *A Critical and Exegetical Commentary on the Epistles to the Ephesians and to the Colossians.* ICC. New York: C. Scribner's Sons, 1897.

Abijole, B. "St. Paul's Concept of Principalities and Powers in African Context. *African Theological Journal* 17 (1988): 118–29.

Acolatse, E. "Cosmology and Pastoral Diagnoses: A Psycho-Theological Anthropology for Pastoral Counseling in Ghana." Ph.D. dissertation, Princeton Theological Seminary, 2002. Ann Arbor, MI: University Microfilms, #3061046.

Alexander, P. S. "Incantations and Books of Magic." In *The History of the Jewish People in the Age of Jesus Christ (175 B.C.E.–A.D. 135): A New English Version,* by E. Schürer, revised and edited by G. Vermes, F. Millar, and M. Goodman; vol. 3, part 1, 342–79. Edinburgh: T & T Clark, 1986.

Anderson, N. *Victory Over the Darkness: Realizing the Power of Your Identity in Christ.* Ventura, CA: Regal, 1990.

Appiah, K. A. *In My Father's House: Africa in Philosophy of Culture.* Oxford: Oxford University Press, 1992.

Apter, A. "Atinga Revisited: Yoruba Witchcraft and the Cocoa Economy, 1950–1951." In *Modernity and Its Malcontents: Ritual and Power in Postcolonial Africa,* edited by J. Comaroff and J. Comaroff, 111–28. Chicago: University of Chicago Press, 1993.

Arnold, C. E. *The Colossian Syncretism: The Interface between Christianity and Folk Belief at Colossae.* WUNT 77. Tübingen: Mohr Siebeck, 1995.

———. *Ephesians: Power and Magic. The Concept of Power in Ephesians in Light of Its Historical Setting.* Society for New Testament Studies Monograph Series 63. Cambridge: Cambridge University Press, 1989.

———. *Powers of Darkness: Principalities and Powers in Paul's Letters.* Downer's Grove, IL: InterVarsity Press, 1992.

———. "Returning to the Domain of the Powers: *Stoicheia* as Evil Spirits in Galatians 4:3, 9." *Novum Testamentum* 38 (1996): 55–76.

———. *3 Crucial Questions about Spiritual Warfare.* Grand Rapids: Baker Books, 1997.

Asamoa, E. A. "The Christian Church and African Heritage." *International Review of Mission* 44 (1955): 292–301.

Asamoah-Gyadu, J. K. "Pulling Down Strongholds: Evangelism, Principalities and Powers and the African Pentecostal Imagination." *International Review of Missions* (2007): 306–16.

Asselin, D. T. "The Notion of Dominion in Gen 1–3." *CBQ* 16 (1954): 277–94.

Attfield, R. "On Translating Myth." *The International Journal for the Philosophy of Religion* 2 (1971): 228–45.

Aulen, G. *Christus Victor: An Historical Study of the Three Main Types of the Idea of Atonement.* Translated by A. G. Hebert. New York: Macmillan, 1951.

Ayers, R. H. "'Myth' in Theological Discourse: A Profusion of Confusion." *AThR* 48 (1966): 200–17.

Balchin, J. F. "Colossians 1:15-20: An Early Christian Hymn? The Arguments from Style." *VE* 15 (1985): 65–94.

Bandstra, A. J. *The Law and the Elements of the World.* Kampen: J. H. Kok, 1964.

Barbour, R. S. "Salvation and Cosmology: The Setting of the Epistle to the Colossians." *SJT* 20 (1967): 257–71.

Barclay, J. M. G. *Colossians and Philemon.* NTG. Sheffield: Sheffield Academic Press, 1997.

———. *Obeying the Truth: A Study of Paul's Ethics in Galatians.* Edinburgh: T & T Clark, 1988.

———. *Pauline Churches and Diaspora Jews.* WUNT 275. Tubingen: Mohr Siebeck, 2011.

Barr, J. "Hypostatization of Linguistic Phenomena in Modern Literary Theory." *JSS* 7 (1962): 85–94.

Barrett, C. K. *A Commentary on the Second Epistle to the Corinthians.* HNTC. New York: Harper and Row, 1973.

———. *The Epistle to the Romans.* HNTC. New York: Harper & Row, 1957.

———. *The First Epistle to the Corinthians.* HNTC. New York: Harper & Row, 1968.

———. *Freedom and Obligation.* Philadelphia: Westminster, 1985.

———. "Things Sacrificed to Idols." In *Essays on Paul*, 40–59. London; SPCK, 1982.

Barth, K. *Church Dogmatics.* Edited by G. W. Bromiley and F. F. Torrance. 4 volumes. Edinburgh: T & T Clark, 1936–1977.

Barth, M. *The Broken Wall: A Study of Ephesians.* Valley Forge: Judson, 1959.

Basham, D. *Deliver Us from Evil: A Pastor's Reluctant Encounters with the Powers of Darkness.* Grand Rapids: Chosen Books, 1972.

Bastian, M. " 'Bloodhounds Who Have No Friends': Witchcraft and Locality in the Nigerian Popular Press." In *Modernity and Its Malcontents: Ritual and*

Power in Postcolonial Africa, edited by J. Comaroff and J. Comaroff, 129–66. Chicago: University of Chicago Press, 1993.

Baugh, S. M. "The Poetic Form of Col 1:15-20." *WTJ* 47 (1995): 227–44.

Baur, F. C. *Paul, the Apostle of Jesus Christ, His Life and Works, His Epistles and Teachings: A Contribution to a Critical History of Primitive Christianity*. 2 vols. Edited by E. Zeller, revised by A. Menzies. London: Williams and Norgate, 1873–75 [repr. 2003; Peabody, MA: Hendrickson].

Bavinck, H. *Reformed Dogmatics*, volume 3: *Sin and Salvation in Christ*. Edited by J. Bolt. Grand Rapids: Baker Academic, 2006.

Beasley-Murray, G. R. *Baptism in the New Testament*. Grand Rapids: Eerdmans, 1962.

Beasley-Murray, P. "Colossians 1:15-20: An Early Christian Hymn Celebrating the Lordship of Christ." In *Pauline Studies: Essays Presented to Professor F. F. Bruce on his 70th Birthday*, edited by D. A. Hagner and M. J. Harris, 169–83. Grand Rapids: Eerdmans, 1980.

Becker, J. *Paul the Apostle to the Gentiles*. Louisville: Westminster John Knox, 1993.

Bediako, K. "Worship as Vital Participation: Some Personal Reflections on Ministry in the African Church." *Journal of African Christian Thought* 8 (2005): 3–7.

Behr, J. "Colossians 1:13-20: A Chiastic Reading." *SVTQ* 40 (1996): 247–64.

Beker, J. C. *Paul's Apocalyptic Gospel: The Coming Triumph of God*. Philadelphia: Fortress Press, 1982.

———. *Paul the Apostle*. Philadelphia: Fortress Press, 1980.

Belleville, L. "'Under Law': Structural Analysis and the Pauline Concept of Law in Galatians 3:21—4:11." *JSNT* 26 (1986): 64–69.

Benoit, P. "L'Hymne Christologique de Col 1.15-20." In *Christianity, Judaism and Other Greco-Roman Cults: Studies for Morton Smith at Sixty*, edited by J. Neusner, 226–63. Leiden: Brill, 1975.

Berkhof, H. *Christ and the Powers*. Scottdale, PA: Herald, 1977 [orig. 1953].

Betz, H. D. "2 Cor 6:14—7:1: An Anti-Pauline Fragment?" *JBL* 42 (1973): 88–108.

———. *Galatians*. Hermeneia. Philadelphia: Fortress Press, 1979.

Bird, P. *Missing Persons and Mistaken Identities: Women and Gender in Ancient Israel*. Minneapolis: Fortress Press, 1997.

Black, C. "Christ Crucified in Paul and Mark: Reflections on an Intracanonical Conversation." In *Theology and Ethics in Paul and His Interpreters: Essays in*

Honor of Victor Paul Furnish, edited by E. H. Lovering and J. L. Sumney, 184–206. Nashville: Abingdon, 1996.

Blanchette, O. "Does the Cheirographon of Col 2,14 Represent Christ Himself?" *CBQ* 23 (1961): 306–12.

Blinzler, J. "Lexikalisches zu dem Terminus τὰ στοιχεῖα τοῦ κόσμου bei Paulus." In *Studiorum Paulinorum Congressus Interntionalis Catholicus (1961)*, 429–44. AnBib 1718. Rome: Pontifical Biblical Institute, 1963.

Böcher, O. *Das Neue Testament und die dämonischen Mächte*. SBS 50. Stuttgart: KBW, 1972.

Boer, M. C. de. "The Meaning of the Phrase τὰ στοιχεῖα τοῦ κόσμου in Galatians." *NTS* 53 (2007): 204–24.

Boers, H. "The Structure and Meaning of Romans 6:1-14." *CBQ* 63 (2001): 664–82.

Bornkamm, G. "The Heresy of Colossians." In Francis and Meeks, *Conflict at Colossae*, 123–45.

———. "Taufe und neues Leben bei Paulus (Röm 6)." In *Das Ende des Gesetzes: Paulusstudien. Gesammelte Afusätze* 1, 34–50. 2nd. ed. BEvT 16. Munich: C. Kaiser, 1958.

Bourdieu, P. *The Logic of Practice*. Translated by Richard Nice. Stanford: Stanford University Press, 1990 [orig. 1980].

———. *Outline of a Theory of Practice*. Translated by Richard Nice. Cambridge Studies in Social Anthropology. Cambridge: Cambridge University Press, 1977 [orig. 1972].

Bousset, J. F. W. *Kyrios Christos: A History of the Belief in Christ from the Beginnings of Christianity to Irenaeus*. Nashville: Abingdon Press, 1970 [orig. 1913].

Bousset, W. and H. Gressmann, *Die Religion des Judentums im späthellenistichen Zeitalter*. 3rded. HNT 21. Tübingen: Mohr, 1966.

Brenk, E. "In the Light of the Moon: Demonology in the Early Imperial Period." *ANRW* 2:16:3 (1986): 2068–2145.

Brett, M. G. *Genesis: Procreation and the Politics of Identity*. New York: Routledge, 2000.

Briggs, C. A. and E. G. *A Critical and Exegetical Commentary on the Book of Psalms*. Vol. 1. New York: Charles Schribner's Sons, 1914.

Bring, R. *Commentary on Galatians*. Philadelphia: Muhlenberg, 1961.

———. "Der Mittler und das Gesetz: Eine Studie zu Gal. 3:20." *KD* 12 (1966): 292–309.

Broekhoven, H. V. "The Social Profiles in the Colossian Debate." *JSNT* 66 (1977): 73–90.

Brown, R. "The Qumran Scrolls and the Johannine Gospel and Epistles." In *The Scrolls and the New Testament*, edited by K. Stendahl, 283–307. New York: Harper & Brothers, 1957.

Bruce, F. F. "Colossian Problems Part 1: Jews and Christians in the Lycus Valley." *BSac* 141 (1984): 3–15.

———. "Colossian Problems Part 2: The 'Christ Hymn' of Colossians 1:15-20." *BSac* 141 (1984): 99–111.

———. "Colossian Problems Part 3: The Colossian Heresy." *BSac* 141 (1984): 195– 208.

———. "Colossian Problems Part 4: Christ as Conqueror and Reconciler." *BSac* 141 (1984): 291–302.

———. *The Epistle to the Galatians*. NIGTC. Grand Rapids: Eerdmans, 1982.

Bullmore, M. A. *St. Paul's Theology of Rhetorical Style: An Examination of 1 Corinthians 2:1-5 in the Light of Century Greco-Roman Rhetorical Culture*. San Francisco: International Scholars Publication, 1995.

Bultmann, R. *Exegetische Probleme des zweiten Korintherbriefs*. Upsala: Wretmans, 1947.

———. *New Testament and Mythology: And Other Basic Writings*. Edited and translated by Schubert M. Ogden. Philadelphia: Fortress Press, 1984.

———. *Theology of the New Testament*. 2 vols. Waco, TX: Baylor University Press, 2007 [orig. 1951–55].

Bundrick, D. R. "TA STOICHEIA TOU KOSMOU (Gal 4:3)." *JETS* 34 (1991): 353–64.

Burney, C. F. "Christ as the APXH of Creation." *JTS* 27 (1926): 160–77.

Burridge, K. *New Heaven, New Earth: A Study of Millenarian Activities*. Oxford: Blackwell, 1969.

Burtness, J. H. "All the Fullness." *Dialog* 3 (1964): 257–63.

Burton, E. D. *A Critical and Exegetical Commentary on the Epistle to the Galatians*. ICC. Edinburgh: T & T Clark, 1921.

Busch, A. "The Figure of Eve in Romans 7:5-25." *Biblical Interpretation* 12 (2004): 1–36.

Byrne, B. "Living Out the Righteousness of God: The Contribution of Rom 6:1—8:13 to an Understanding of Paul's Ethical Presuppositions." *CBQ* 83 (1981): 557–81.

———. *Romans*. Sacra Pagina 6. Collegeville, MN: Liturgical Press, 1996.

———. *Sons of God –"Seed of Abraham": A Study of the Idea of the Sonship of God of All Christians in Paul against the Jewish Background.* AnBib 83. Rome: Biblical Institute Press, 1979.

———. "'The Type of the One to Come' (Rom 5:14): Fate and Responsibility in Romans 5:12-21." *Australian Biblical Review* 36 (1988): 19–30.

Caird, G. B. *The Language and Imagery of the Bible.* Philadelphia: Westminster, 1980.

———. *Paul's Letters from Prison: In the Revised Standard Version.* Oxford: Oxford University Press, 1976.

———. *Principalities and Powers: A Study in Pauline Theology.* Eugene, OR: Wipf and Stock, 1956.

Cambier, J. "La Chair et l'Espirit en 1 Cor v. 5." *NTS* 15 (1968–69): 221–32.

Campbell, B. "Flesh and Spirit in 1 Cor 5:5: An Exercise in Rhetorical Criticism of the NT." *JETS* 36.3 (1993): 331–42.

Campbell, D. *Deliverance of God: An Apocalyptic Rereading of Justification in Paul.* Grand Rapids: Eerdmans, 2009.

———. *The End of Religion* (forthcoming).

Carr, W. *Angels and Principalities: The Background Meaning and Development of the Pauline Phrase Hai Archai kai hai Exousiai.* SNTSMS 43. Cambridge: Cambridge University Press, 1981.

———. "The Rulers of This Age—1 Cor. ii:6-8." *NTS* 23 (1976): 20–35.

Certeau, M. de. "How is Christianity Thinkable Today?" *Theology Digest* 19 (1971): 334–45.

———. *The Practice of Everyday Life.* Vol. 1. Berkeley: University of California Press, 1984.

Chang, H.-K. "The Christian Life in a Dialectical Tension? Romans 7:7-25 Reconsidered." *NovT* 49 (2007): 257–80.

Cheung, A. T. *Idol Food in Corinth: Jewish Background and Pauline Legacy.* JSNTSup 176. Sheffield: Sheffield Academic Press, 1999.

Clarke, A. D. *Secular and Christian Leadership in Corinth: A Socio-Historical and Exegetical Study of 1 Corinthians 1–6.* Leiden: Brill, 1993.

Clines, D. J. A. "The Image of God in Man." *TynBul* 19 (1968): 53–103.

———. "The Tree of Knowledge and the Law of Yahweh (Psalm XIX)." *VT* 24 (1974): 8– 14.

Cole, G. A. "1 Cor 5:4 ' . . . Wwith My Spirit,'" *ExpTim* 98 (1987): 205.

Collins, A. Y. "The Function of 'Excommunication' in Paul." *HTR* 73 (1980): 251–63.

Collins, J. J. *The Apocalyptic Imagination: An Introduction to Jewish Apocalyptic Literature*. Grand Rapids: Eerdmans, 1998.

———. *The Apocalyptic Imagination: An Introduction to the Jewish Matrix of Christianity*. New York: Crossroad, 1984.

Collins, R. F. *First Corinthians*. Sacra Pagina 7. Collegeville, MN: Liturgical Press, 1999.

Colpe, C. *Die religionsgeschichtliche Schule: Darstellung und Kritik ihres Bildes vom gnostichen Erlösermythus*. FRLANT 78. Göttingen: Vandenhoeck & Ruprecht, 1961.

Conzelmann, H. *1 Corinthians: A Commentary on the First Epistle to the Corinthians*. Hermeneia. Philadelphia: Fortress Press, 1975.

Cotter, A. C. "The Divinity of Jesus Christ in Saint Paul." *CBQ* 7 (1945): 259–89.

Cousar, C. B. *Galatians*. Interpretation. Louisville: John Knox Press, 1982.

Craddock, F. B. "'All Things in Him': A Critical Note on Col. I. 15-20." *NTS* 12 (1965): 78–80.

Cranfield, C. E. B. *The Epistle to the Romans*. Vol. 1. ICC. Edinburgh: T & T Clark, 1975.

———. "Romans 6:1-14 Revisited." *ExpTim* 106 (1994): 40–43.

Crossan, J. D. and J. L. Reed. *In Search of Paul: How Jesus' Apostle Opposed Rome's Empire with God's Kingdom*. San Francisco: HarperSanFrancisco, 2004.

Cullmann, O. *Christ and Time: The Primitive Christian Conception of Time and History*. Philadelphia: Westminster, 1950.

———. *The State in the New Testament*. New York: Charles Schribner's Sons, 1956.

Curtin, P., S. Feierman, L. Thompson, and J. Vansina. *African History*. Boston: Little Brown, 1978.

Dahl, N. A. Appendix I: A Synopsis of Rom 5:1-11 and 8:1-39." In *Studies in Paul: Theology of the Early Christian Mission*, 88–90. Minneapolis: Augsburg, 1977.

———. "Two Notes on Romans 5." *ST* (1951): 37–48.

Dahood, M. *Psalms I: 1–50*. AB. Garden City, NY: Doubleday, 1966.

Daniélou, J. *The Theology of Jewish Christianity*. Vol. 1 of *The Development of Christian Doctrine before the Council of Nicaea*. London: Darton, Longman and Todd, 1964.

Davidson, R. *Genesis 1–11*. 3rd ed. CBC. Cambridge: Cambridge University Press, 1980.

Davies, W. D. "Paul and the Dead Sea Scrolls: Flesh and Spirit." In *The Scrolls and the New Testament*, edited by K. Stendahl, 157–82. New York: Harper & Brothers, 1957.

———. *Paul and Rabbinic Judaism*. Mifflintown, Pa: Sigler, 1998 [orig. 1948].

Davis, J. A. *Wisdom and Spirit: An Investigation of 1 Cor. 1:18—3:20 against the Background of Jewish Sapiential Traditions in the Greco-Roman Period*. Lanham, MD: University Press of America, 1984.

Dawes, G. W. "The Danger of Idolatry: First Corinthians 8:7-13." *CBQ* 58 (1996): 82–98.

Dawn, M. J. *Powers, Weakness, and the Tabernacling of God*. Grand Rapids: Eerdmans, 2001.

Deissmann, A. *Light from the Ancient East: the New Testament Illustrated by Recently Discovered Texts from the Graeco-Roman World*. London: Hodder and Stoughton, 1927 [1911].

DeMaris, R. "Element, Elemental Spirit." In *ABD* 2:445.

Derrett, J. D. M. "'Handing Over to Satan': An Explanation of 1 Cor. 5:1-7." *Revue internationale des droits de l'antiquité* 26 (1979): 11–30.

Dibelius, M. *A Fresh Approach to the New Testament and Early Christian Literature*. London: Ivor Nicholson and Watson, 1936.

———. *Die Geisterwelt im Glauben des Paulus*. Göttingen: Vandenhoeck & Ruprecht, 1909.

———. "The Isis Initiation in Apuleius and Related Initiatory Rites." In Francis Meeks, *Conflict at Colossae*, 61–121.

Dickson, K. and P. Ellingworth, eds. *Biblical Revelation and African Beliefs*. London: Lutterworth, 1969.

Dodd, C. H. *The Epistle of Paul to the Romans*. MNTC. New York: Harper 1932.

Dunn, J. D. G. "The Colossian Philosophy: A Confident Jewish Apologia." *Bib* 76 (1995): 153– 81.

———. *The Epistle to the Galatians*. BNTC. Peabody, MA: Hendrickson, 1993.

———. *Jesus, Paul and the Law: Studies in Mark and Galatians*. Louisville: Westminster/John Knox, 1990.

———. *Jesus and the Spirit: A Study of the Religious and Charismatic Experience of Jesus and the First Christians as Reflected in the New Testament*. London: SCM, 1975.

———. *Romans 1–8*. WBC 38A. Nashville: Thomas Nelson, 1988.

———. *The Theology of Paul the Apostle*. Edinburgh: T & T Clark, 1998.

Eastman, S. "'The Evil I Do Not Want Is What I Do': Sin and Evil in Romans." Paper presented to the Society of Biblical Literature, Atlanta, 2010.

Edelstein, E. J. and L. Edelstein. *Asclepius: A Collection and Interpretation of the Testimonies*. Baltimore: John Hopkins Press, 1945.

Eitrem, S. *Some Notes on the Demonology of the New Testament*. Symbolae Osloenses 20. Oslo: Universitetsforlaget, 1964.

Ejenobo, D. T. "'Union with Christ': A Critique of Romans 6:1-11." *AJT* 22 (2008): 309–23.

Ellingworth, P. "Colossians i. 15-20 and Its Context." *ExpTim* 73 (1961–62): 252–53.

Ellingworth, P. and H. Hatton. *A Translators Guide on Paul's First Letter to the Corinthians*. London: United Bible Societies, 1985.

Elliott, N. *The Arrogance of Nations: Reading Romans in the Shadow of Empire*. Minneapolis: Fortress Press, 2008.

———. *Liberating Paul: The Justice of God and the Politics of the Apostle*. Maryknoll, NY: Orbis Books, 1994.

Engberg-Pedersen, T. *Cosmology and Self in the Apostle Paul*. Oxford: Oxford University Press, 2010.

Evans, C. A. "The Colossian Mystics." *Bib* 63 (1982): 188–205.

Everling, O. *Die paulinische Angelologie und Dämonologie: Ein biblisch-theologischer Versuch*. Göttingen: Vandenhoeck & Ruprecht, 1888.

Farmer, W. R., C. F. D. Moule, and R. R. Niebuhr, eds. *Christian History and Interpretation: Studies Presented to John Knox*. Cambridge: Cambridge University Press, 1967.

Fascher, E. *Der erster Brief des Paulus an die Korinther*. 1st ed. THKNT 7/1. Berlin: Evangelische Verlagsanstalt, 1975.

Fee, G. D. "II Corinthians VI.4—VII.1 and Food Offered to Idols." *NTS* 23 (1977): 140–61.

———. "Εἰδωλόθυτα Once Again: An Interpolation of 1 Corinthians 8–10." *Bib* 61 (1980): 172–97.

———. *The First Epistle to the Corinthians*. NICNT. Grand Rapids: Eerdmans, 1987.

———. *God's Empowering Presence: The Holy Spirit in the Letters of Paul*. Peabody: Hendrickson, 1994.

Ferdinando, K. "Screwtape Revisited: Demonology Western, African and Biblical." In *The Unseen World: Christian Reflections on Angels, Demons and the Heavenly Realm*, edited by A. N. S. Lane, 103–32. Carlisle: Paternoster Press, 1996.

Findlay, G. G. "St. Paul's First Epistle to the Corinthians." In *The Expositor's Greek Testament*, edited by W. R. Nicoll. Grand Rapids: Eerdmans 1961 [orig. 1900].

Fisk, B. N. "Eating Meat Offered to Idols: Corinthian Behavior and Pauline Response in 1 Corinthians 8–10 (A Response to Gordon Fee)." *TJ* 10 (1989): 49–70.

Fitzmeyer, J. A. "Qumran and the Interpolated Paragraph in 2 Cor 6:1—7:1." *Catholic Biblical Quarterly* 23 (1961): 271–80.

Forbes, C. "Pauline Demonology and/or Cosmology? Principalities, Powers, and the Elements of the World in their Hellenistic Context." *JSNT* 85 (2002): 51–73.

———. "Paul's Principalities and Powers: Demythologizing Apocalyptic?" *JSNT* 82 (2001): 61–88.

Forkman, G. *The Limits of the Religious Community: Expulsion from the Religious Community within the Qumran Sect, within Rabbinic Judaism, and within Primitive Christianity*. Lund: CWK Gleerup, 1972.

Forsyth, N. *The Old Enemy: Satan and the Combat Myth*. Princeton: Princeton University Press, 1987.

Fossum, J. "Colossians 1.15-18a in the Light of Jewish Mysticism and Gnosticism." *NTS* 35 (1989): 183–201.

Francis, F. O. "The Christological Argument of Colossians." In *God's Christ and His People: Studies in Honour of Nils Alstrup Dahl*, edited by J. Jervell and W. A. Meeks, 192–208. Oslo: Universitetsforlaget, 1977.

———. "The Background of Embateuein (Col 2:18) in Legal Papyri and Oracle Inscriptions." In Francis and Meeks, *Conflict at Colossae* 197–207.

———. "Humility and Angel Worship in Col. 2:18." In Francis and Meeks, *Conflict at Colossae*, 163–95.

Francis, F. O. and W. A. Meeks, eds. *Conflict at Colossae: A Problem in the Interpretation of Early Christianity, Illustrated by Selected Modern Studies*. Missoula, Mont.: Society of Biblical Literature, 1973.

Friedrich, G. "*Hamartia . . . ouk ellogeitai*—Rom. 5,13." *TLZ* 77 (1952): 523–28.

Fung, R. Y. *The Epistle to the Galatians*. NICNT. Grand Rapids: Eerdmans, 1988.

Furnish, V. P. *II Corinthians*. AB 32A. Garden City, NY: Doubleday, 1984.

———. *Theology and Ethics in Paul*. Nashville: Abingdon, 1968.

Gadamer, H.-G. *Truth and Method*. Second revised edition. New York: Continuum, 2004 [orig. 1975].

Gaffin, R. B., Jr. "Some Epistemological Reflections on 1 Cor 2:6-16." *WTJ* 57 (1995): 103–24.

Gagnon, R. A. J. "Heart of Wax and a Teaching That Stamps: (Rom 6:17b): Once More." *JBL* 112 (1993): 667–87.

Garland, D. E. "The Dispute Over Food Sacrificed to Idols (1 Cor 8:1—11:1)." *PRSt* 30 (2003): 173–97.

Garlington, D. B. "Romans 7:14-25 and the Creation Theology of Paul." *TJ* 11 (1990): 197–235.

Garrett, S. R. *The Demise of the Devil: Magic and the Demonic in Luke's Writings.* Minneapolis: Fortress Press, 1989.

———. *The Temptations of Jesus in Mark's Gospel.* Grand Rapids: Eerdmans, 1998.

Gaston, L. *Paul and the Torah.* Vancouver: University of British Colombia, 1987.

Gaventa, B. "The Cosmic Power of Sin in Paul's Letter to the Romans: Toward a Widescreen Edition." *Interpretation* 58 (2004): 229–40.

———. "Neither Height Nor Depth: Discerning the Cosmology of Romans." *SJT* 64 (2011): 265–78.

Ghana Evangelism Committee. *National Church Survey, 1993 Update: Facing the Unfinished Task of the Church in Ghana.* Accra: Assemblies of God Literature Centre, 1993.

Gifford, P. *African Christianity: Its Public Role.* Bloomington: Indiana University Press, 1998.

Goen, C. C. *Broken Churches, Broken Nation: Denominational Schisms and the Coming of the American Civil War.* Macon, Ga.: Mercer University Press, 1985.

Goldingay, J. *Psalms 1–41.* Vol. 1. Grand Rapids: Baker, 2006.

Gooch, P. D. *Dangerous Food: 1 Corinthians 8–10 in Its Context.* SCJ 5. Waterloo: Wilfred Laurier University Press, 1993.

Gordon, T. D. "A Note on ΠΑΙΔΑΓΩΓΟΣ in Galatians 3.24-25." *NTS* 35 (1989): 150–54.

Graf, F. *Magic in the Ancient World.* Cambridge: Harvard University Press, 1997.

Grundmann, W. *Der Begriff der Kraft in der neutestamentlichen Gedankenwelt.* BWANT 4:8. Stuttgart: Kohlhammer, 1932.

Gundry, R. H. "The Moral Frustration of Paul before his Conversion." In *Pauline Studies: Essays Presented to F.F. Bruce*, edited by D. A. Hagner and M. J. Harris, 228–45. Exeter: Paternoster, 1980.

Gundry-Volf, J. M. *Paul & Perseverance: Staying In and Falling Away.* Louisville: Westminster/John Knox, 1991 [orig. 1990].

Gunkel, J. F. H. *The Influence of the Holy Spirit: the Popular View of the Apostolic Age and the Teaching of the Apostle Paul.* Philadelphia: Fortress Press, 1979 [orig. 1888].

Gunton, C. *The Actuality of Atonement: A Study of Metaphor, Rationality and the Christian Tradition.* Grand Rapids: Eerdmans, 1989.

Gyekye, K. *An Essay on African Philosophical Thought: The Akan Conceptual Scheme.* Revised edition. Philadelphia: Temple University Press, 1995.

Hackett, R. I. J. "Discourses of Demonization in Africa and Beyond." *Diogenes* 50 (2003): 61–75.

Halter, H. *Taufe und Ethos: paulinische Kriterien für das Proprium christlicher Moral.* FThSt 106. Freiburg im Breisgau: Herder, 1977.

Hammer, P. L. "Element (Elemental Spirit)." In *IDB* (1962): 2:82.

Hammond, F. and I. Mae. *Pigs in the Parlor: A Practical Guide to Deliverance.* Kirkwood, MO: Impact Christian Books, 1973.

Hanson, A. T. "The Origin of the Paul's Use of ΠΑΙΔΑΓΩΓΟΣ for the Law." *JSNT* 34 (1988): 71–76.

Harris, G. "The Beginnings of Church Discipline: 1 Corinthians 5." *NTS* 37 (1991): 1–21.

Hart, I. "Genesis 1:1—2:3 as Prologue to the Book of Genesis." *TynBul* 46 (1995): 315–36.

Hatch, W. H. P. "Τὰ στοιχεῖα in Paul and Bardaisan." *JTS* 28 (1927): 181–82.

Hauerwas, S. *The Peacable Kingdom: A Primer in Christian Ethics.* Notre Dame, IN: University of Notre Dame Press, 1983.

Hays, R. B. "Christology and Ethics in Galatians: The Law of Christ." *CBQ* 49 (1987): 268–90.

———. *The Conversion of the Imagination: Paul as Interpreter of Israel's Scripture.* Grand Rapids: Eerdmans, 2005.

———. *The Faith of Jesus Christ: The Narrative Substructure of Galatians 3:1—4:11.* 2nd ed. Grand Rapid: Eerdmans, 2002 [orig. 1983].

———. *First Corinthians.* Interpretation. Louisville: Knox, 1997.

———. "Justification." *ABD* 3:1129–33.

———. "The Letter to the Galatians." *NIB.* Vol. 11. Nashville: Abingdon, 2000.

———. *The Moral Vision of the New Testament: Community, Cross, New Creation: A Contemporary Introduction to New Testament Ethics.* San Francisco: HarperSanFrancisco, 1996.

———. "Operation Evil Power: If Christ Has Truly Defeated the Powers of Satan on the Cross (Col 2:15), Why Do the Powers of Evil Effectively Operate in the World?" *Christianity Today* 48 (2004): 74.

Helyer, L. R. "Colossians 1:15-20: Pre-Pauline or Pauline?" *JETS* 26 (1983): 167–79.

———. "Cosmic Christology and Col 1:15-20." *JETS* 37 (1994): 235–46.

———. "Recent Research on Col 1:15-20." *Grace Theological Journal* 12 (1992): 51–67.

Henderson, S. W. "'If Anyone Hungers . . . ': An Integrated Reading of 1 Cor 11.17-34." *NTS* 48 (2002): 195–208.

Henten, J. W. van. "Mastemah משטמה." In *Dictionary of Deities and Demons in the Bible*, edited by K. van der Toorn, B. Becking, and P. W. van der Horst, 553–54. Leiden: Brill, 1999.

Hincks, E. Y. "The Meaning of the Phrase τὰ στοιχεῖα τοῦ κόσμου in Gal. 4.3 and Col. 2.8." *JBL* 15 (1896): 183–92.

Hitchens, C. *God Is Not Great: How Religion Poisons Everything.* New York: Warner 12, 2007.

Holtz, T. "'Euer Glaube an Gott': Zu Form und Inhalt von 1 Thess 1,9f." In R. *Die Kirche des Anfangs. Für Heiny Schürmann*, edited by Schnackenburg, J. Ernst, and J. Wanke, 459–88. Freiburg: Herder, 1978.

Hong, I. *The Law in Galatians.* JSNTSup 81. Sheffield: JSOT Press, 1993.

Hooker, M. D. "Were There False Teachers in Colossae?" In *Christ and Spirit in the New Testament: Studies in Honour of C.F.D. Moule*, edited by B. Lindars and S. S. Smalley, 121–34. Cambridge: Cambridge University Press, 1990.

Horbury, W. "Extirpation and Excommunication." *VT* 35 (1985): 13–38.

Horsley, R. A. "Gnosis in Corinth: 1 Corinthians 8.1-6." *NTS* 27 (1980): 32–51.

———, ed. *Paul and Empire: Religion and Power in Roman Imperial Society.* Harrisburg, PA: Trinity Press International, 1997.

———, ed. *Paul and Politics: Ekklesia, Israel, Imperium, Interpretatio: Essays in Honor of Krister Stendahl.* Harrisburg, PA: Trinity Press International, 2000.

———, ed. *Paul and the Roman Imperial Order.* Harrisburg, PA: Trinity Press International, 2004.

———. "Wisdom of Word and Words of Wisdom." *CBQ* 39 (1977): 224–39.

Horton, R. "African Traditional Religion and Western Science." *Africa* 32 (1967): 50–71.

Hourfeld, K. "Churches Involved in Torture, Murder of Thousands of African Children." LA Times. Posted on 19 October 2009 at http://www.loonwatch.com/2009/10/churches-involved-in-torture-murder-of-thousands-of-african-children-denounced-as-witches/. Accessed 29 February 2012.

Howard, G. *Paul: Crisis in Galatia.* SNTSMS 35. Cambridge: Cambridge University Press, 1979.

Hübner, H. *Das Gesetz bei Paulus.* FRLANT 119. Göttingen: Vandenhoeck & Ruprecht, 1978.

———. "Paulusforschung seit 1945: Ein Kritischer Literaturbericht." *ANRW* 2-25-4 (1987): 2691–94.

Huggins, R. V. "Alleged Classical Parallels to Paul's 'What I Want to Do I Do Not Do, but What I Hate, That I Do' (Rom 7:15)." *WTJ* 54 (1992): 153–61.

Hurd, J. C., Jr. *The Origin of I Corinthians.* London: SPCK, 1965.

Igwe, L. "Witch Hunt: Africa's Hidden War on Women." The Independent (12 March 2009). Accessed 28 February 2012. Online: http://www.independent.co.uk/news/world/africa/witch-hunt-africas-hidden-war-on-women-1642907.html.

———. "Witches of Africa." *Independent World Report* 4 (April 2010): n.p. Accessed 28 February 2012. Online: http://www.independentworldreport.com/2010/04/witches-of-africa/.

Imasogie, O. *Guidelines for Christian Theology in Africa.* Achimota, Ghana: Africa Christian Press, 1983.

Jervis, L. A. "'The Commandment Which Is for Life' (Romans 7.10): Sin's Use of the Obedience of Faith." *JSNT* 27.2 (2004): 193–216.

Jewett, R. "The Basic Human Dilemma: Weakness or Zealous Violence? (Romans 7:7-25 and Romans 10:1-18)." *Ex Auditu* 13 (1997): 96–109.

———. *Paul's Anthropological Terms: A Study of Their Use in Conflict Settings.* Leiden: Brill, 1971.

———. *Romans: A Commentary.* Hermeneia. Minneapolis: Fortress Press, 2007.

Johnson, D. H. "The Image of God in Colossians." *Didaskalia* 3 (1992): 9–15.

Johnson, L. T. *Hebrews: A Commentary.* NTL. Louisville: Westminster John Knox, 2006.

Johnson, S. L., Jr. "Romans 5:12—An Exercise in Exegesis and Theology." In *New Dimensions in New Testament Study*, edited by R. N. Longenecker and M. C. Tenney, 298–316. Grand Rapids: Zondervan, 1974.

Joy, N. G. "Is the Body Really to Be Destroyed? (1 Corinthians 5:5)." *BT* 39 (1988): 429–36.

Kaiser, W., Jr. *Towards an Old Testament Theology.* Grand Rapids: Zondervan, 1978.

Käsemann, E. *Commentary on Romans.* Translated by Geoffrey W. Bromiley. Grand Rapids: Eerdmans, 1980.

———. "The Eschatological Royal Reign of God." In *Your Kingdom Come: Mission Perspectives. Report on the World Conference on Mission and Evangelism, Melbourne, Australia, 12–25 May, 1980*, 61–71. Geneva: World Council of Churches, 1980.

———. *Essays on New Testament Themes.* Translated by J. W. Montague. Philadelphia: Fortress Press, 1982 [orig. 1964].

———. *New Testament Questions of Today.* Philadelphia: Fortress Press, 1969 [orig. 1957].

———. *Perspectives on Paul.* Translated by Margaret Kohl. Mifflintown, PA: Sigler, 1971 [orig. 1969].

Keck, L. E. "What Makes Romans Tick?" In *Pauline Theology, Volume III: Romans*, edited by D. M. Hay and E. E. Johnson, 3–29. Minneapolis: Fortress Press, 1995.

Kehl, N. *Der Christushymnus im Kolosserbrief: eine motivgeschichtliche Untersuchung, zu Kol. 1, 12-20.* Stuttgart: Katholisches Biblewerk, 1967.

———. "Erniedrigung und Erhöhung in Qumran und Kolossä." *ZKT* 91 (1969): 364–94.

Kelly, G. B. and F. B. Nelson, eds. *A Testament to Freedom: The Essential Writings of Dietrich Bonhoeffer.* Rev. ed. San Francisco: HarperSanFrancisco, 1995.

Kempthorne, R. "Incest in the Body of Christ." *NTS* 14 (1968): 568–74.

Kirby, J. T. "The Syntax of Romans 5.12: A Rhetorical Approach." *NTS* 33 (1987): 283–86.

Kistemaker, S. K. "'Deliver This Man to Satan' (1 Cor 5:5): A Case Study in Church Discipline." *MSJ* 3, no. 1 (1992): 33–45.

Klauck, H.-J. *The Religious Context of Early Christianity: A Guide to Graeco-Roman Religions.* Edinburgh: T & T Clark, 2000.

Koep, L. *Das himmlische Buch in Antike und Christentum: Eine religionsgeschichtliche Untersuchung zur altchristlichen Bidlersprache.* Bonn: Peter Hanstein, 1952.

Konradt, M. *Gericht und Gemeinde: Eine Studie zur Bedeutung und Funktion von Gerichtsaussagen im Rahmen der paulinischen Ekklesiologie und Ethik im 1 Thess und 1 Kor.* BZNW 117. Berlin: Walter de Gruyter, 2003.

Kooten, G. H. van. *Paul's Anthropology in Context: The Image of God, Assimilation to God, and Tripartite Man in Ancient Judaism, Ancient Philosophy and Early Christianity.* WUNT. Tübingen: Mohr Siebeck, 2008.

Kopytoff, I., ed. *The African Frontier: The Reproduction of Traditional African Societies.* Bloomington: Indiana University Press, 1987.

Kovacs, J. "The Archons, the Spirit, and the Death of Christ: Do We Really Need the Hypothesis of Gnostic Opponents to Explain 1 Cor. 2:2-16?" In *Apocalyptic in the NT: Essays in Honor of J. Louis Martyn*, edited by J. Marcus and M. L. Soards, 217–36. JSNTSup 24. Sheffield: JSOT Press, 1989.

Kraft, C. H. *Defeating Dark Angels: Breaking Demonic Oppression in the Believer's Life*. Ann Arbor, MI: Vine Books, 1992.

Kraft, C. H., T. White, and E. Murphy, eds. *Behind Enemy Lines: An Advanced Guide to Spiritual Warfare*. Ann Arbor: Vine Books, 1994.

Krentz, E. *Galatians, Philippians, Philemon, 1 Thessalonians*. ACNT. Minneapolis: Augsburg, 1985.

Kuhn, K. G. "Les rouleaux de cuivre de Qumran." *Revue Biblique* 61 (1954): 193–205.

Kümmel, W. G. *Römer 7 und die Bekehrung des Paulus*. Leipzig: J. C. Hinrichs'sche Buchhandlung, 1929.

Kurapati, C. J. "Spiritual Bondage and Christian Freedom According to Paul." Ph.D. Dissertation, Princeton Theological Seminary, 1976.

Laato, T. *Paul and Judaism: An Anthropological Approach*. Atlanta: Scholars Press, 1995.

Lamp, J. S. "Wisdom in Col 1:15-20: Contribution and Significance." *JETS* 41 (1998): 45–53.

Landes, G. M. "Creation and Liberation." *USQR* 33 (1978): 79–89.

Levenson, J. D. "Is There a Counterpart in the Hebrew Bible to New Testament Antisemitism?" *JETS* 22 (1985): 242–60.

———. "Yehezkel Kaufmann and Mythology." *Conservative Judaism* 36 (1982): 36–43.

Liftin, D. *St. Paul's Theology of Proclamation: 1 Corinthians 1–4 and Greco-Roman Rhetoric*. SNTSMS 79. Cambridge: Cambridge University Press, 1994.

Lightfoot, J. B. *Notes on the Epistles of St Paul from Unpublished Commentaries*. London: Macmillan, 1895.

———. *Saint Paul's Epistle to the Galatians: A Revised Text with Introduction, Notes, and Dissertations*. London: Macmillan, 1887.

———. *Saint Paul's Epistles to the Colossians and to Philemon: A Revised Text with Introductions, Notes, and Dissertations*. London: Macmillan, 1904 [orig. 1875].

Lindemann, A. *Der erste Korintherbrief*. HNT 9/1. Tübingen: Mohr Siebeck, 2000.

Little, J. A. "Paul's Use of Analogy: A Structural Analysis of Romans 7:1-6." *CBQ* 46 (1984): 82–90.

Lohmeyer, E. *Die Briefe an die Kolosser und an Philemon.* 12 Aufl. Göttingen: Vandenhoeck & Ruprecht, 1961.

Longenecker, R. N. *Galatians.* WBC 41. Dallas: Word, 1990.

———. "The Pedagogical Nature of the Law in Galatians." *JETS* 25 (1985): 53–61.

Lüdemann, G. *Opposition to Paul in Jewish Christianity.* Minneapolis: Fortress Press, 1989.

Lull, D. J. "'The Law Was Our Pedagogue': A Study in Galatians 3:19-25." *JBL* 105 (1986): 481–98.

Lyonnet, S. "L'histoire du salut selon le chapitre VII de l'épître aux Romains." *Bib* 43 (1962): 117–51.

———. "'Tu ne convoiteras pas,'" In *Neotestamentica et Patristica. Eine Freunsgabe Herrn Prof. Dr. Oscar Cullmann zu seinem 60. Geburtstag uberreicht,* 157–65. Leiden: Brill, 1962.

MacArthur, S. D. "'Spirit' in Pauline Usage: 1 Corinthians 5.5." In *Studia Biblica* 3, edited by E. A. Livingstone, 249–56. JSNTSup 3. Sheffield: JSOT Press, 1978.

MacGregor, G. H. C. "Principalities and Powers: The Cosmic Background of Paul's Thought." *NTS* 1 (1954): 17–28.

MacIntyre, A. *After Virtue: A Study in Moral Theory.* 3rd ed. Notre Dame, IN: University of Notre Dame Press, 2007 [orig. 1981].

———. *Three Rival Versions of Moral Enquiry: Encyclopaedia, Genealogy, and Tradition.* Notre Dame, IN: University of Notre Dame Press, 1988.

———. *Whose Justice, Which Rationality?* Notre Dame, IN: University of Notre Dame Press, 1988.

MacNutt, F. *Deliverance from Evil Spirits: A Practical Manual.* Grand Rapids: Chosen Books, 1995.

———. *Healing.* Notre Dame, IN: Ave Maria Press, 1974.

Malherbe, A. J. *The Letters to the Thessalonians.* AB 32B. New York: Doubleday, 2000.

———. *Paul and the Thessalonians: The Philosophical Tradition of Pastoral Care.* Philadelphia: Fortress Press, 1987.

Manns, F. "Col. 1, 15-20: Midrash Chrétien de Gen. 1, 1." *RevScRel* 53 (1979): 100–10.

Marcus, J. "The Evil Inclination in the Epistle of James." *CBQ* 44 (1982): 606–21.

———. "The Evil Inclination in the Letters of Paul." *IBS* 8 (1986): 8–21.

———. "Idolatry in the New Testament." *Int* (2006): 152–64.

————. "Mark—Interpreter of Paul." *NTS* 46 (2000): 473–87.

————. *Mark 8–16*. AB 27A. New Haven: Yale University Press, 2009.

Marshal, A. J. "Flaccus and the Jews in Asia (*Pro Flacco* 28:67–69)." *Phoenix* 29 (1975): 139–54.

Marshall, I. H. "The Meaning of Reconciliation." In *Unity and Diversity in the New Testament: Essays in Honor of George E. Ladd*, R. A. Guelich, 117–32. Grand Rapids: Eerdmans, 1978.

Marshall, R. "'God Is Not a Democrat': Pentecostalism and Democratisation in Nigeria." In *The Christian Churches and the Democratisation of Africa*, edited by P. Gifford, 239–60. Leiden: Brill, 1995.

Martin, D. B. *The Corinthian Body*. New Haven: Yale University Press, 1995.

Martin, R. P. *Colossians and Philemon*. NCB. Grand Rapids: Eerdmans, 1973.

Martin, T. W. "Pagan and Judeo-Christian Time-Keeping Schemes in Gal 4:10 and Col 2:16." *NTS* 42 (1996): 105–19.

Martyn, J. L. *Galatians: A New Translation with Introduction and Commentary*. AB. New Haven: Yale University Press, 1997.

————. *History and Theology in the Fourth Gospel*. 3rd ed. NTL. Louisville: Westminster John Knox, 2003 [orig. 1968].

————. *Theological Issues in the Letters of Paul*. Nashville: Abingdon, 1997.

Masson, C. *L'Épître de saint Paul aux Colossiens* (CNT 10; Neuchâtel: Delachaux, 1950): 97–107.

Matera, F. J. *Galatians*. Sacra Pagina 9. Collegeville, MN: Liturgical, 1992.

Mbiti, J. S. *African Religions and Philosophy*. Oxford: Heinemann, 1990.

————. *Introduction to African Religion*. London: Heinemann, 1975.

McAll, K. *Healing the Family Tree*. London: Sheldon, 1982.

McMillan, E. "An Aspect of Recent Wisdom Studies in the New Testament." *ResQ* 10 (1967): 201–10.

McVeigh, T. "Children are Targets of Nigerian Witch Hunt." *The Observer* (8 December 2007): 34. Accessed 28 February 2012. Online: http://www.guardian.co.uk/world/2007/dec/09/tracymcveigh.theobserver.

Meeks, W. *The First Urban Christians: The Social World of the Apostle Paul*. 2nd ed. New Haven: Yale University Press, 2003 [orig. 1983].

————. "Social Function of Apocalyptic Language in Pauline Christianity." In *Apocalypticism in the Mediterranean World and the Near East. Proceedings of the International Colloquium on Apocalypticism. Uppsala, August 12–17, 1979*, edited by D. Hellholm, 687–705. Tübingen: Mohr, 1983.

Meyer, B. *Translating the Devil: Religion and Modernity among the Ewe in Ghana*. Edinburgh: Edinburgh University Press, 1999.

Meyer, P. W. "Augustine's *The Spirit and the Letter* as a Reading of Paul's Romans." In *The Word in This World: Essays in New Testament Exegesis and Theology*, 133–48. Louisville: Westminster John Knox, 2004.

———. "The Worm at the Core of the Apple." In *The Word in This World: Essays in New Testament Exegesis and Theology*, 57–77. Louisville: Westminster John Knox, 2004.

Middleton, J. R. *The Liberating Image: The Imago Dei in Genesis 1*. Grand Rapids: Baker, 2005.

Millard, A. R. and P. Bordreuil, "A Statue from Syria with Assyrian and Aramaic Inscriptions." *BA* 45 (1982): 135–41.

Miller, G. "ΑΡΧΟΝΤΩΝ ΤΟΥ ΑΙΩΝΟΣ ΤΟΥΤΟΥ — A New Look at 1 Corinthians 2:6-8." *JBL* 91 (1972): 522–28.

Mitchell, M. *Paul, the Corinthians, and the Birth of Christian Hermeneutics*. Cambridge: Cambridge University Press, 2010.

Moffat, J. "The Interpretation of Romans 6:17-18." *JBL* 48 (1929): 233–38.

Moo, D. J. "Israel and Paul in Romans 7:7-12." *NTS* 32 (1986): 122–35.

———. *The Letters to the Colossians and to Philemon*. PNTC. Grand Rapids: Eerdmans, 2008.

Moo, J. "Romans 8.19-22 and Isaiah's Cosmic Covenant." *NTS* 54 (2008): 74–89.

Moore-Crispin, D. R. "Galatians 4:1-9: The Use and Abuse of Parallels." *EvQ* 60 (1989): 203–23.

Moreau, A. S. *Essentials of Spiritual Warfare: Equipped to Win the Battle*. Wheaton, IL: Harold Shaw Publishers, 1997.

Morris, L. *The Cross in the New Testament*. Grand Rapids: Eerdmans, 1965.

Moses, R. "Physical and/or Spiritual Exclusion? Ecclesial Discipline in 1 Corinthians 5." *NTS* 59 (2013): 172–91.

———. "'The *Satan*' in Light of the Creation Theology of Job." *HBT* 34 (2012): 19–34.

Moule, C. F. D. *The Epistles of Paul the Apostle to the Colossians and to Philemon*. CGTC. Cambridge: Cambridge University Press, 1957.

Mowinckel, S. *The Psalms in Israel's Worship*. 2 vols. Oxford: Oxford University Press, 1962.

Muga, E. *African Response to Western Christian Religion: A Sociological Analysis of African Separatist Religious and Political Movements in East Africa*. Kampala, Nairobi, Dar es Salaam: East African Literature Bureau, 1975.

Murphy, E. *The Handbook for Spiritual Warfare*. Nashville: Thomas Nelson, 1992.

Murphy-O'Connor, J. "Freedom or Ghetto (1 Cor. viii, 1–13; x, 23—xi, 1)." *RB* 85 (1978): 543– 74.

———. "Interpolations in 1 Corinthians." *CBQ* 48 (1986): 81–94.

———. *Keys to First Corinthians: Revisiting Major Issues.* Oxford: Oxford University Press, 2009.

Napier, D. "Paul's Analysis of Sin and Torah in Romans 7:7-25." *Restoration Quarterly* 44, no. 1 (2002): 15–32.

Noble, G. and M. Watkins. "So, How Did Bourdieu Learn to Play Tennis? Habitus, Consciousness and Habituation." *Cultural Studies* 17 (2003): 520–38.

O'Brien, D. B. C. "Satan Steps Out from the Shadows: Religion and Politics in Africa." *Africa* 70 (2000): 520–25.

O'Brien, P. T. *Colossians, Philemon.* WBC 44. Waco, TX: Word Books, 1982.

———. "Principalities and the Relationship to Structures." *Evangelical Theological Review* 6 (1982): 50–61.

O'Neill, J. C. "The Source of Christology in Colossians." *NTS* 26 (1979): 87–100.

Overfield, P. D. "Pleroma: A Study in Content and Context." *NTS* 25 (1979): 384–96.

Pagels, E. *The Gnostic Paul: Gnostic Exegesis of the Pauline Letters.* Philadelphia: Fortress
Press, 1975.

Parratt, J. *Reinventing Christianity: African Theology Today.* Grand Rapids: Eerdmans, 1995.

Parrinder, E. G. *Religion in Africa.* Baltimore: Penguin Books, 1969.

Peck, M. S. *People of the Lie: The Hope for Healing Human Evil.* New York: Touchstone, 1983.

Peretti, F. *Piercing the Darkness.* Westchester, IL: Crossway Books, 1989.

———. *This Present Darkness.* Westchester, IL: Crossway Books, 1986.

Peterson, R. A. " 'To Reconcile to Himself All Things": Colossians 1:20." *Presbyterion* 36 (2010): 37–46.

Pew Forum on Religion & Public Life, *U.S. Religious Landscape Survey* (2008). Accessed on October 22, 2012. Online: http://religions.pewforum.org/pdf/report2religious-landscape-study-key-findings.pdf.

Pfizner, V. C. "Purified Community—Purified Sinner: Expulsion from the Community according to Matt 18:15-18 and 1 Cor 5:1-5." *ABR* (1982): 34–55.

Pinker, S. *The Language Instinct.* New York: W. Morrow and Co., 1994.

Pogoloff, S. M. *Logos and Sophia: The Rhetorical Situation of 1 Corinthians.* SBLDS 134. Atlanta: Scholars, 1992.

Porter, S. E. "The Pauline Concept of Original Sin, in Light of Rabbinic Background." *Tyndale Bulletin* 41, no. 1 (1990): 3–30.

Powlison, D. *Power Encounters: Reclaiming Spiritual Warfare.* Grand Rapids: Baker, 1995.

Prince, D. *They Shall Expel Demons: What You Need to Know about Demons-Your Invisible Enemies.* Grand Rapids: Chosen Books, 1998.

Pryke, J. "'Spirit' and 'Flesh' in the Qumran Documents and Some New Testament Texts." *RevQ* 19 (1965): 345–60.

Ramsay, W. M. "Sketches in the Religious Antiquities of Asia Minor (Plates I–IV)." *ABSA* 18 (1911–12): 37–79.

Reicke, B. "The Law and This World According to Paul: Some Thoughts Concerning Gal 4:1- 11." *JBL* 70 (1951): 259–76.

———. *The Rule of Metaphor: Multi-Disciplinary Studies of the Creation of Meaning in Language.* Toronto: University of Toronto Press, 1981 [orig. 1975].

Roberts, J. W. "The Preposition *Eis* after the Verbs *Pisteuo* and *Baptizo*." *ResQ* 5 (1961): 157–59.

Robertson, A. T. and A. Plummer. *First Epistle to the Corinthians.* 2d ed. ICC. Edinburgh: T & T Clark, 1914 [orig. 1911].

Robinson, J. M. "A Formal Analysis of Colossians 1 [15-20]." *JBL* 76 (1957): 270–87.

———. *The Problem of History in Mark and Other Marcan Studies.* Philadelphia: Fortress Press, 1982 [orig. 1957].

Roetzel, C. J. *Judgement in the Community: A Study of the Relationship between Eschatology and Ecclesiology in Paul.* Leiden: Brill, 1972.

Rohde, J. *Der Brief des Paulus an die Galater.* THKNT 9. Berlin: Evangelische Verlagsanstalt, 1989.

Rosner, B. "'ΟΥΧΙ ΜΑΛΛΟΝ ΕΠΕΝΘΗΣΑΤΕ': Corporate Responsibility in 1 Corinthians 5." *NTS* 38 (1992): 470–473.

———. *Paul, Scripture and Ethics: A Study of 1 Corinthians 5–7.* Leiden: Brill, 1994.

Rowland, C. "Apocalyptic Visions and the Exaltation of Christ in the Letter to the Colossians." *JSNT* 19 (1983): 73–83.

———. *The Open Heaven: A Study of Apocalyptic in Judaism and Early Christianity.* London: SPCK, 1982.

Rupp, G. E. *Principalities and Powers: Studies in the Christian Conflict in History.* London: Epworth, 1952.

Rusam, D. "Neue Belege zu den στοιχεῖα τοῦ κόσμου." *ZNW* 83 (1992): 119–25.

Russell, J. B. *The Devil: Perceptions of Evil from Antiquity to Primitive Christianity.* Ithaca, NY: Cornell University Press, 1977.

———. *Lucifer: The Devil in the Middle Ages.* Ithaca, NY: Cornell University Press, 1984.

———. *Mephistopheles: The Devil in the Modern World.* Ithaca, NY: Cornell University Press, 1986.

———. *Satan: The Early Christian Tradition.* Ithaca, NY: Cornell University Press, 1981.

Sabou, S. "A Note on Romans 6:5: The Representation (ὁμοίωμα): of His Death." *Tyndale Bulletin* 55, no. 2 (2004): 220–29.

Saggs, H. W. F. *The Encounter with the Divine in Mesopotamia and Israel.* London: Athlone Press, 1978.

Sanders, E. P. *Paul and Palestinian Judaism.* Minneapolis: Fortress Press, 1977.

———. *Paul, the Law, and the Jewish People.* Minneapolis: Fortress Press, 1983.

Schäfer, P. "Jewish Magic Literature in Late Antiquity and Early Middle Ages." *JJS* 41 (1990): 75–91.

———. *The Origins of Jewish Mysticism.* Tübingen: Mohr Siebeck, 2009.

———. *Synopse zur Hekhalot-Literatur.* Tübingen: Mohr Siebeck, 1981.

Scheu, L. E. *Die "Weltelemente" beim Apostel Paulus (Gal. 4,3.9 und Kol 2,8.20).* Universitas Catholica Americae 37. Washington: Catholic University of America Press, 1933.

Schlier, H. *Der Brief an die Galater.* 12th ed. KEK 7. Gottingen: Vandenhoeck & Ruprecht, 1962.

———. *Principalities and Powers in the New Testament.* New York: Herder and Herder, 1961.

Schmithals, W. *Gnosticism in Corinth: An Investigation of the Letters to the Corinthians.* Nashville: Abingdon, 1971.

Schnelle, U. *Gerechtigkeit und Christusgegenwart.* Göttingen: Vadenhoeck & Ruprecht, 1983.

Schniewind, J. *Nachgelassene Reden und Aufsätze.* Berlin: A. Töpelmann, 1952.

Scholem, G. *Jewish Gnosticism, Merkabah Mysticism and Talmudic Tradition.* New York: Jewish Theological Seminary of America, 1965 [orig. 1960].

———. *Major Trends in Jewish Mysticism.* New York: Schocken, 1961 [orig. 1954].

Schrage, W. *Der erste Brief an die Korinther*. EKKNT 7/1. Zürich: Benziger Verlag, 1991.

Schüle, A. "Made in the 'Image of God': The Concepts of Divine Images in Gen 1–3." *ZAW* 117 (2005): 1–20.

Schweitzer, A. *The Mysticism of Paul the Apostle*. New York: Macmillan, 1956 [orig. 1931].

Schweizer, E. *The Church as the Body of Christ*. Richmond: John Knox, 1964.

———. "The Church as the Missionary Body of Christ." *NTS* 8 (1961): 1–11.

———. "Dying and Rising with Christ." *NTS* 14 (1967–68): 1–14.

———. *The Letter to the Colossians*. Minneapolis: Augsburg, 1982 [orig. 1976].

———. "Slaves of the Elements and Worshipers of Angels: Gal 4:3, 9 and Col 2:8, 18, 20." *JBL* 107 (1988): 455–68.

———. "Col 1:15-20." *RevExp* 87 (1990): 97–104.

Scott, C. A. A. *Christianity according to St. Paul*. Cambridge: Cambridge University Press, 1927.

Scott, J. *Adoption as Sons of God*. WUNT 2.48. Tubingen: Mohr, 1992.

Scott Peck, M. *People of the Lie: The Hope for Healing Human Evil*. New York: Touchstone, 1983.

Scroggs, R. *The Last Adam*. Oxford: Blackwell, 1966.

———. "Paul as Rhetorician: Two Homilies in Romans 1–11." In *Jews, Greeks and Christians: Religious Cultures in Late Antiquity: Essays in Honor of William David Davies*, edited by R. Hammerton-Kelly and R. Scroggs, 71– 98. SJLA 21. Leiden: Brill 1976.

Seifrid, M. A. "The Subject of Rom 7:14-25." *NovT* 34 (1992): 313–333.

Shillington, V. G. "Atonement Texture in 1 Corinthians 5:5." *JSNT* 71 (1998): 29–50.

Shogren, G. S. "Presently Entering the Kingdom of Christ: The Background and Purpose of Col 1:12-14." *JETS* 31 (1988): 173–80.

Shultz, G. L., Jr. "The Reconciliation of All Things in Christ." *Bibliotheca Sacra* 167 (2010): 442–59.

Sider, R. J. "Christ and Power." *International Review of Mission* 69 (1980): 8–20.

Sieffert, F. *Der Brief an die Galater*. 8th ed. KEK 7. Göttingen: Vandenhoeck & Ruprecht, 1894.

Siegert, F. *Philon von Alexandrien: Uber die Gottesbezeichnung "wohltätig verzehendes Feuer" (De Deo)*. Tübingen: Mohr Siebeck, 1988.

Silberman, L. H. "Prophets/Angels: LXX and Qumran Psalm 151 and the Epistle to the Hebrews." In *Standing before God: Studies on Prayer in Scriptures in Tradition with Essays (FS J. M. Oestereicher)*, edited by A. Finkel and L. Frizzell, 91–101. New York: KTAV, 1981.

Smit, J. *"About the Idol Offerings": Rhetoric, Social Context and Theology of Paul's Discourse in First Corinthians 8:1—11:1.* BETL 27. Leuven: Peeters, 2000.

———. "'Do Not Be Idolaters': Paul's Rhetoric in First Corinthians 10:1-22." *NovT* 39 (1997): 40–53.

Smith, D. R. *"Hand This Man Over to Satan": Curse, Exclusion and Salvation in 1 Corinthians 5.* LNTS 386. London: T & T Clark, 2008.

Smith, E. W. *The Secret of the African.* London: Student Christian Movement, 1930.

Smith, M. S. "The Levitical Compilation of the Psalter." *ZAW* 103 (1991): 258–63.

Snodgrass, K. "Spheres of Influence: A Possible Solution to the Problem of Paul and the Law." *JSNT* 32 (1988): 93–113.

South, J. T. "A Critique of the 'Curse/Death' Interpretation of 1 Corinthians 5.1-8." *NTS* 39 (1993): 539–61.

———. *Disciplinary Practices in Pauline Texts.* Lewiston, NY: Mellen Biblical Press, 1992.

Southall, D. J. *Rediscovering Righteousness in Romans: Personified Dikaiosyne within Metaphoric and Narratorial Settings.* WUNT 240. Tübingen: Mohr Siebeck, 2008.

Sperber, D. "Some Rabbinic Themes in Magical Papyri." *JSJ* 16 (1983): 93–108.

Spitaler, P. "Analogical Reasoning in Romans 7:2-4: A Woman and the Believers in Rome." *JBL* 125 (2006): 715–47.

Steindorff, G. *Die Apokalypse der Elias, eine unbekannte Apokalypse, und Bruchstücke der Sophonias-Apokalypse.* TUGAL 17. Leipzig: J. C. Hinrichs, 1899.

Stendahl, K. *Final Account: Paul's Letter to the Romans.* Minneapolis: Fortress Press, 1995.

———. *Paul among Jews and Gentiles: And Other Essays.* Minneapolis: Fortress Press, 1976.

Stenger, V. J. *God: The Failed Hypothesis—How Science Shows That God Does Not Exist.* Amherst, NY: Prometheus Books, 2007.

Stewart, J. S. "On a Neglected Emphasis in New Testament Theology." *SJT* 4 (1951): 292–301.

Stott, J. R. W. *God's New Society: The Message of Ephesians.* Downers Grove, IL: InterVarsity Press, 1979.

Stringfellow, W. *Free in Obedience.* New York: Seabury, 1964.

Talmon, Y. "Millenarism." In *International Encyclopedia of the Social Sciences X*, edited by D. L. Sills, 349–62. New York: Macmillan, 1968.

Tannehill, R. C. *Dying and Rising with Christ*. Berlin: Töpelmann, 1967.

Terrien, S. *The Psalms: Strophic Structure and Theological Commentary*. Grand Rapids: Eerdmans, 2003.

Theissen, G. *Psychological Aspects of Pauline Theology*. Minneapolis: Fortress Press, 1987 [orig. 1983].

Thielmann, F. *From Plight to Solution*. NovTSup 61. Leiden: Brill, 1989.

Thiselton, A. C. *First Epistle to the Corinthians*. NIGTC. Grand Rapids: Eerdmans, 2000.

———. "The Meaning of ΣΑΡΞ in 1 Corinthians 5.5: A Fresh Approach in the Light of Logical and Semantic Factors." *SJT* 26 (1973): 204–28.

Thornton, T. C. G. "Jewish New Moon Festivals, Galatians 4:3-11 and Colossians 2:16." *JTS* 40, no. 1 (1989): 97–100.

———. "Satan—God's Agent for Punishing." *ExpTim* 83 (1972): 151–52.

Thrall, M. *The Second Epistle to the Corinthians*. 2 vols. ICC. London: T & T Clark: 1994.

Toepel, A. "Planetary Demons in Early Jewish Literature." *JSP* 14 (2005): 231–38.

Tonstad, S. K. "The Restrainer Removed: A Truly Alarming Thought (2 Thess 2:1-12)." *HBT* 29 (2007): 133–51.

Torres, S. and V. Fabella, eds. *The Emergent Gospel: Theology from the Underside of History: Papers from the Ecumenical Dialogue of Third World Theologians, Dar es Salaam, August 5–12, 1976*. Maryknoll, NY: Orbis Books, 1978.

Toussaint, S. D. "The Contrast between the Spiritual Conflict in Romans 7 and Galatians 5." *Bibliotheca Sacra* 123 (1966): 310–14.

Tripp, D. "ΚΑΤΟΙΚΗΣΑΙ, ΚΑΤΟΙΚΕΙ (Colossians 1:19, 2:9): Christology, or Soteriology Also?" *ExpTim* 116 (2004): 78–79.

Twelftree, G. *Christ Triumphant: Exorcism Then and Now*. London: Hodder & Stoughton, 1985.

Vander Broek, L. "Discipline and Community: Another Look at 1 Corinthians 5." *RefR* 48 (1994): 5–13.

VanderKam, J. C. "The Angel of the Presence in the Book of Jubilees." *DSD* 7 (2000): 378–93.

Vawter, B. "The Colossians Hymn and the Principle of Redaction." *CBQ* 33 (1971): 62–81.

Versnel, H. S. *Triumphus: An Inquiry into the Origin, Development and Meaning of the Roman Triumph.* Leiden: Brill, 1970.

Vielhauer, P. "Gesetzesdienst und Stoicheiadienst im Galaterbrief." In *Rechtfertigung: Festscrift für Ernst Käsemann zum 70 Geburtstag*, edited by J. Friedrich, W. Pöhlmann, and P. Stuhlmacher, 543–55. Tübingen: Mohr, 1976.

———. "On the 'Paulinism' of Acts." In *Studies in Luke-Acts*, edited by L. E. Keck and J. L. Martyn, 33–50. Philadelphia: Fortress Press, 1980 [orig. 1963].

Viser, W. C. *The Darkness among Us.* Nashville: Broadman & Holman, 1994.

Visser't Hooft, W. A. *The Kingship of Christ: An Interpretation of Recent European Theology.* New York: Harper and Brothers, 1948.

Vos, C. S. de. "Stepmothers, Concubines and the Case of πορνεία in 1 Corinthians 5." *NTS* 44 (1998): 104–14.

Wagner, C. P. *Confronting the Powers: How the New Testament Church Experienced the Power of Strategic-Level Spiritual Warfare.* Ventura, CA: Regal, 1996.

———. *Engaging the Enemy: How to Fight and Defeat Territorial Spirits.* Ventura, CA: Regal, 1991.

Wagner, C. P. and F. D. Pennoyer. *Wrestling with Dark Angels: Towards a Deeper Understanding of the Supernatural Forces in Spiritual Warfare.* Ventura, CA: Regal Books, 1990.

Wagner, G. *Pauline Baptism and the Pagan Mysteries: The Problem of the Pauline Doctrine of Baptism in Romans VI.1-11, in the Light of its Religio-historical "Parallels."* Edinburgh: Oliver & Boyd, 1967.

Walker, W., Jr. "1 Corinthians 2.6-16: A Non-Pauline Interpolation?" *JSNT* 47 (1992): 75–94.

Walsh, B. "Late/Post Modernity and Idolatry: A Contextual Reading of Colossians 2:8—3:4." *ExAud* 15 (1999): 1–17.

Walsh, B. J. and S. C. Keesmaat. *Colossians Remixed: Subverting the Empire.* Downers Grove, IL: InterVarsity, 2004.

Walter, N. "Christusglaube und Heidnische Religiosität in Paulinischen Gemeinden." *NTS* 25 (1979): 425–36.

Wanamaker, C. A. "Apocalypticism at Thessalonica." *Neot* 21 (1987): 1–10.

———. *The Epistles to the Thessalonians: A Commentary on the Greek Text.* NIGTC. Grand Rapids: Eerdmans, 1990.

Waters, L. J. "Paradoxes in the Pauline Epistles." *BSac* 167 (2010): 423–41.

Webber, R. E. *The Church in the World: Opposition, Tension, or Transformation.* Grand Rapids: Zondervan, 1986.

Wedderburn, A. J. M. *Baptism and Resurrection: Studies in Pauline Theology against Its Graeco-Roman Background.* WUNT. Tubingen: Mohr, 1987.

———. "The Soteriology of the Mysteries and Pauline Baptismal Theology." *NovT* 29 (1987): 53–72.

———. "The Theological Structure of Romans v. 12." *NTS* 19 (1972–73): 332–54.

Weiss, H. "The Law in the Epistle to the Colossians." *CBQ* 34 (1972): 294–314.

Weiß, J. *Der erste Korintherbrief.* 9th ed. KEK 5. Göttingen: Vandenhoeck & Ruprecht, 1910.

Werner, M. *The Formation of Christian Dogma.* New York: Harper and Brothers, 1957.

Whitley, D. E. H. *The Theology of Saint Paul.* Oxford: Blackwell, 1964.

Wilckens, U. *Der Brief an die Römer.* Vol. 2. Neukirchen-Vluyn: Neukirchener Verlag, 1980.

———. *Weisheit und Torheit. Eine exegetisch-religionsgeschichtliche Untersuchung zu 1 Kor 1 und 2.* Tübingen: Mohr, 1959.

Wilder, A. N. *Kerygma, Eschatology and Social Ethics.* Philadelphia: Fortress Press, 1966.

Williams, G. *The Spirit World in the Letters of Paul the Apostle: A Critical Examination of the Role of Spiritual Beings in the Authentic Pauline Epistles.* FRLANT. Göttingen: Vandenhoeck & Ruprecht, 2009.

Williamson, L., Jr. "Led in Triumph: Paul's Use of *Thriambeuo.*" *Interpretation* 22 (1968): 317– 32.

Willis, W. L. *Idol Meat in Corinth: The Pauline Argument in 1 Corinthians 8 and 10.* SBLDS 68. Chico: Scholars, 1985.

Wilson, R. McL. "How Gnostic Were the Corinthians?" *NTS* 19 (1972): 65–74.

———. "Slippery Words: II. Gnosis, Gnostic, Gnosticism." *ExpTim* 89 (1978): 296–301.

Windmann, M. "1 Kor 2:6-16: Ein Einspruch gegen Paulus." *ZNW* 70 (1979): 44–53.

Wink, W. *Engaging the Powers: Discernment and Resistance in a World of Domination.* Minneapolis: Fortress Press, 1992.

———. *Naming the Powers: The Language of the Powers in the New Testament.* Philadelphia: Fortress Press, 1984.

———. *The Powers That Be.* New York: Doubleday, 1999.

———. *Unmasking the Powers: The Invisible Forces That Determine Human Existence.* Philadelphia: Fortress Press, 1986.

———. *When the Powers Fall.* Minneapolis: Augsburg-Fortress, 1998.

Winter, B. W. *Philo and Paul among the Sophists.* SNTSMS 96. Cambridge: Cambridge University Press, 1997.

Wolff, C. *Der erste Brief des Paulus an die Korinther.* THKNT 7. Leipzig: Evangelische Verlagsanstalt, 1996.

Wright, N. T. *The Climax of the Covenant: Christ and the Law in Pauline Theology.* Minneapolis: Fortress Press, 1991.

———. "The Letter to the Romans: Introduction, Commentary, and Reflections. In *The New Interpreter's Bible.* Vol. 10, 395–770. Nashville: Abingdon, 2002.

———. "Paul and Caesar: A New Reading of Romans." In *A Royal Priesthood? The Use of the Bible Ethically and Politically*, edited by C. Bartholomew, J. Chaplin, R. Song, and A. Wolters, 173–93. Grand Rapids: Zondervan, 2002.

———. *Paul: In Fresh Perspective.* Minneapolis: Fortress Press, 2005.

———. "Poetry and Theology in Colossians 1.15-20." *NTS* 36 (1990): 444–68.

Yamauchi, E. M. *Pre-Christian Gnosticism: A Survey of the Proposed Evidences.* Grand Rapids: Eerdmans, 1973.

Yates, R. "Colossians 2:15: Christ Triumphant." *NTS* 37 (1991): 573–91.

———. "Colossians and Gnosis." *JSNT* 27 (1986): 49–68.

———. "'The Worship of Angels (Col 2:18),'" *ExpTim* 97 (1985): 12–15.

Yoder, J. H. *The Politics of Jesus.* Second Edition. Grand Rapids: Eerdmans, 1994.

Young, N. H. "The Figure of the *Paidagogos* in Art and Literature." *BA* 53 (1990): 80–86.

———. "*Paidagogos*: The Social Setting of a Pauline Metaphor." *NovT* 29 (1987): 150–76.

Ziesler, J. *Paul's Letter to the Romans.* TPINTC. Philadelphia: Trinity, 1989.

———. "The Role of the Tenth Commandment in Romans 7." *JSNT* 33 (1988): 41–56.

Zuendel, F. *The Awakenings: One Man's Battle with Darkness.* Farmington, PA: Plough, 1999.

Index of Authors

Index of Scripture and Ancient Author

1. Where OG chapter and verse numbers differ from MT, OG is in parenthesis.

CPSIA information can be obtained
at www.ICGtesting.com
Printed in the USA
LVHW051313090321
680923LV00019B/246

9 781451 476644